# ICON COMICS PRESENTS

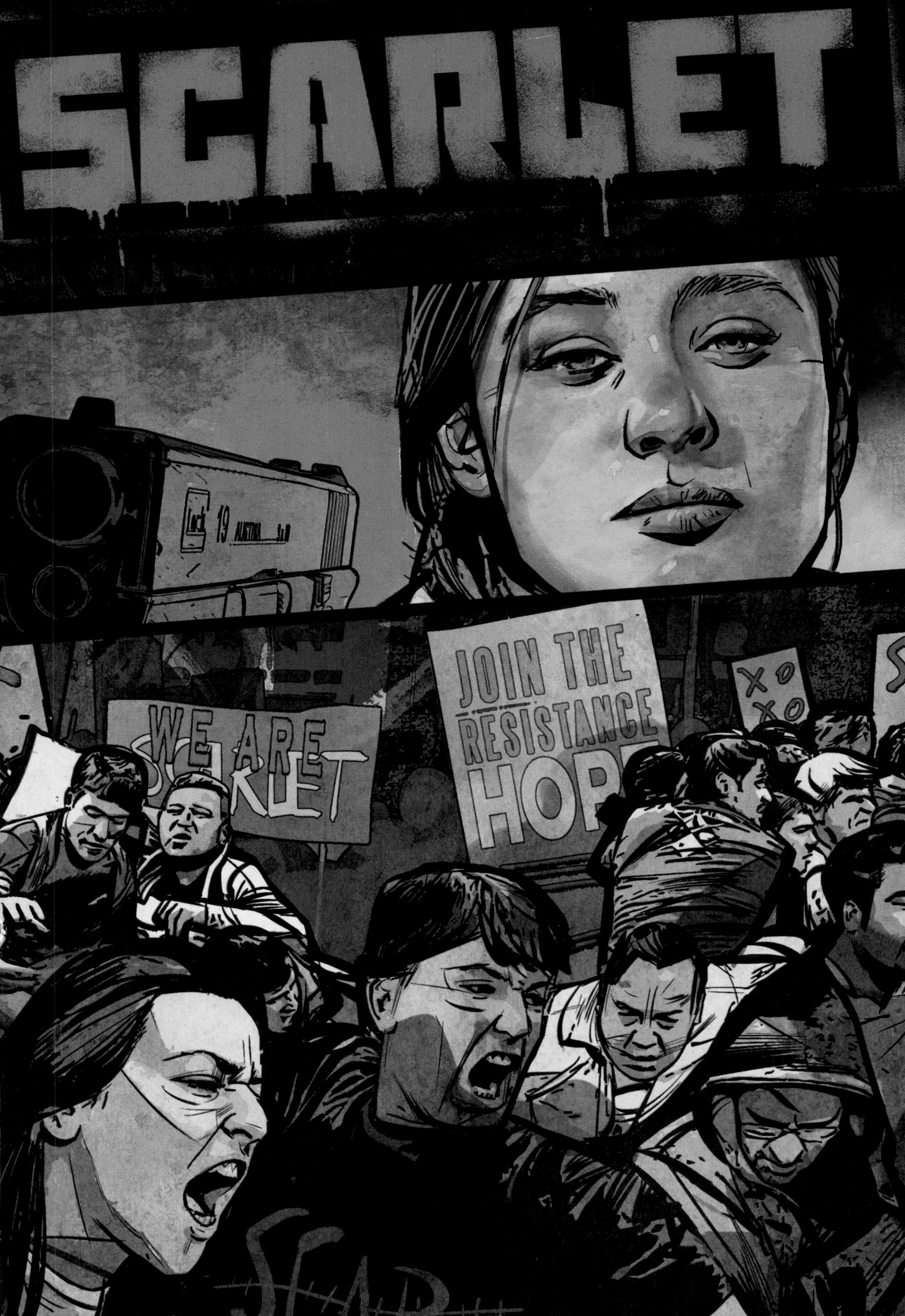
SCARLET
WE ARE
JOIN THE RESISTANCE

# CREATED & PRODUCED BY

# BRIAN MICHAEL BENDIS & ALEX MALEEV

**LETTERS:** CHRIS ELIOPOULOS (#6-7)
& JOE SABINO (#8-10)

**EDITOR:** JENNIFER GRÜNWALD

**BOOK DESIGN:** PATRICK MCGRATH

**BUSINESS AFFAIRS:** ALISA BENDIS

**SCARLET MODELED BY** IVA

OK 2. Contains material originally published in magazine form as SCARLET #6-10. First printing 2016. ISBN# 978-0-7851-8429-4. Published by MARVEL WORLDWIDE, INC., a MARVEL ENTERTAINMENT, LLC. OFFICE OF PUBLICATION: 135 West 50th Street, New York, NY 10020. Copyright © 2015 and 2016 Jinxworld, Inc. All rights reserved. Scarlet, its and all characters featured in or on this issue and the distinctive names and likenesses thereof, and all related indicia are trademarks of Jinxworld, Inc. ICON and its logos are TM Characters, Inc. No similarity between any of the names, characters, persons, and/or institutions in this magazine with those of any living or dead person or institution is intended, similarity that may exist is purely coincidental. $24.99 per copy in the U.S. and $32.99 in Canada (GST #R127032852). Canadian Agreement #40668537. Printed in the U.S.A.

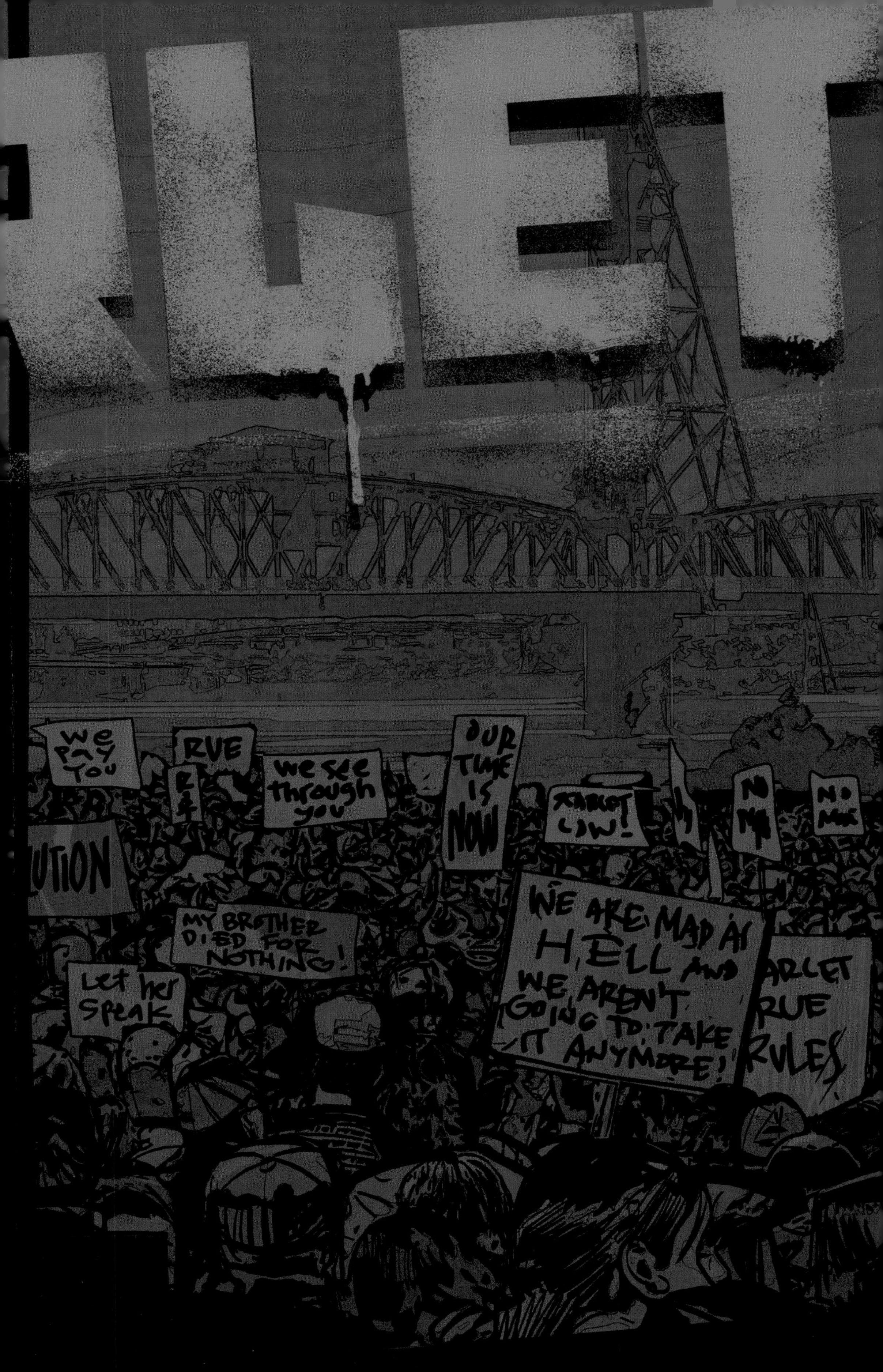
WE PAY YOU
RUE
WE SEE THROUGH YOU
OUR TIME IS NOW
LUTION
MY BROTHER DIED FOR NOTHING!
LET HER SPEAK
WE ARE MAD AS HELL AND WE AREN'T GOING TO TAKE IT ANYMORE!
ARLET RUE RULES

WHERE HAVE I BEEN?
I'VE BEEN PLANNING.


WHERE HAVE
*YOU* BEEN?




OH THAT'S
RIGHT... YOU'VE
BEEN OCCUPYING.




YOU'VE BEEN SCREAMING
AND YELLING AND CARRYING
ON. LIVING IN TENTS.




JUMPING IN FRONT OF
CAMERAS AND LETTING
THE BAD MAN HAVE A
GOOD OLD PIECE OF
YOUR MIND.




HOW DID THAT WORK
OUT FOR YOU?




NOW THAT IT'S ALL OVER
AND DONE, AND THE DUST
IS CLEAR, THE GRASS HAS
GROWN BACK, YOU'RE
HOME SAFE AND SOUND...




I'M NOT BEING
CONDESCENDING.
I KNOW YOU MEANT
WELL.




I'M ASKING YOU: DID
ANYTHING CHANGE?




NO. NOTHING
CHANGED.




NOBODY LEARNED A
LESSON. NOBODY PAID
THE PRICE FOR THEIR
GREED AND CORRUPTION.




WALL STREET IS STILL
WALL STREET. CORRUPTION
IS STILL CORRUPT.




THE BIG MONEY PEOPLE
WHO YOU WERE RAILING
AGAINST OWN THE AIRWAVES
THAT YOU WERE USING
TO RAIL.




THEY PUT YOU ON
THEIR AIR AND THEY
LAUGHED AT YOU.




I'M SAYING: YOU
TRIED YOUR WAY.




NOW I'M GOING
TO TRY MINE.

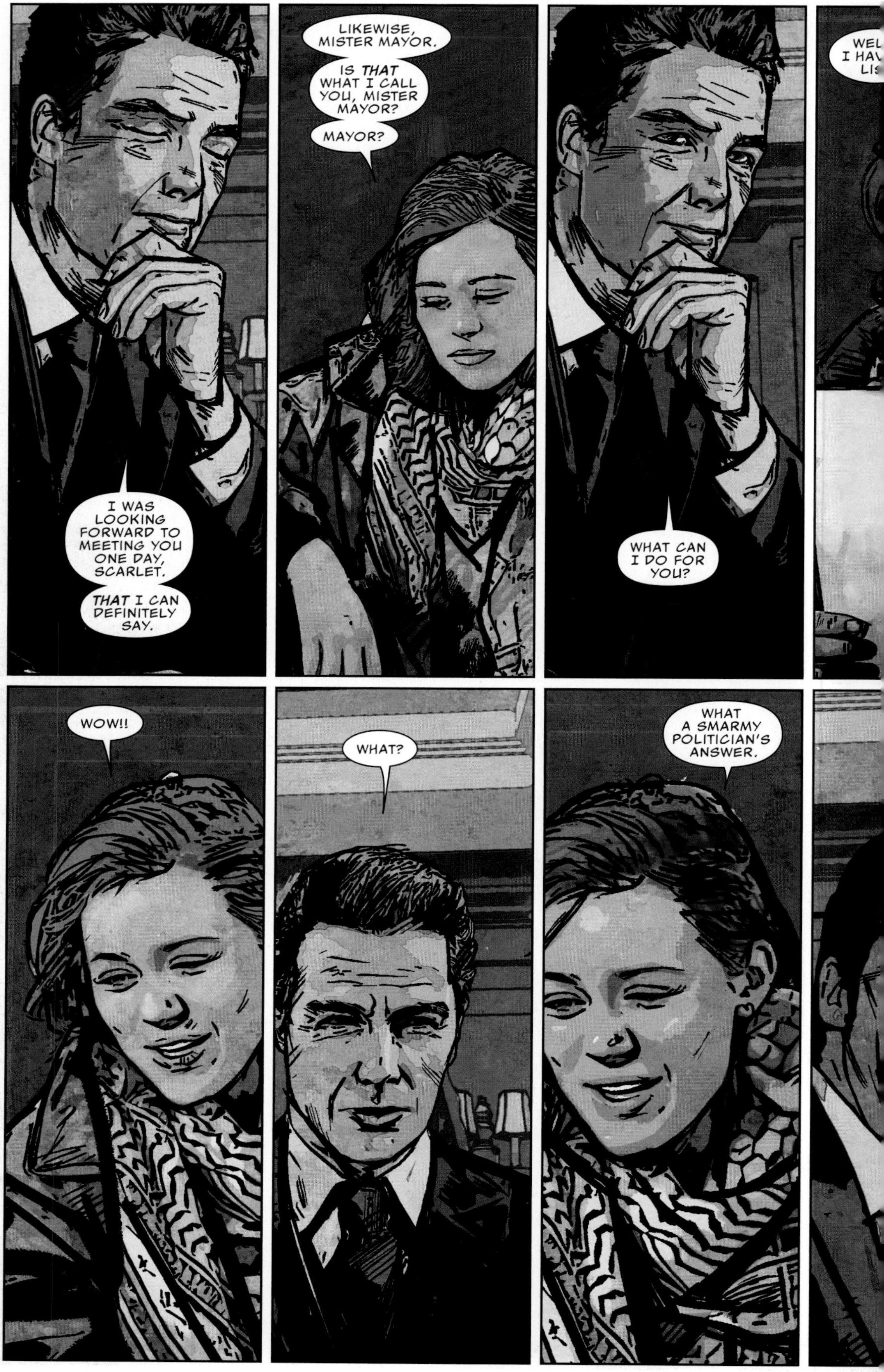
I WAS LOOKING FORWARD TO MEETING YOU ONE DAY, SCARLET.
THAT I CAN DEFINITELY SAY.
LIKEWISE, MISTER MAYOR.
IS THAT WHAT I CALL YOU, MISTER MAYOR?
MAYOR?
WHAT CAN I DO FOR YOU?
WOW!!
WHAT?
WHAT A SMARMY POLITICIAN'S ANSWER.

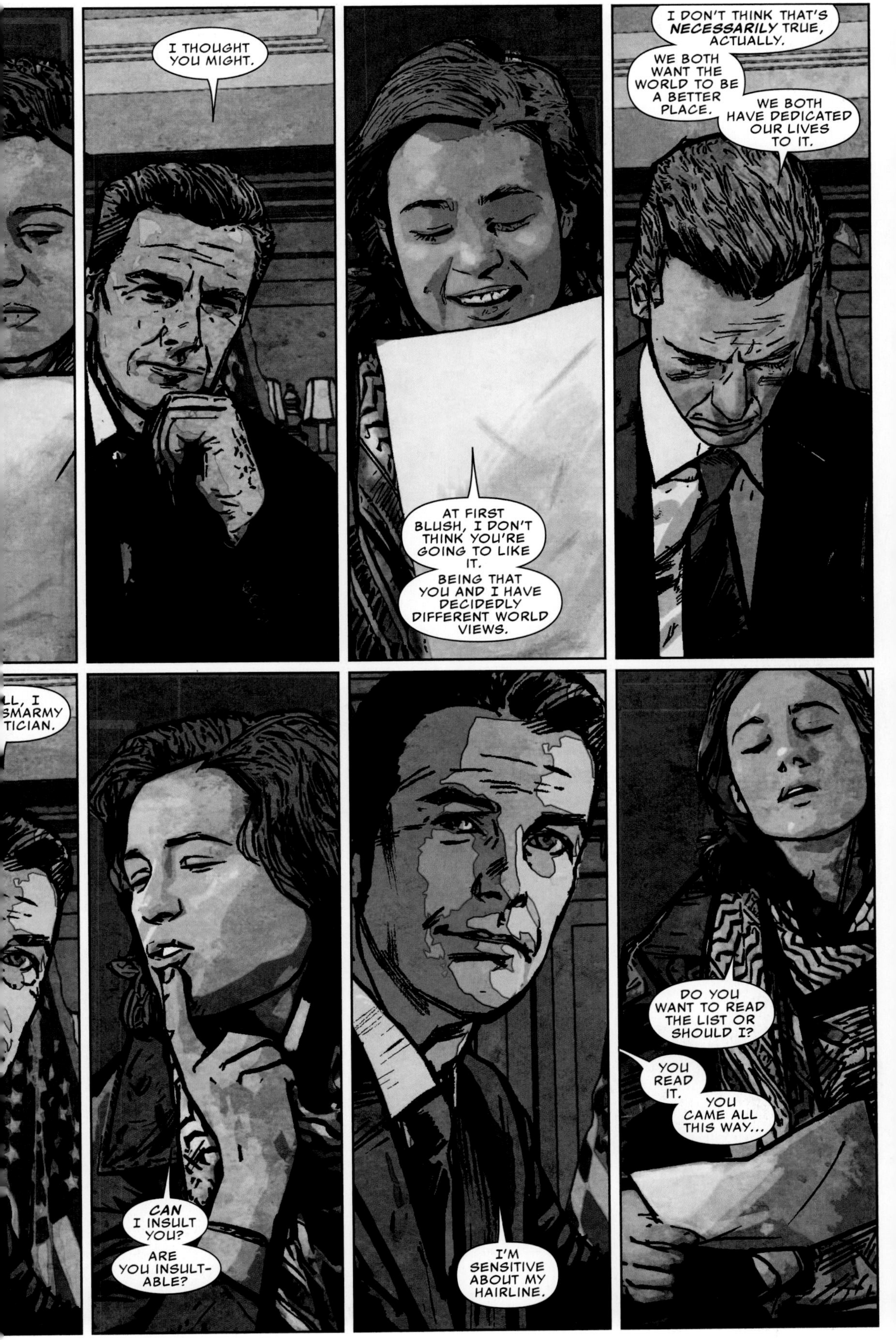
I THOUGHT YOU MIGHT.
AT FIRST BLUSH, I DON'T THINK YOU'RE GOING TO LIKE IT.
BEING THAT YOU AND I HAVE DECIDEDLY DIFFERENT WORLD VIEWS.
I DON'T THINK THAT'S *NECESSARILY* TRUE, ACTUALLY.
WE BOTH WANT THE WORLD TO BE A BETTER PLACE.
WE BOTH HAVE DEDICATED OUR LIVES TO IT.
LL, I SMARMY TICIAN.
*CAN* I INSULT YOU?
ARE YOU INSULT-ABLE?
I'M SENSITIVE ABOUT MY HAIRLINE.
DO YOU WANT TO READ THE LIST OR SHOULD I?
YOU READ IT.
YOU CAME ALL THIS WAY...

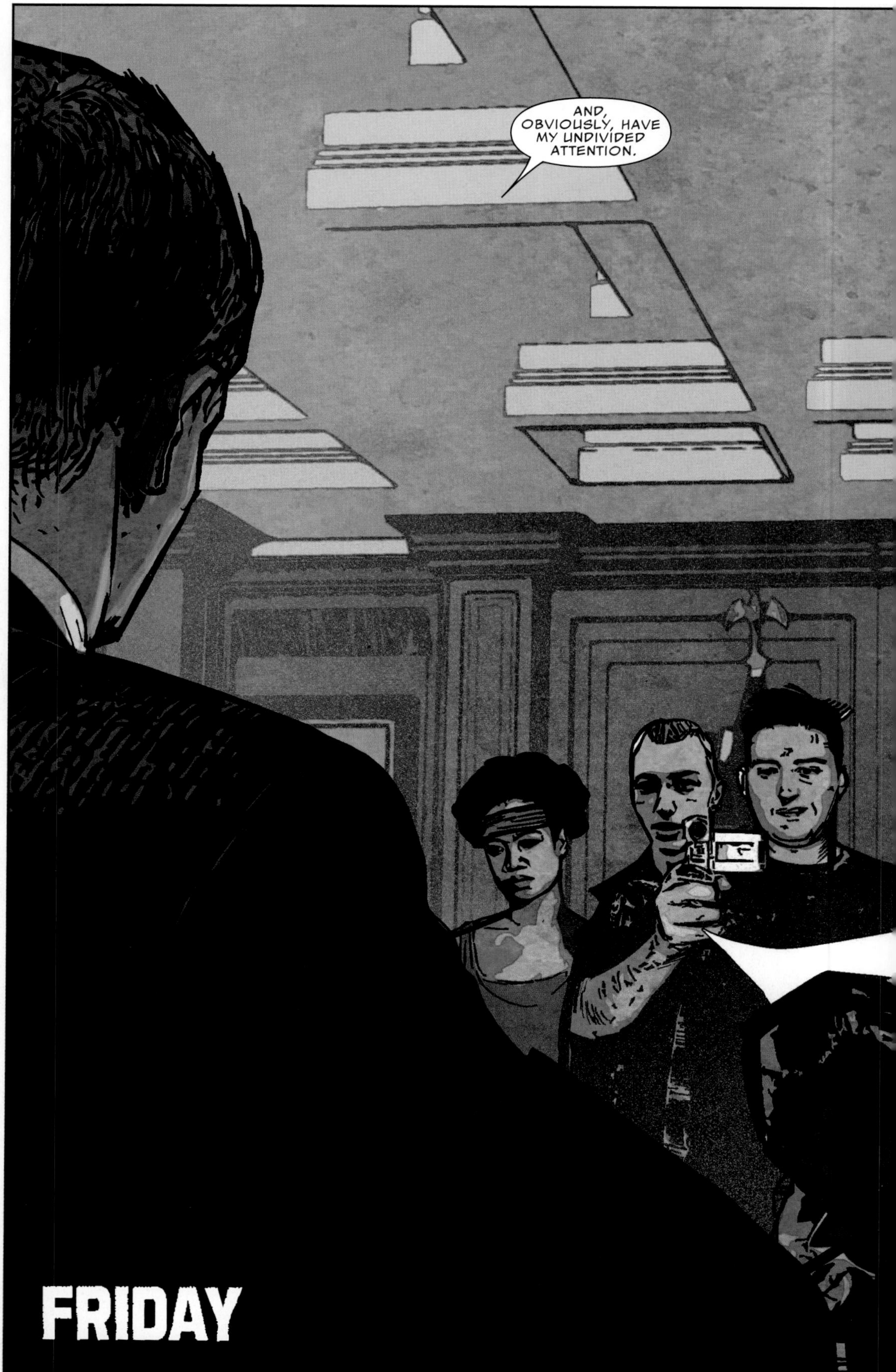
AND, OBVIOUSLY, HAVE MY UNDIVIDED ATTENTION.
FRIDAY

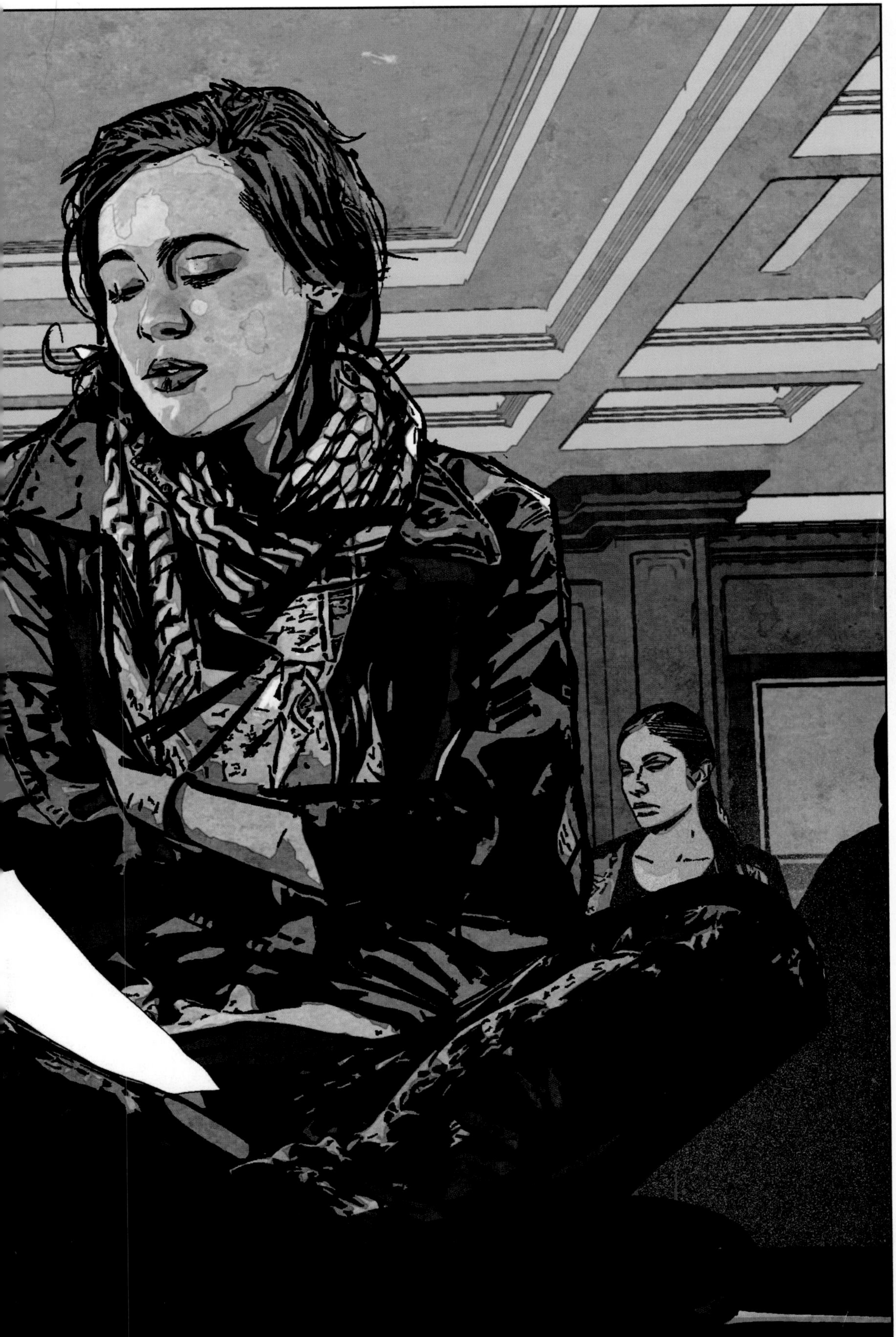

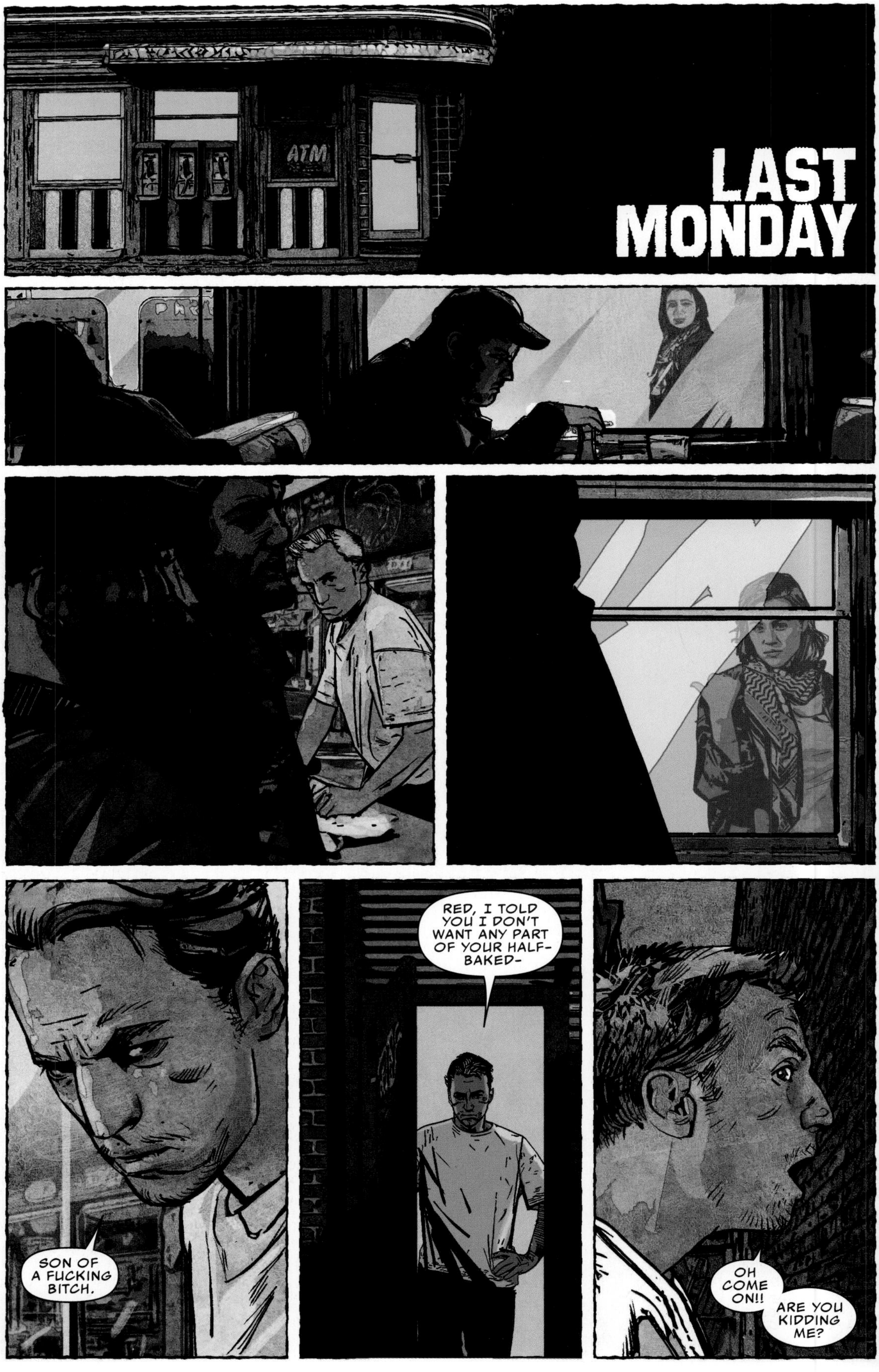
LAST MONDAY
ATM
SON OF A FUCKING BITCH.
RED, I TOLD YOU I DON'T WANT ANY PART OF YOUR HALF-BAKED-
OH COME ON!!
ARE YOU KIDDING ME?

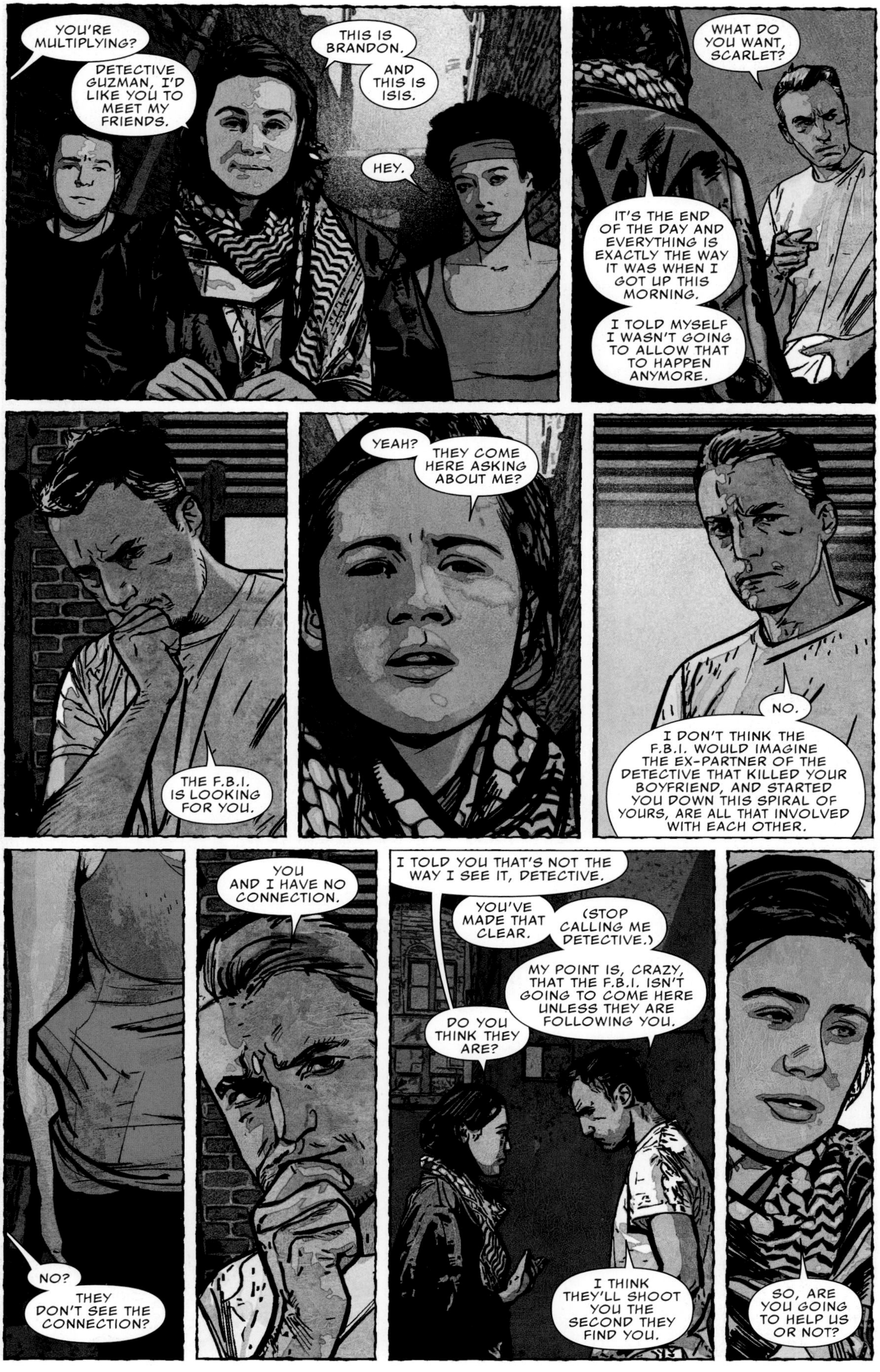
YOU'RE MULTIPLYING?
DETECTIVE GUZMAN, I'D LIKE YOU TO MEET MY FRIENDS.
THIS IS BRANDON.
AND THIS IS ISIS.
HEY.
WHAT DO YOU WANT, SCARLET?
IT'S THE END OF THE DAY AND EVERYTHING IS EXACTLY THE WAY IT WAS WHEN I GOT UP THIS MORNING.
I TOLD MYSELF I WASN'T GOING TO ALLOW THAT TO HAPPEN ANYMORE.
THE F.B.I. IS LOOKING FOR YOU.
YEAH?
THEY COME HERE ASKING ABOUT ME?
NO.
I DON'T THINK THE F.B.I. WOULD IMAGINE THE EX-PARTNER OF THE DETECTIVE THAT KILLED YOUR BOYFRIEND, AND STARTED YOU DOWN THIS SPIRAL OF YOURS, ARE ALL THAT INVOLVED WITH EACH OTHER.
NO?
THEY DON'T SEE THE CONNECTION?
YOU AND I HAVE NO CONNECTION.
I TOLD YOU THAT'S NOT THE WAY I SEE IT, DETECTIVE.
YOU'VE MADE THAT CLEAR.
(STOP CALLING ME DETECTIVE.)
MY POINT IS, CRAZY, THAT THE F.B.I. ISN'T GOING TO COME HERE UNLESS THEY ARE FOLLOWING YOU.
DO YOU THINK THEY ARE?
I THINK THEY'LL SHOOT YOU THE SECOND THEY FIND YOU.
SO, ARE YOU GOING TO HELP US OR NOT?

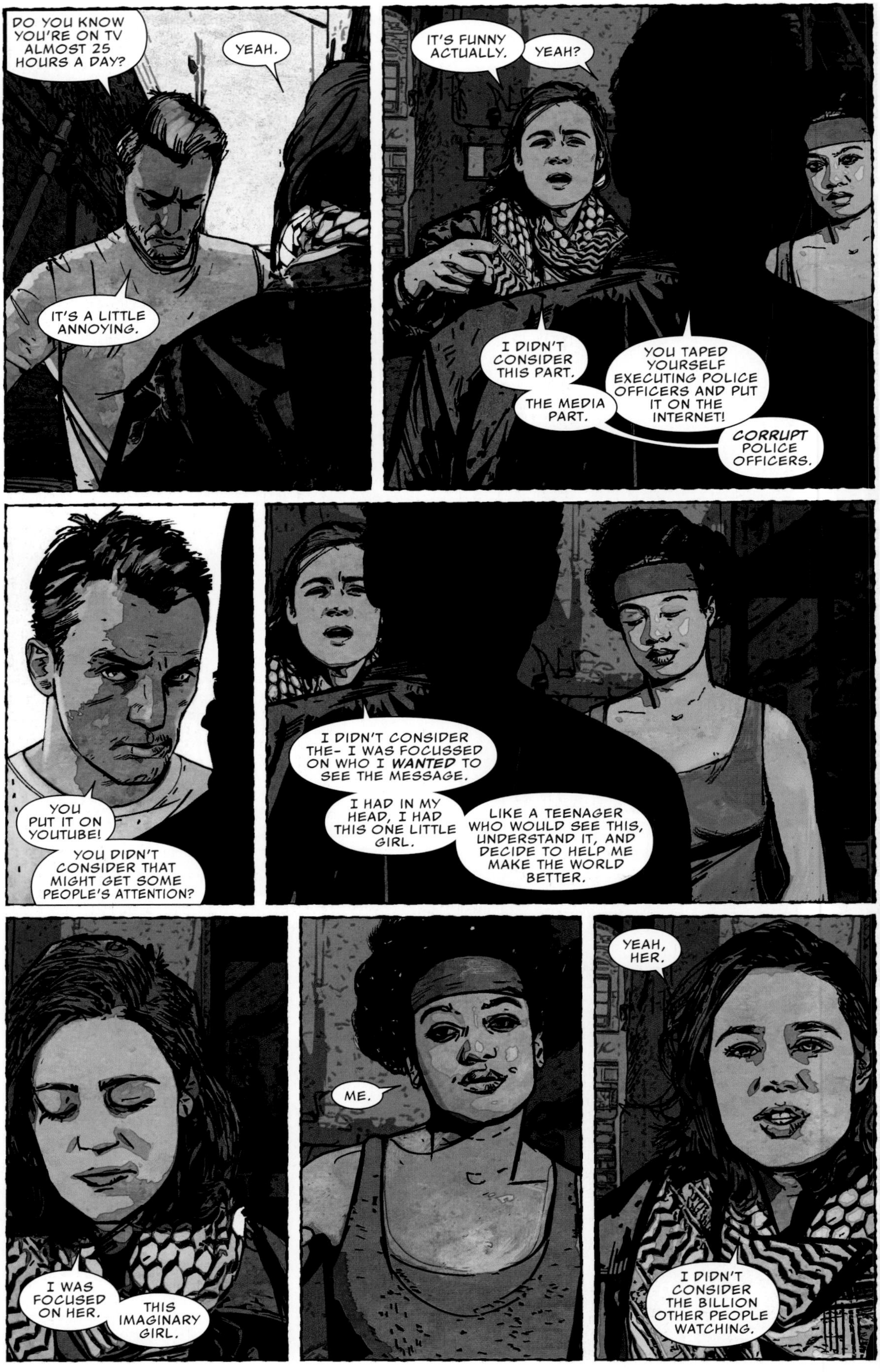
DO YOU KNOW YOU'RE ON TV ALMOST 25 HOURS A DAY?
YEAH.
IT'S A LITTLE ANNOYING.
IT'S FUNNY ACTUALLY.
YEAH?
I DIDN'T CONSIDER THIS PART.
THE MEDIA PART.
YOU TAPED YOURSELF EXECUTING POLICE OFFICERS AND PUT IT ON THE INTERNET!
CORRUPT POLICE OFFICERS.
YOU PUT IT ON YOUTUBE!
YOU DIDN'T CONSIDER THAT MIGHT GET SOME PEOPLE'S ATTENTION?
I DIDN'T CONSIDER THE- I WAS FOCUSSED ON WHO I WANTED TO SEE THE MESSAGE.
I HAD IN MY HEAD, I HAD THIS ONE LITTLE GIRL.
LIKE A TEENAGER WHO WOULD SEE THIS, UNDERSTAND IT, AND DECIDE TO HELP ME MAKE THE WORLD BETTER.
I WAS FOCUSED ON HER.
THIS IMAGINARY GIRL.
ME.
YEAH, HER.
I DIDN'T CONSIDER THE BILLION OTHER PEOPLE WATCHING.

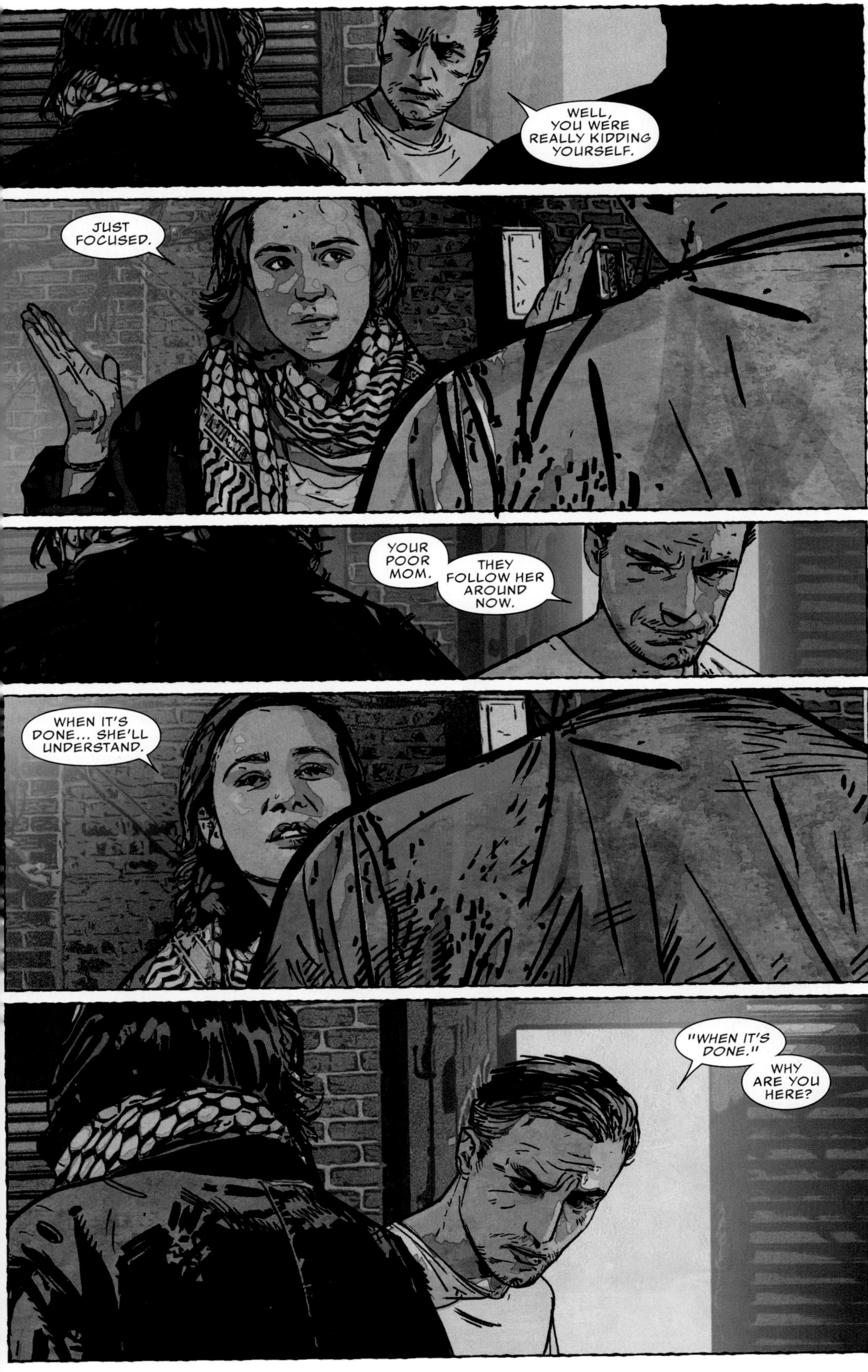
WELL, YOU WERE REALLY KIDDING YOURSELF.
JUST FOCUSED.
YOUR POOR MOM.
THEY FOLLOW HER AROUND NOW.
WHEN IT'S DONE... SHE'LL UNDERSTAND.
"WHEN IT'S DONE."
WHY ARE YOU HERE?

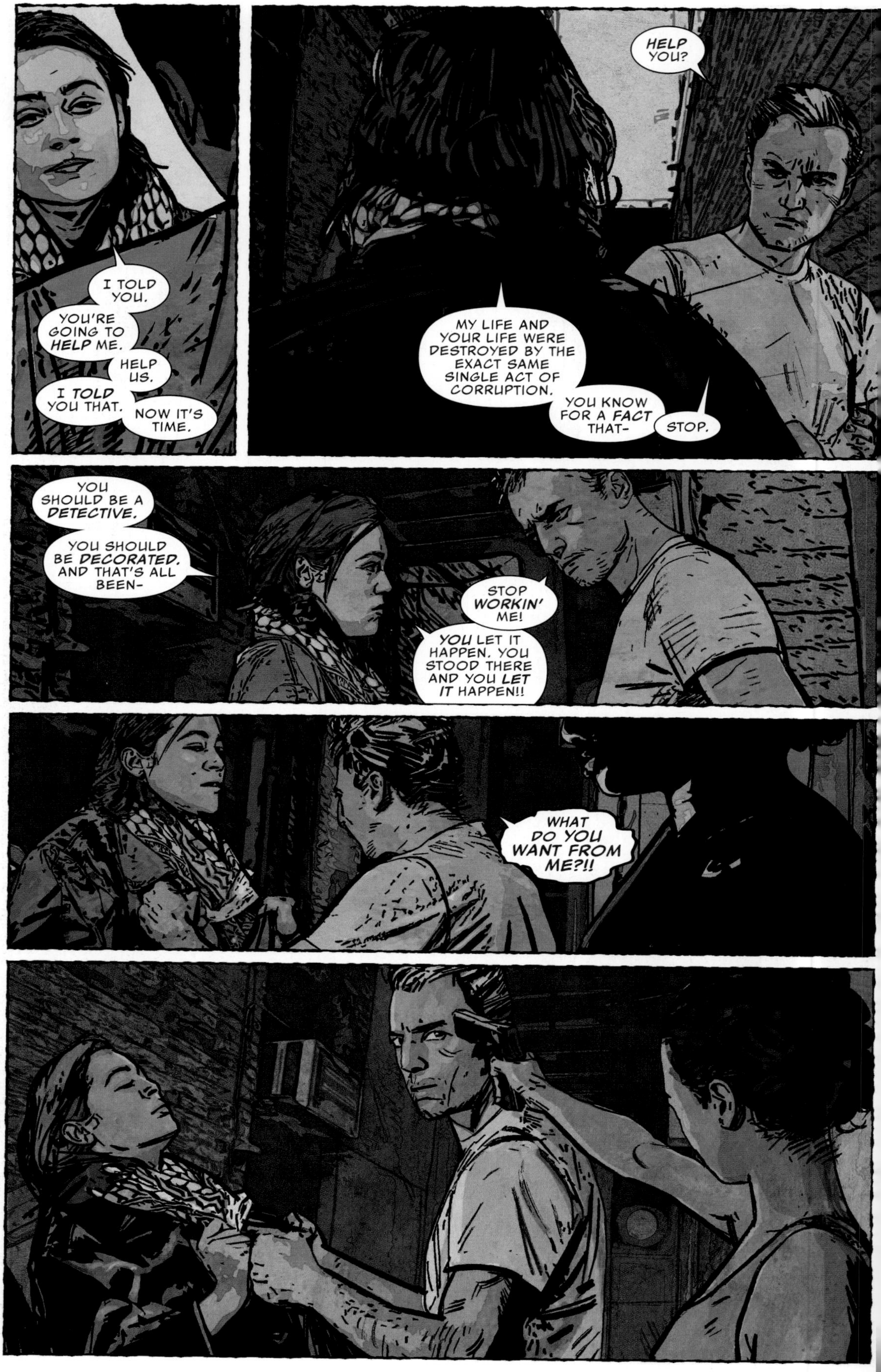
I TOLD YOU.
YOU'RE GOING TO HELP ME.
HELP US.
I TOLD YOU THAT.
NOW IT'S TIME.
HELP YOU?
MY LIFE AND YOUR LIFE WERE DESTROYED BY THE EXACT SAME SINGLE ACT OF CORRUPTION.
YOU KNOW FOR A FACT THAT-
STOP.
YOU SHOULD BE A DETECTIVE.
YOU SHOULD BE DECORATED. AND THAT'S ALL BEEN-
STOP WORKIN' ME!
YOU LET IT HAPPEN. YOU STOOD THERE AND YOU LET IT HAPPEN!!
WHAT DO YOU WANT FROM ME?!!

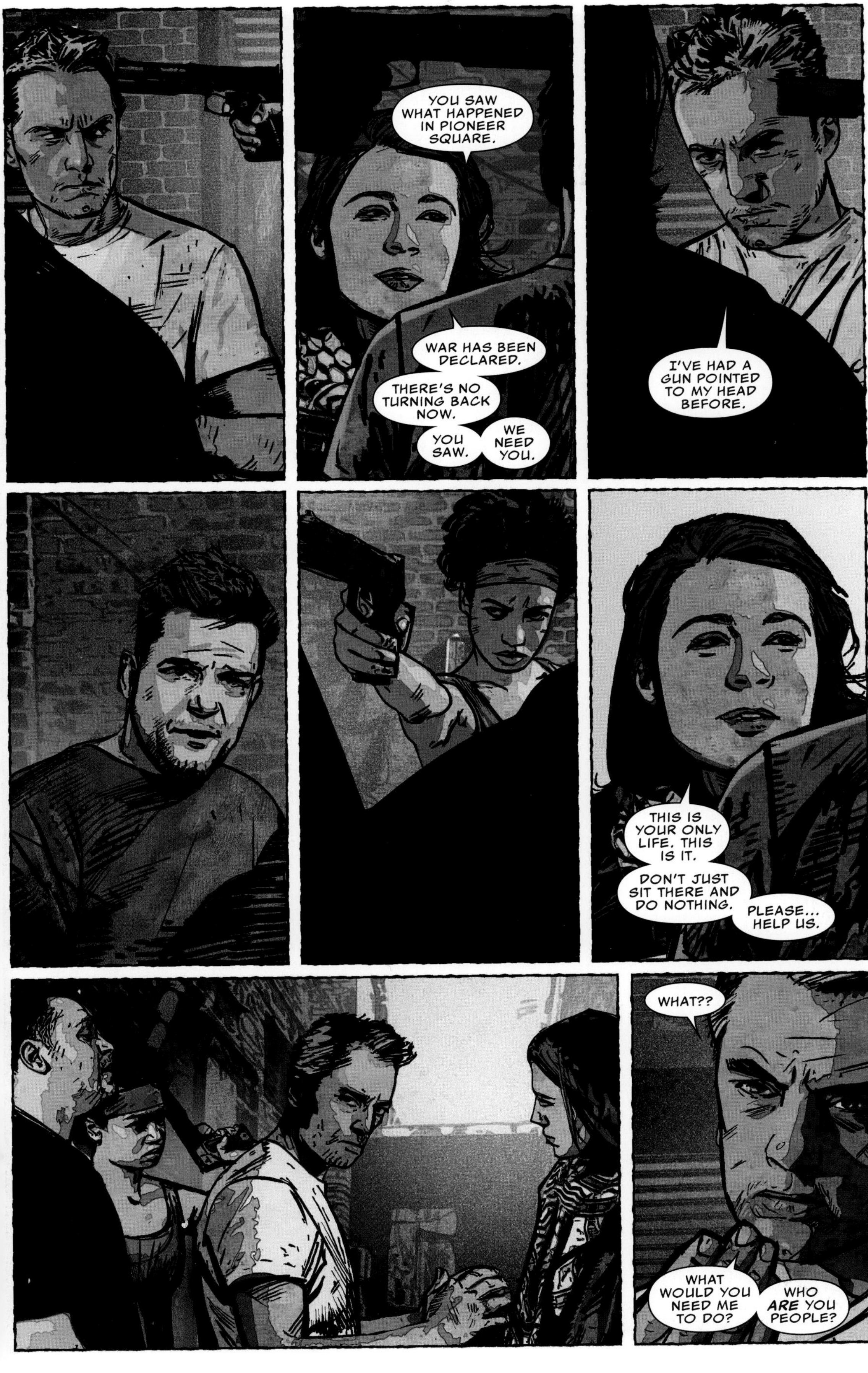
YOU SAW WHAT HAPPENED IN PIONEER SQUARE.
WAR HAS BEEN DECLARED.
THERE'S NO TURNING BACK NOW.
YOU SAW.
WE NEED YOU.
I'VE HAD A GUN POINTED TO MY HEAD BEFORE.
THIS IS YOUR ONLY LIFE. THIS IS IT.
DON'T JUST SIT THERE AND DO NOTHING.
PLEASE... HELP US.
WHAT??
WHAT WOULD YOU NEED ME TO DO?
WHO ARE YOU PEOPLE?

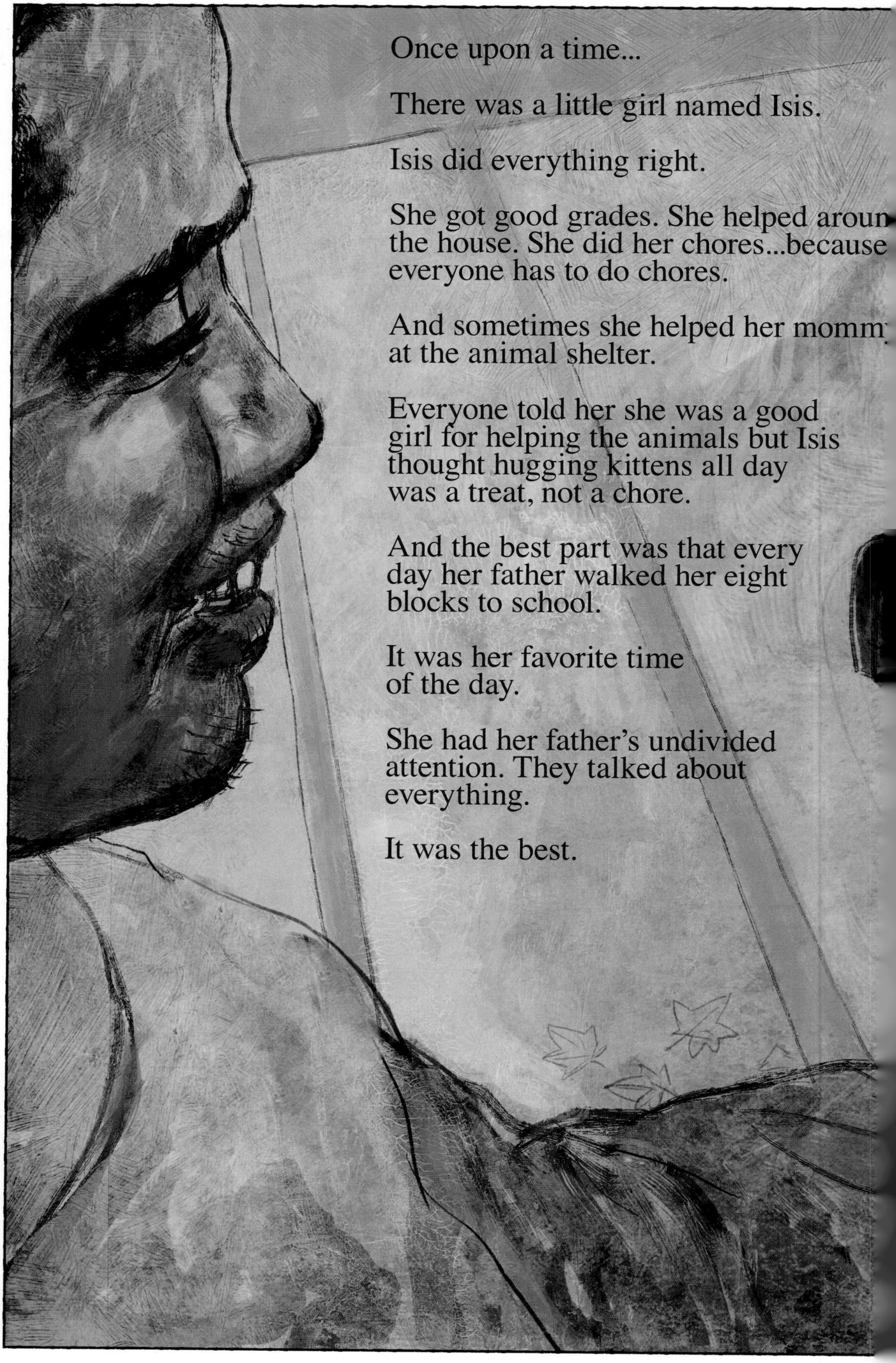

Once upon a time...

There was a little girl named Isis.

Isis did everything right.

She got good grades. She helped aroun
the house. She did her chores...because
everyone has to do chores.

And sometimes she helped her momm
at the animal shelter.

Everyone told her she was a good girl for helping the animals but Isis thought hugging kittens all day was a treat, not a chore.

And the best part was that every day her father walked her eight blocks to school.

It was her favorite time of the day.

She had her father's undivided attention. They talked about everything.

It was the best.

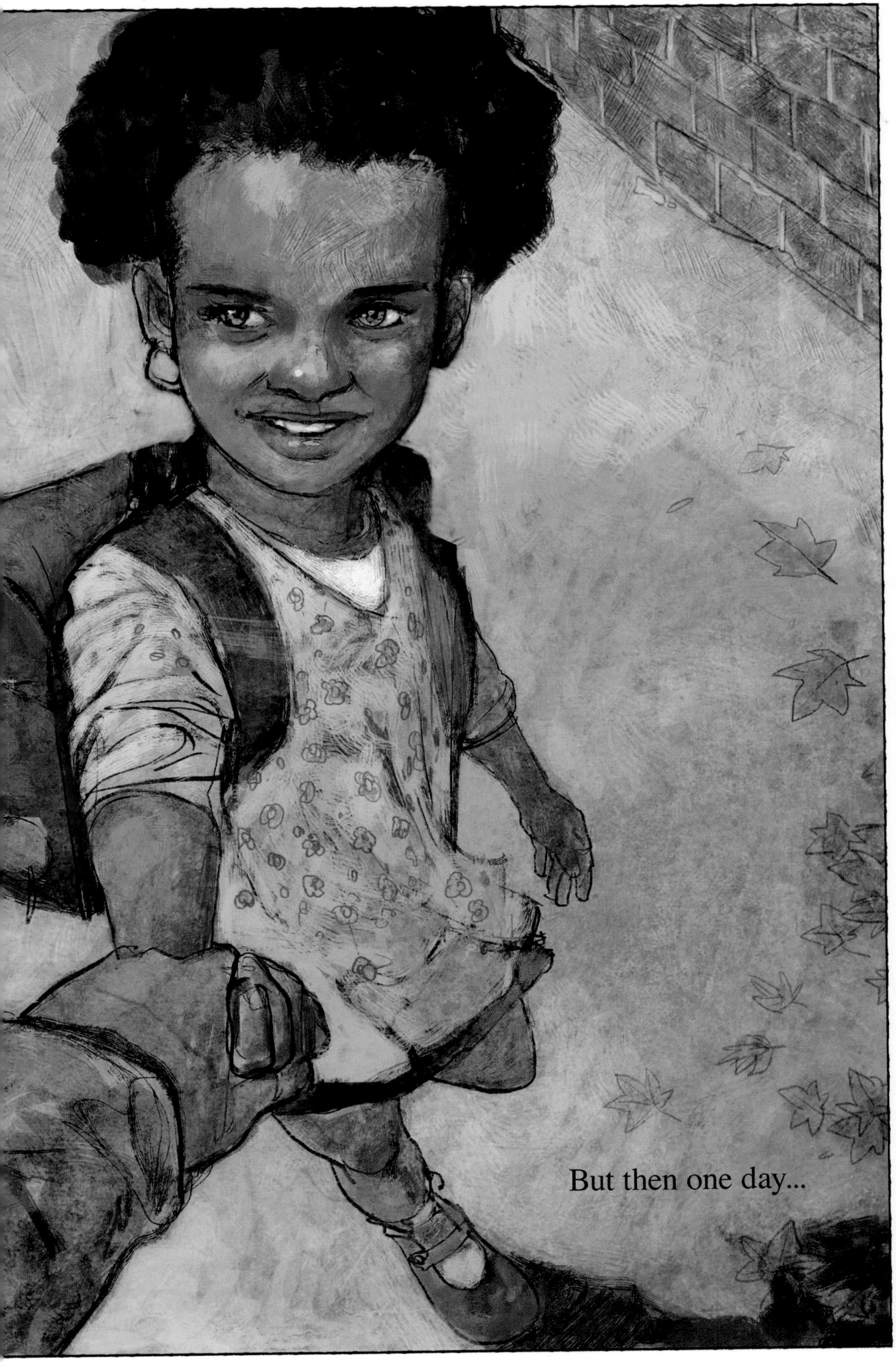
But then one day...

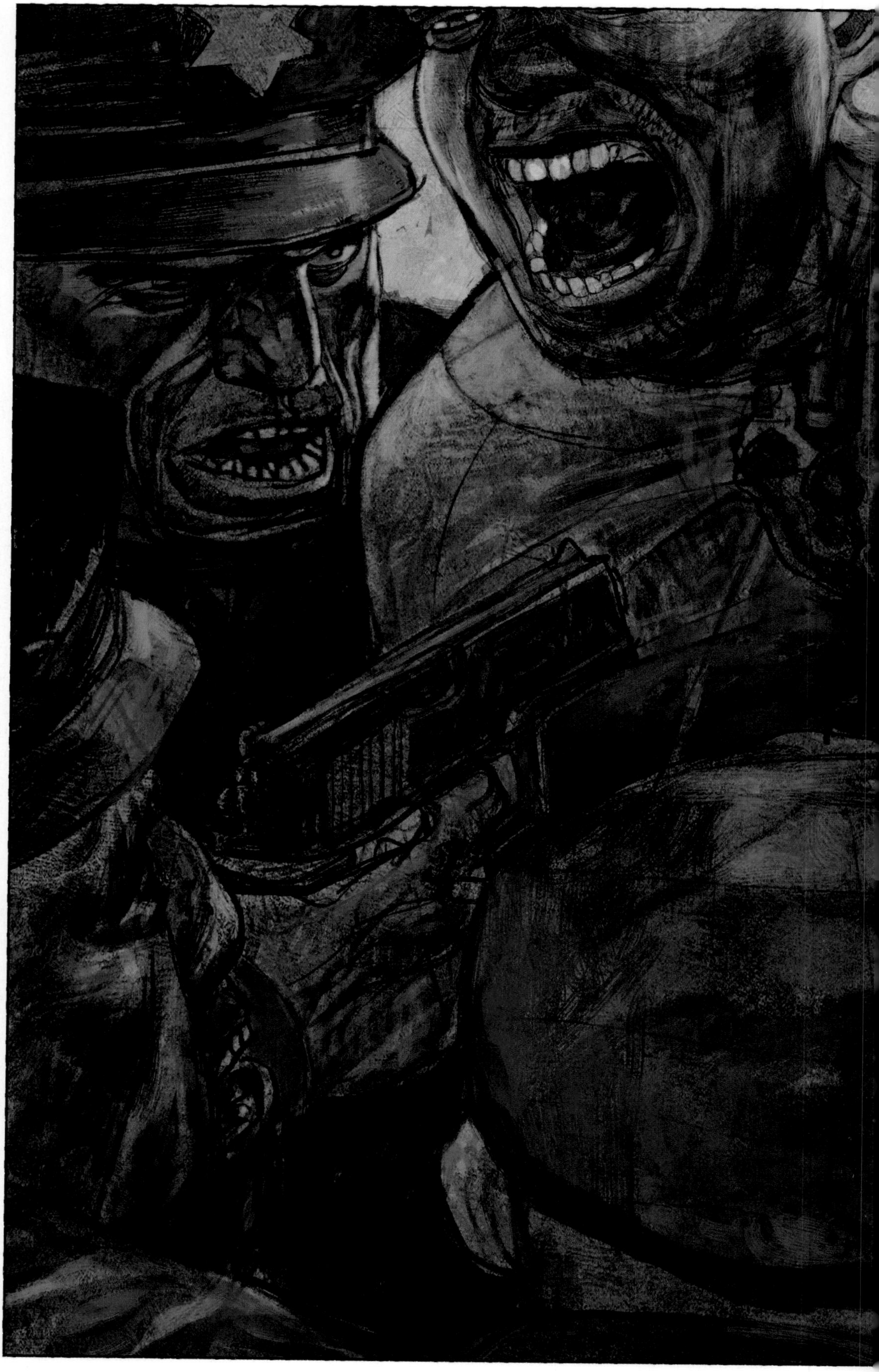

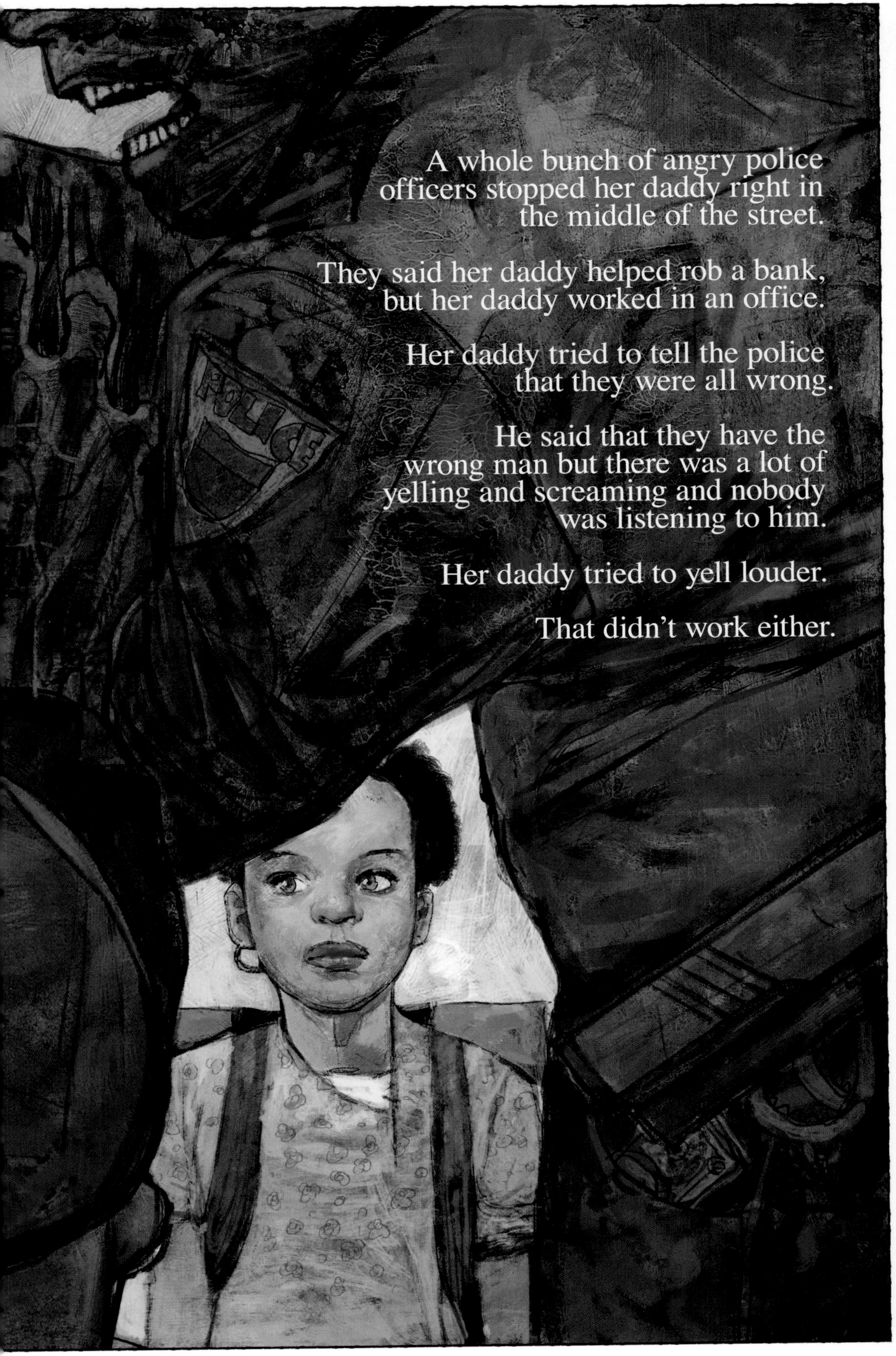
A whole bunch of angry police officers stopped her daddy right in the middle of the street.
They said her daddy helped rob a bank, but her daddy worked in an office.
Her daddy tried to tell the police that they were all wrong.
He said that they have the wrong man but there was a lot of yelling and screaming and nobody was listening to him.
Her daddy tried to yell louder.
That didn't work either.

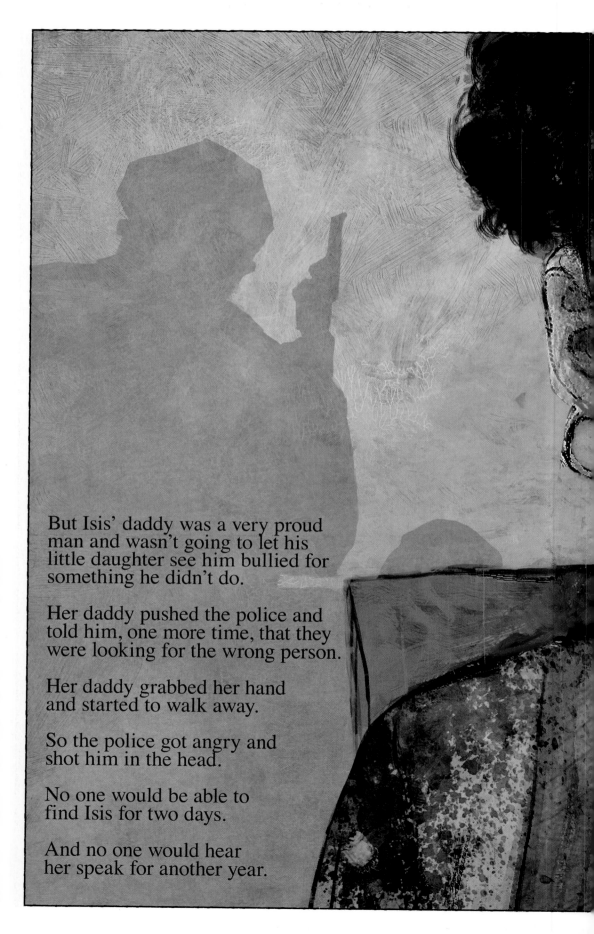

But Isis' daddy was a very proud man and wasn't going to let his little daughter see him bullied for something he didn't do.

Her daddy pushed the police and told him, one more time, that they were looking for the wrong person.

Her daddy grabbed her hand and started to walk away.

So the police got angry and shot him in the head.

No one would be able to find Isis for two days.

And no one would hear her speak for another year.

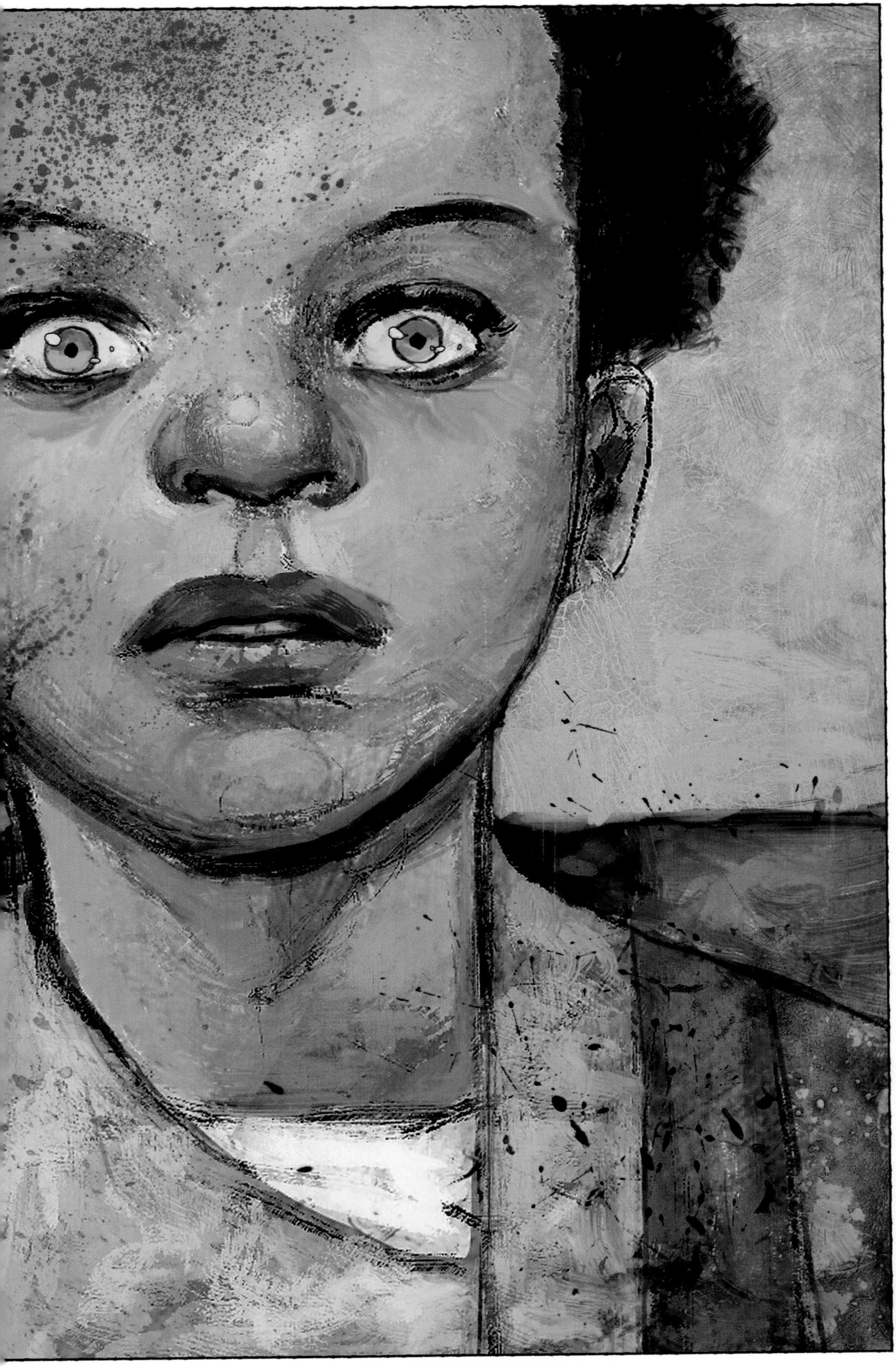

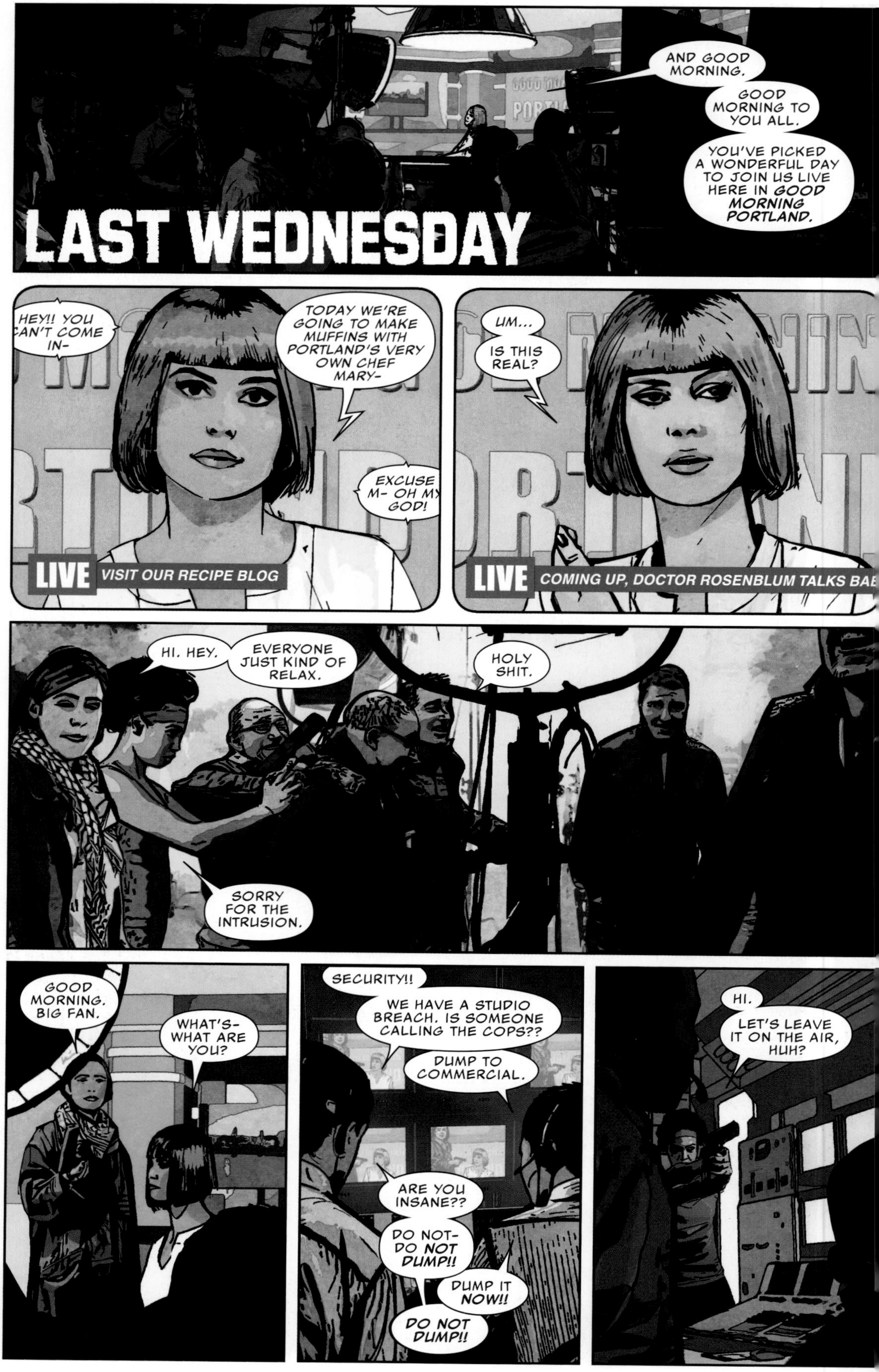
LAST WEDNESDAY
AND GOOD MORNING.
GOOD MORNING TO YOU ALL.
YOU'VE PICKED A WONDERFUL DAY TO JOIN US LIVE HERE IN GOOD MORNING PORTLAND.
HEY!! YOU CAN'T COME IN-
TODAY WE'RE GOING TO MAKE MUFFINS WITH PORTLAND'S VERY OWN CHEF MARY-
EXCUSE M- OH MY GOD!
LIVE
VISIT OUR RECIPE BLOG
UM...
IS THIS REAL?
LIVE
COMING UP, DOCTOR ROSENBLUM TALKS BAB
HI. HEY.
EVERYONE JUST KIND OF RELAX.
HOLY SHIT.
SORRY FOR THE INTRUSION.
GOOD MORNING. BIG FAN.
WHAT'S- WHAT ARE YOU?
SECURITY!!
WE HAVE A STUDIO BREACH. IS SOMEONE CALLING THE COPS??
DUMP TO COMMERCIAL.
ARE YOU INSANE??
DO NOT- DO NOT DUMP!!
DUMP IT NOW!!
DO NOT DUMP!!
HI.
LET'S LEAVE IT ON THE AIR, HUH?

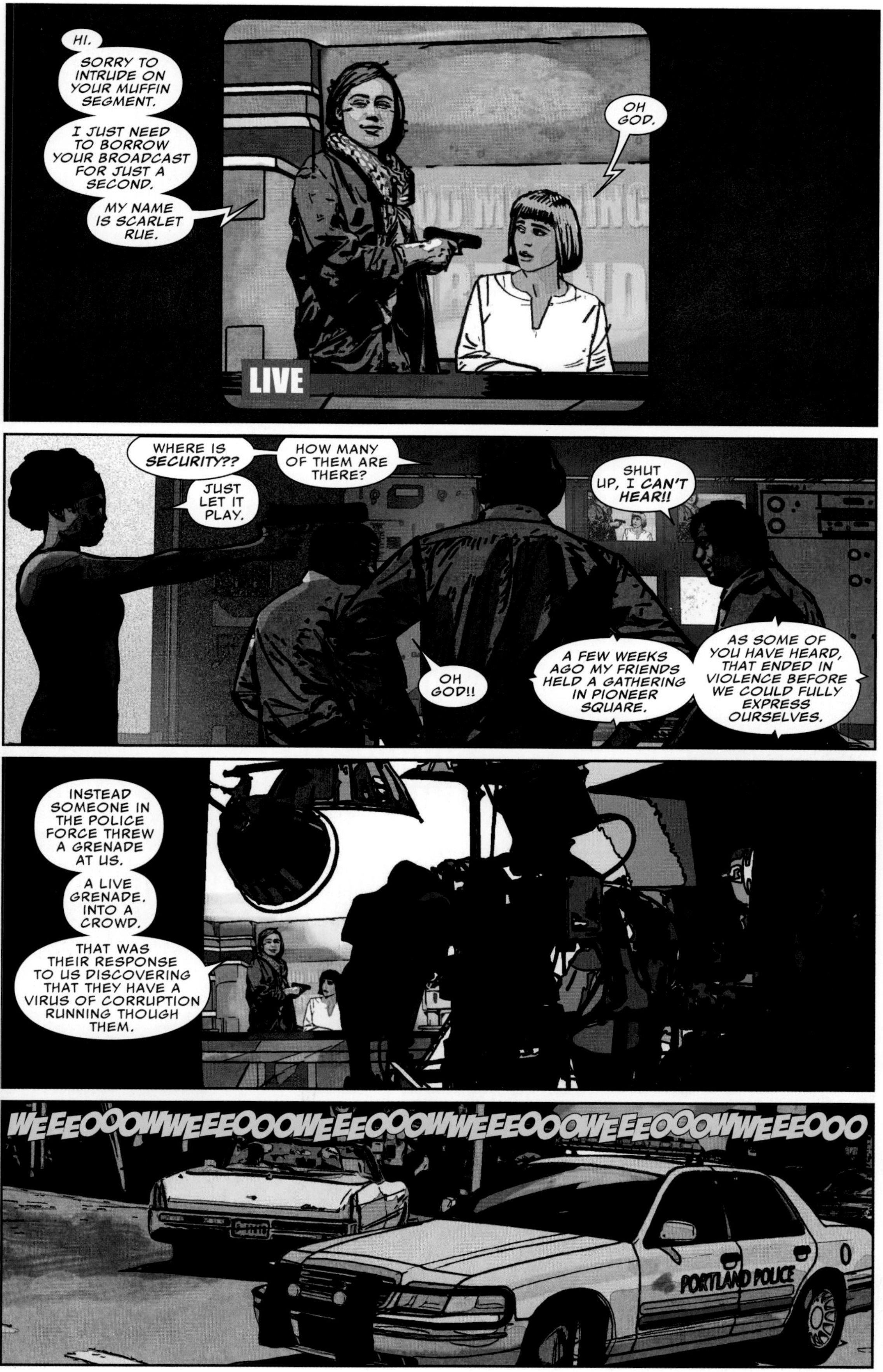
HI.
SORRY TO INTRUDE ON YOUR MUFFIN SEGMENT.
I JUST NEED TO BORROW YOUR BROADCAST FOR JUST A SECOND.
MY NAME IS SCARLET RUE.
OH GOD.
LIVE
WHERE IS SECURITY??
HOW MANY OF THEM ARE THERE?
JUST LET IT PLAY.
SHUT UP, I CAN'T HEAR!!
OH GOD!!
A FEW WEEKS AGO MY FRIENDS HELD A GATHERING IN PIONEER SQUARE.
AS SOME OF YOU HAVE HEARD, THAT ENDED IN VIOLENCE BEFORE WE COULD FULLY EXPRESS OURSELVES.
INSTEAD SOMEONE IN THE POLICE FORCE THREW A GRENADE AT US.
A LIVE GRENADE. INTO A CROWD.
THAT WAS THEIR RESPONSE TO US DISCOVERING THAT THEY HAVE A VIRUS OF CORRUPTION RUNNING THOUGH THEM.
WEEEOOOWWEEEOOOWEEEOOOWWEEEOOOWEEEOOOWWEEEOOO
PORTLAND POLICE

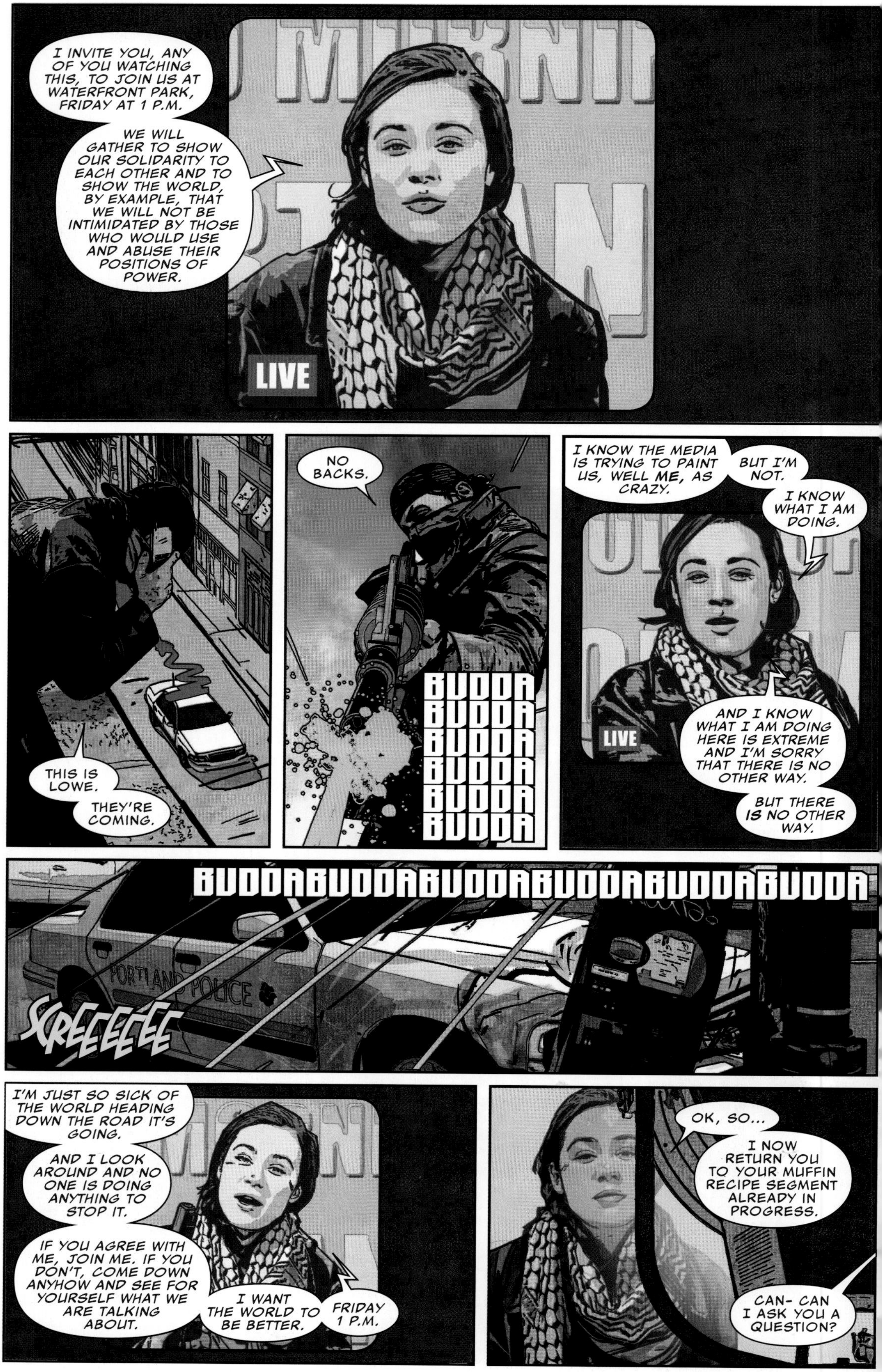
I INVITE YOU, ANY OF YOU WATCHING THIS, TO JOIN US AT WATERFRONT PARK, FRIDAY AT 1 P.M.
WE WILL GATHER TO SHOW OUR SOLIDARITY TO EACH OTHER AND TO SHOW THE WORLD, BY EXAMPLE, THAT WE WILL NOT BE INTIMIDATED BY THOSE WHO WOULD USE AND ABUSE THEIR POSITIONS OF POWER.
LIVE
THIS IS LOWE.
THEY'RE COMING.
NO BACKS.
BUDDA BUDDA BUDDA BUDDA BUDDA BUDDA
I KNOW THE MEDIA IS TRYING TO PAINT US, WELL ME, AS CRAZY.
BUT I'M NOT.
I KNOW WHAT I AM DOING.
LIVE
AND I KNOW WHAT I AM DOING HERE IS EXTREME AND I'M SORRY THAT THERE IS NO OTHER WAY.
BUT THERE IS NO OTHER WAY.
BUDDABUDDABUDDABUDDABUDDABUDDA
PORTLAND POLICE
SCREEEEEE
I'M JUST SO SICK OF THE WORLD HEADING DOWN THE ROAD IT'S GOING.
AND I LOOK AROUND AND NO ONE IS DOING ANYTHING TO STOP IT.
IF YOU AGREE WITH ME, JOIN ME. IF YOU DON'T, COME DOWN ANYHOW AND SEE FOR YOURSELF WHAT WE ARE TALKING ABOUT.
I WANT THE WORLD TO BE BETTER.
FRIDAY 1 P.M.
OK, SO...
I NOW RETURN YOU TO YOUR MUFFIN RECIPE SEGMENT ALREADY IN PROGRESS.
CAN- CAN I ASK YOU A QUESTION?

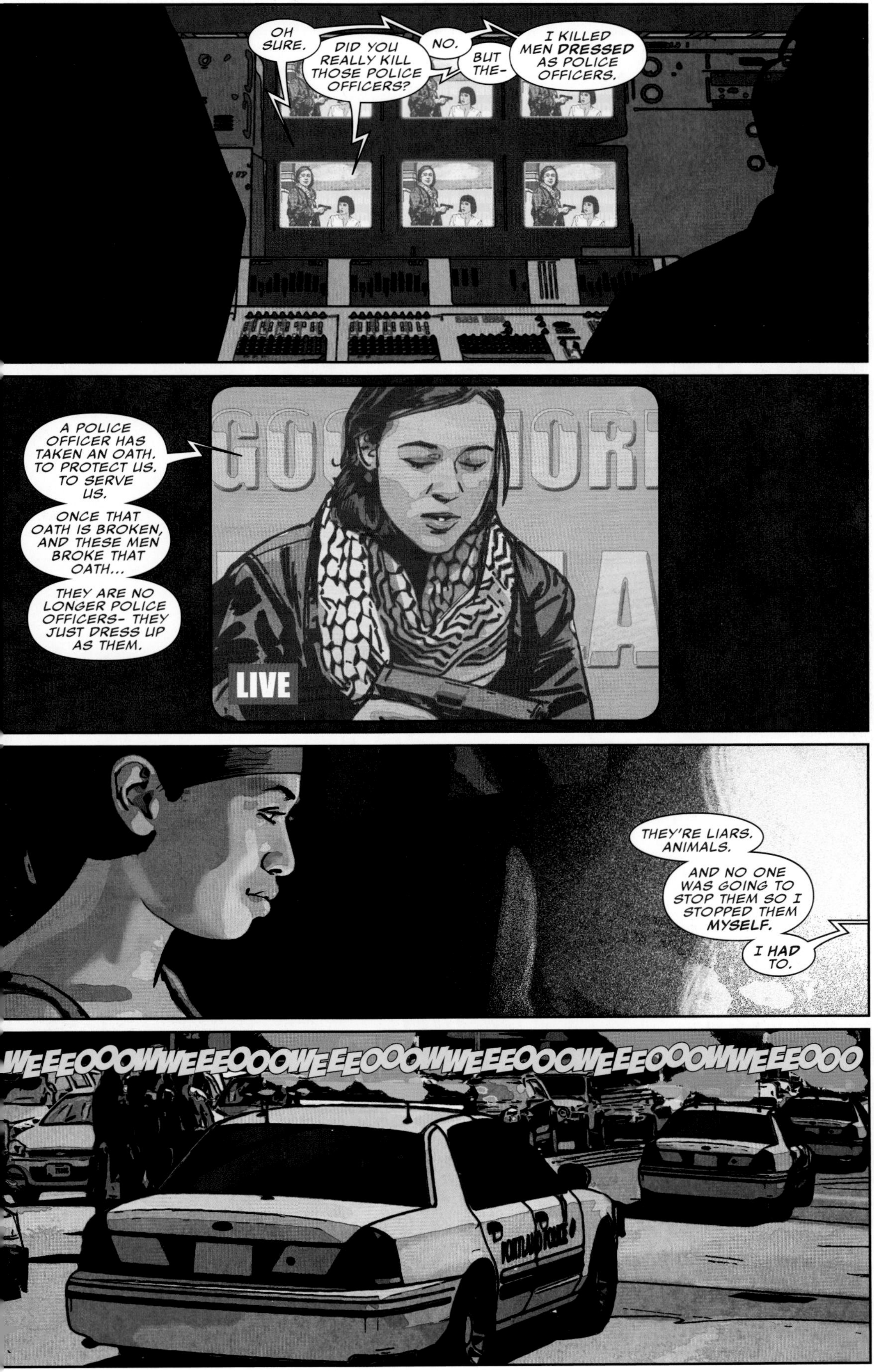
OH SURE.
DID YOU REALLY KILL THOSE POLICE OFFICERS?
NO.
BUT THE-
I KILLED MEN DRESSED AS POLICE OFFICERS.
A POLICE OFFICER HAS TAKEN AN OATH. TO PROTECT US. TO SERVE US.
ONCE THAT OATH IS BROKEN, AND THESE MEN BROKE THAT OATH...
THEY ARE NO LONGER POLICE OFFICERS- THEY JUST DRESS UP AS THEM.
LIVE
THEY'RE LIARS. ANIMALS.
AND NO ONE WAS GOING TO STOP THEM SO I STOPPED THEM MYSELF.
I HAD TO.
WEEEOOOWWEEEOOOWEEEOOOWWEEEOOOWEEEOOOWWEEEOOO
PORTLAND POLICE

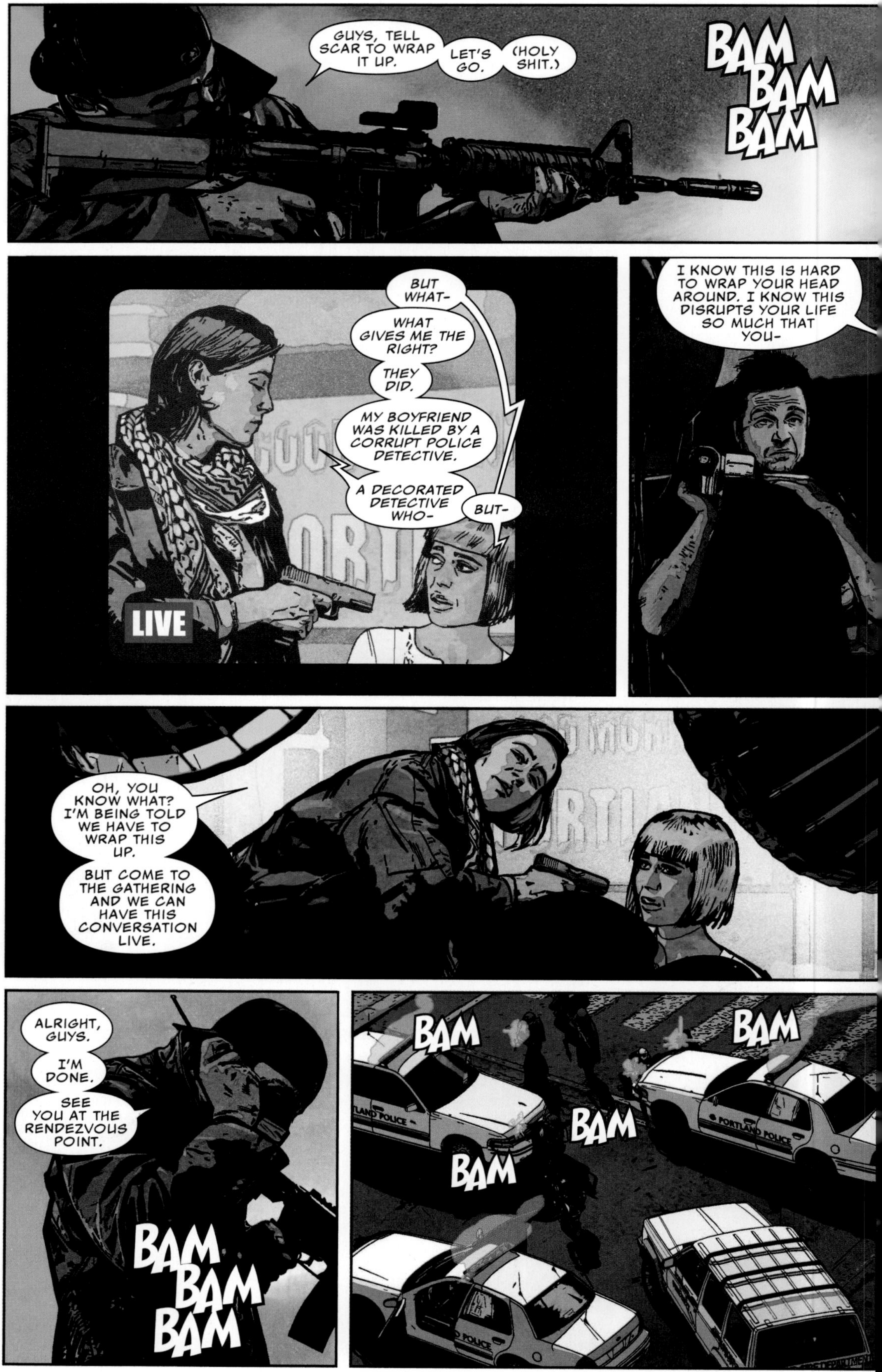
GUYS, TELL SCAR TO WRAP IT UP.
LET'S GO.
(HOLY SHIT.)
BAM BAM BAM
BUT WHAT-
WHAT GIVES ME THE RIGHT?
THEY DID.
MY BOYFRIEND WAS KILLED BY A CORRUPT POLICE DETECTIVE.
A DECORATED DETECTIVE WHO-
BUT-
LIVE
I KNOW THIS IS HARD TO WRAP YOUR HEAD AROUND. I KNOW THIS DISRUPTS YOUR LIFE SO MUCH THAT YOU-
OH, YOU KNOW WHAT? I'M BEING TOLD WE HAVE TO WRAP THIS UP.
BUT COME TO THE GATHERING AND WE CAN HAVE THIS CONVERSATION LIVE.
ALRIGHT, GUYS.
I'M DONE.
SEE YOU AT THE RENDEZVOUS POINT.
BAM BAM BAM
BAM
BAM
BAM
BAM
PORTLAND POLICE

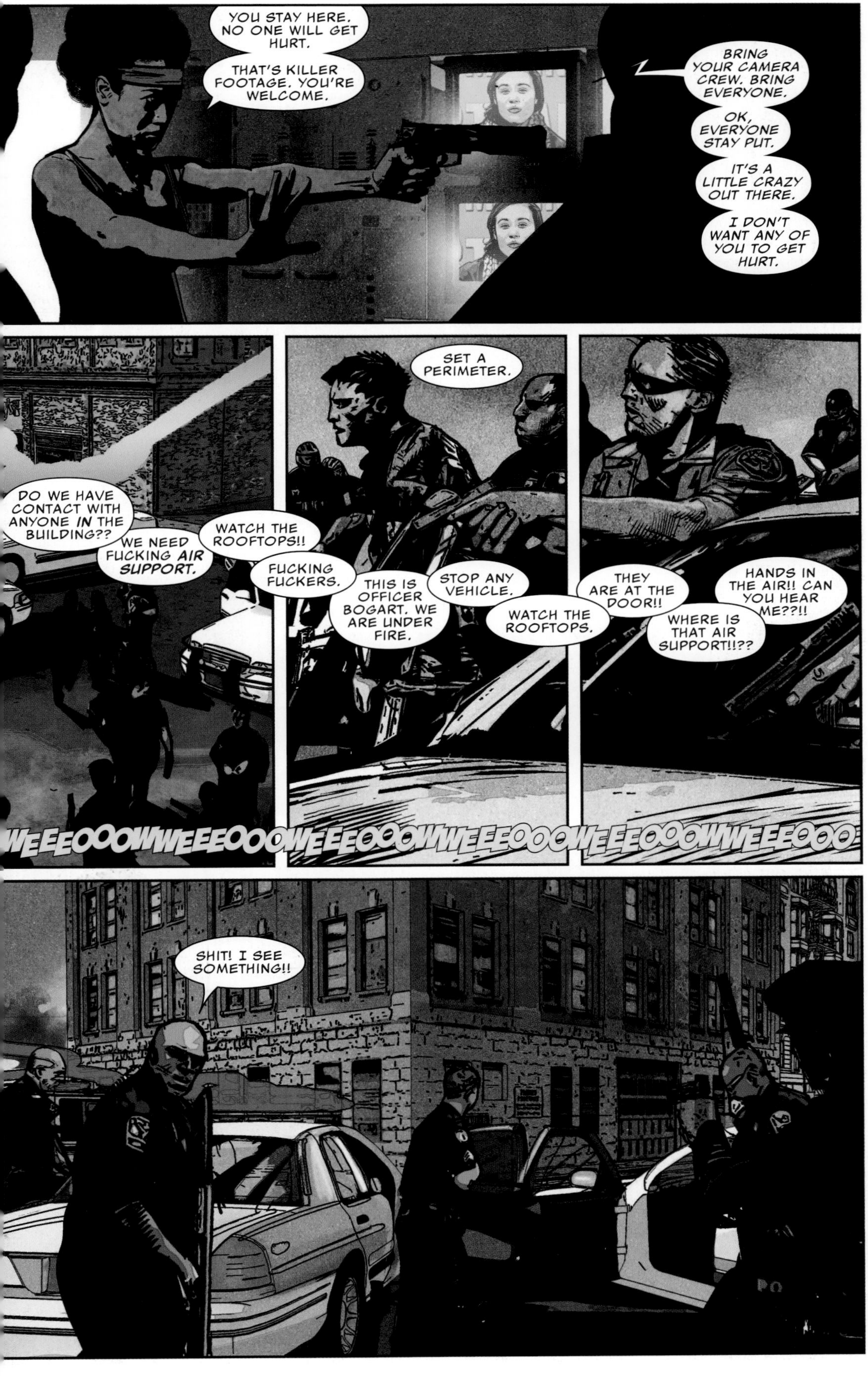
YOU STAY HERE. NO ONE WILL GET HURT.
THAT'S KILLER FOOTAGE. YOU'RE WELCOME.
BRING YOUR CAMERA CREW. BRING EVERYONE.
OK, EVERYONE STAY PUT.
IT'S A LITTLE CRAZY OUT THERE.
I DON'T WANT ANY OF YOU TO GET HURT.
DO WE HAVE CONTACT WITH ANYONE IN THE BUILDING??
WE NEED FUCKING AIR SUPPORT.
WATCH THE ROOFTOPS!!
FUCKING FUCKERS.
SET A PERIMETER.
THIS IS OFFICER BOGART. WE ARE UNDER FIRE.
STOP ANY VEHICLE.
WATCH THE ROOFTOPS.
THEY ARE AT THE DOOR!!
HANDS IN THE AIR!! CAN YOU HEAR ME??!!
WHERE IS THAT AIR SUPPORT!!??
WEEEOOOWWEEEOOOWEEEOOOWWEEEOOOWEEEOOOWWEEEOOO
SHIT! I SEE SOMETHING!!

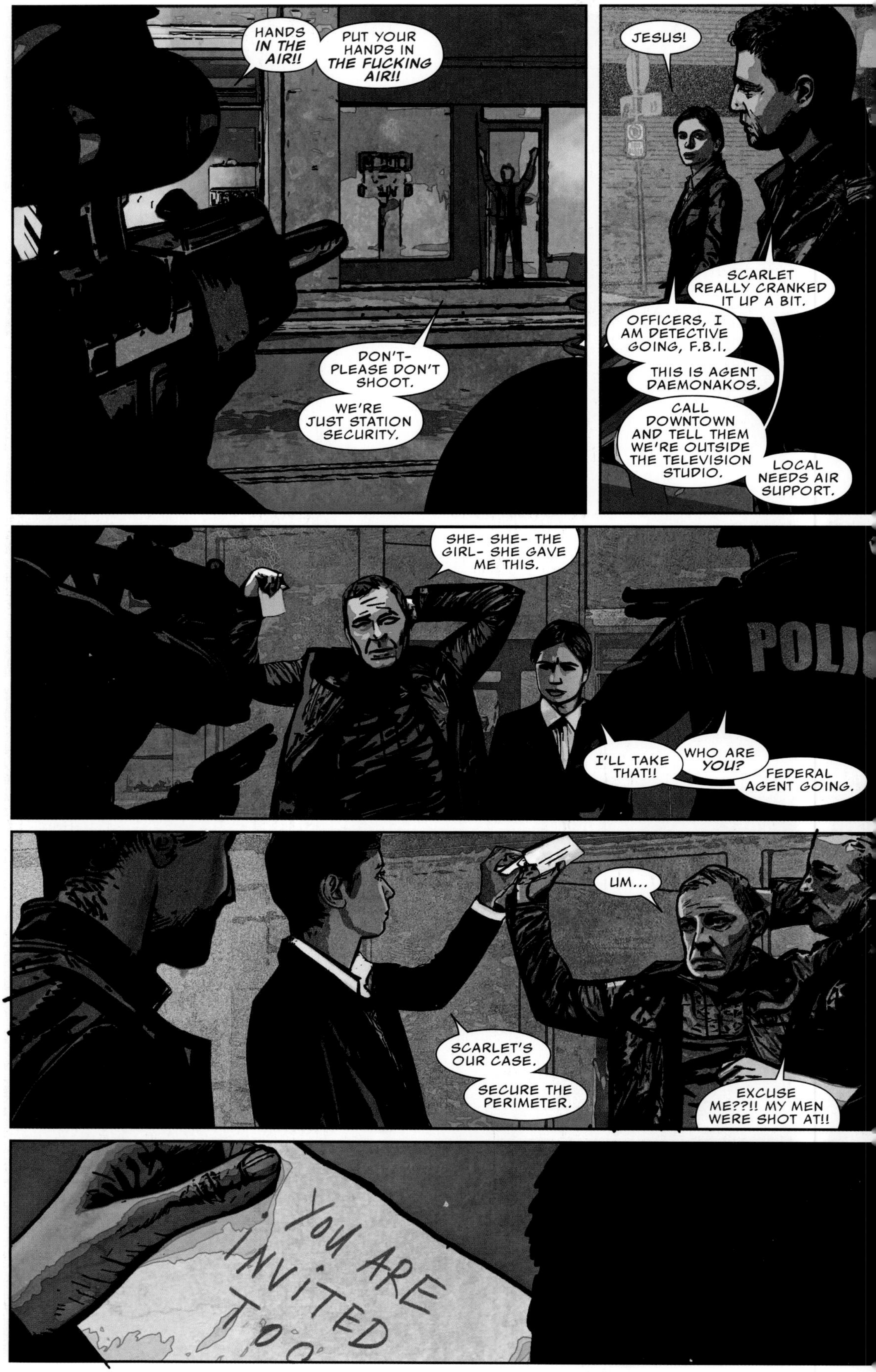
HANDS IN THE AIR!!
PUT YOUR HANDS IN THE FUCKING AIR!!
DON'T- PLEASE DON'T SHOOT.
WE'RE JUST STATION SECURITY.
JESUS!
SCARLET REALLY CRANKED IT UP A BIT.
OFFICERS, I AM DETECTIVE GOING, F.B.I.
THIS IS AGENT DAEMONAKOS.
CALL DOWNTOWN AND TELL THEM WE'RE OUTSIDE THE TELEVISION STUDIO.
LOCAL NEEDS AIR SUPPORT.
SHE- SHE- THE GIRL- SHE GAVE ME THIS.
POLIC
I'LL TAKE THAT!!
WHO ARE YOU?
FEDERAL AGENT GOING.
UM...
SCARLET'S OUR CASE.
SECURE THE PERIMETER.
EXCUSE ME??!! MY MEN WERE SHOT AT!!
YOU ARE INVITED TOO

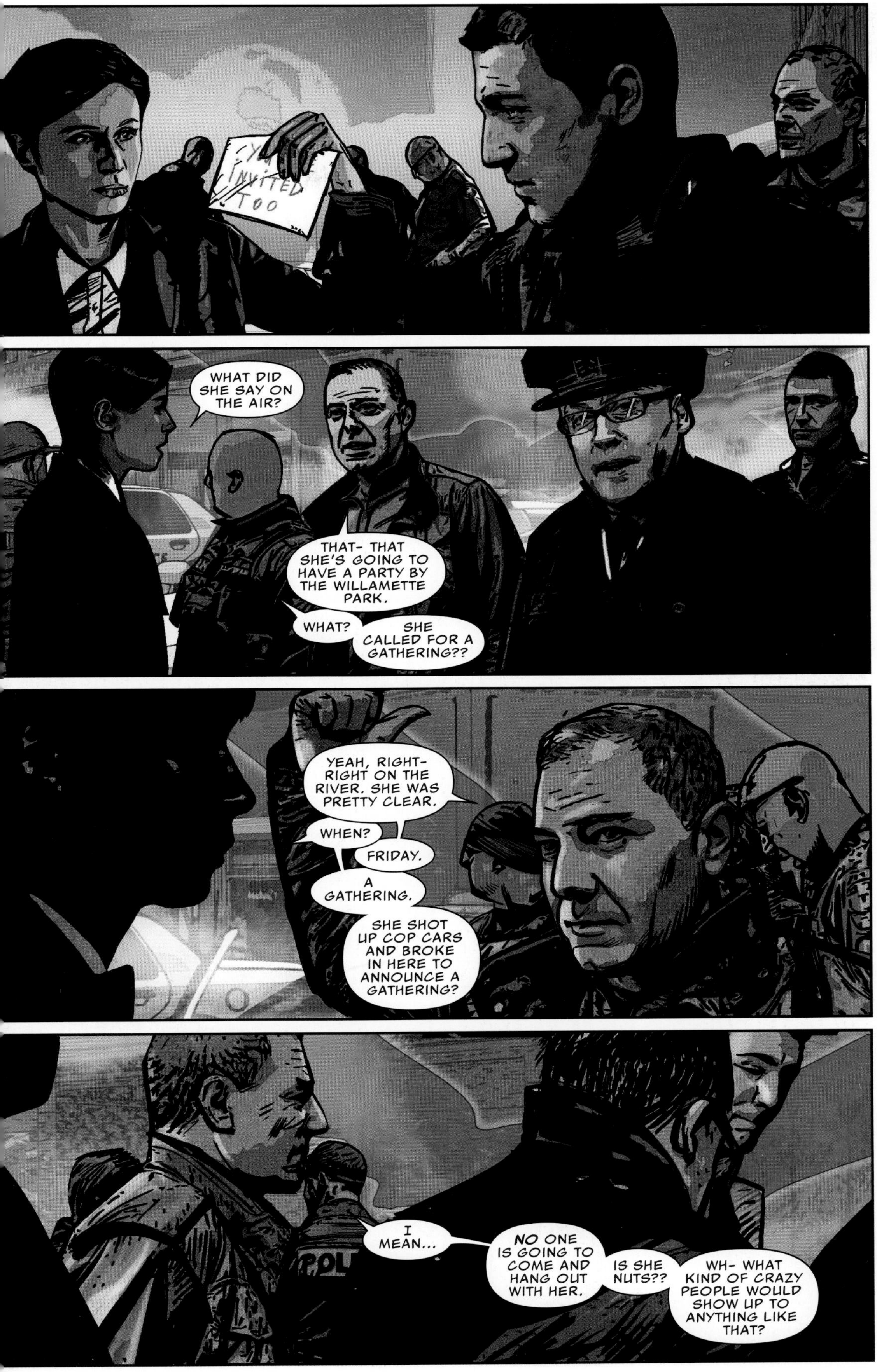
INVITED TOO
WHAT DID SHE SAY ON THE AIR?
THAT- THAT SHE'S GOING TO HAVE A PARTY BY THE WILLAMETTE PARK.
WHAT?
SHE CALLED FOR A GATHERING??
YEAH, RIGHT- RIGHT ON THE RIVER. SHE WAS PRETTY CLEAR.
WHEN?
FRIDAY.
A GATHERING.
SHE SHOT UP COP CARS AND BROKE IN HERE TO ANNOUNCE A GATHERING?
I MEAN...
NO ONE IS GOING TO COME AND HANG OUT WITH HER.
IS SHE NUTS??
WH- WHAT KIND OF CRAZY PEOPLE WOULD SHOW UP TO ANYTHING LIKE THAT?

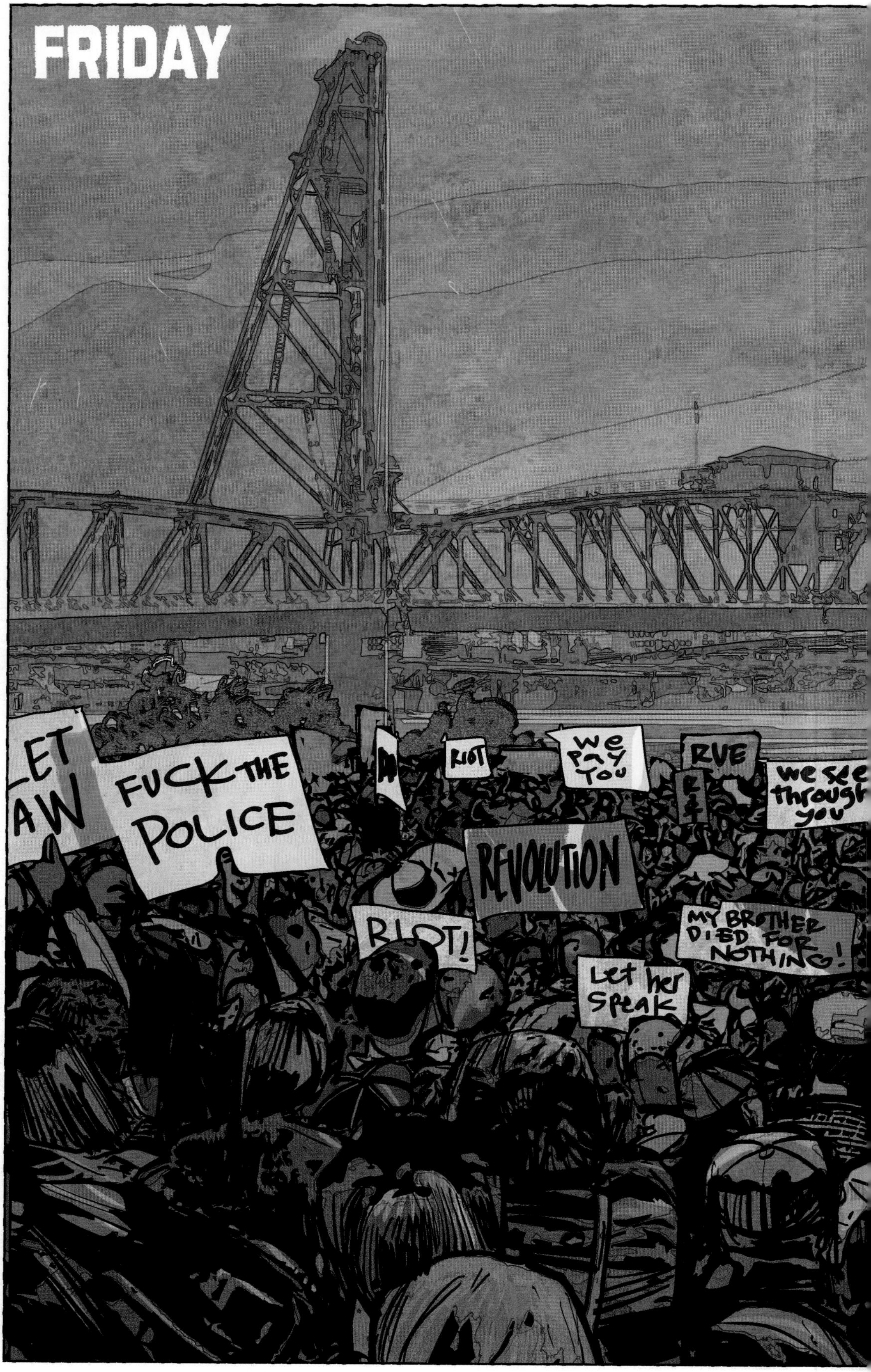
FRIDAY
FUCK THE POLICE
RIOT
we pay you
REVOLUTION
RIOT!
MY BROTHER DIED FOR NOTHING!
Let her speak

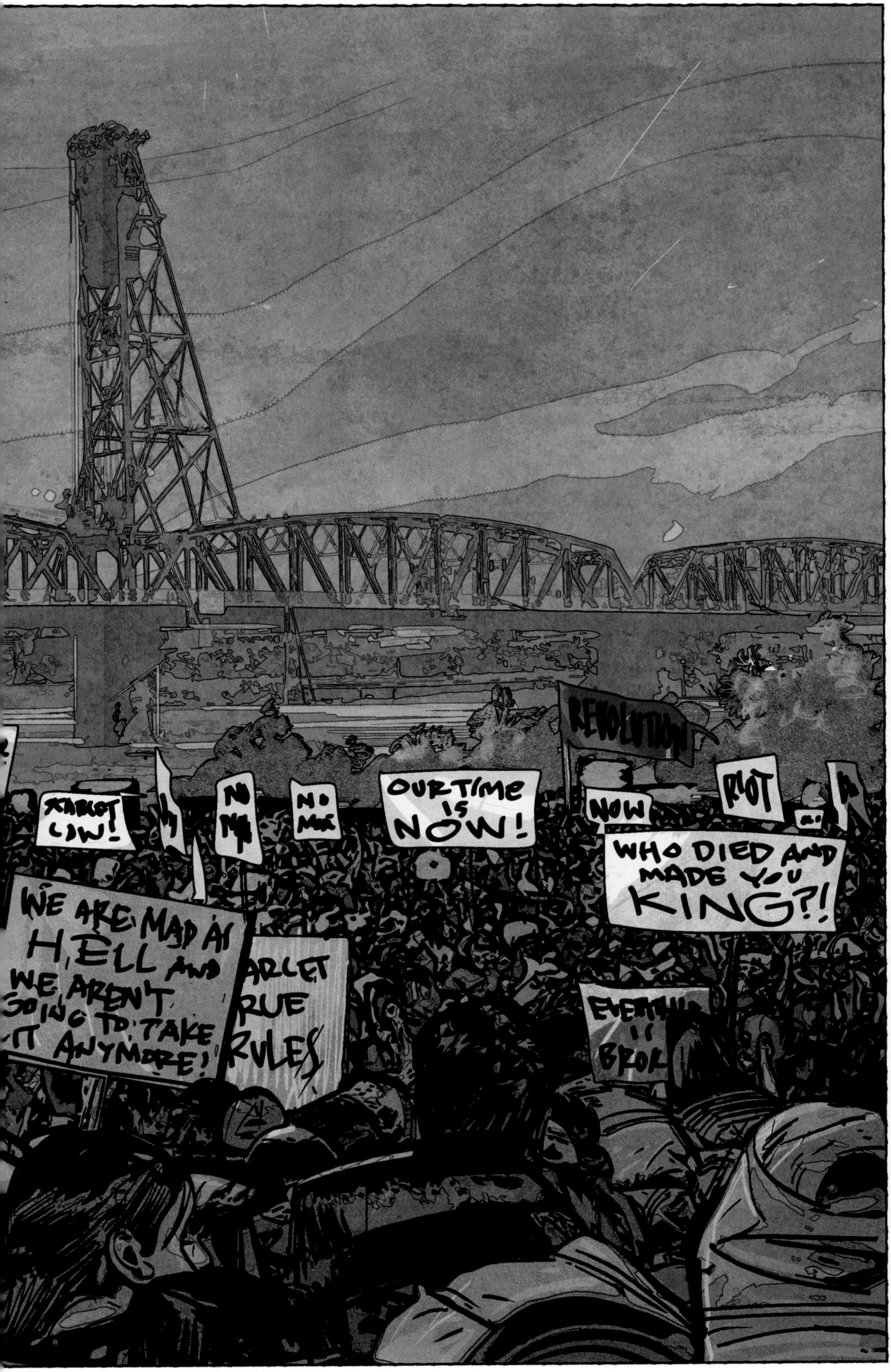
REVOLUTION
OUR TIME IS NOW!
NOW
RIOT
WHO DIED AND MADE YOU KING?!
WE ARE MAD AS HELL AND WE AREN'T GOING TO TAKE IT ANYMORE!

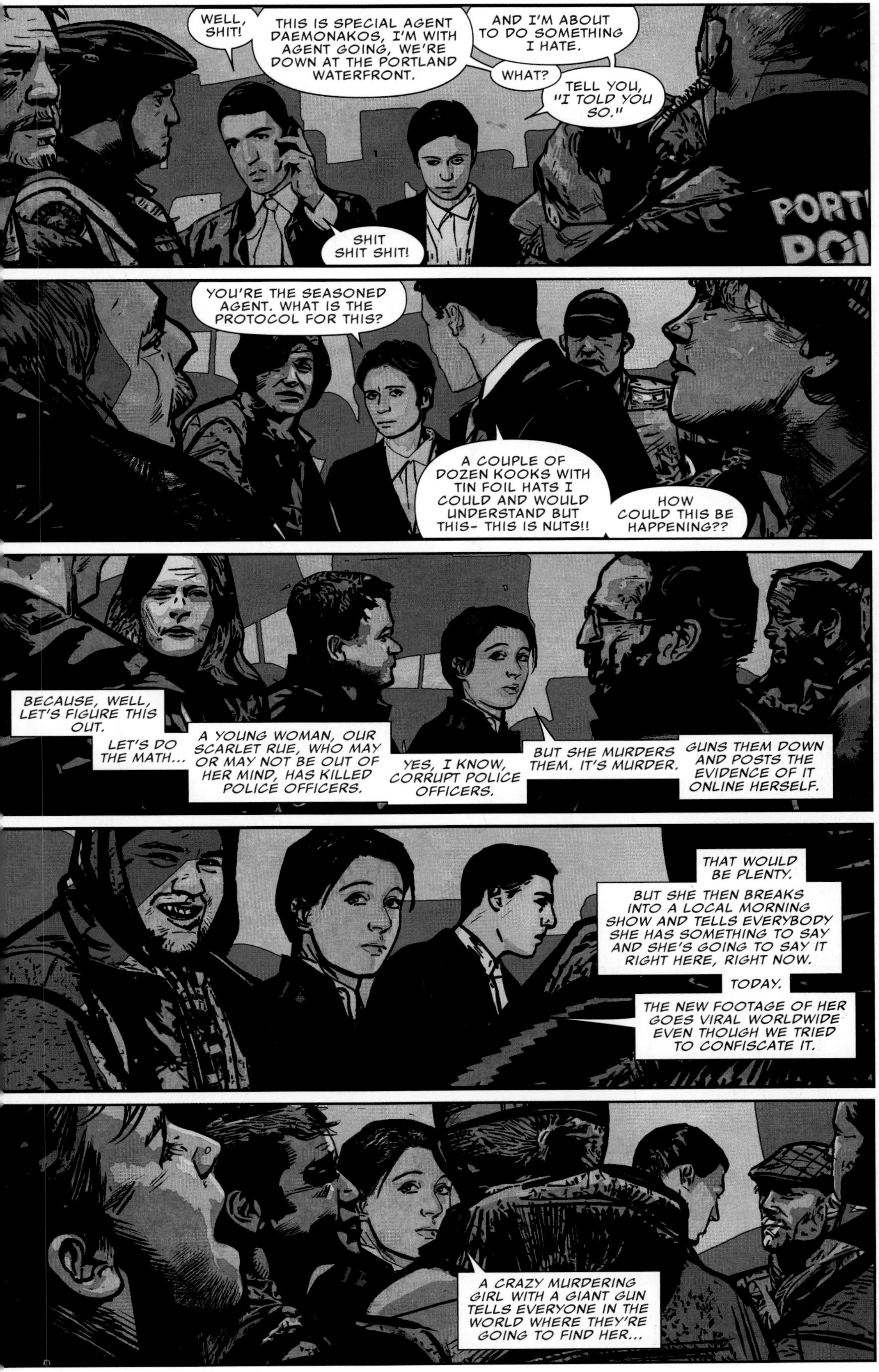
WELL, SHIT!
THIS IS SPECIAL AGENT DAEMONAKOS, I'M WITH AGENT GOING, WE'RE DOWN AT THE PORTLAND WATERFRONT.
AND I'M ABOUT TO DO SOMETHING I HATE.
WHAT?
TELL YOU, "I TOLD YOU SO."
SHIT SHIT SHIT!
PORT
POL
YOU'RE THE SEASONED AGENT. WHAT IS THE PROTOCOL FOR THIS?
A COUPLE OF DOZEN KOOKS WITH TIN FOIL HATS I COULD AND WOULD UNDERSTAND BUT THIS- THIS IS NUTS!!
HOW COULD THIS BE HAPPENING??
BECAUSE, WELL, LET'S FIGURE THIS OUT.
LET'S DO THE MATH...
A YOUNG WOMAN, OUR SCARLET RUE, WHO MAY OR MAY NOT BE OUT OF HER MIND, HAS KILLED POLICE OFFICERS.
YES, I KNOW, CORRUPT POLICE OFFICERS.
BUT SHE MURDERS THEM. IT'S MURDER.
GUNS THEM DOWN AND POSTS THE EVIDENCE OF IT ONLINE HERSELF.
THAT WOULD BE PLENTY.
BUT SHE THEN BREAKS INTO A LOCAL MORNING SHOW AND TELLS EVERYBODY SHE HAS SOMETHING TO SAY AND SHE'S GOING TO SAY IT RIGHT HERE, RIGHT NOW.
TODAY.
THE NEW FOOTAGE OF HER GOES VIRAL WORLDWIDE EVEN THOUGH WE TRIED TO CONFISCATE IT.
A CRAZY MURDERING GIRL WITH A GIANT GUN TELLS EVERYONE IN THE WORLD WHERE THEY'RE GOING TO FIND HER...

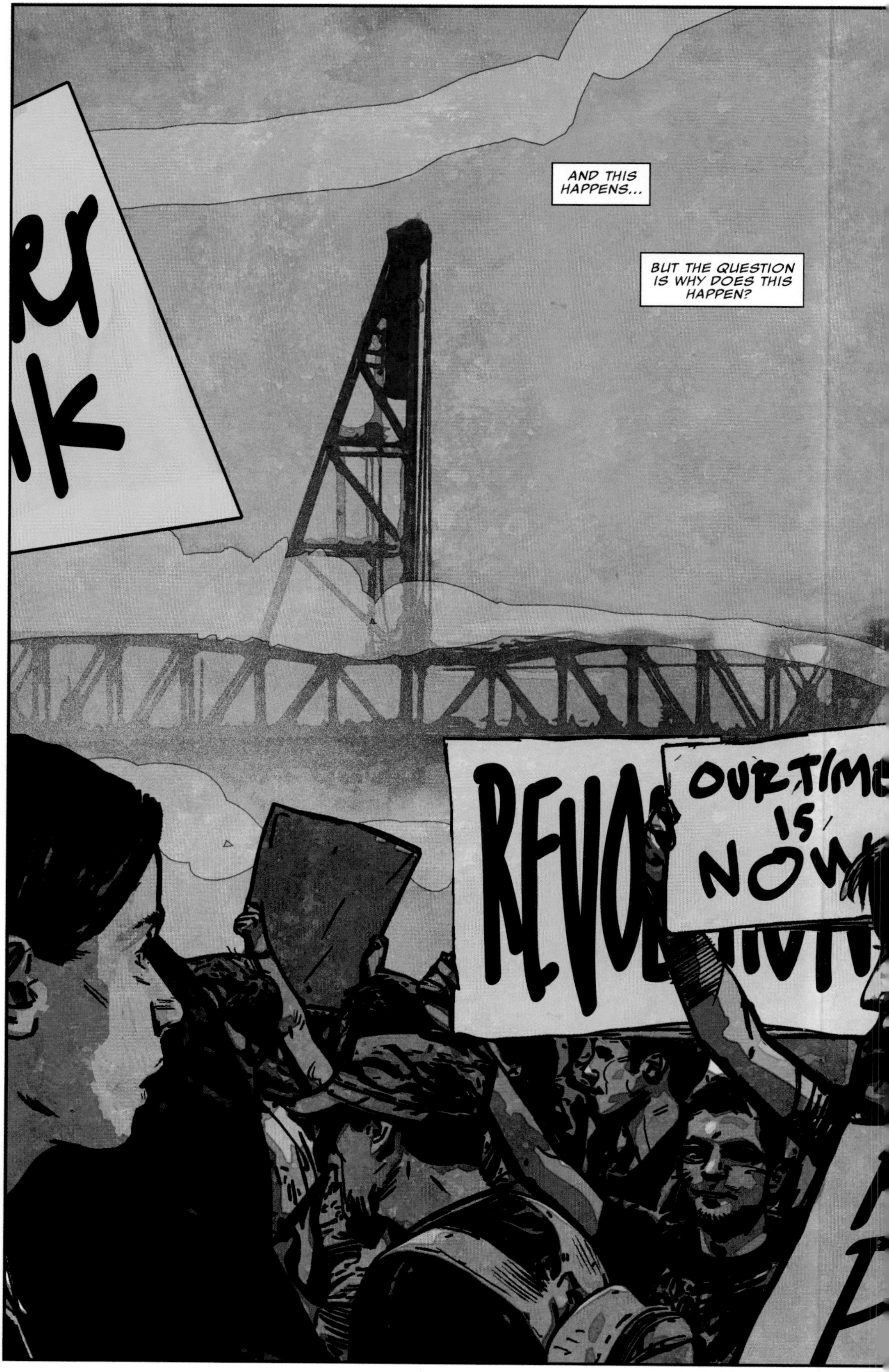
AND THIS HAPPENS...
BUT THE QUESTION IS WHY DOES THIS HAPPEN?
OUR TIME IS NOW

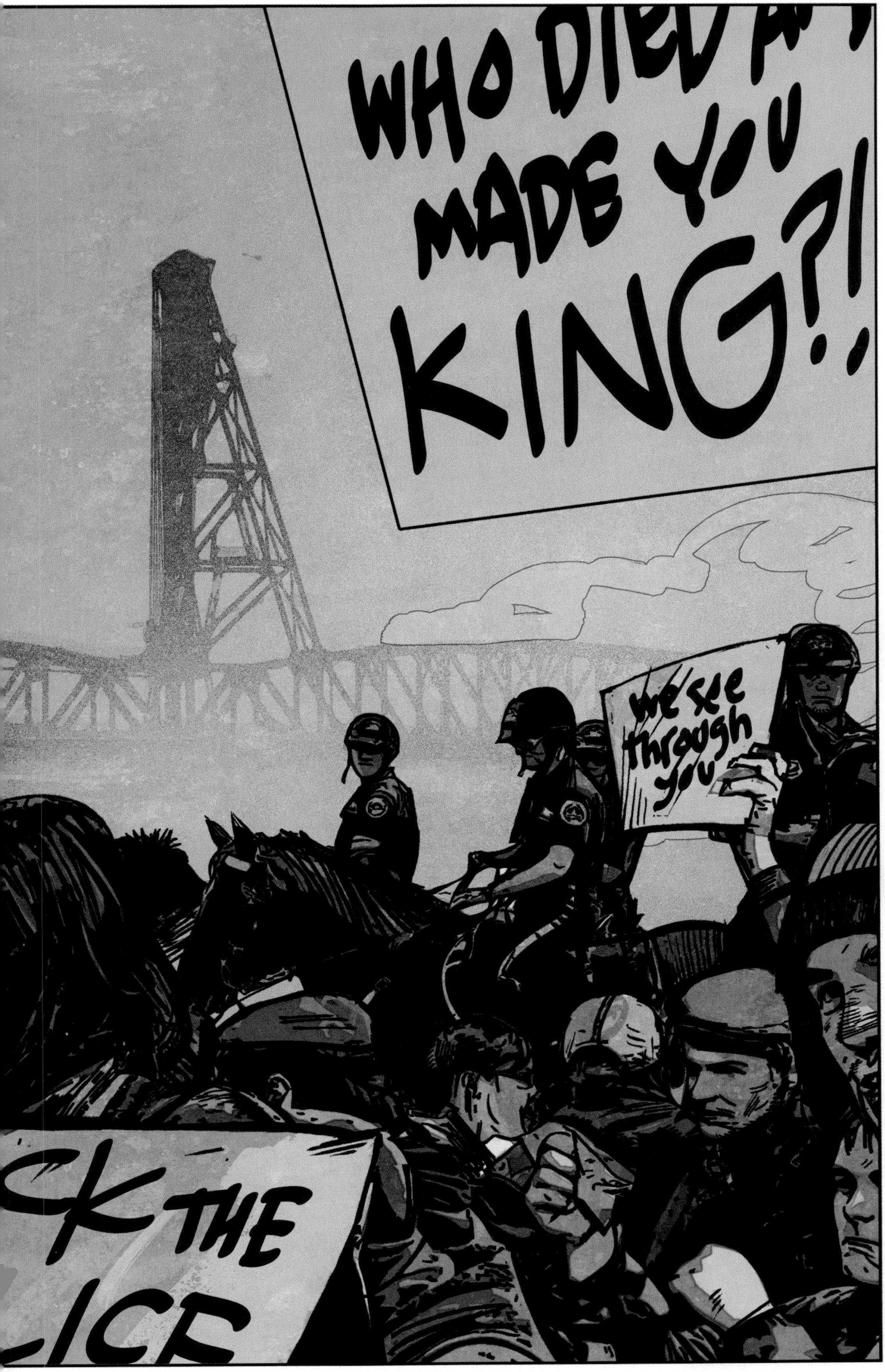

MADE YOU
KING?!
we see through you
CK THE
LICE

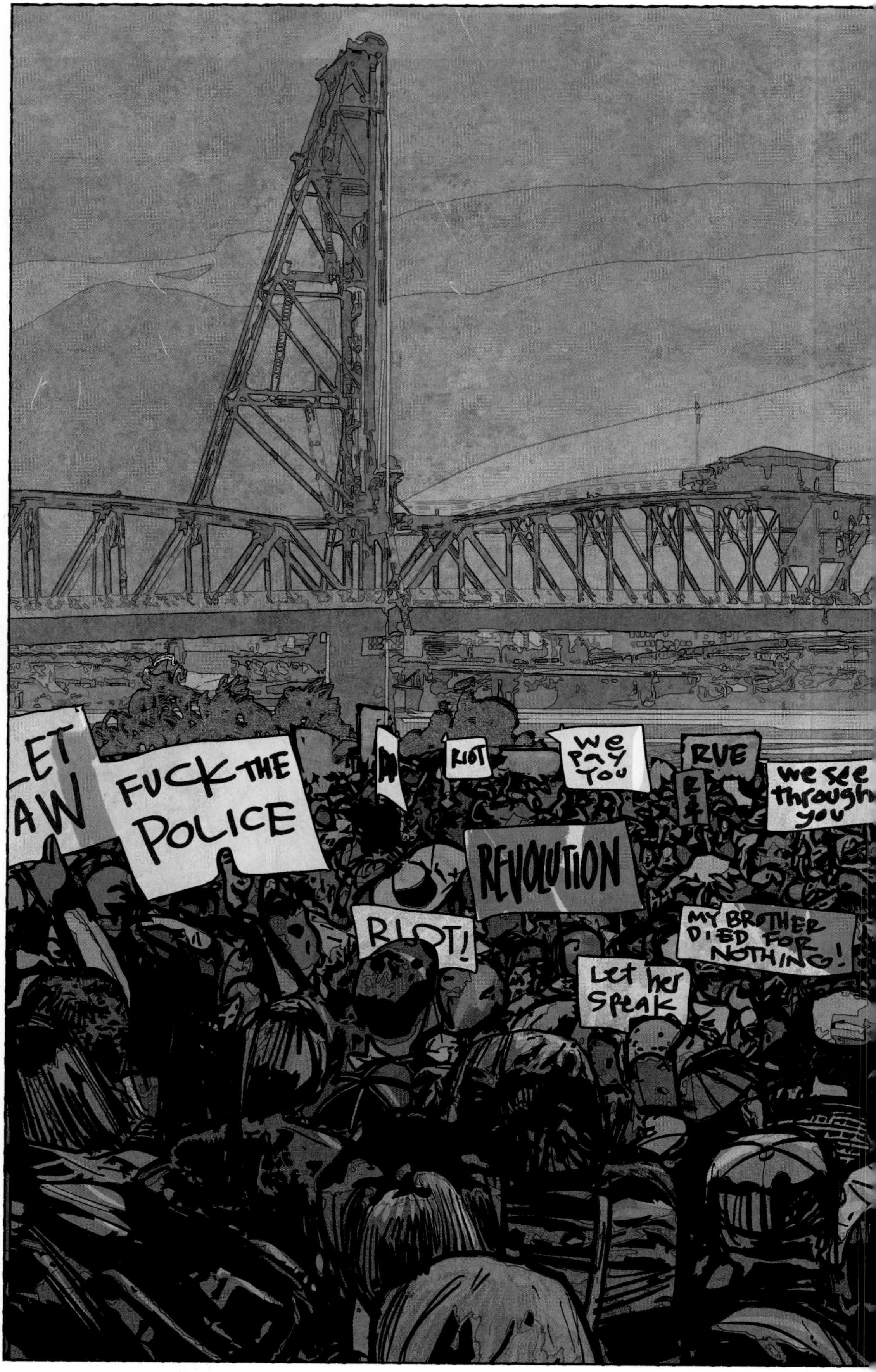
LET
AW
FUCK THE POLICE
RIOT
We pay you
RVE
we see through you
REVOLUTION
RIOT!
MY BROTHER DIED FOR NOTHING!
Let her speak

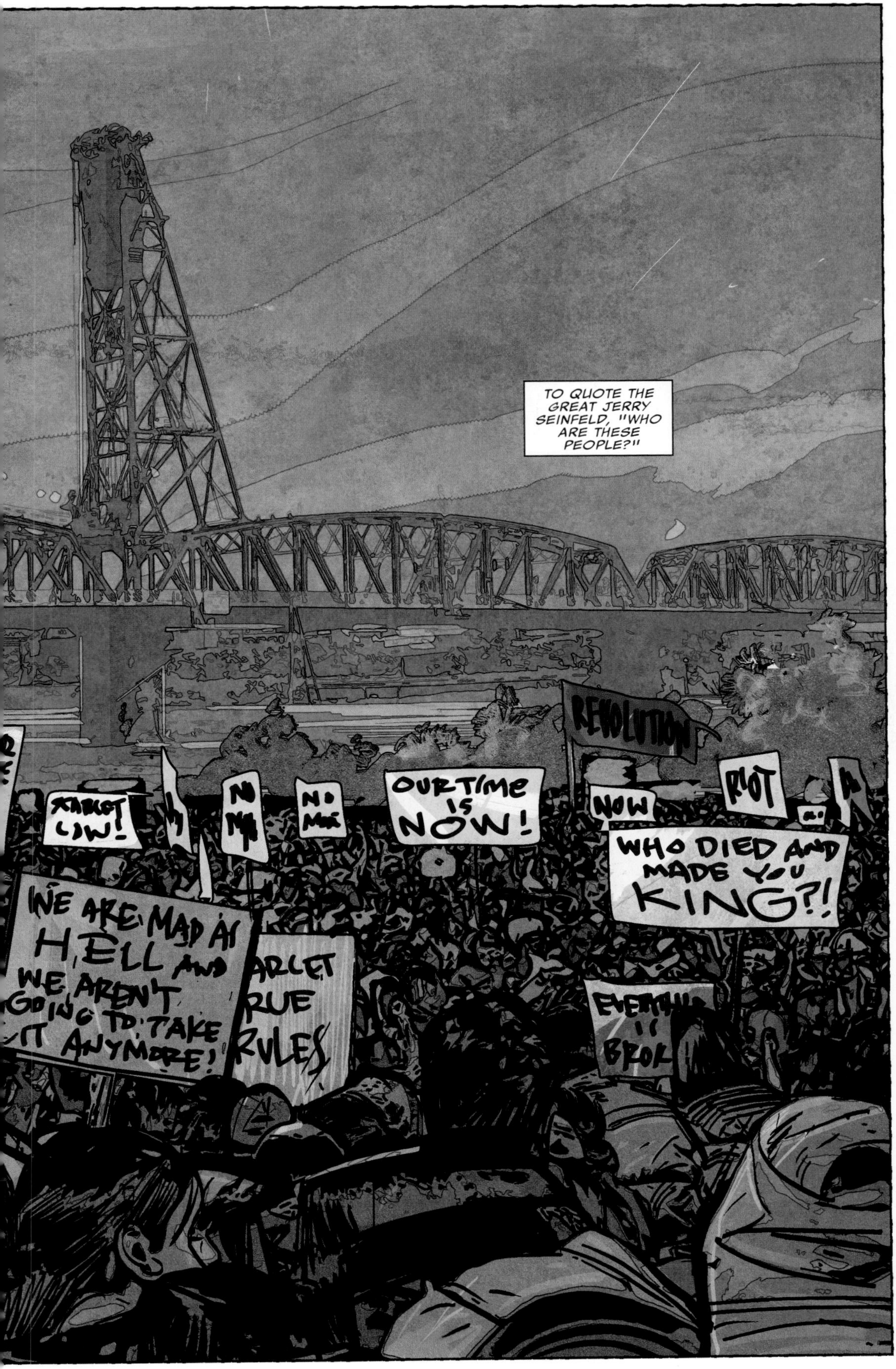
TO QUOTE THE GREAT JERRY SEINFELD, "WHO ARE THESE PEOPLE?"
REVOLUTION
OUR TIME IS NOW!
NOW
RIOT
WHO DIED AND MADE YOU KING?!
WE ARE MAD AS HELL AND WE AREN'T GOING TO TAKE IT ANYMORE!
RULES

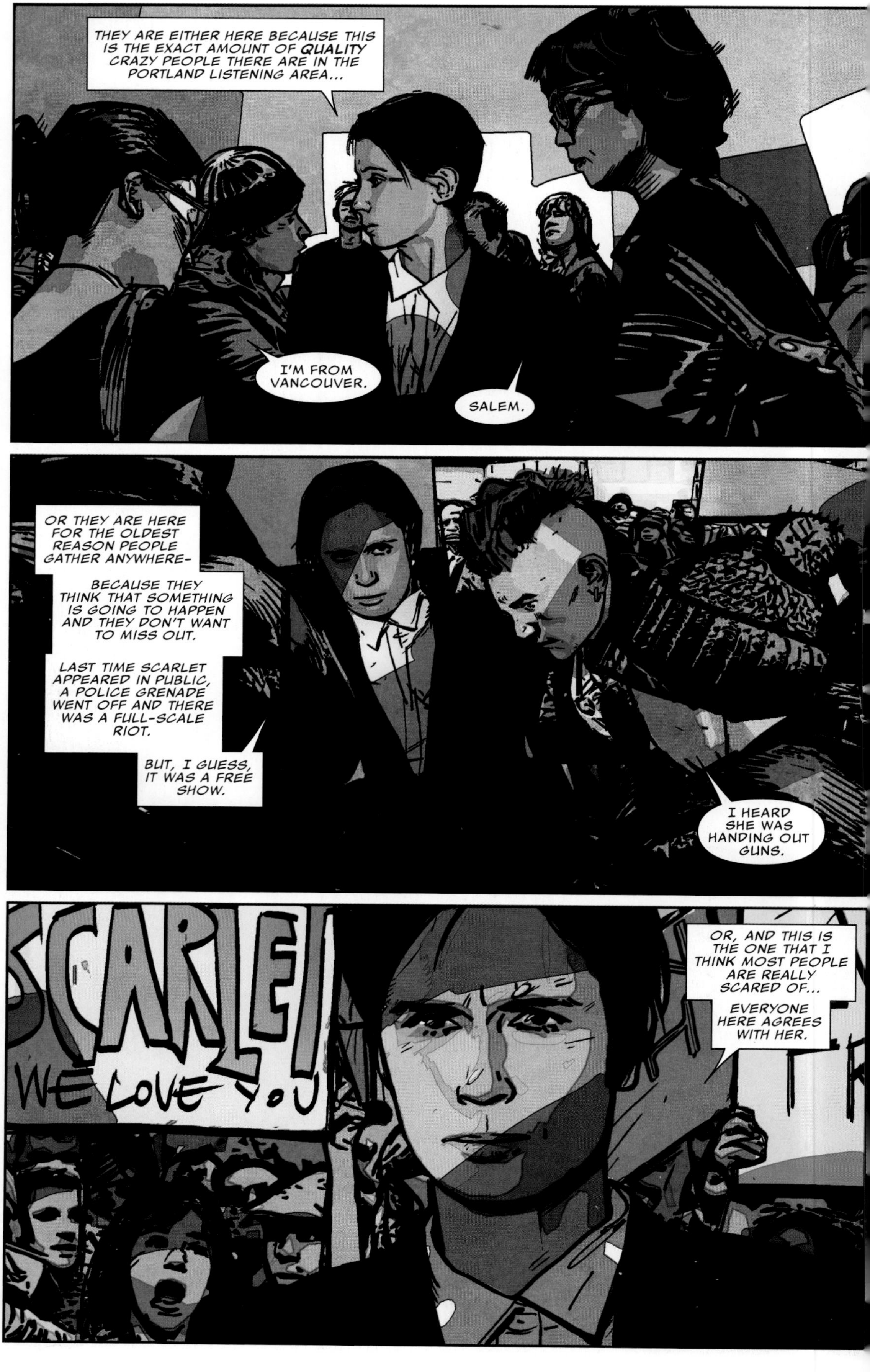
THEY ARE EITHER HERE BECAUSE THIS IS THE EXACT AMOUNT OF QUALITY CRAZY PEOPLE THERE ARE IN THE PORTLAND LISTENING AREA...
I'M FROM VANCOUVER.
SALEM.
OR THEY ARE HERE FOR THE OLDEST REASON PEOPLE GATHER ANYWHERE-
BECAUSE THEY THINK THAT SOMETHING IS GOING TO HAPPEN AND THEY DON'T WANT TO MISS OUT.
LAST TIME SCARLET APPEARED IN PUBLIC, A POLICE GRENADE WENT OFF AND THERE WAS A FULL-SCALE RIOT.
BUT, I GUESS, IT WAS A FREE SHOW.
I HEARD SHE WAS HANDING OUT GUNS.
SCARLET
WE LOVE YOU
OR, AND THIS IS THE ONE THAT I THINK MOST PEOPLE ARE REALLY SCARED OF...
EVERYONE HERE AGREES WITH HER.

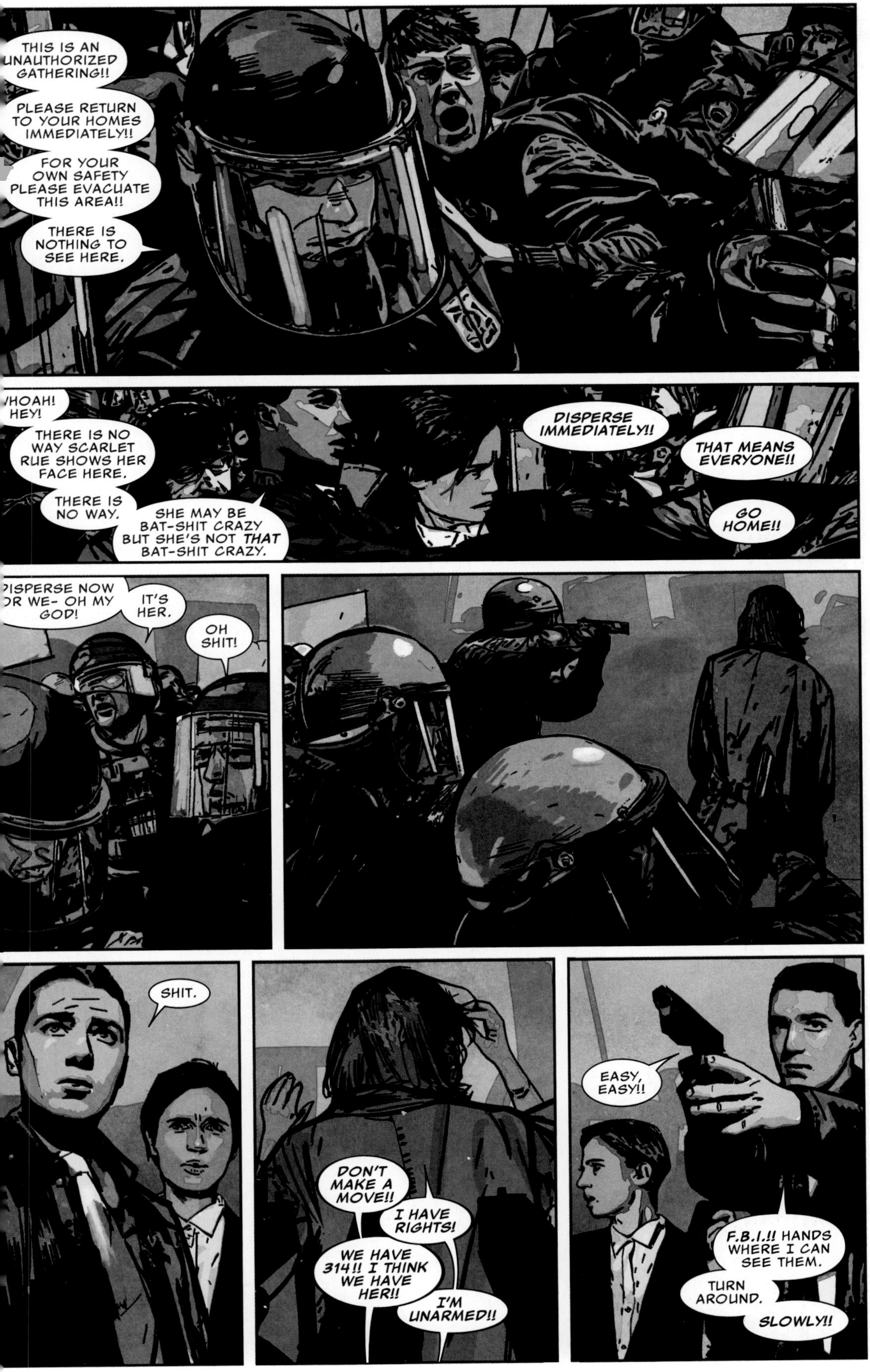
THIS IS AN UNAUTHORIZED GATHERING!!
PLEASE RETURN TO YOUR HOMES IMMEDIATELY!!
FOR YOUR OWN SAFETY PLEASE EVACUATE THIS AREA!!
THERE IS NOTHING TO SEE HERE.
WHOAH! HEY!
THERE IS NO WAY SCARLET RUE SHOWS HER FACE HERE.
THERE IS NO WAY.
SHE MAY BE BAT-SHIT CRAZY BUT SHE'S NOT *THAT* BAT-SHIT CRAZY.
*DISPERSE IMMEDIATELY!!*
*THAT MEANS EVERYONE!!*
*GO HOME!!*
DISPERSE NOW OR WE- OH MY GOD!
IT'S HER.
OH SHIT!
SHIT.
*DON'T MAKE A MOVE!!*
*I HAVE RIGHTS!*
*WE HAVE 314!! I THINK WE HAVE HER!!*
*I'M UNARMED!!*
EASY, EASY!!
F.B.I.!! HANDS WHERE I CAN SEE THEM.
TURN AROUND.
*SLOWLY!!*

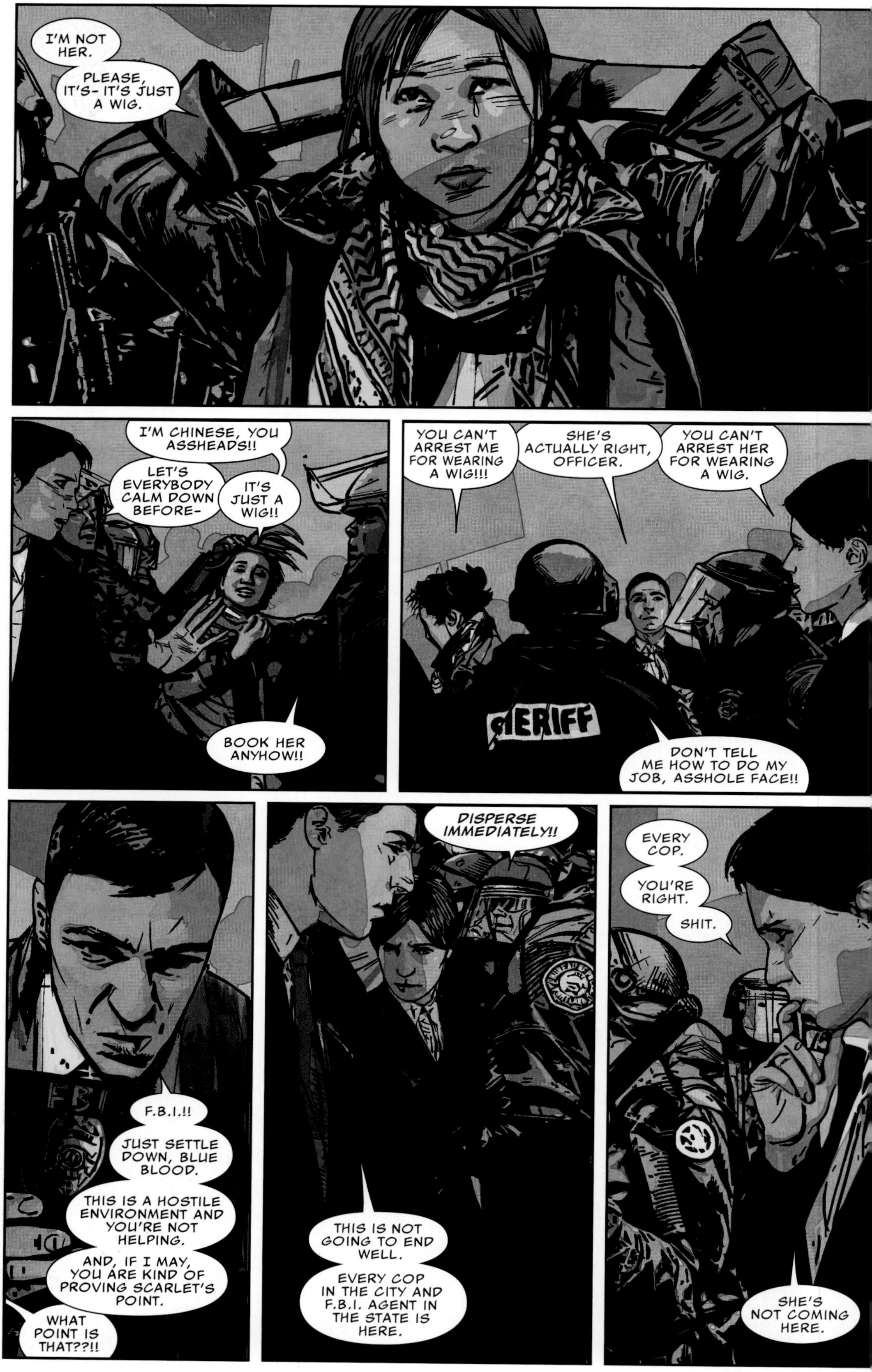

I'M NOT HER.
PLEASE, IT'S- IT'S JUST A WIG.
I'M CHINESE, YOU ASSHEADS!!
LET'S EVERYBODY CALM DOWN BEFORE-
IT'S JUST A WIG!!
BOOK HER ANYHOW!!
YOU CAN'T ARREST ME FOR WEARING A WIG!!!
SHE'S ACTUALLY RIGHT, OFFICER.
YOU CAN'T ARREST HER FOR WEARING A WIG.
DON'T TELL ME HOW TO DO MY JOB, ASSHOLE FACE!!
F.B.I.!!
JUST SETTLE DOWN, BLUE BLOOD.
THIS IS A HOSTILE ENVIRONMENT AND YOU'RE NOT HELPING.
AND, IF I MAY, YOU ARE KIND OF PROVING SCARLET'S POINT.
WHAT POINT IS THAT??!!
DISPERSE IMMEDIATELY!!
THIS IS NOT GOING TO END WELL.
EVERY COP IN THE CITY AND F.B.I. AGENT IN THE STATE IS HERE.
EVERY COP.
YOU'RE RIGHT.
SHIT.
SHE'S NOT COMING HERE.

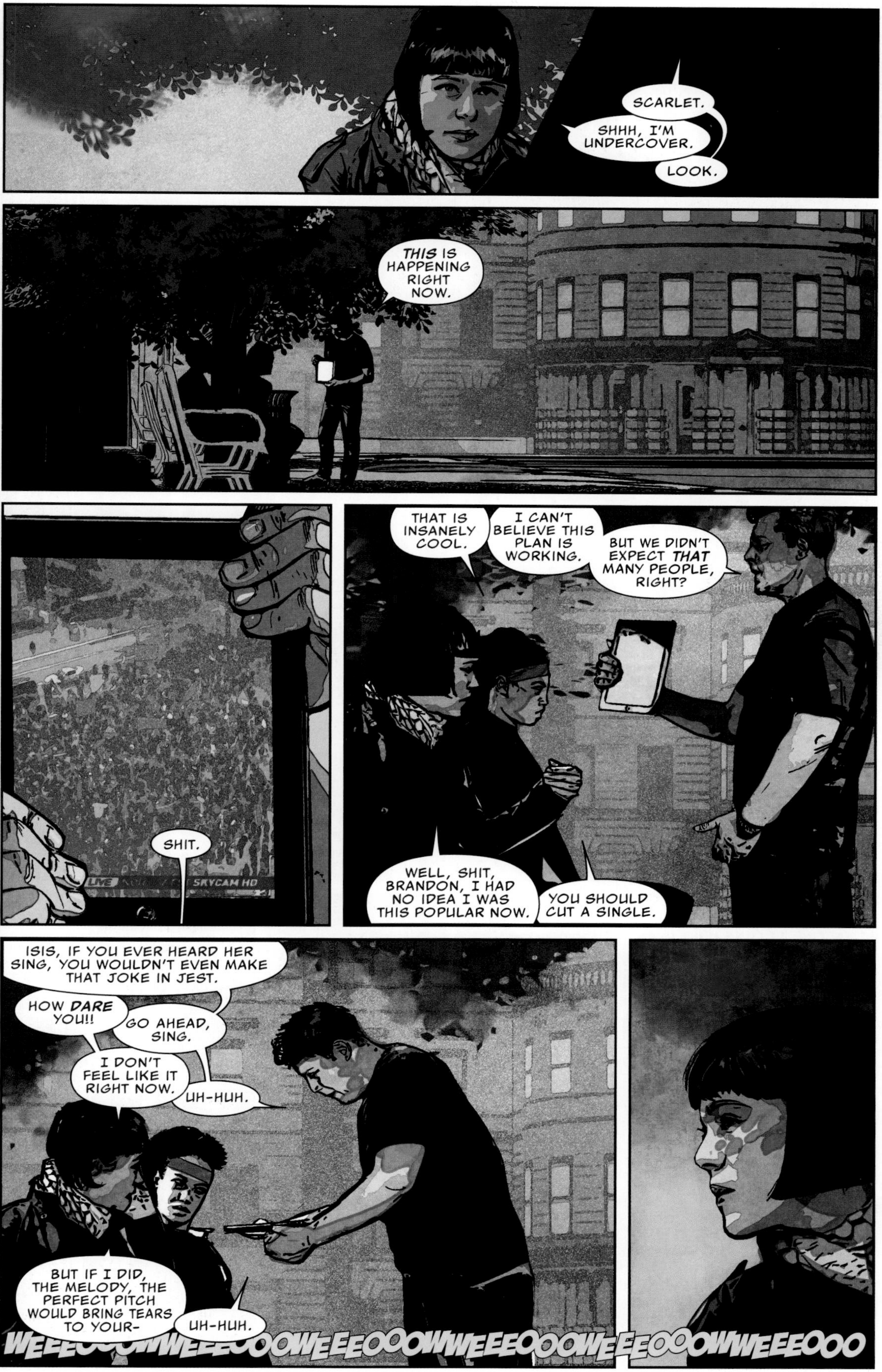
SCARLET.
SHHH, I'M UNDERCOVER.
LOOK.
THIS IS HAPPENING RIGHT NOW.
LIVE
SKYCAM HD
SHIT.
THAT IS INSANELY COOL.
I CAN'T BELIEVE THIS PLAN IS WORKING.
BUT WE DIDN'T EXPECT THAT MANY PEOPLE, RIGHT?
WELL, SHIT, BRANDON, I HAD NO IDEA I WAS THIS POPULAR NOW.
YOU SHOULD CUT A SINGLE.
ISIS, IF YOU EVER HEARD HER SING, YOU WOULDN'T EVEN MAKE THAT JOKE IN JEST.
HOW DARE YOU!!
GO AHEAD, SING.
I DON'T FEEL LIKE IT RIGHT NOW.
UH-HUH.
BUT IF I DID, THE MELODY, THE PERFECT PITCH WOULD BRING TEARS TO YOUR-
UH-HUH.
WEEEOOOWWEEEOOOWWEEEOOOWWEEEOOOWWEEEOOO

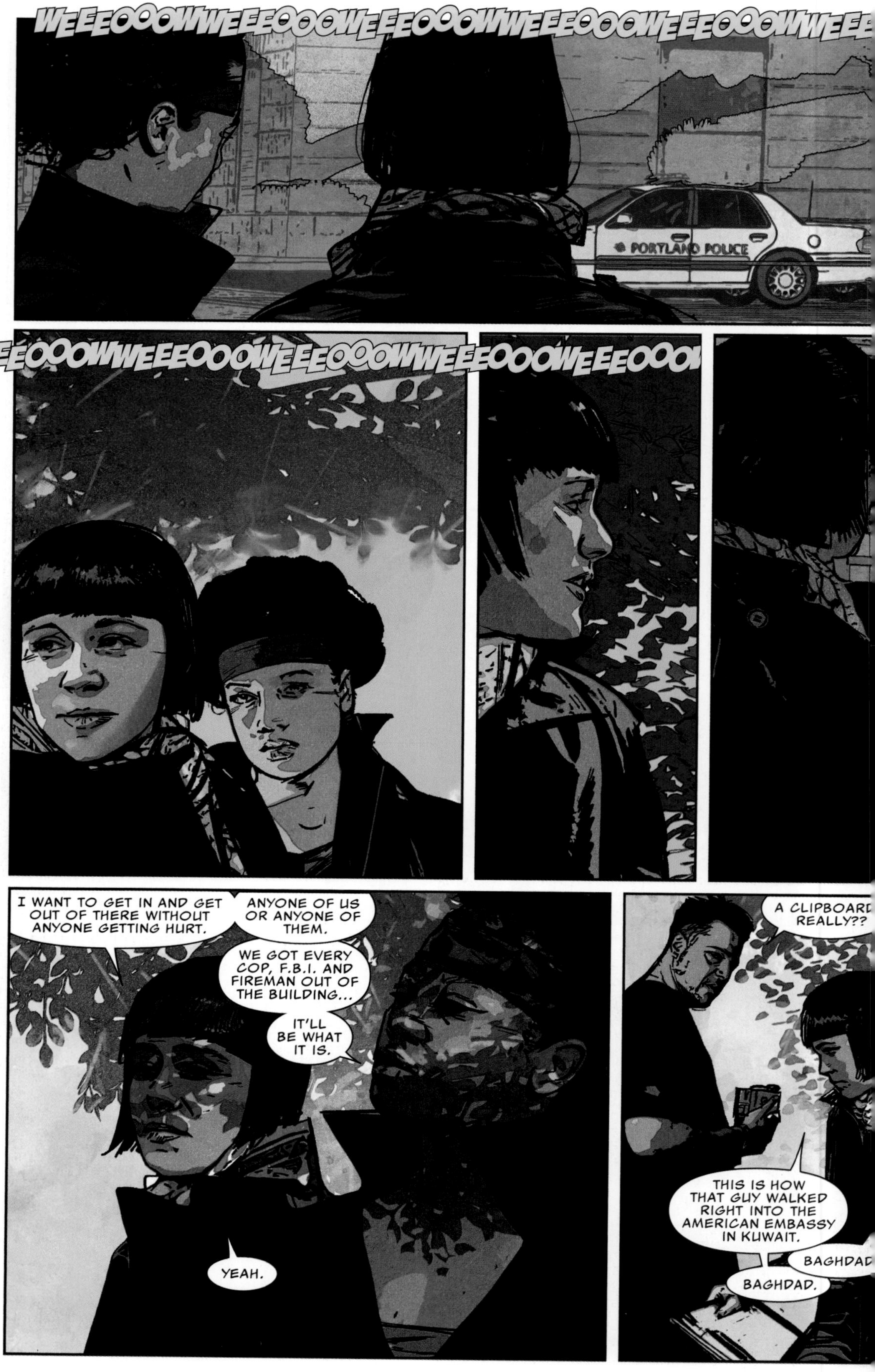
WEEEOOOWWEEEOOOWEEEOOOWWEEEOOOWEEEOOOWWEEE
PORTLAND POLICE
WEEEOOOWWEEEOOOWEEEOOOWWEEEOOOWEEEOOOW
I WANT TO GET IN AND GET OUT OF THERE WITHOUT ANYONE GETTING HURT.
ANYONE OF US OR ANYONE OF THEM.
WE GOT EVERY COP, F.B.I. AND FIREMAN OUT OF THE BUILDING...
IT'LL BE WHAT IT IS.
YEAH.
A CLIPBOARD REALLY??
THIS IS HOW THAT GUY WALKED RIGHT INTO THE AMERICAN EMBASSY IN KUWAIT.
BAGHDAD
BAGHDAD.

EOOOWWEEEOOOWWEEEOOOWWEEEOOOWWEEEOOOWWEEEOOO

THAT'S HIS CAR? NO LIMO?

HE'S THE MAYOR OF PORTLAND, NOT THE KING OF SIAM.

IS EVERYONE IN POSITION?

EVERYONE IN POSITIONS.

NO ONE WHO WORKS FOR THE GOVERNMENT WANTS TO TALK TO SOMEONE WITH A BRIEFCASE AND A CLIPBOARD.

IT MIGHT BE THE PERSON WHO'S COME TO FIRE THEM.

YOU LOOK GOOD IN A SUIT.

YOU SHOULD GET A JOB.

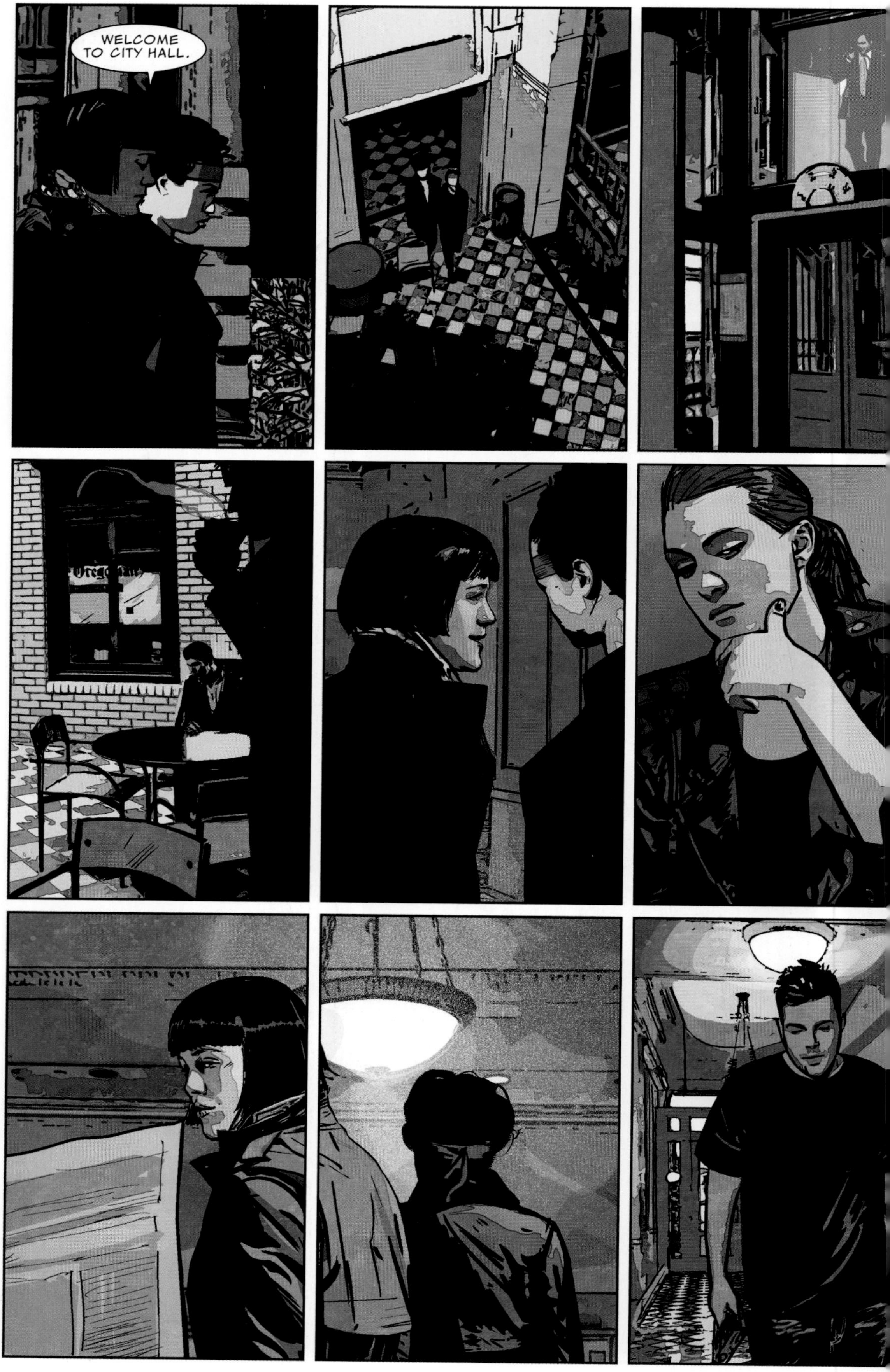
WELCOME TO CITY HALL.

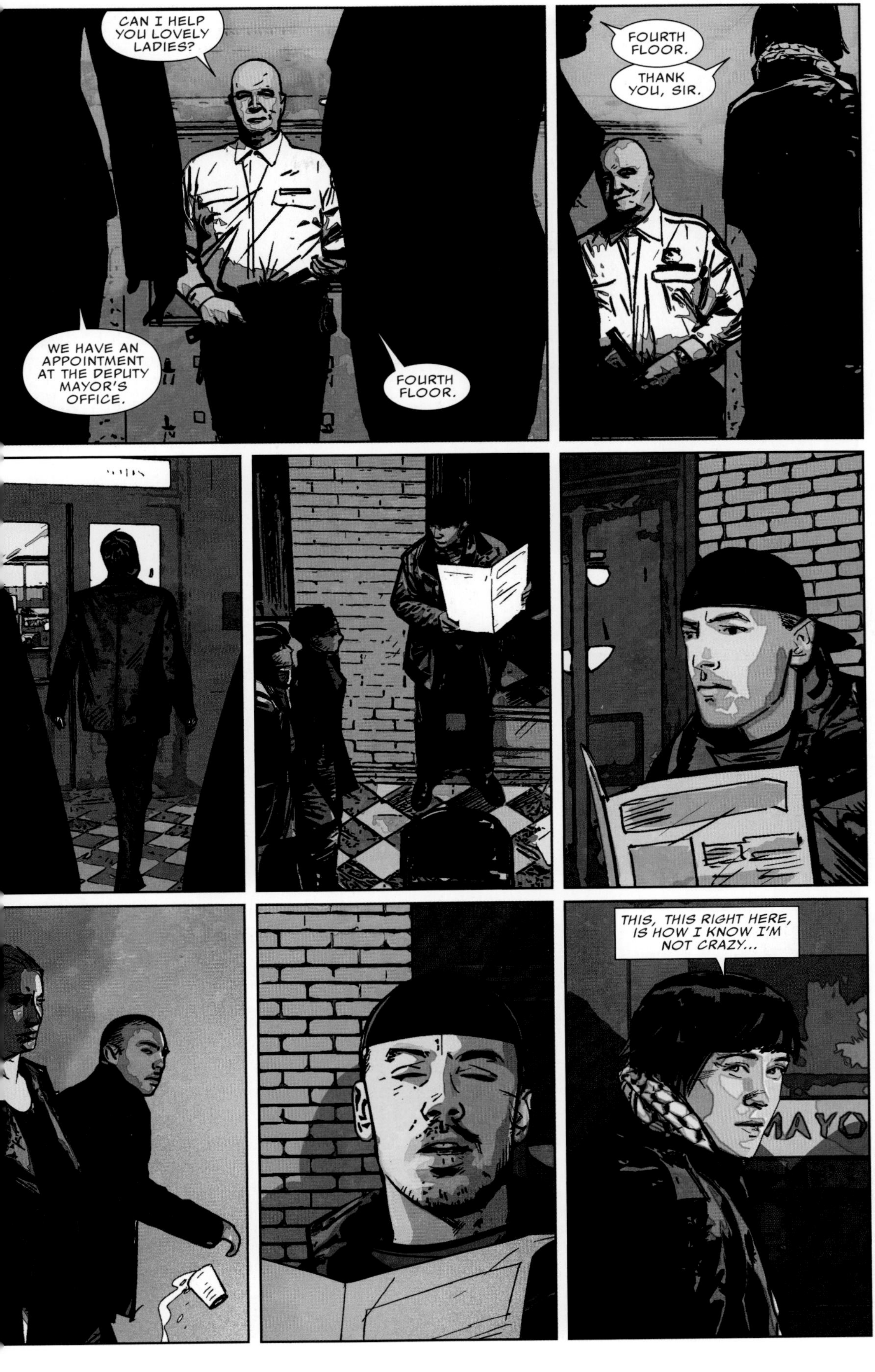
CAN I HELP YOU LOVELY LADIES?
WE HAVE AN APPOINTMENT AT THE DEPUTY MAYOR'S OFFICE.
FOURTH FLOOR.
FOURTH FLOOR.
THANK YOU, SIR.
MAYO
THIS, THIS RIGHT HERE, IS HOW I KNOW I'M NOT CRAZY...

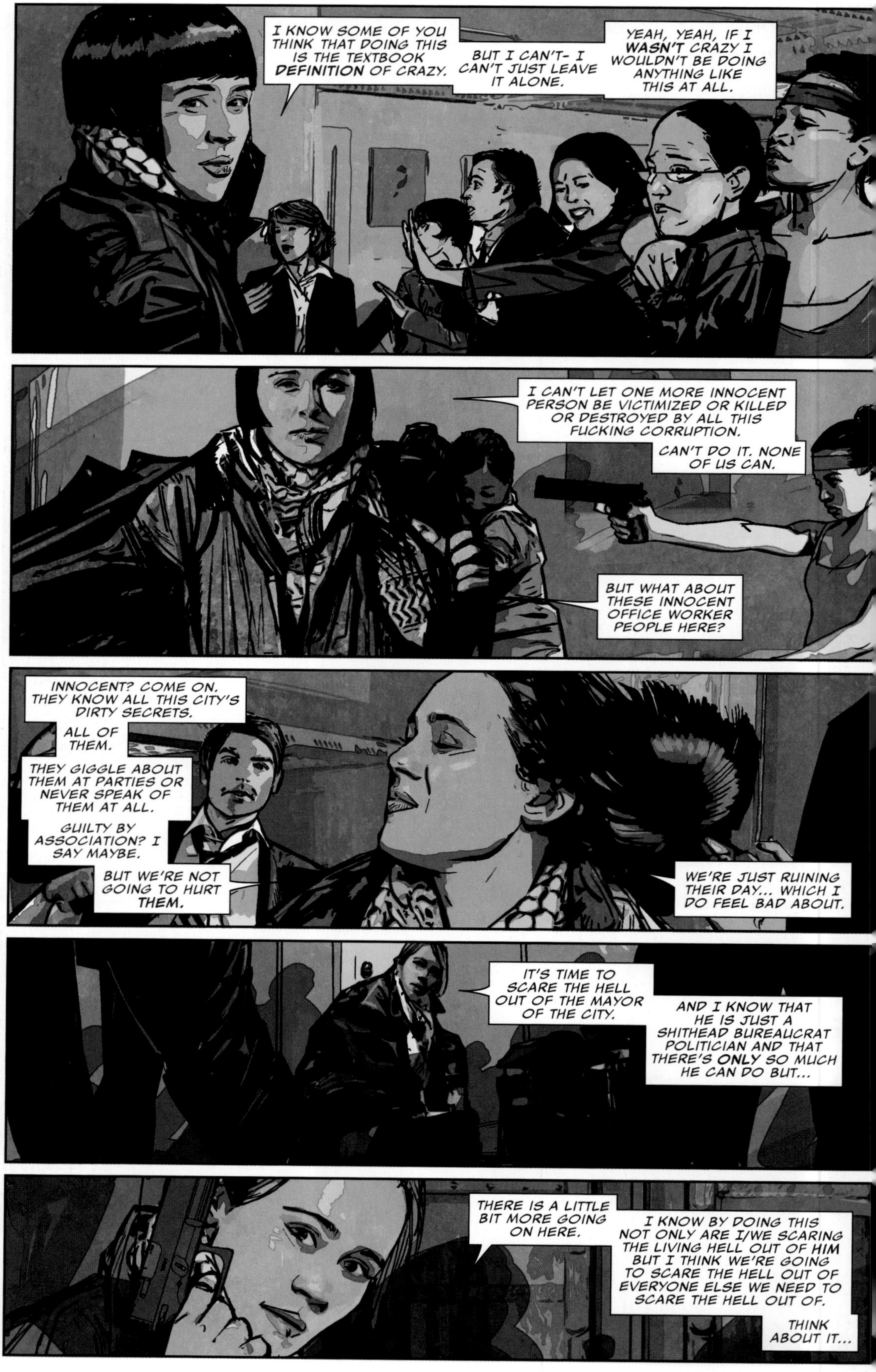
I KNOW SOME OF YOU THINK THAT DOING THIS IS THE TEXTBOOK DEFINITION OF CRAZY.
BUT I CAN'T- I CAN'T JUST LEAVE IT ALONE.
YEAH, YEAH, IF I WASN'T CRAZY I WOULDN'T BE DOING ANYTHING LIKE THIS AT ALL.
I CAN'T LET ONE MORE INNOCENT PERSON BE VICTIMIZED OR KILLED OR DESTROYED BY ALL THIS FUCKING CORRUPTION.
CAN'T DO IT. NONE OF US CAN.
BUT WHAT ABOUT THESE INNOCENT OFFICE WORKER PEOPLE HERE?
INNOCENT? COME ON. THEY KNOW ALL THIS CITY'S DIRTY SECRETS.
ALL OF THEM.
THEY GIGGLE ABOUT THEM AT PARTIES OR NEVER SPEAK OF THEM AT ALL.
GUILTY BY ASSOCIATION? I SAY MAYBE.
BUT WE'RE NOT GOING TO HURT THEM.
WE'RE JUST RUINING THEIR DAY... WHICH I DO FEEL BAD ABOUT.
IT'S TIME TO SCARE THE HELL OUT OF THE MAYOR OF THE CITY.
AND I KNOW THAT HE IS JUST A SHITHEAD BUREAUCRAT POLITICIAN AND THAT THERE'S ONLY SO MUCH HE CAN DO BUT...
THERE IS A LITTLE BIT MORE GOING ON HERE.
I KNOW BY DOING THIS NOT ONLY ARE I/WE SCARING THE LIVING HELL OUT OF HIM BUT I THINK WE'RE GOING TO SCARE THE HELL OUT OF EVERYONE ELSE WE NEED TO SCARE THE HELL OUT OF.
THINK ABOUT IT...

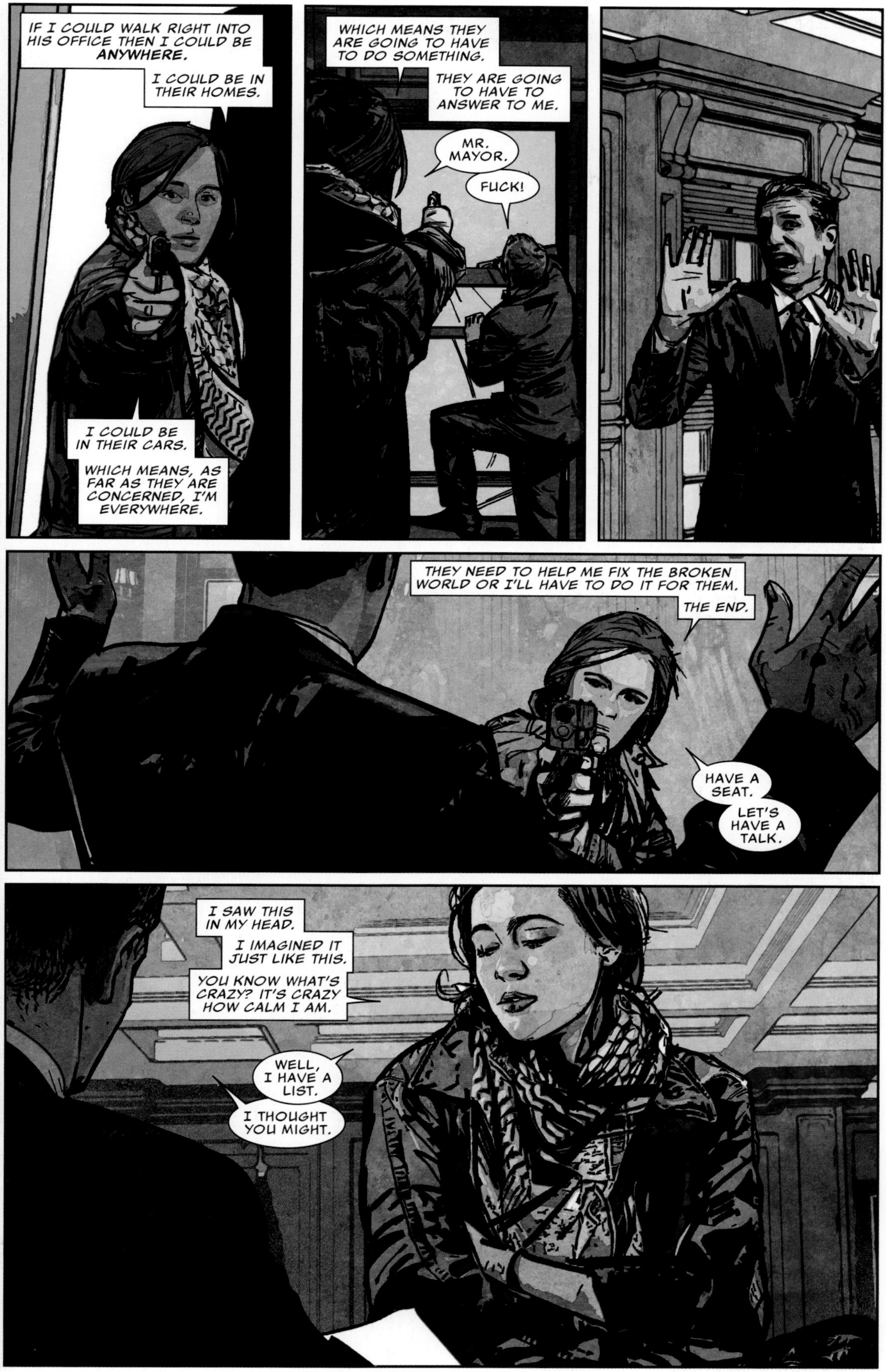
IF I COULD WALK RIGHT INTO HIS OFFICE THEN I COULD BE **ANYWHERE.**
I COULD BE IN THEIR HOMES.
I COULD BE IN THEIR CARS.
WHICH MEANS, AS FAR AS THEY ARE CONCERNED, I'M EVERYWHERE.
WHICH MEANS THEY ARE GOING TO HAVE TO DO SOMETHING.
THEY ARE GOING TO HAVE TO ANSWER TO ME.
MR. MAYOR.
FUCK!
THEY NEED TO HELP ME FIX THE BROKEN WORLD OR I'LL HAVE TO DO IT FOR THEM.
THE END.
HAVE A SEAT.
LET'S HAVE A TALK.
I SAW THIS IN MY HEAD.
I IMAGINED IT JUST LIKE THIS.
YOU KNOW WHAT'S CRAZY? IT'S CRAZY HOW CALM I AM.
WELL, I HAVE A LIST.
I THOUGHT YOU MIGHT.

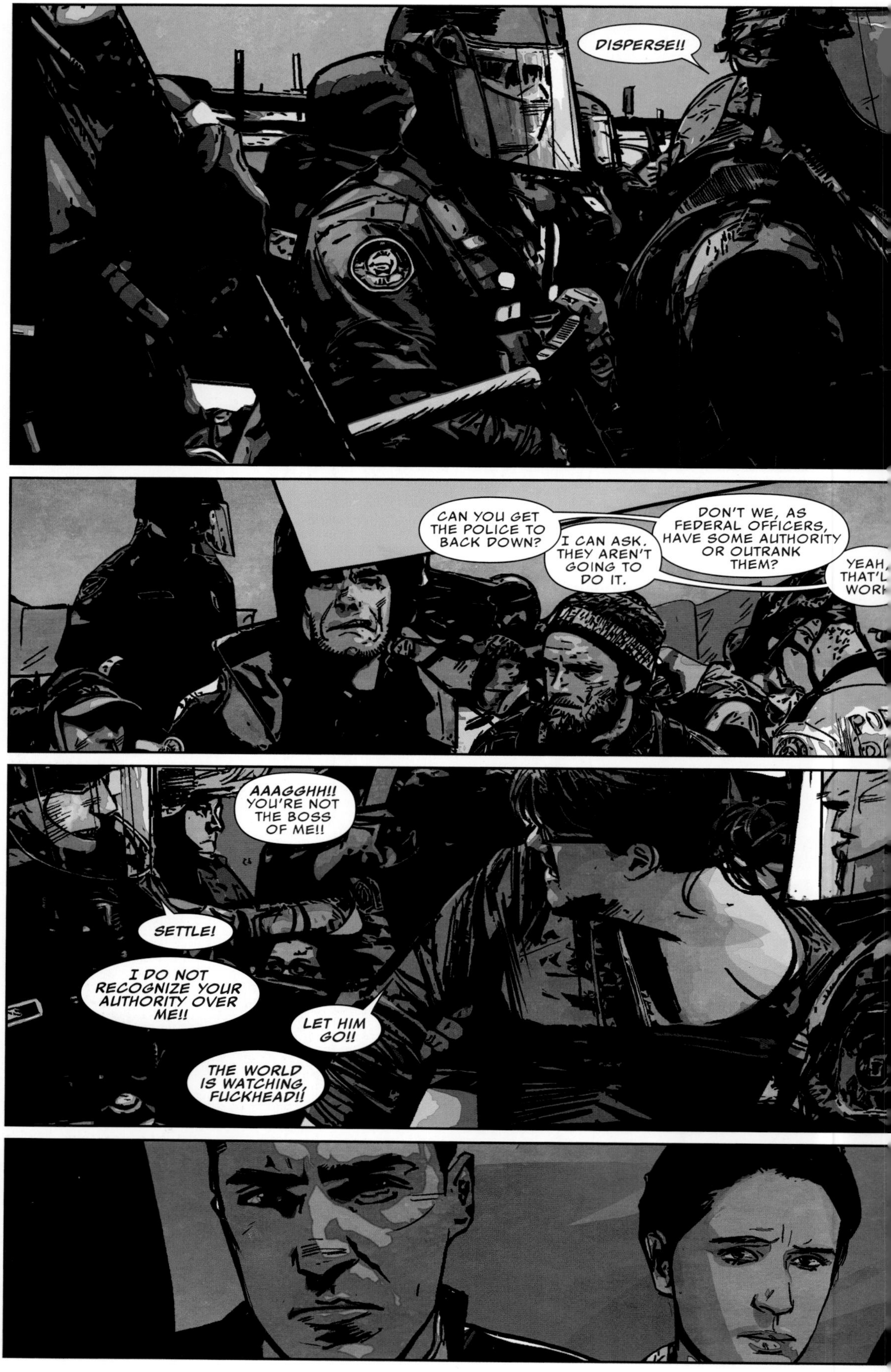
DISPERSE!!
CAN YOU GET THE POLICE TO BACK DOWN?
I CAN ASK. THEY AREN'T GOING TO DO IT.
DON'T WE, AS FEDERAL OFFICERS, HAVE SOME AUTHORITY OR OUTRANK THEM?
YEAH, THAT'L WORK
AAAGGHH!! YOU'RE NOT THE BOSS OF ME!!
SETTLE!
I DO NOT RECOGNIZE YOUR AUTHORITY OVER ME!!
LET HIM GO!!
THE WORLD IS WATCHING, FUCKHEAD!!

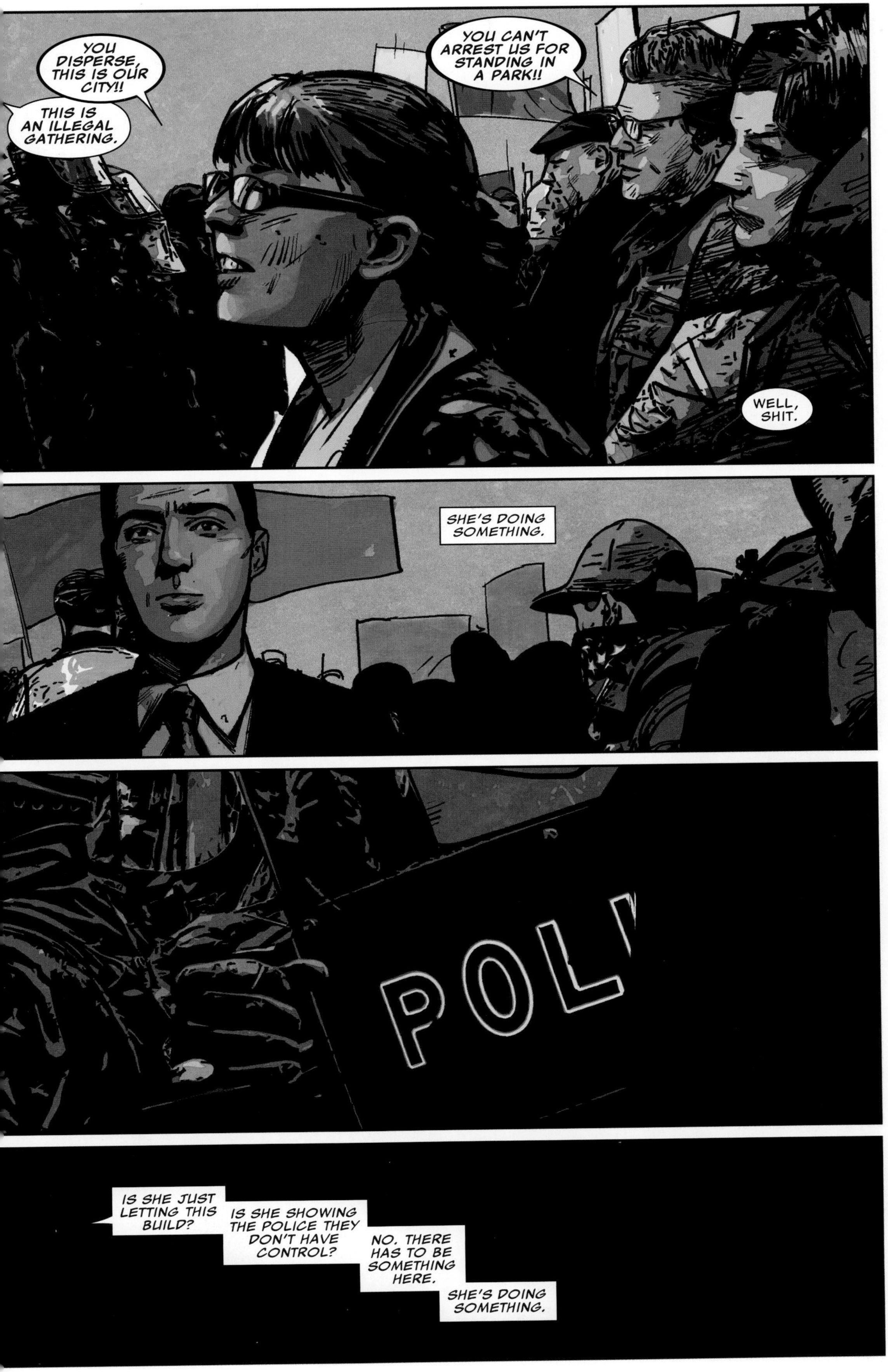
YOU DISPERSE, THIS IS OUR CITY!!
THIS IS AN ILLEGAL GATHERING.
YOU CAN'T ARREST US FOR STANDING IN A PARK!!
WELL, SHIT.
SHE'S DOING SOMETHING.
POL
IS SHE JUST LETTING THIS BUILD?
IS SHE SHOWING THE POLICE THEY DON'T HAVE CONTROL?
NO. THERE HAS TO BE SOMETHING HERE.
SHE'S DOING SOMETHING.

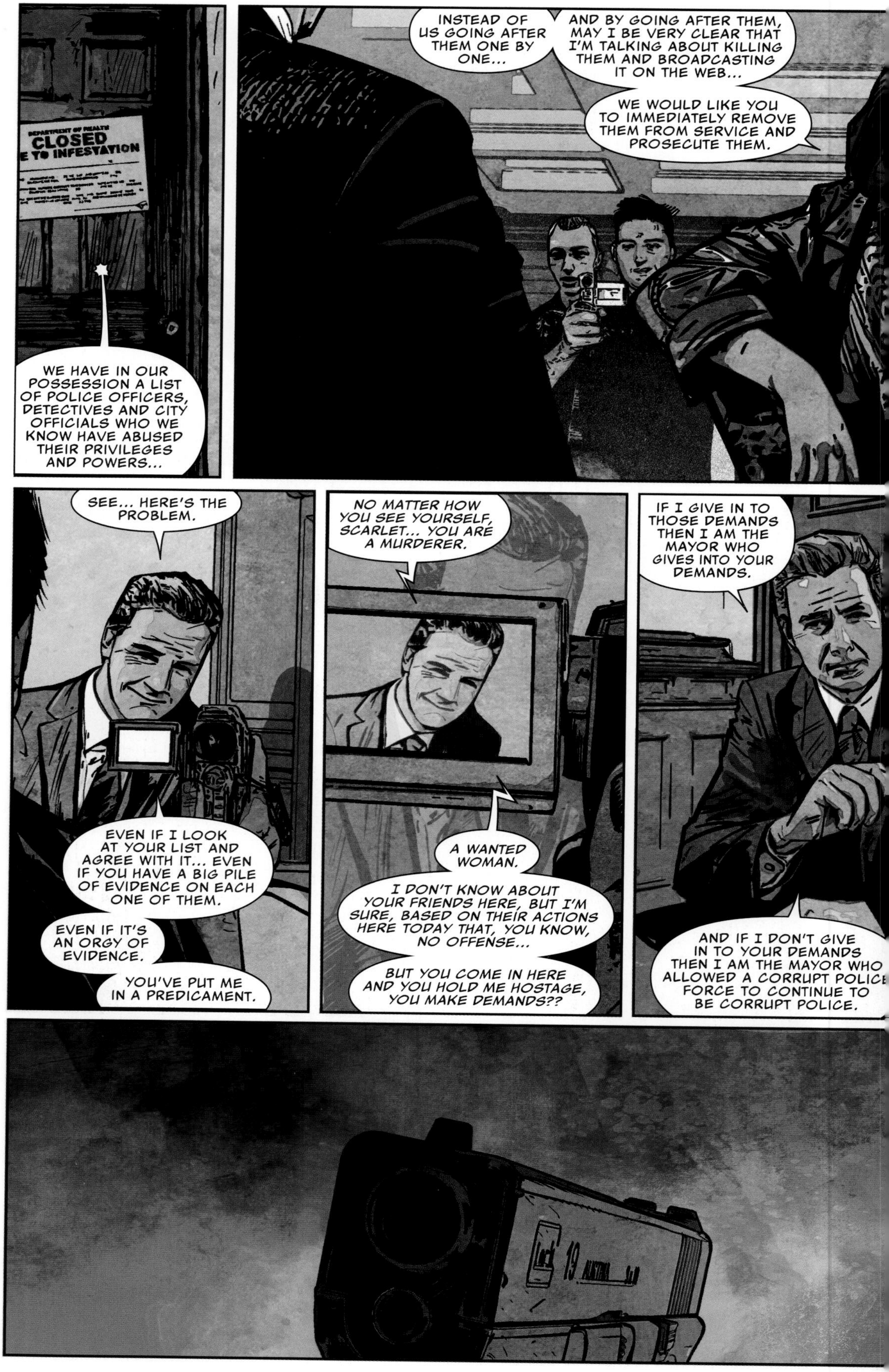
DEPARTMENT OF HEALTH
CLOSED
E TO INFESTATION
WE HAVE IN OUR POSSESSION A LIST OF POLICE OFFICERS, DETECTIVES AND CITY OFFICIALS WHO WE KNOW HAVE ABUSED THEIR PRIVILEGES AND POWERS...
INSTEAD OF US GOING AFTER THEM ONE BY ONE...
AND BY GOING AFTER THEM, MAY I BE VERY CLEAR THAT I'M TALKING ABOUT KILLING THEM AND BROADCASTING IT ON THE WEB...
WE WOULD LIKE YOU TO IMMEDIATELY REMOVE THEM FROM SERVICE AND PROSECUTE THEM.
SEE... HERE'S THE PROBLEM.
EVEN IF I LOOK AT YOUR LIST AND AGREE WITH IT... EVEN IF YOU HAVE A BIG PILE OF EVIDENCE ON EACH ONE OF THEM.
EVEN IF IT'S AN ORGY OF EVIDENCE.
YOU'VE PUT ME IN A PREDICAMENT.
NO MATTER HOW YOU SEE YOURSELF, SCARLET... YOU ARE A MURDERER.
A WANTED WOMAN.
I DON'T KNOW ABOUT YOUR FRIENDS HERE, BUT I'M SURE, BASED ON THEIR ACTIONS HERE TODAY THAT, YOU KNOW, NO OFFENSE...
BUT YOU COME IN HERE AND YOU HOLD ME HOSTAGE, YOU MAKE DEMANDS??
IF I GIVE IN TO THOSE DEMANDS THEN I AM THE MAYOR WHO GIVES INTO YOUR DEMANDS.
AND IF I DON'T GIVE IN TO YOUR DEMANDS THEN I AM THE MAYOR WHO ALLOWED A CORRUPT POLICE FORCE TO CONTINUE TO BE CORRUPT POLICE.
19 AUSTRIA

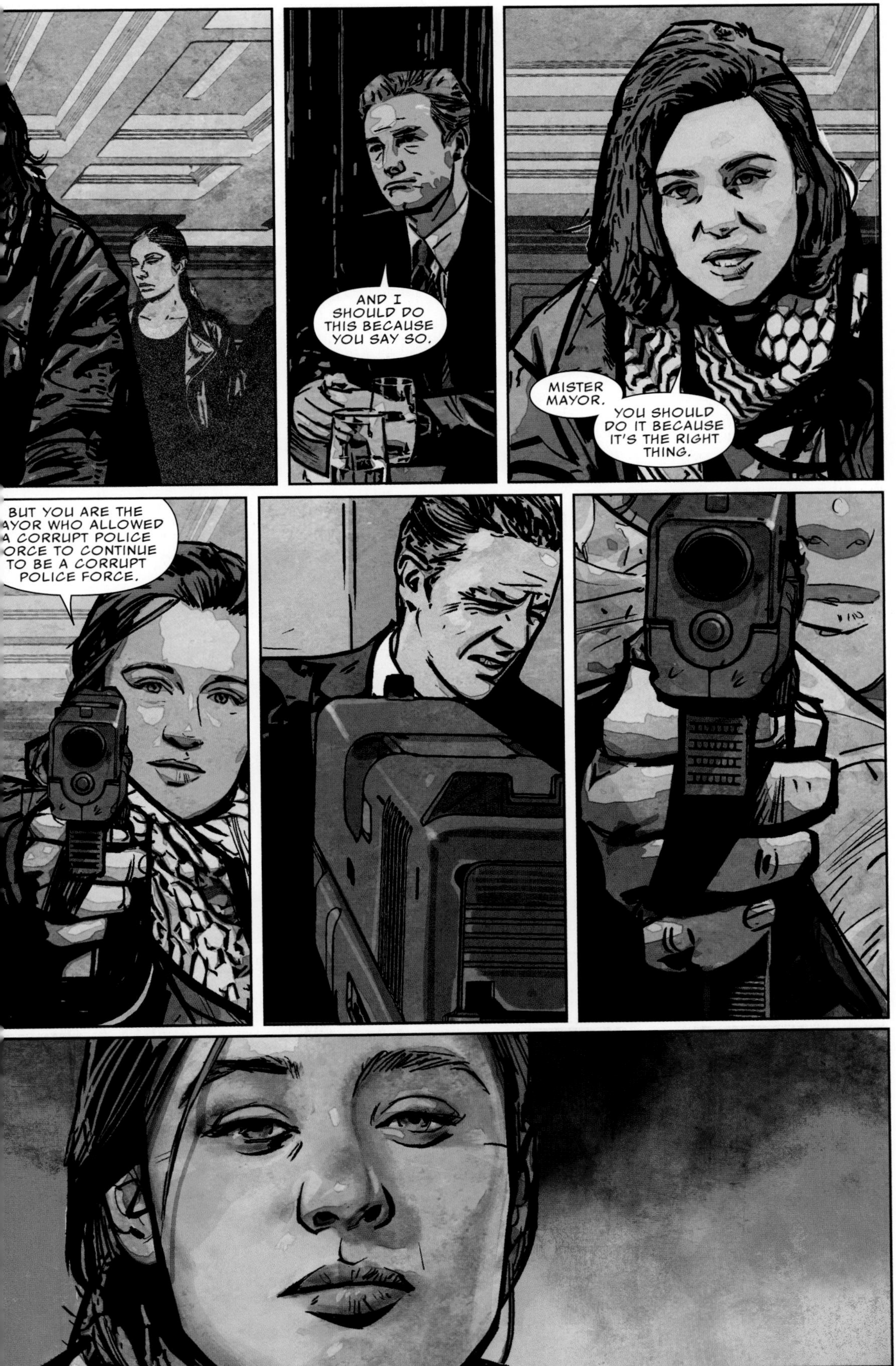
AND I SHOULD DO THIS BECAUSE YOU SAY SO.
MISTER MAYOR.
YOU SHOULD DO IT BECAUSE IT'S THE RIGHT THING.
BUT YOU ARE THE MAYOR WHO ALLOWED A CORRUPT POLICE FORCE TO CONTINUE TO BE A CORRUPT POLICE FORCE.

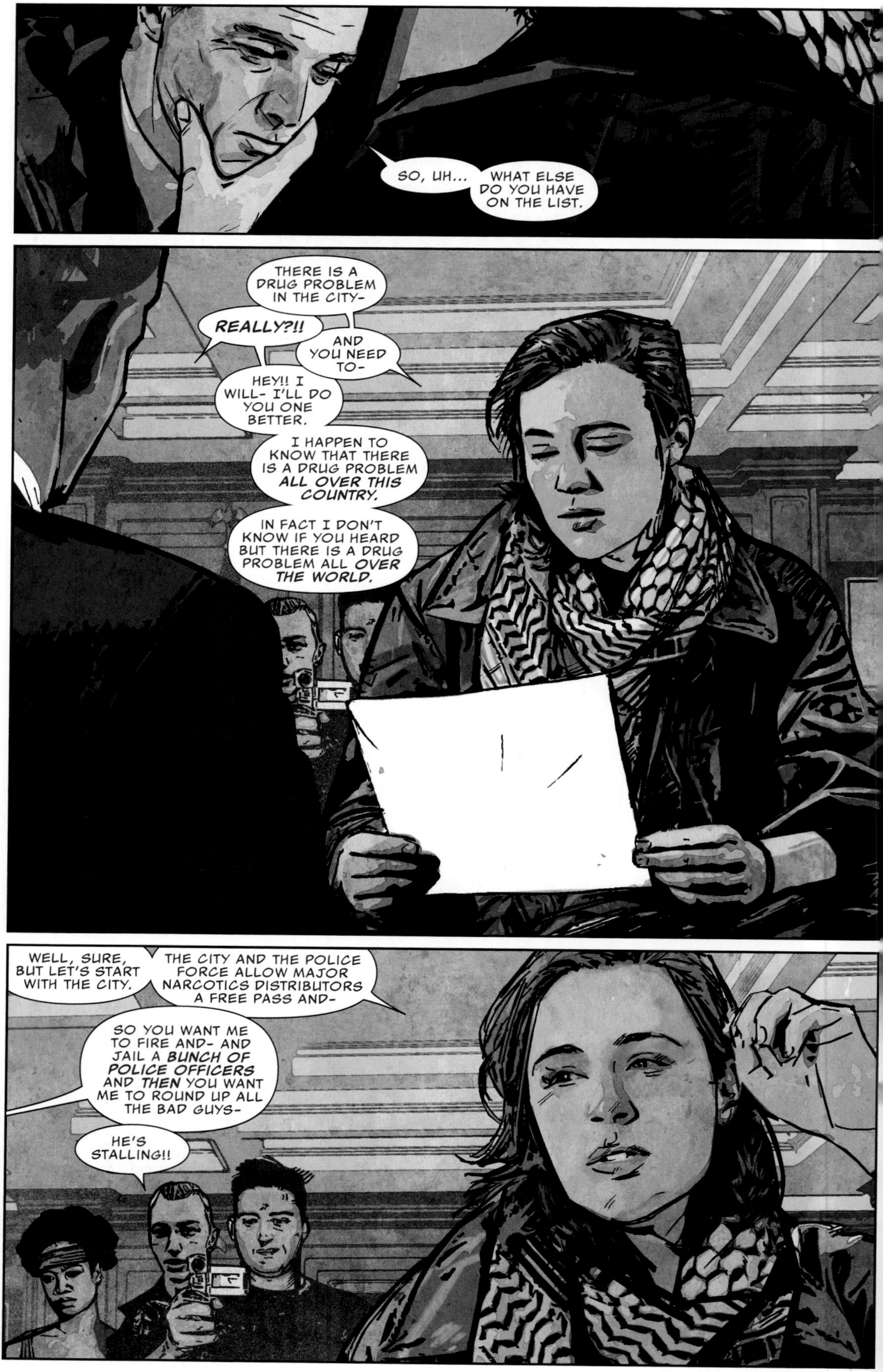
SO, UH...
WHAT ELSE DO YOU HAVE ON THE LIST.
THERE IS A DRUG PROBLEM IN THE CITY-
REALLY?!!
AND YOU NEED TO-
HEY!! I WILL- I'LL DO YOU ONE BETTER.
I HAPPEN TO KNOW THAT THERE IS A DRUG PROBLEM ALL OVER THIS COUNTRY.
IN FACT I DON'T KNOW IF YOU HEARD BUT THERE IS A DRUG PROBLEM ALL OVER THE WORLD.
WELL, SURE, BUT LET'S START WITH THE CITY.
THE CITY AND THE POLICE FORCE ALLOW MAJOR NARCOTICS DISTRIBUTORS A FREE PASS AND-
SO YOU WANT ME TO FIRE AND- AND JAIL A BUNCH OF POLICE OFFICERS AND THEN YOU WANT ME TO ROUND UP ALL THE BAD GUYS-
HE'S STALLING!!

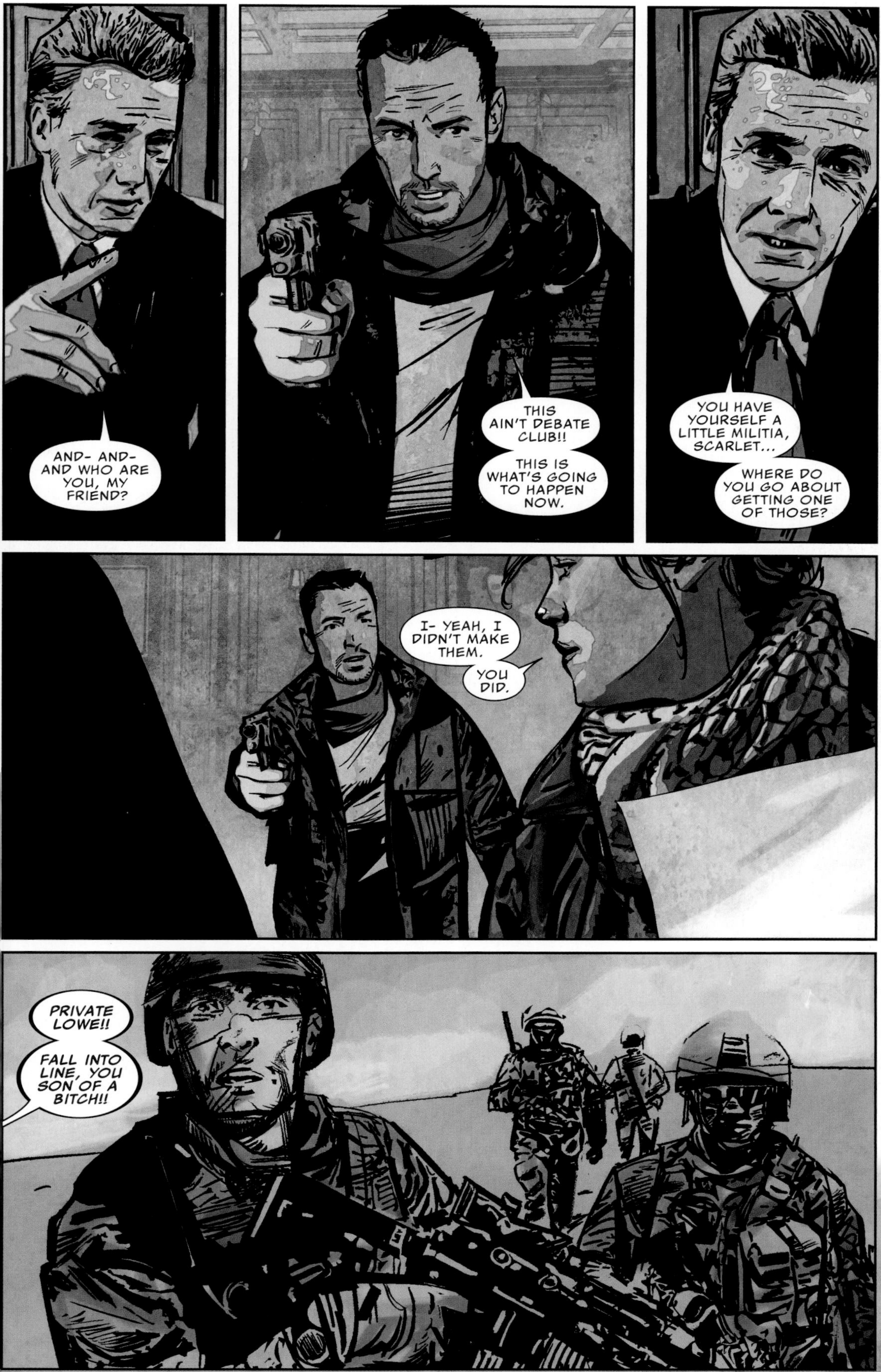
AND- AND- AND WHO ARE YOU, MY FRIEND?
THIS AIN'T DEBATE CLUB!!
THIS IS WHAT'S GOING TO HAPPEN NOW.
YOU HAVE YOURSELF A LITTLE MILITIA, SCARLET...
WHERE DO YOU GO ABOUT GETTING ONE OF THOSE?
I- YEAH, I DIDN'T MAKE THEM.
YOU DID.
PRIVATE LOWE!!
FALL INTO LINE, YOU SON OF A BITCH!!

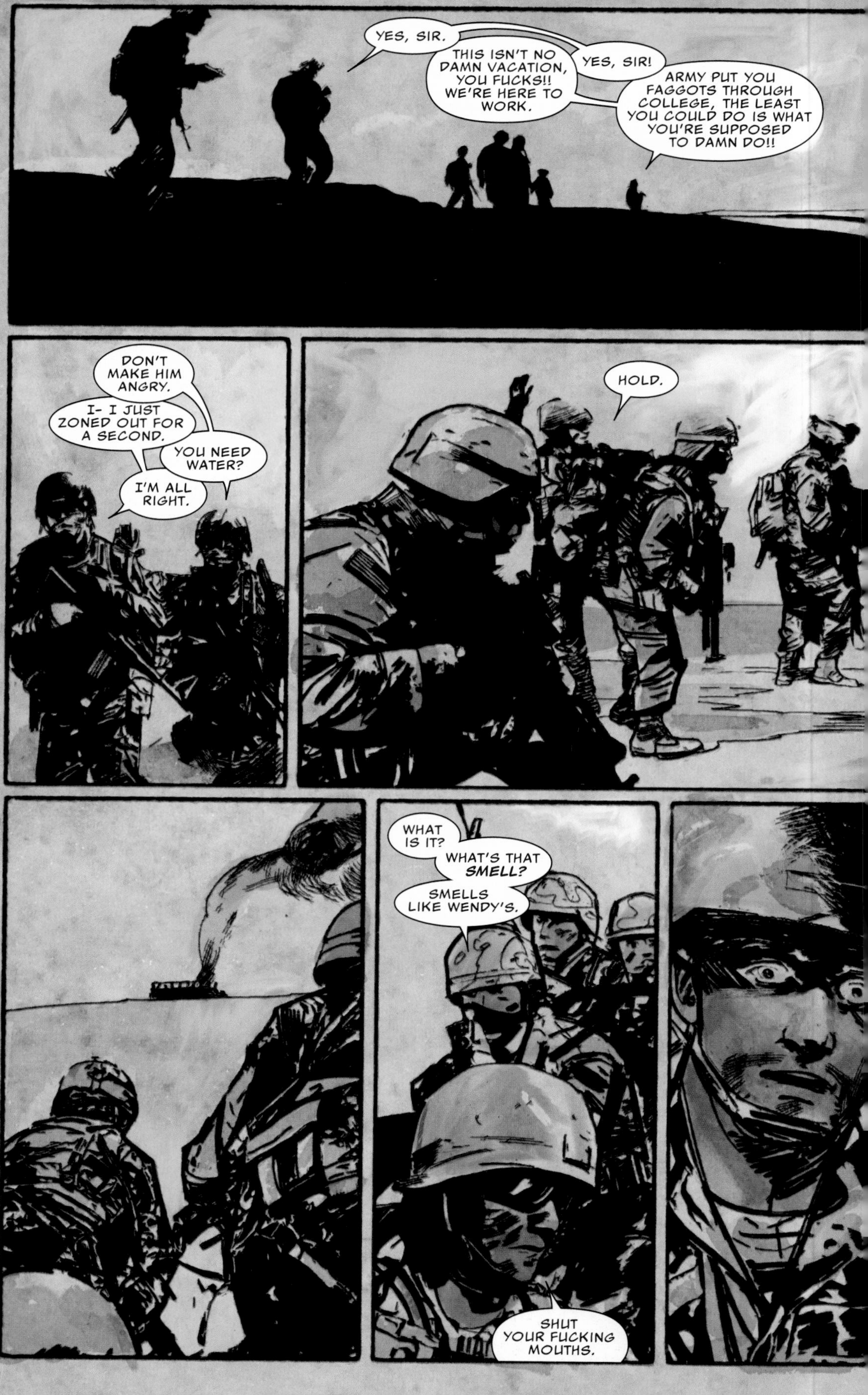
YES, SIR.
THIS ISN'T NO DAMN VACATION, YOU FUCKS!! WE'RE HERE TO WORK.
YES, SIR!
ARMY PUT YOU FAGGOTS THROUGH COLLEGE, THE LEAST YOU COULD DO IS WHAT YOU'RE SUPPOSED TO DAMN DO!!
DON'T MAKE HIM ANGRY.
I- I JUST ZONED OUT FOR A SECOND.
YOU NEED WATER?
I'M ALL RIGHT.
HOLD.
WHAT IS IT?
WHAT'S THAT SMELL?
SMELLS LIKE WENDY'S.
SHUT YOUR FUCKING MOUTHS.

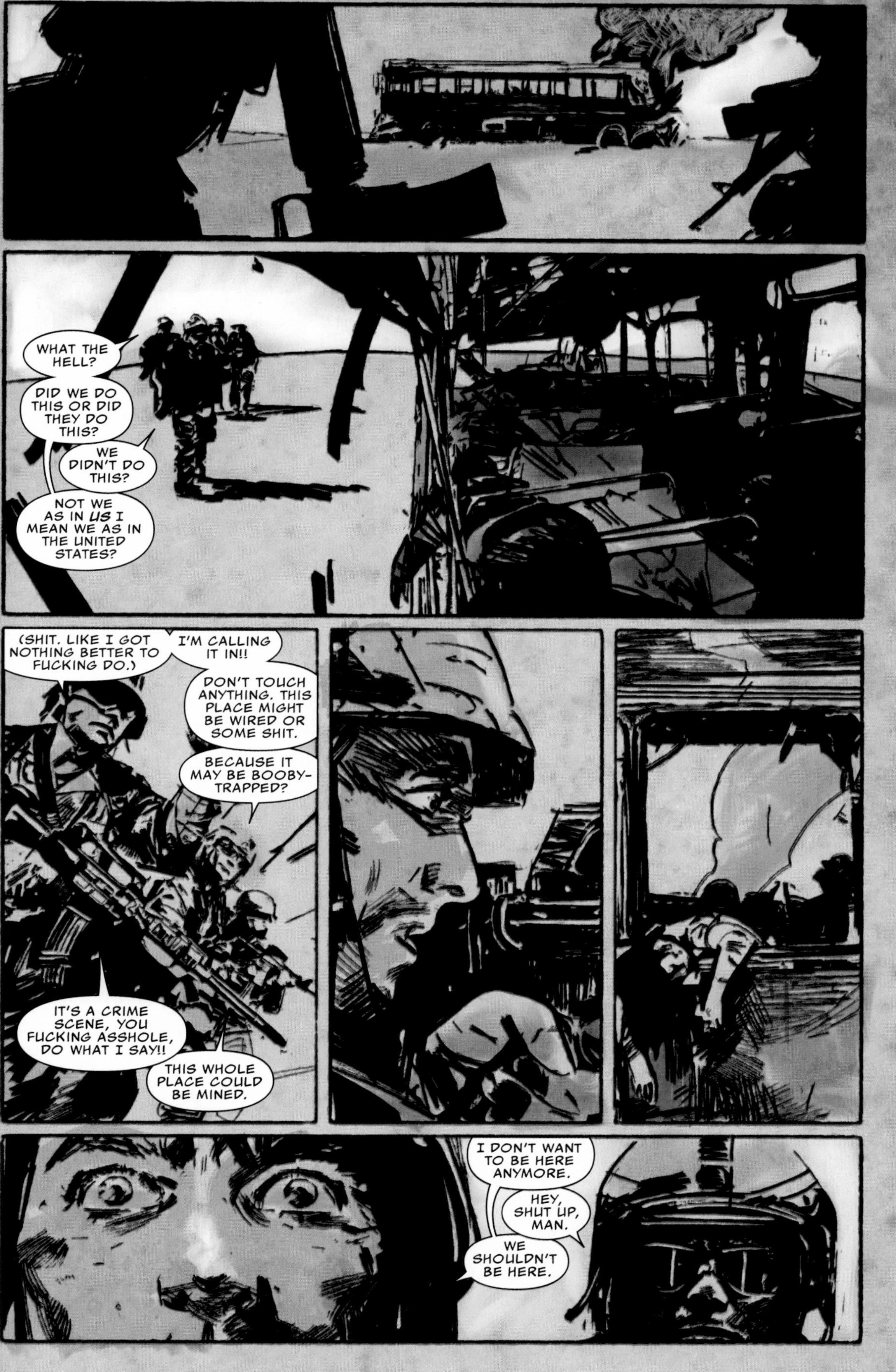
WHAT THE HELL?
DID WE DO THIS OR DID THEY DO THIS?
WE DIDN'T DO THIS?
NOT WE AS IN US I MEAN WE AS IN THE UNITED STATES?
(SHIT. LIKE I GOT NOTHING BETTER TO FUCKING DO.)
I'M CALLING IT IN!!
DON'T TOUCH ANYTHING. THIS PLACE MIGHT BE WIRED OR SOME SHIT.
BECAUSE IT MAY BE BOOBY-TRAPPED?
IT'S A CRIME SCENE, YOU FUCKING ASSHOLE, DO WHAT I SAY!!
THIS WHOLE PLACE COULD BE MINED.
I DON'T WANT TO BE HERE ANYMORE.
HEY, SHUT UP, MAN.
WE SHOULDN'T BE HERE.

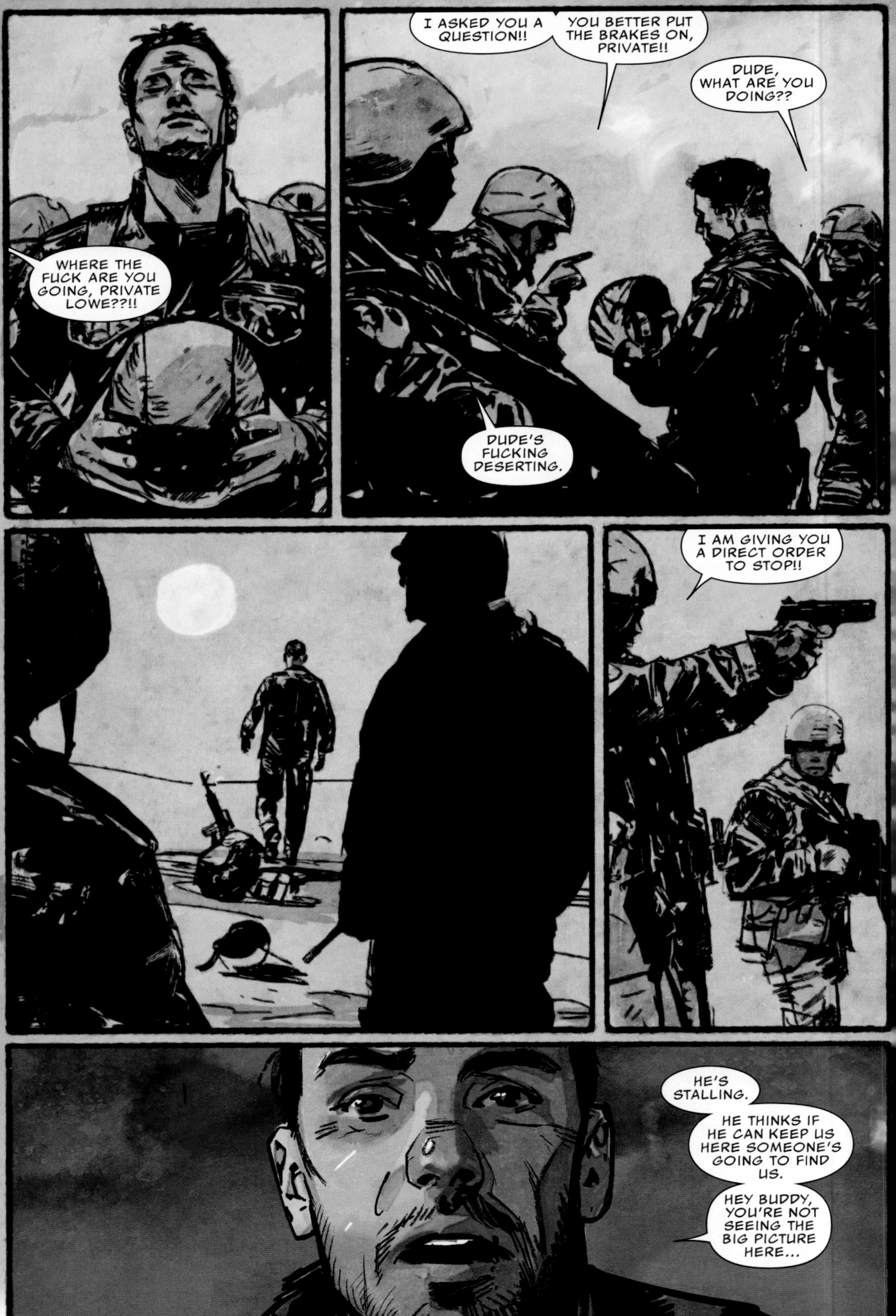
WHERE THE FUCK ARE YOU GOING, PRIVATE LOWE??!!
I ASKED YOU A QUESTION!!
YOU BETTER PUT THE BRAKES ON, PRIVATE!!
DUDE, WHAT ARE YOU DOING??
DUDE'S FUCKING DESERTING.
I AM GIVING YOU A DIRECT ORDER TO STOP!!
HE'S STALLING.
HE THINKS IF HE CAN KEEP US HERE SOMEONE'S GOING TO FIND US.
HEY BUDDY, YOU'RE NOT SEEING THE BIG PICTURE HERE...

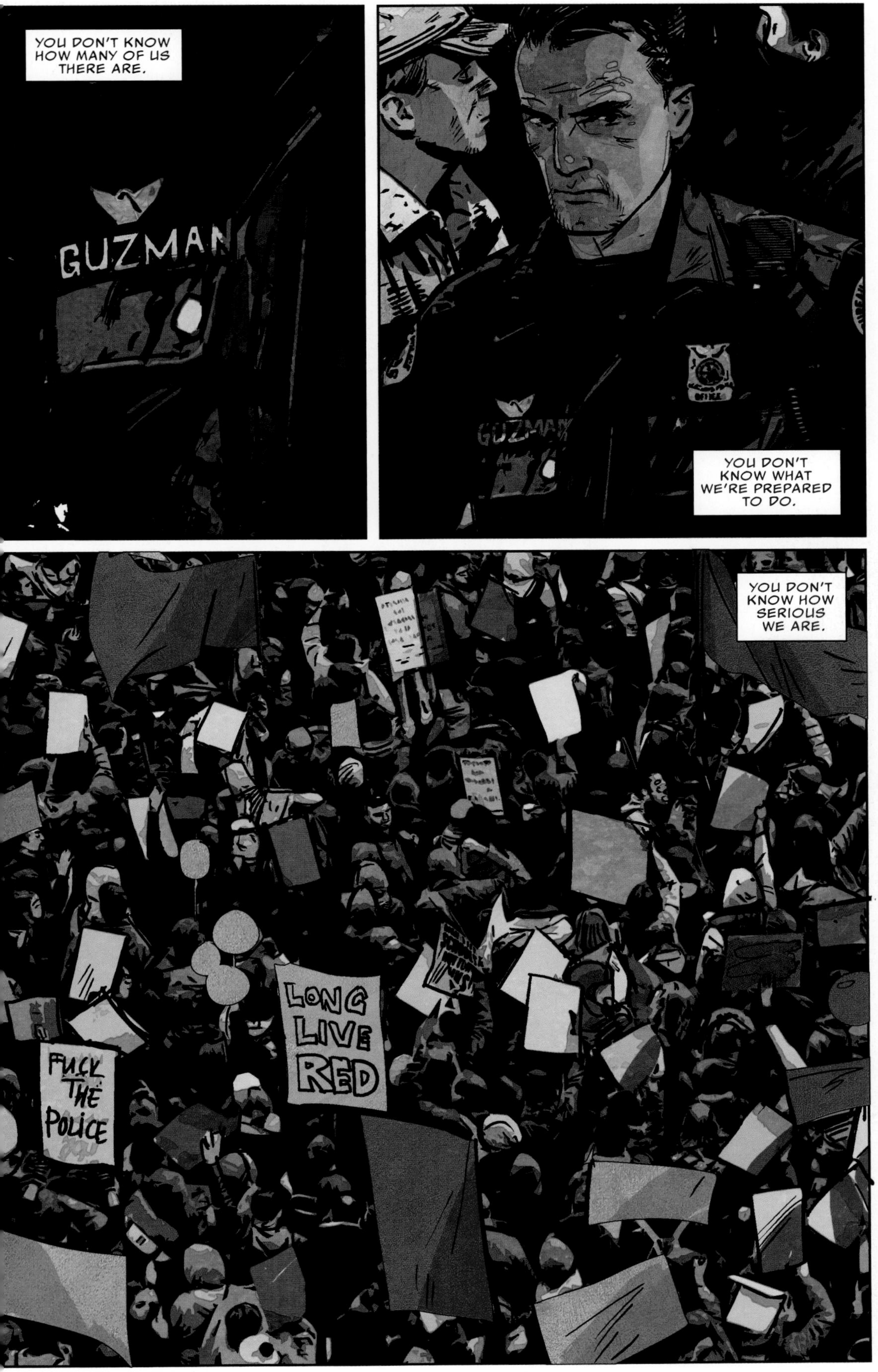
YOU DON'T KNOW HOW MANY OF US THERE ARE.
GUZMAN
GUZMAN
YOU DON'T KNOW WHAT WE'RE PREPARED TO DO.
YOU DON'T KNOW HOW SERIOUS WE ARE.
LONG LIVE RED
FUCK THE POLICE

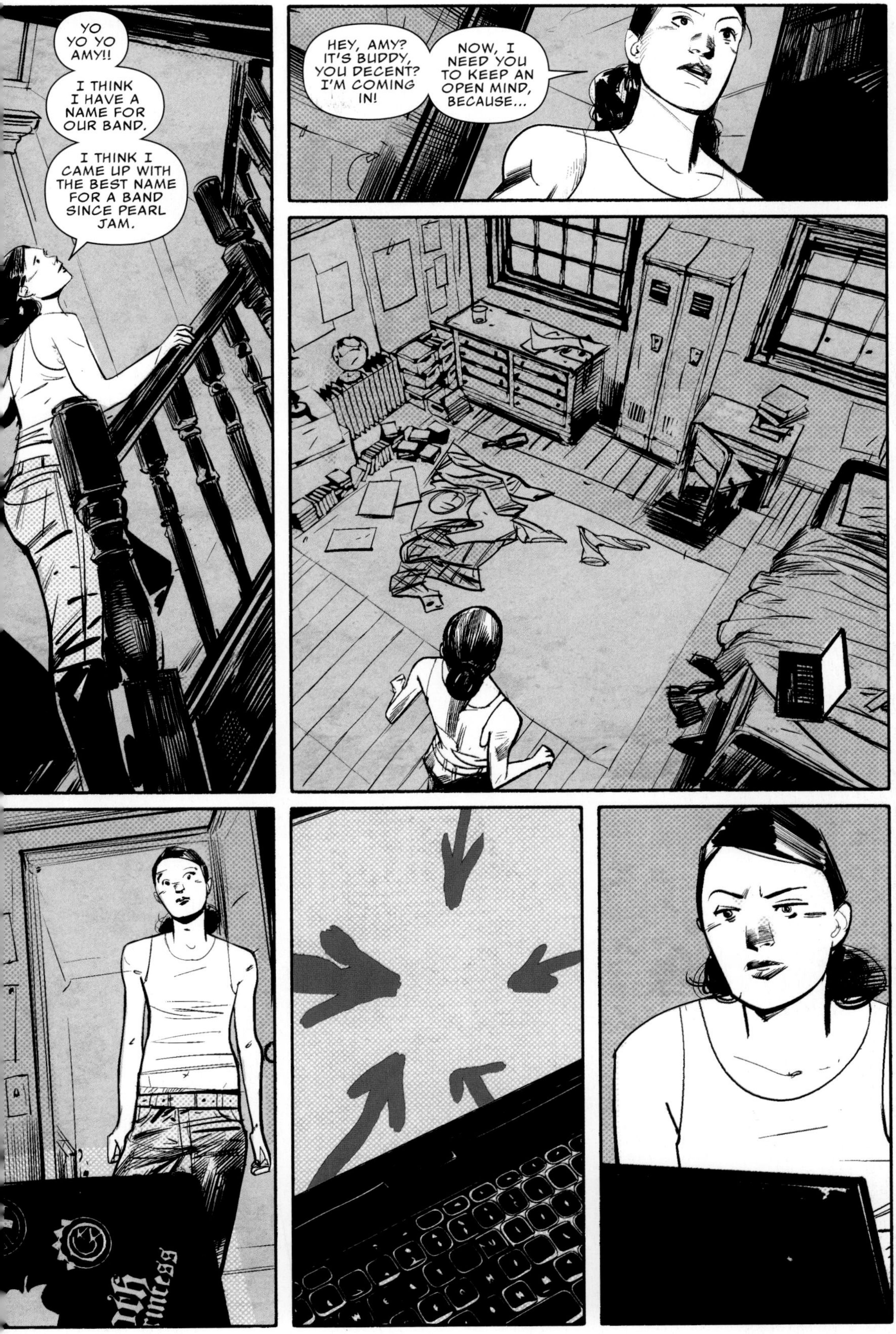
YO YO YO AMY!!
I THINK I HAVE A NAME FOR OUR BAND.
I THINK I CAME UP WITH THE BEST NAME FOR A BAND SINCE PEARL JAM.
HEY, AMY? IT'S BUDDY, YOU DECENT? I'M COMING IN!
NOW, I NEED YOU TO KEEP AN OPEN MIND, BECAUSE...

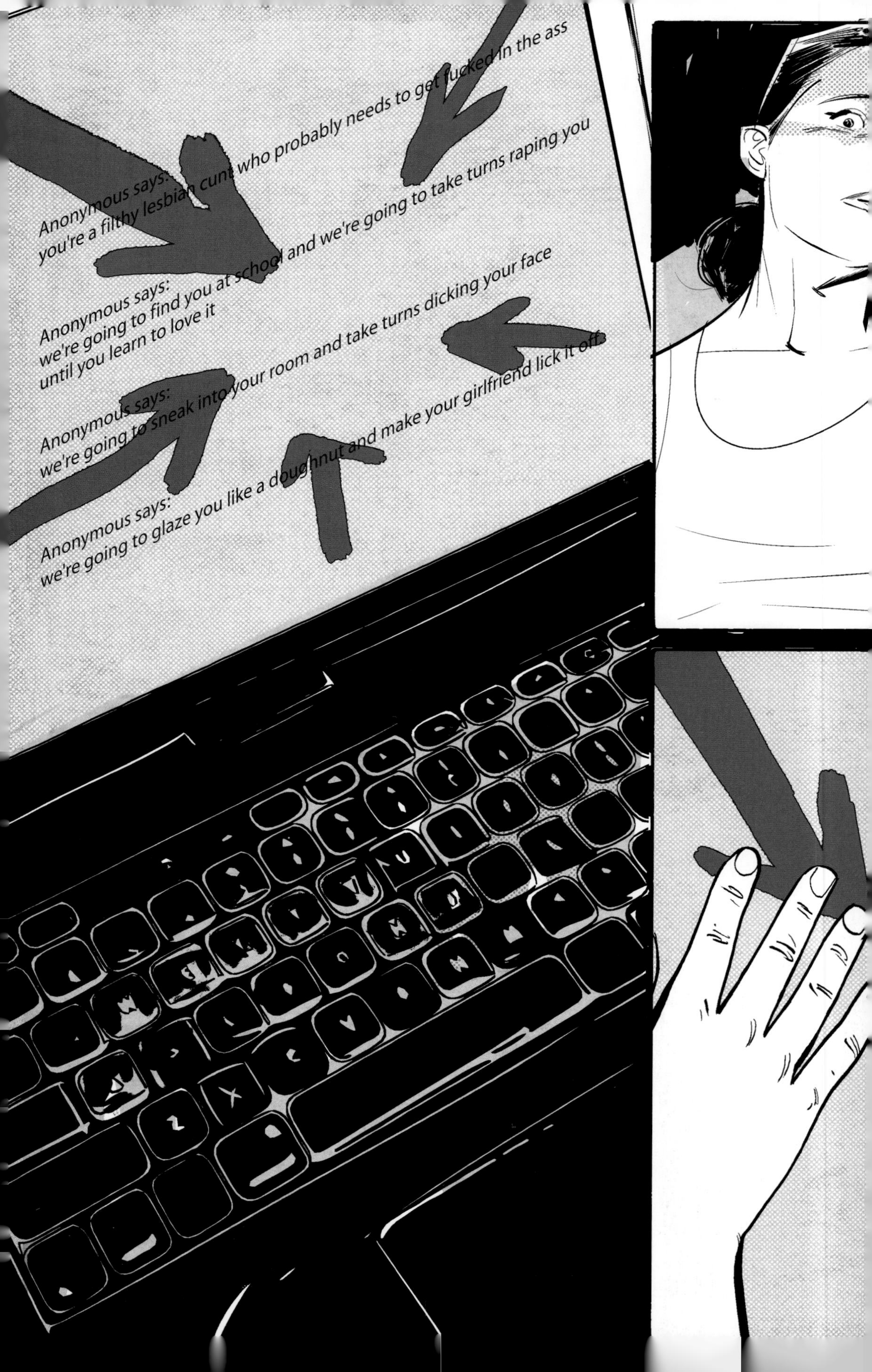
Anonymous says:
you're a filthy lesbian cunt who probably needs to get fucked in the ass
Anonymous says:
we're going to find you at school and we're going to take turns raping you
until you learn to love it
Anonymous says:
we're going to sneak into your room and take turns dicking your face
Anonymous says:
we're going to glaze you like a doughnut and make your girlfriend lick it off

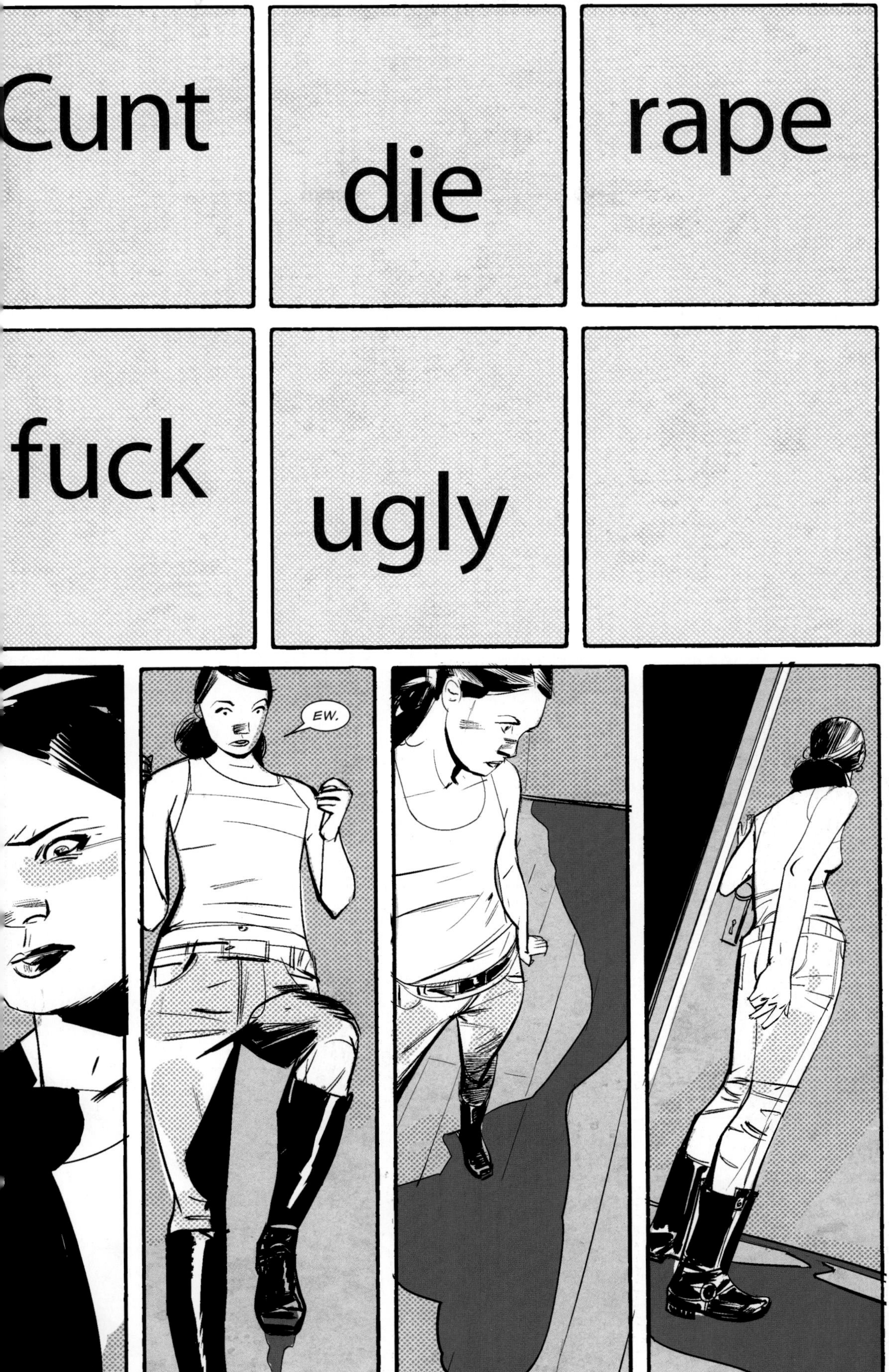
Cunt
die
rape
fuck
ugly
EW.

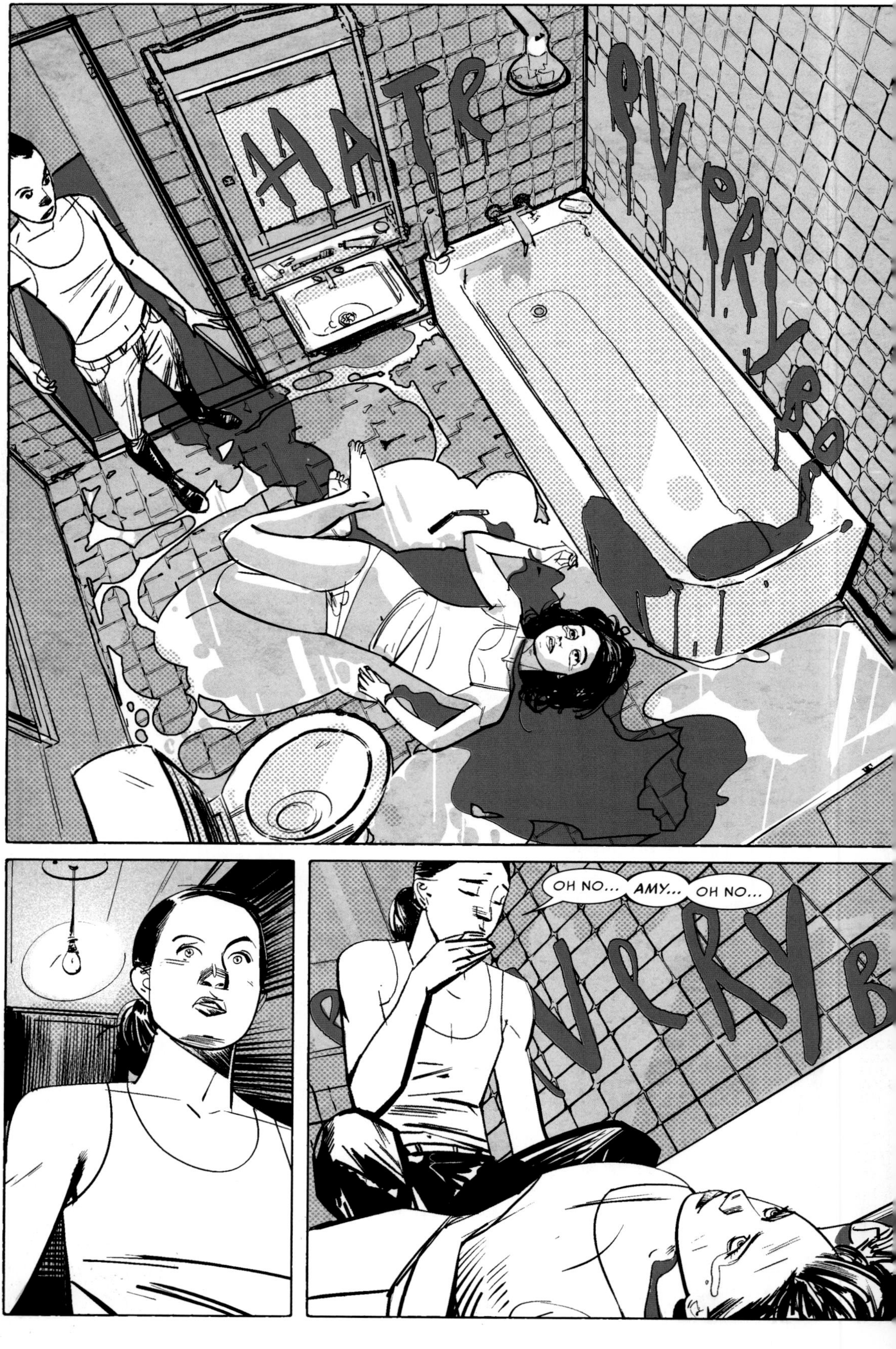
OH NO...
AMY...
OH NO...

LISTEN, RACHEL-

DAD, PLEASE DON'T CALL ME THAT...

YOU REALLY WANT ME TO CALL YOU BUDDY?

I DON'T CARE.

SORRY I HAVE TO TELL YOU THIS...

TO- TODAY OF ALL TIMES, THE FUNERAL AND ALL...

THEY'RE NOT GOING TO PRESS CHARGES ON THE BOYS.

I KNOW- I KNOW HOW YOU FEEL ABOUT THIS, BUT...

YOU KNOW HOW THIS CITY IS ABOUT ITS FOOTBALL, AND THE BOYS ARE GOOD PLAYERS.

THEY'RE GOOD BOYS AND THEY JUST DID SOMETHING STUPID.

I'M SURE IF THEY KNEW IT WOULD LEAD TO-

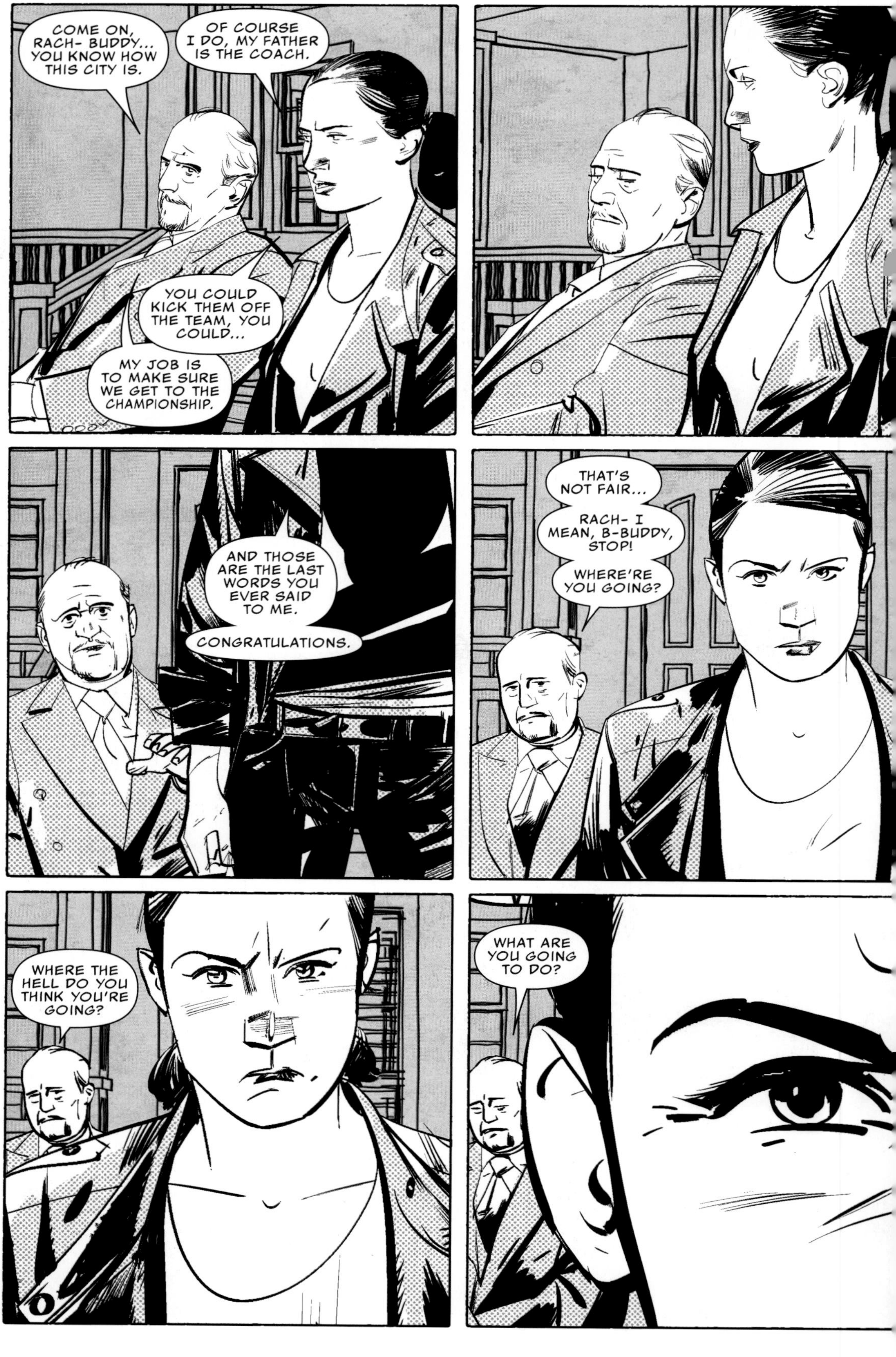
COME ON, RACH- BUDDY... YOU KNOW HOW THIS CITY IS.
OF COURSE I DO, MY FATHER IS THE COACH.
YOU COULD KICK THEM OFF THE TEAM, YOU COULD...
MY JOB IS TO MAKE SURE WE GET TO THE CHAMPIONSHIP.
AND THOSE ARE THE LAST WORDS YOU EVER SAID TO ME.
CONGRATULATIONS.
THAT'S NOT FAIR...
RACH- I MEAN, B-BUDDY, STOP!
WHERE'RE YOU GOING?
WHERE THE HELL DO YOU THINK YOU'RE GOING?
WHAT ARE YOU GOING TO DO?

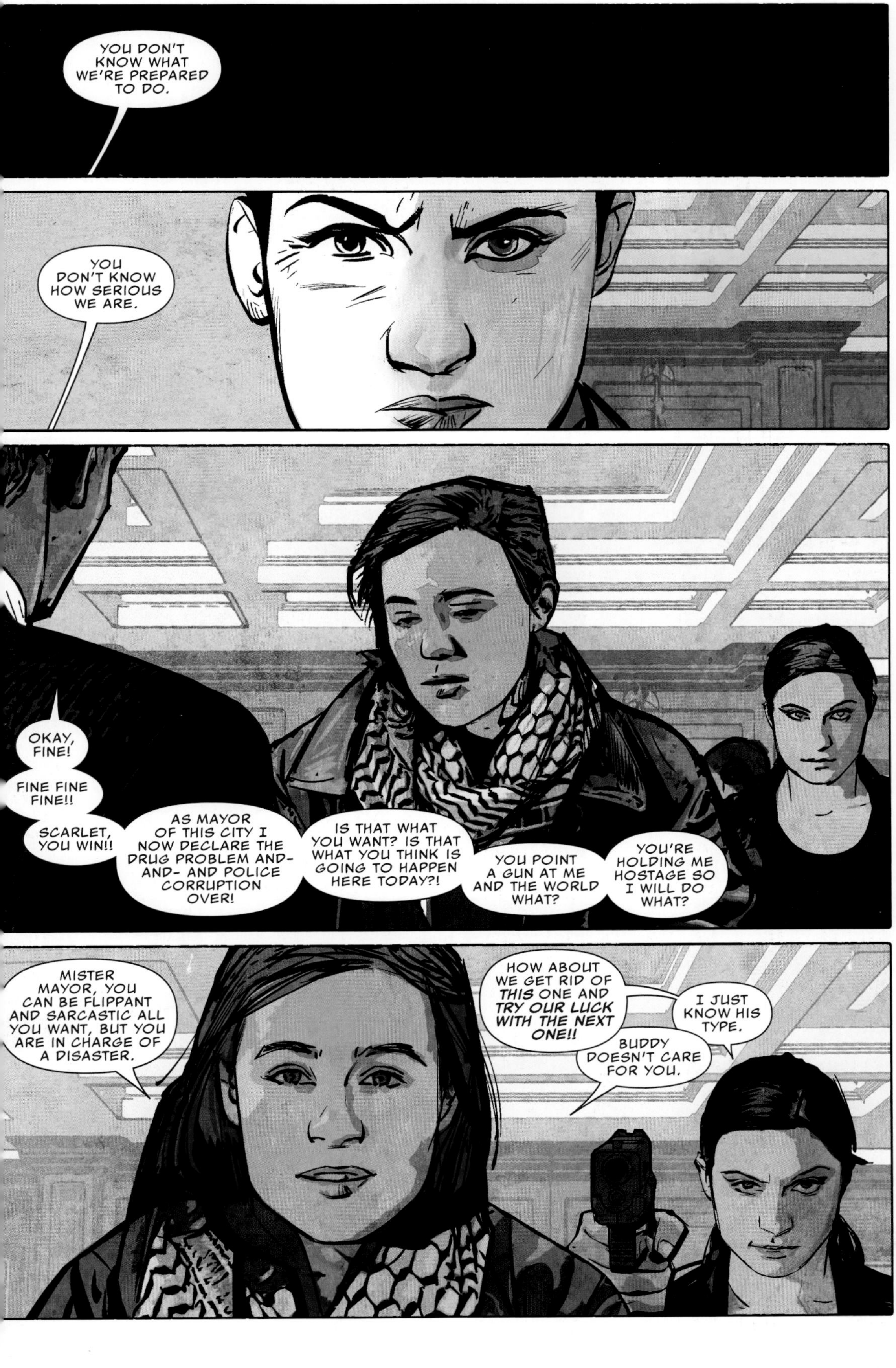
YOU DON'T KNOW WHAT WE'RE PREPARED TO DO.
YOU DON'T KNOW HOW SERIOUS WE ARE.
OKAY, FINE!
FINE FINE FINE!!
SCARLET, YOU WIN!!
AS MAYOR OF THIS CITY I NOW DECLARE THE DRUG PROBLEM AND- AND- AND POLICE CORRUPTION OVER!
IS THAT WHAT YOU WANT? IS THAT WHAT YOU THINK IS GOING TO HAPPEN HERE TODAY?!
YOU POINT A GUN AT ME AND THE WORLD WHAT?
YOU'RE HOLDING ME HOSTAGE SO I WILL DO WHAT?
MISTER MAYOR, YOU CAN BE FLIPPANT AND SARCASTIC ALL YOU WANT, BUT YOU ARE IN CHARGE OF A DISASTER.
HOW ABOUT WE GET RID OF *THIS* ONE AND *TRY OUR LUCK WITH THE NEXT ONE!!*
I JUST KNOW HIS TYPE.
BUDDY DOESN'T CARE FOR YOU.

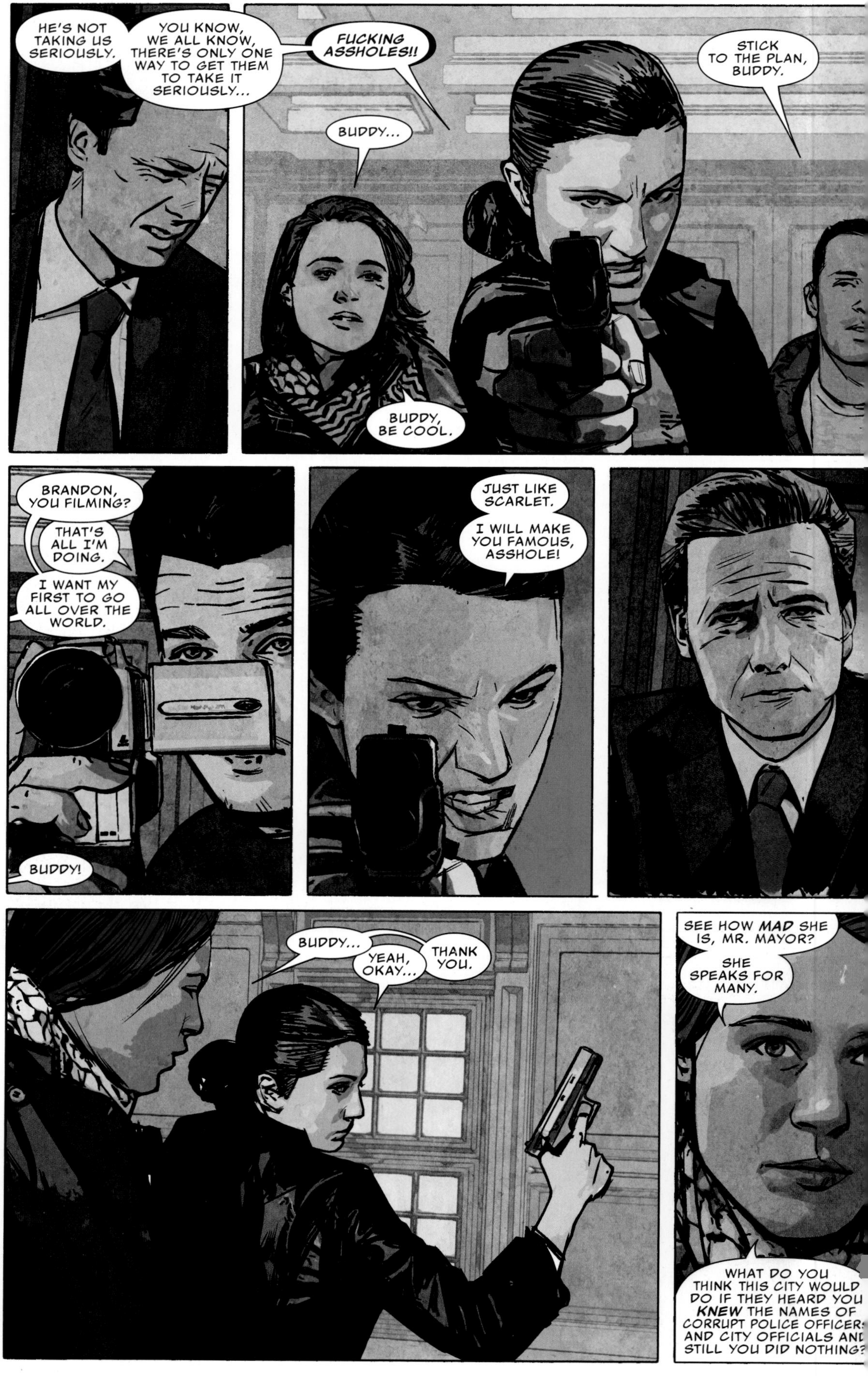
HE'S NOT TAKING US SERIOUSLY.
YOU KNOW, WE ALL KNOW, THERE'S ONLY ONE WAY TO GET THEM TO TAKE IT SERIOUSLY...
FUCKING ASSHOLES!!
BUDDY...
STICK TO THE PLAN, BUDDY.
BUDDY, BE COOL.
BRANDON, YOU FILMING?
THAT'S ALL I'M DOING.
I WANT MY FIRST TO GO ALL OVER THE WORLD.
BUDDY!
JUST LIKE SCARLET.
I WILL MAKE YOU FAMOUS, ASSHOLE!
BUDDY...
THANK YOU.
YEAH, OKAY...
SEE HOW MAD SHE IS, MR. MAYOR?
SHE SPEAKS FOR MANY.
WHAT DO YOU THINK THIS CITY WOULD DO IF THEY HEARD YOU KNEW THE NAMES OF CORRUPT POLICE OFFICERS AND CITY OFFICIALS AND STILL YOU DID NOTHING?

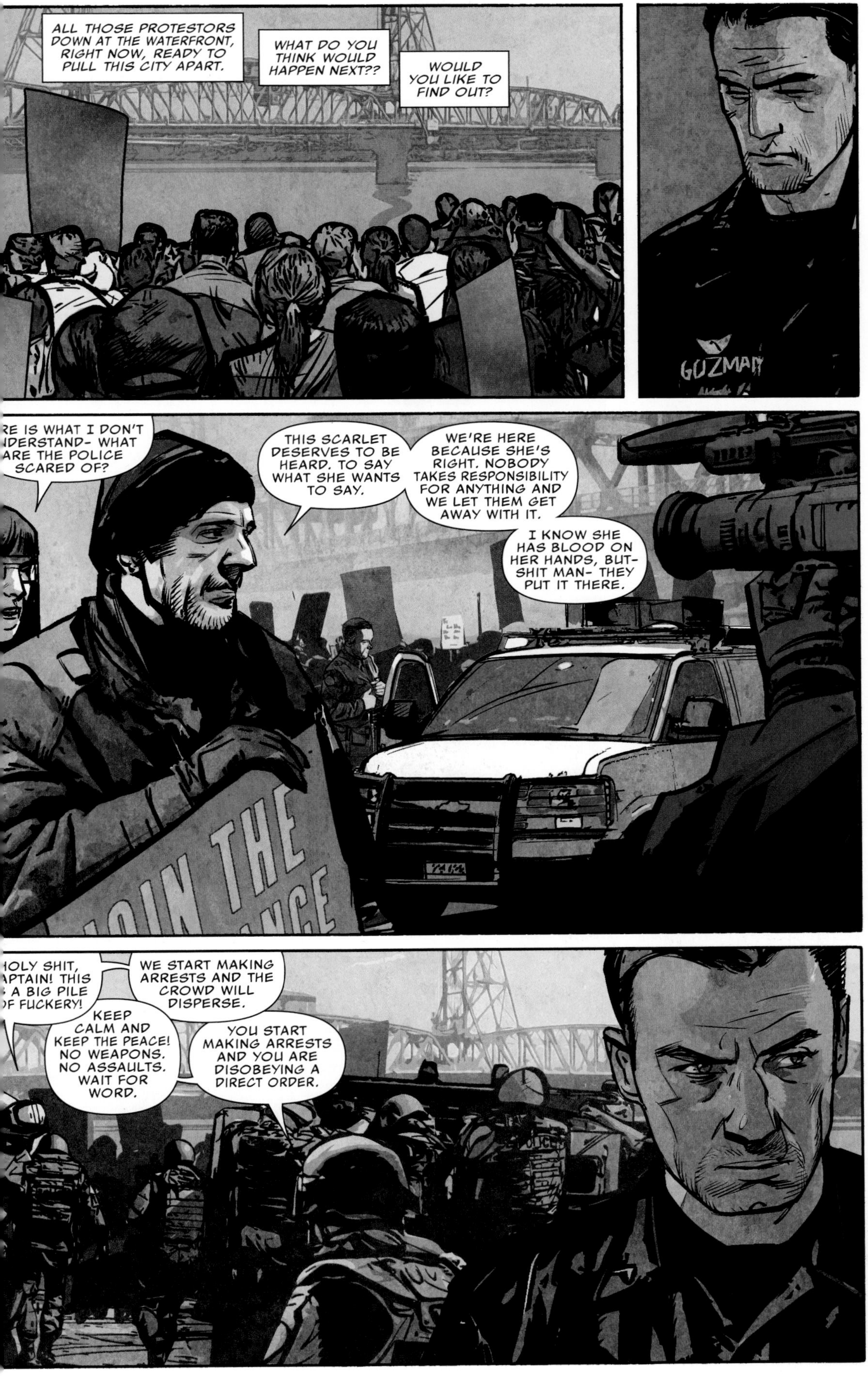
ALL THOSE PROTESTORS DOWN AT THE WATERFRONT, RIGHT NOW, READY TO PULL THIS CITY APART.
WHAT DO YOU THINK WOULD HAPPEN NEXT??
WOULD YOU LIKE TO FIND OUT?
RE IS WHAT I DON'T NDERSTAND- WHAT ARE THE POLICE SCARED OF?
THIS SCARLET DESERVES TO BE HEARD. TO SAY WHAT SHE WANTS TO SAY.
WE'RE HERE BECAUSE SHE'S RIGHT. NOBODY TAKES RESPONSIBILITY FOR ANYTHING AND WE LET THEM GET AWAY WITH IT.
I KNOW SHE HAS BLOOD ON HER HANDS, BUT- SHIT MAN- THEY PUT IT THERE.
HOLY SHIT, APTAIN! THIS A BIG PILE OF FUCKERY!
WE START MAKING ARRESTS AND THE CROWD WILL DISPERSE.
KEEP CALM AND KEEP THE PEACE! NO WEAPONS. NO ASSAULTS. WAIT FOR WORD.
YOU START MAKING ARRESTS AND YOU ARE DISOBEYING A DIRECT ORDER.

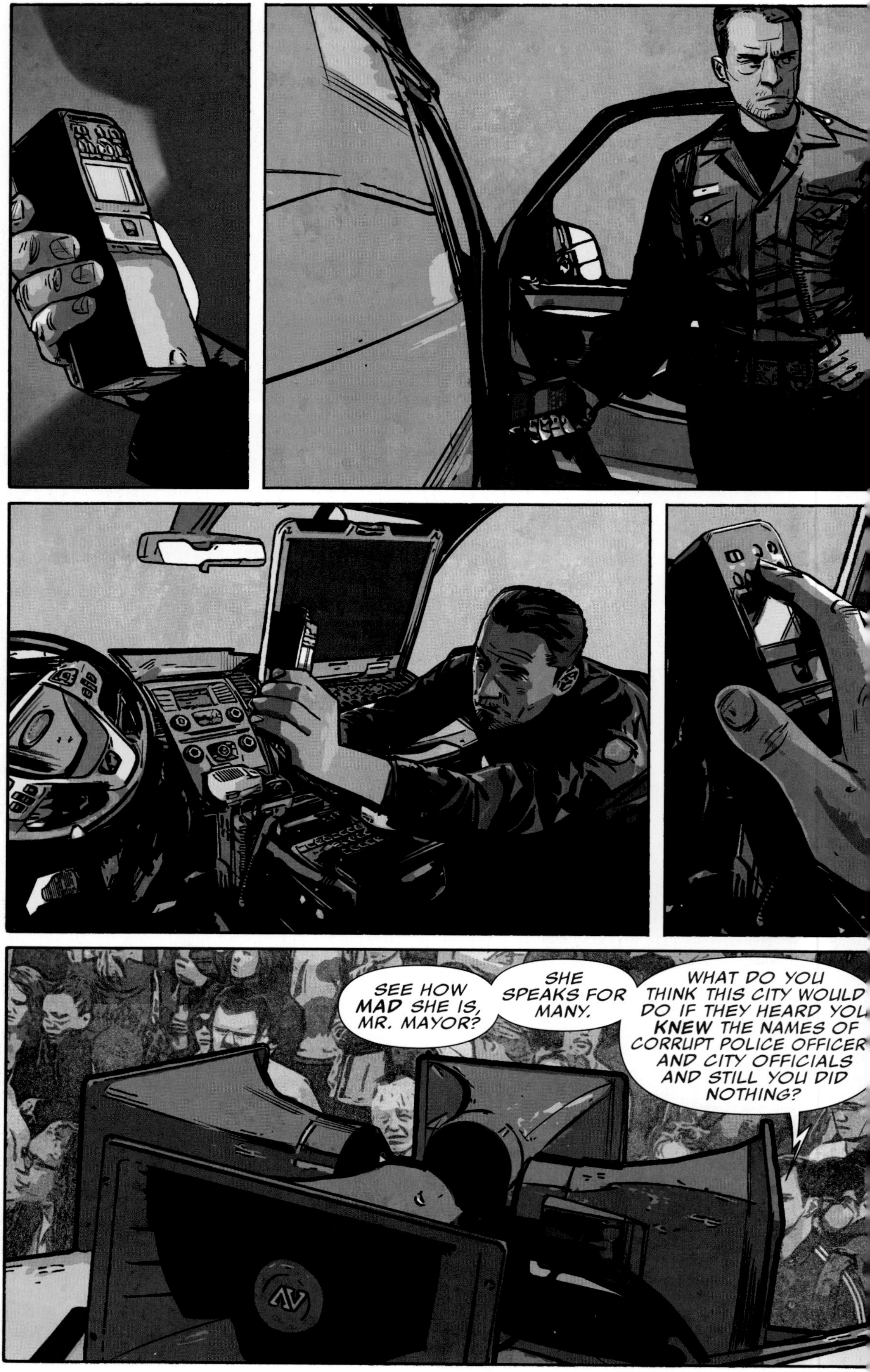
SEE HOW MAD SHE IS, MR. MAYOR?
SHE SPEAKS FOR MANY.
WHAT DO YOU THINK THIS CITY WOULD DO IF THEY HEARD YOU KNEW THE NAMES OF CORRUPT POLICE OFFICER AND CITY OFFICIALS AND STILL YOU DID NOTHING?

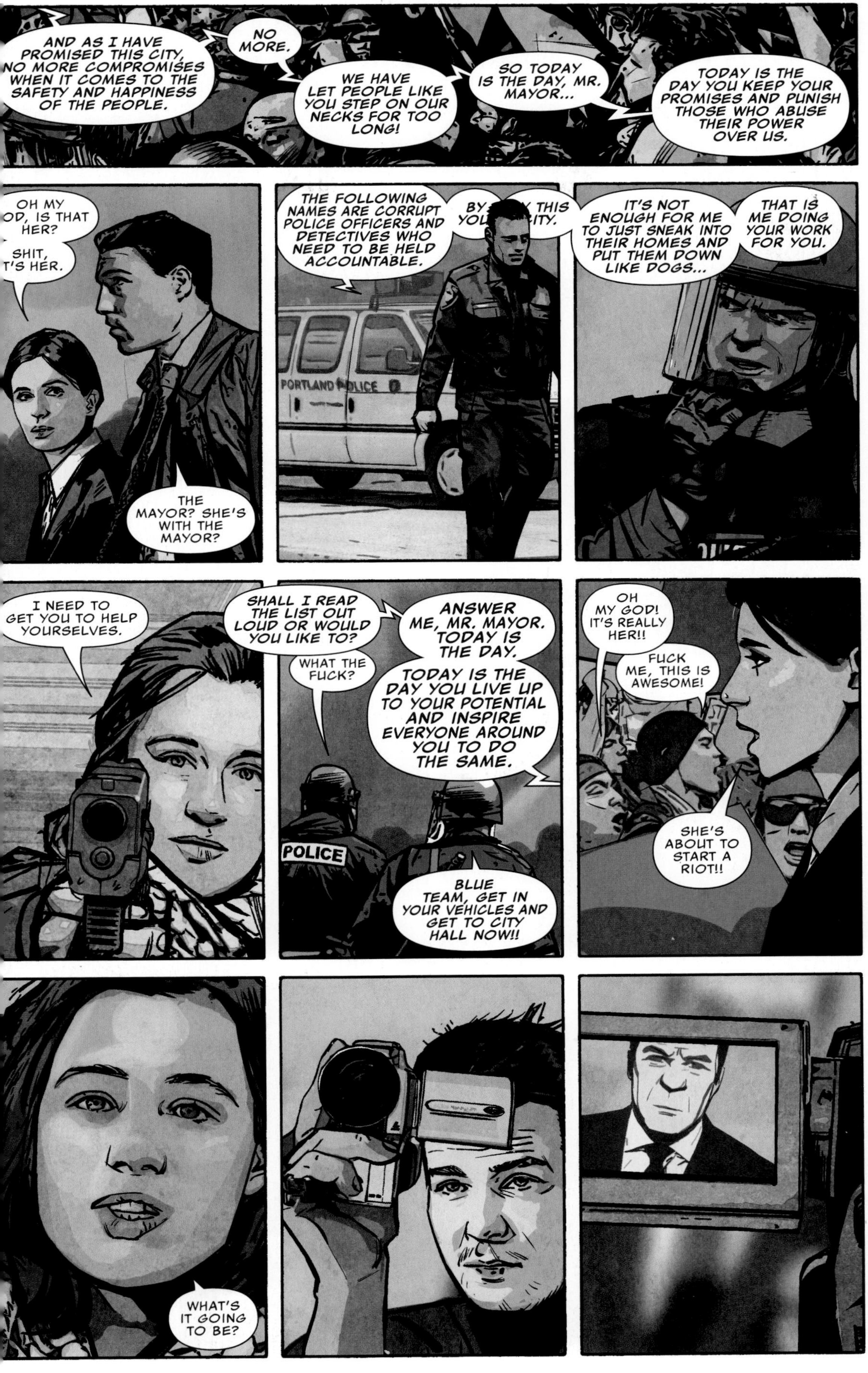
AND AS I HAVE PROMISED THIS CITY, NO MORE COMPROMISES WHEN IT COMES TO THE SAFETY AND HAPPINESS OF THE PEOPLE.
NO MORE.
WE HAVE LET PEOPLE LIKE YOU STEP ON OUR NECKS FOR TOO LONG!
SO TODAY IS THE DAY, MR. MAYOR...
TODAY IS THE DAY YOU KEEP YOUR PROMISES AND PUNISH THOSE WHO ABUSE THEIR POWER OVER US.
OH MY
OD, IS THAT HER?
SHIT,
T'S HER.
THE MAYOR? SHE'S WITH THE MAYOR?
THE FOLLOWING NAMES ARE CORRUPT POLICE OFFICERS AND DETECTIVES WHO NEED TO BE HELD ACCOUNTABLE.
BY YOU THIS ITY.
PORTLAND POLICE
IT'S NOT ENOUGH FOR ME TO JUST SNEAK INTO THEIR HOMES AND PUT THEM DOWN LIKE DOGS...
THAT IS ME DOING YOUR WORK FOR YOU.
I NEED TO GET YOU TO HELP YOURSELVES.
SHALL I READ THE LIST OUT LOUD OR WOULD YOU LIKE TO?
WHAT THE FUCK?
ANSWER ME, MR. MAYOR. TODAY IS THE DAY.
TODAY IS THE DAY YOU LIVE UP TO YOUR POTENTIAL AND INSPIRE EVERYONE AROUND YOU TO DO THE SAME.
POLICE
BLUE TEAM, GET IN YOUR VEHICLES AND GET TO CITY HALL NOW!!
OH MY GOD! IT'S REALLY HER!!
FUCK ME, THIS IS AWESOME!
SHE'S ABOUT TO START A RIOT!!
WHAT'S IT GOING TO BE?

WHAT DO YOU THINK WOULD HAPPEN NEXT??

JOIN THE RESISTANCE HOPE

WOULD YOU LIKE TO FIND OUT?

SCARLET

OH MY GOD...

I NEED YOU TO TAKE THIS VERY SERIOUSLY.

OR YOU'LL KILL ME?

WE DON'T WANT TO KILL ANYONE.

YOU'RE NOT GETTING OFF THAT EASY.

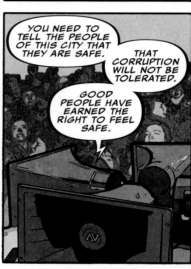

YOU NEED TO TELL THE PEOPLE OF THIS CITY THAT THEY ARE SAFE.

THAT CORRUPTION WILL NOT BE TOLERATED.

GOOD PEOPLE HAVE EARNED THE RIGHT TO FEEL SAFE.

THIS IS THE CAREER YOU CHOSE, MR. MAYOR.

YOU TOOK THIS TITLE, YOU MADE AN OATH.

YOU MADE A PROMISE TO EVERYONE TO KEEP THEM SAFE.

IF YOU CAN'T KEEP THIS PROMISE

...YOU FORFEIT YOUR PLACE–

WHY IS THAT COMING FROM THE CARS??

TURN IT OFF!!

IT'S COMING FROM ALL OF THEM!!!

THE FUCK DO YOU EXPECT ME TO DO?!!

WATCH YOUR LANGUAGE, MR. MAYOR.

THERE MIGHT BE CHILDREN LISTENING.

I SAID TURN IT OFF!!

IT WON'T TURN OFF!!

THEN RIP IT OUT OF THE GOD-DAMN STEERING WHEEL!!

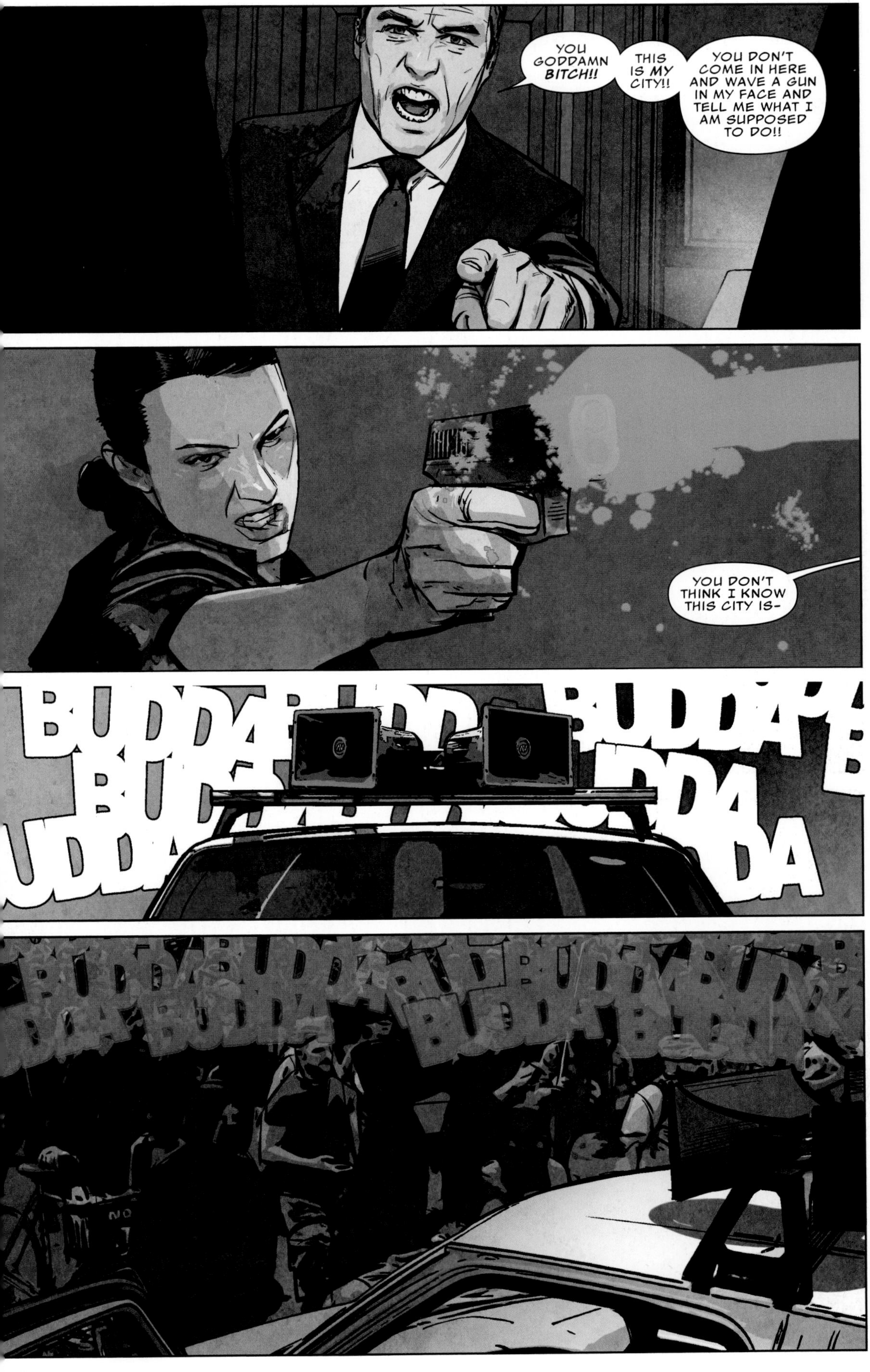
YOU GODDAMN BITCH!!
THIS IS MY CITY!!
YOU DON'T COME IN HERE AND WAVE A GUN IN MY FACE AND TELL ME WHAT I AM SUPPOSED TO DO!!
YOU DON'T THINK I KNOW THIS CITY IS-
BUDDA

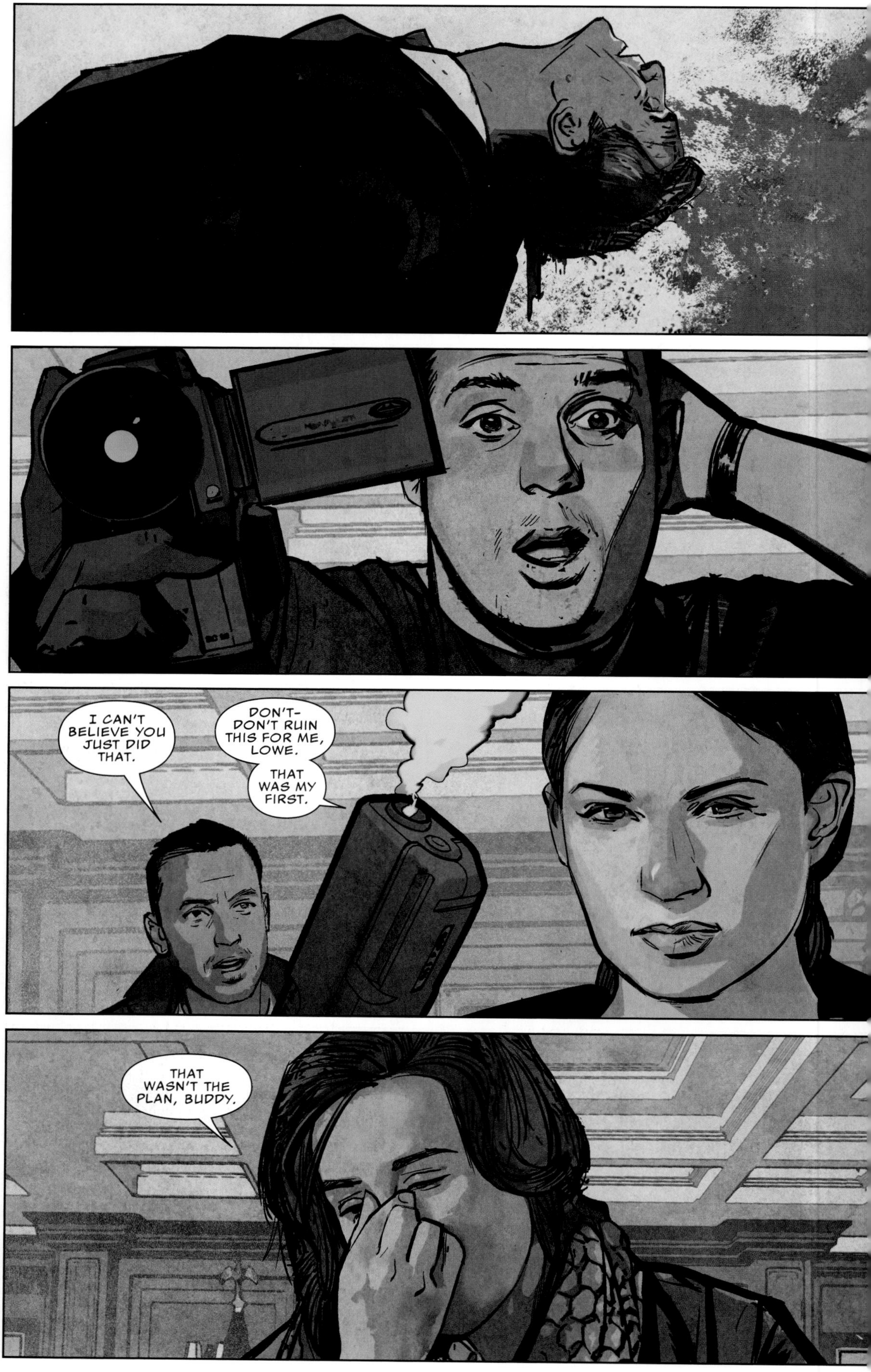
I CAN'T BELIEVE YOU JUST DID THAT.
DON'T- DON'T RUIN THIS FOR ME, LOWE.
THAT WAS MY FIRST.
THAT WASN'T THE PLAN, BUDDY.

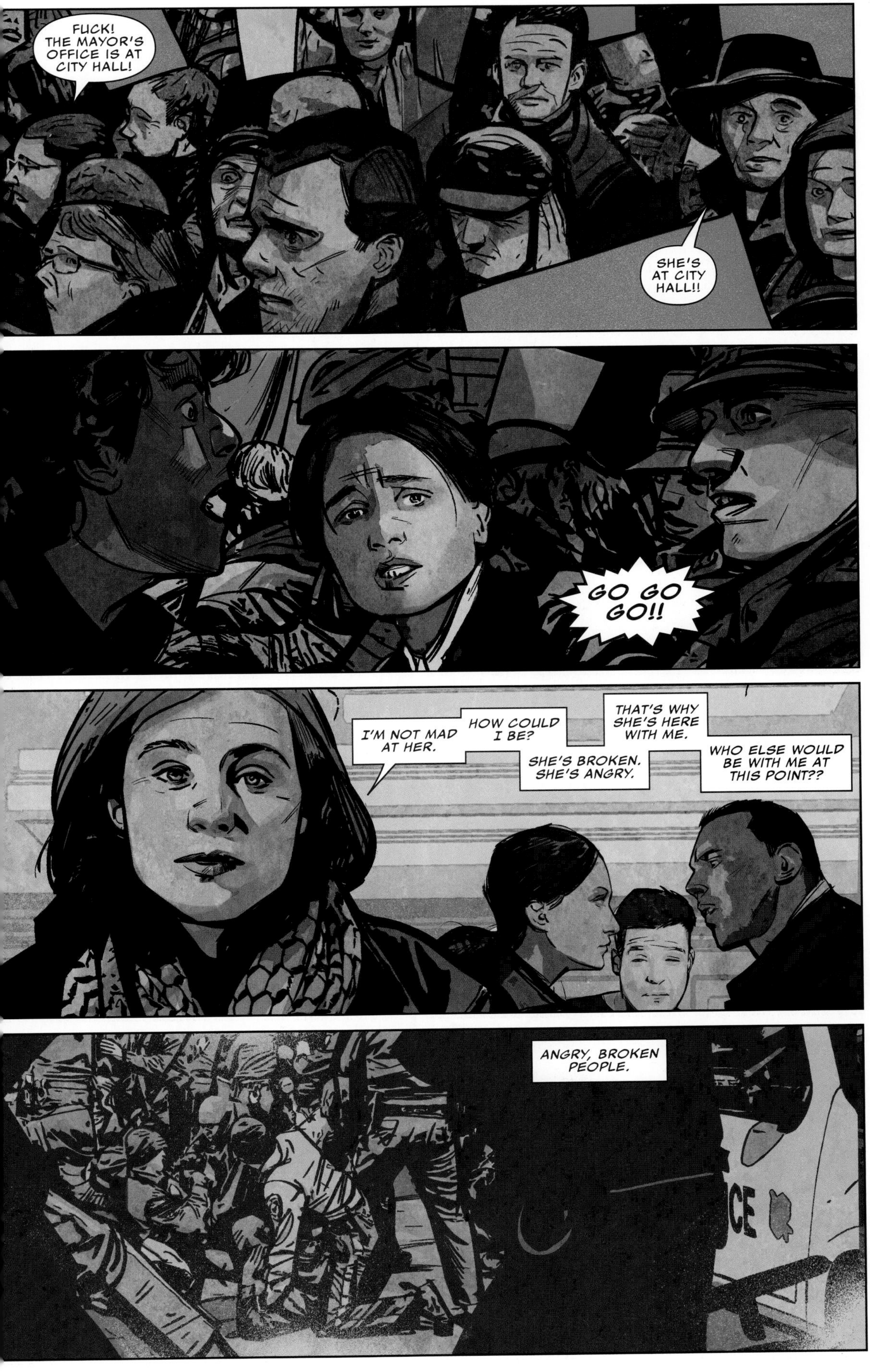
FUCK! THE MAYOR'S OFFICE IS AT CITY HALL!
SHE'S AT CITY HALL!!
GO GO GO!!
I'M NOT MAD AT HER.
HOW COULD I BE?
SHE'S BROKEN. SHE'S ANGRY.
THAT'S WHY SHE'S HERE WITH ME.
WHO ELSE WOULD BE WITH ME AT THIS POINT??
ANGRY, BROKEN PEOPLE.

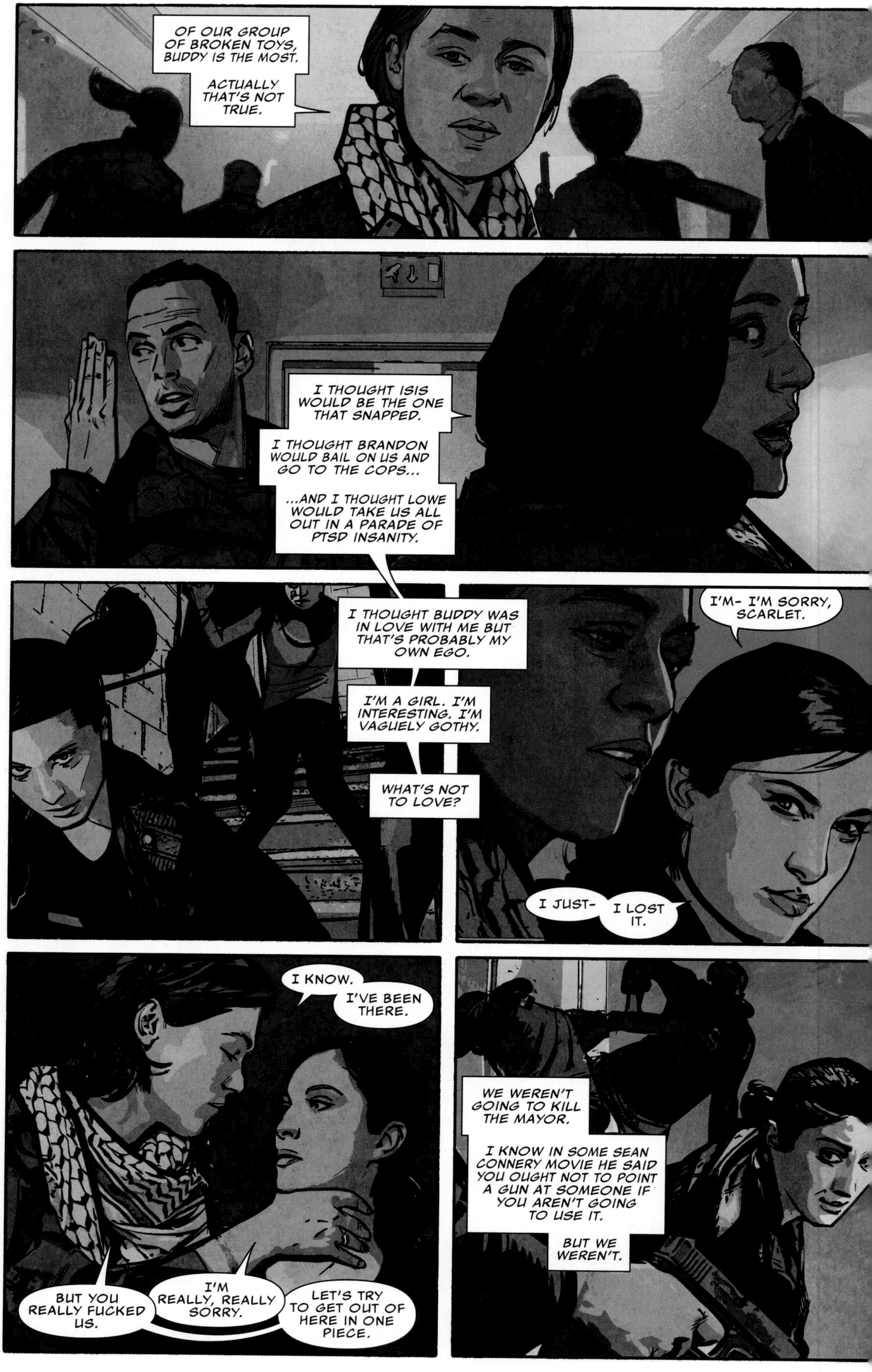

OF OUR GROUP OF BROKEN TOYS, BUDDY IS THE MOST.
ACTUALLY THAT'S NOT TRUE.
I THOUGHT ISIS WOULD BE THE ONE THAT SNAPPED.
I THOUGHT BRANDON WOULD BAIL ON US AND GO TO THE COPS...
...AND I THOUGHT LOWE WOULD TAKE US ALL OUT IN A PARADE OF PTSD INSANITY.
I THOUGHT BUDDY WAS IN LOVE WITH ME BUT THAT'S PROBABLY MY OWN EGO.
I'M A GIRL. I'M INTERESTING. I'M VAGUELY GOTHY.
WHAT'S NOT TO LOVE?
I'M- I'M SORRY, SCARLET.
I JUST-
I LOST IT.
I KNOW.
I'VE BEEN THERE.
BUT YOU REALLY FUCKED US.
I'M REALLY, REALLY SORRY.
LET'S TRY TO GET OUT OF HERE IN ONE PIECE.
WE WEREN'T GOING TO KILL THE MAYOR.
I KNOW IN SOME SEAN CONNERY MOVIE HE SAID YOU OUGHT NOT TO POINT A GUN AT SOMEONE IF YOU AREN'T GOING TO USE IT.
BUT WE WEREN'T.

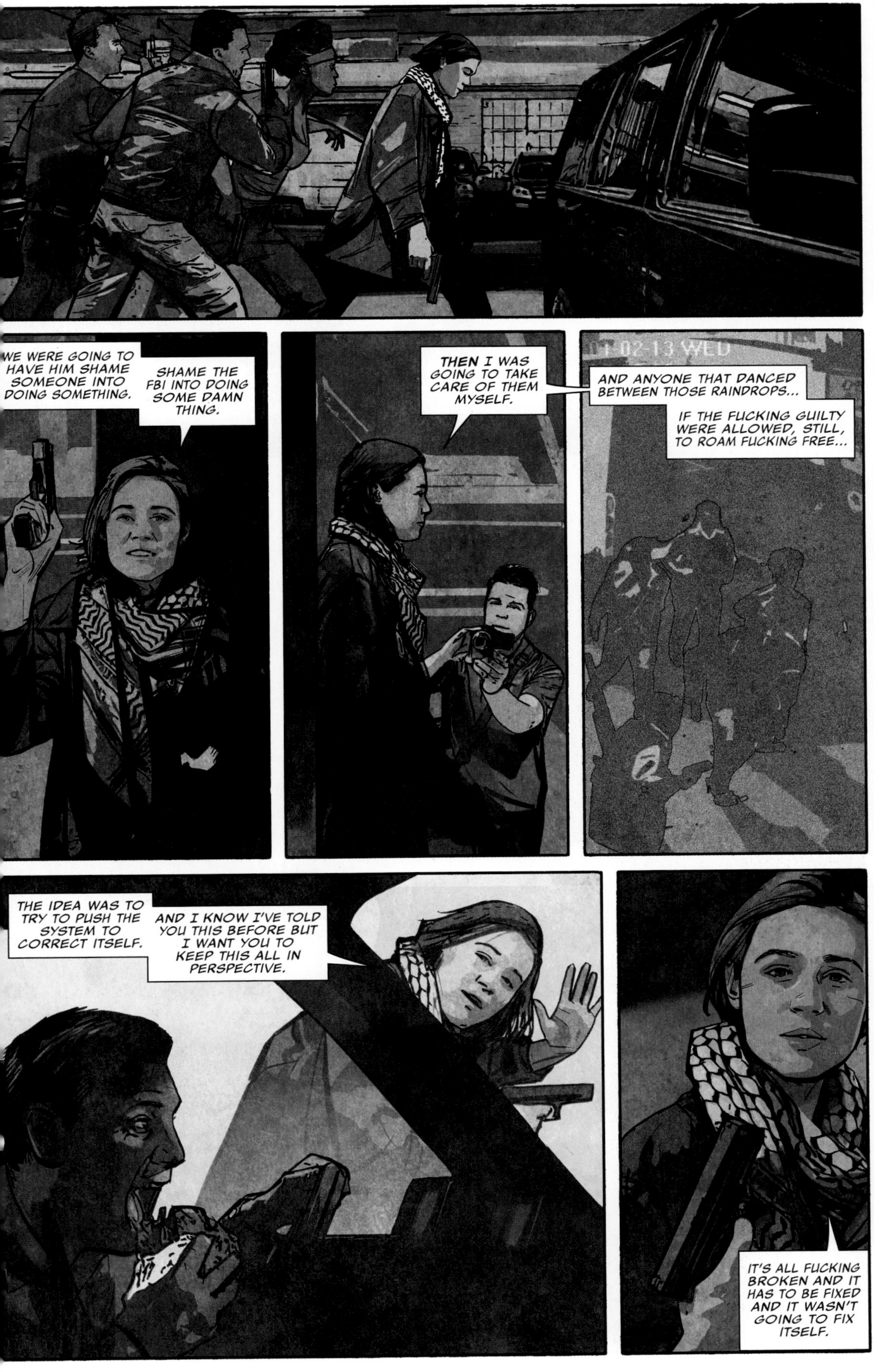
WE WERE GOING TO HAVE HIM SHAME SOMEONE INTO DOING SOMETHING.
SHAME THE FBI INTO DOING SOME DAMN THING.
THEN I WAS GOING TO TAKE CARE OF THEM MYSELF.
01-02-13 WED
AND ANYONE THAT DANCED BETWEEN THOSE RAINDROPS...
IF THE FUCKING GUILTY WERE ALLOWED, STILL, TO ROAM FUCKING FREE...
THE IDEA WAS TO TRY TO PUSH THE SYSTEM TO CORRECT ITSELF.
AND I KNOW I'VE TOLD YOU THIS BEFORE BUT I WANT YOU TO KEEP THIS ALL IN PERSPECTIVE.
IT'S ALL FUCKING BROKEN AND IT HAS TO BE FIXED AND IT WASN'T GOING TO FIX ITSELF.

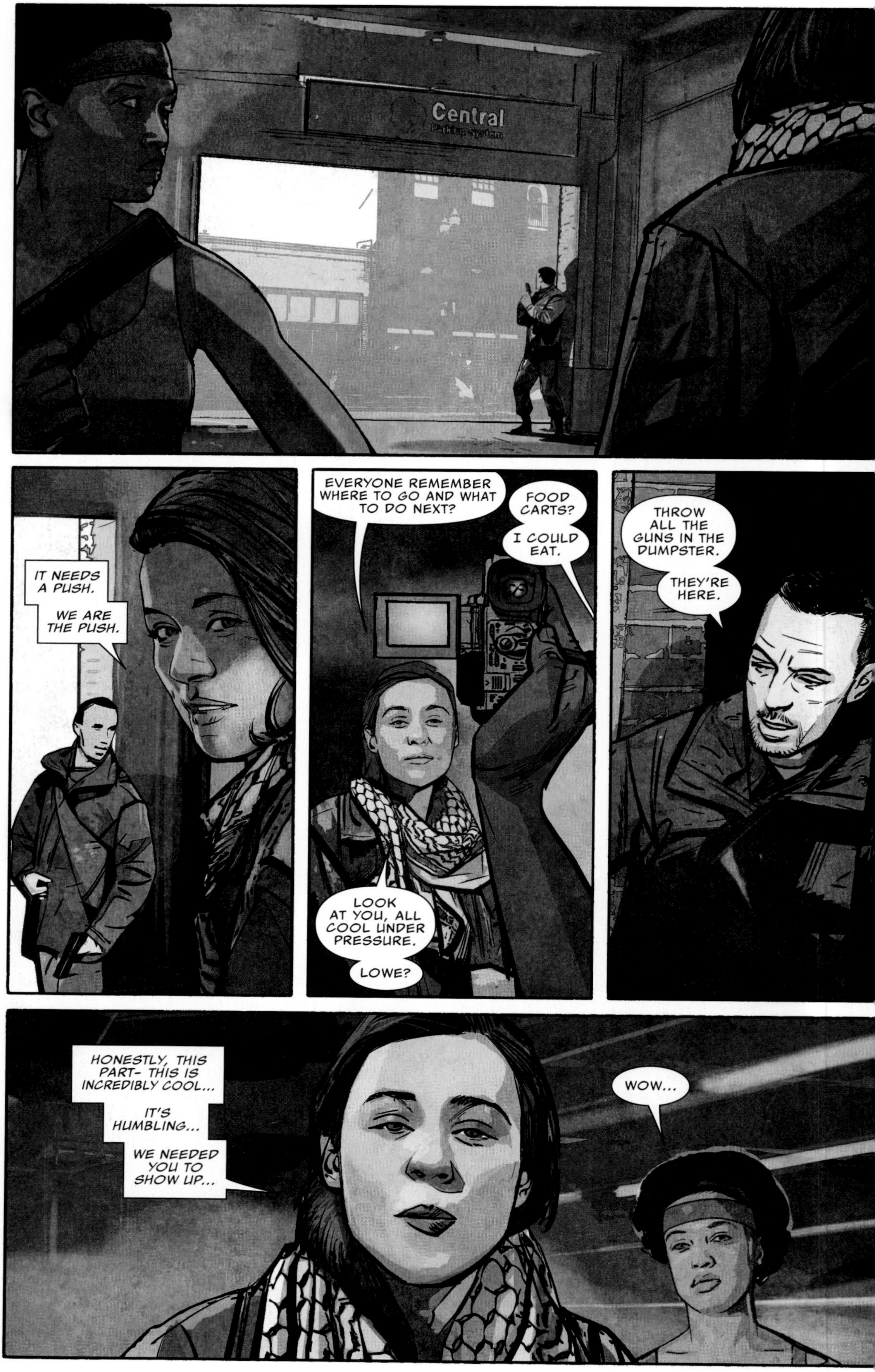
Central
IT NEEDS A PUSH.
WE ARE THE PUSH.
EVERYONE REMEMBER WHERE TO GO AND WHAT TO DO NEXT?
FOOD CARTS?
I COULD EAT.
LOOK AT YOU, ALL COOL UNDER PRESSURE.
LOWE?
THROW ALL THE GUNS IN THE DUMPSTER.
THEY'RE HERE.
HONESTLY, THIS PART- THIS IS INCREDIBLY COOL...
IT'S HUMBLING...
WE NEEDED YOU TO SHOW UP...
WOW...

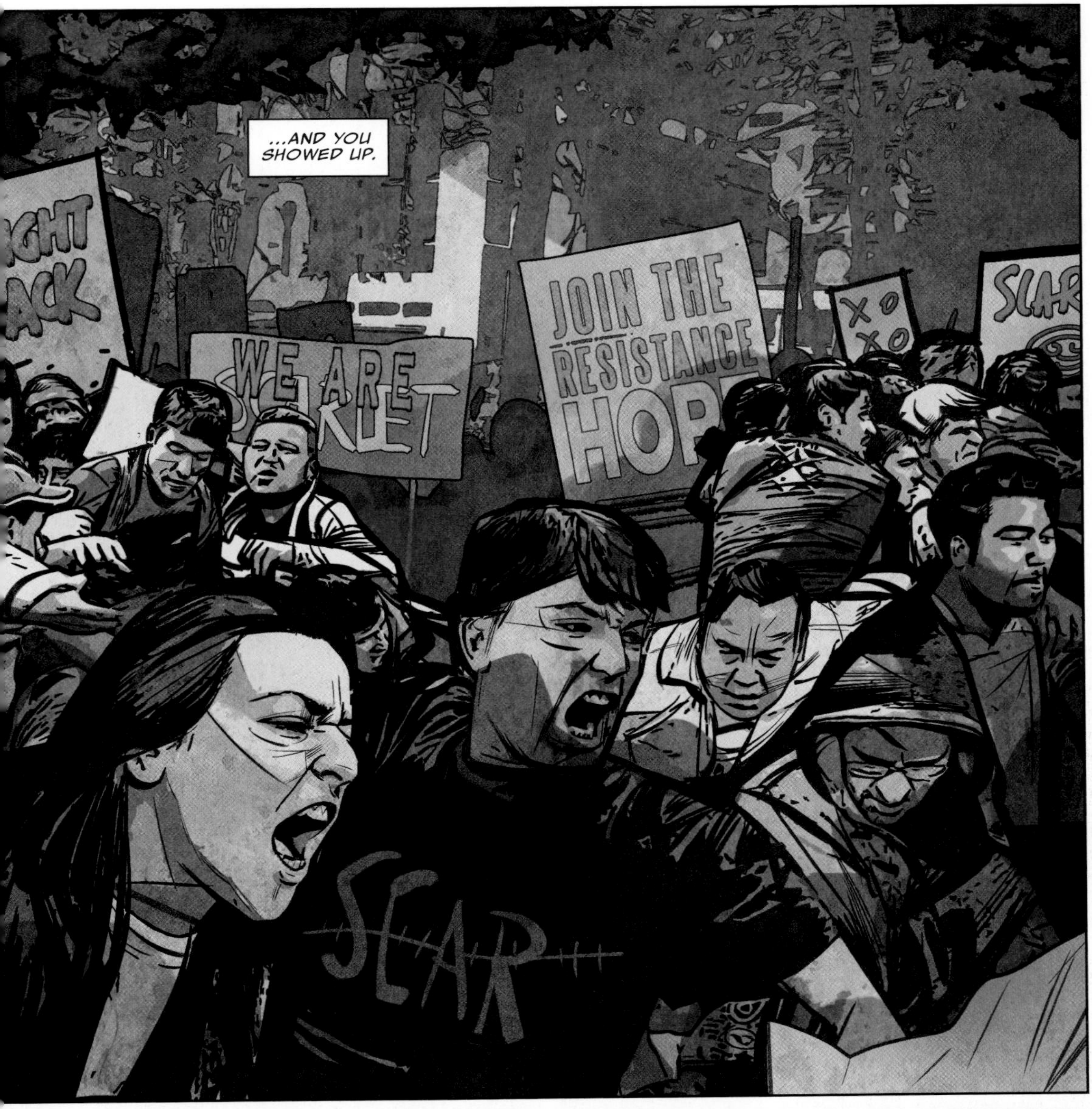
...AND YOU SHOWED UP.
WE ARE
JOIN THE RESISTANCE
SCAR

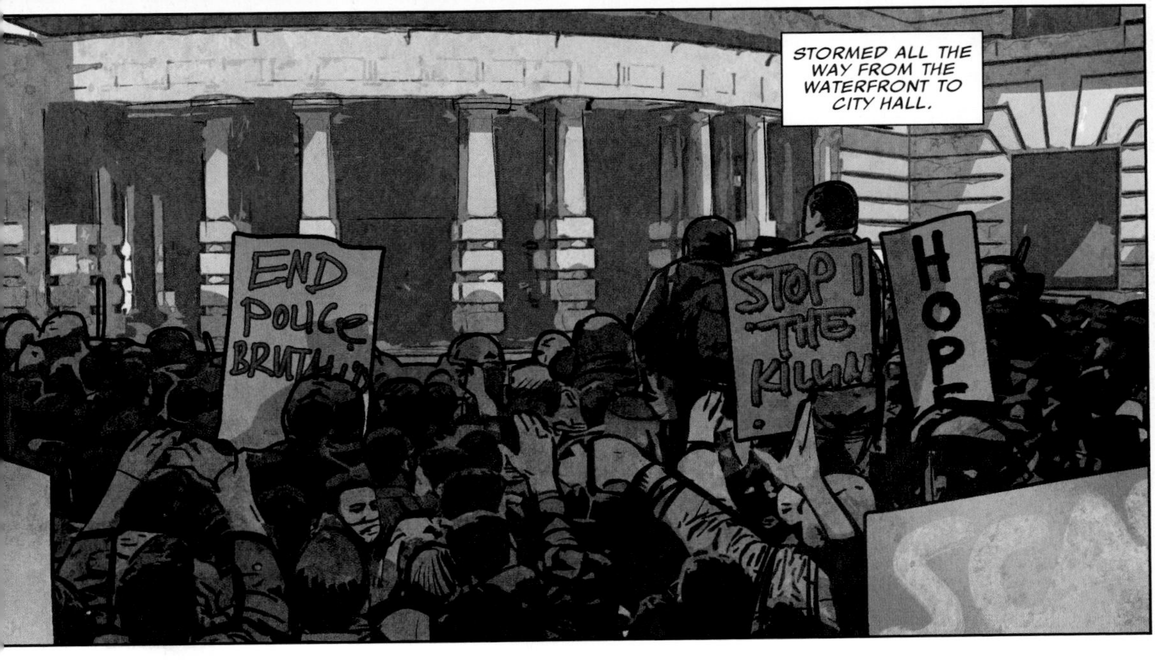
STORMED ALL THE WAY FROM THE WATERFRONT TO CITY HALL.
END
HOPE

WEEEOOOOOOOOWWEEEEOOOOO

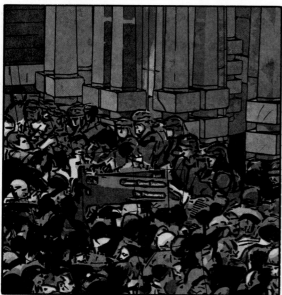

OKAY, YES, SOME OF YOU SHOWED UP JUST TO SEE A SHOW.

SOME OF YOU SHOWED UP BECAUSE YOU HAD TO SEE IT FOR YOURSELF...

BUT SOME OF YOU ARE HERE BECAUSE, WELL, LIKE ME, THIS IS WHERE YOU NEED TO BE.

POLICE

STAND DOWN!!

YOU MUST DISPERSE IMMEDIATELY!!!

FUCK YOU!!

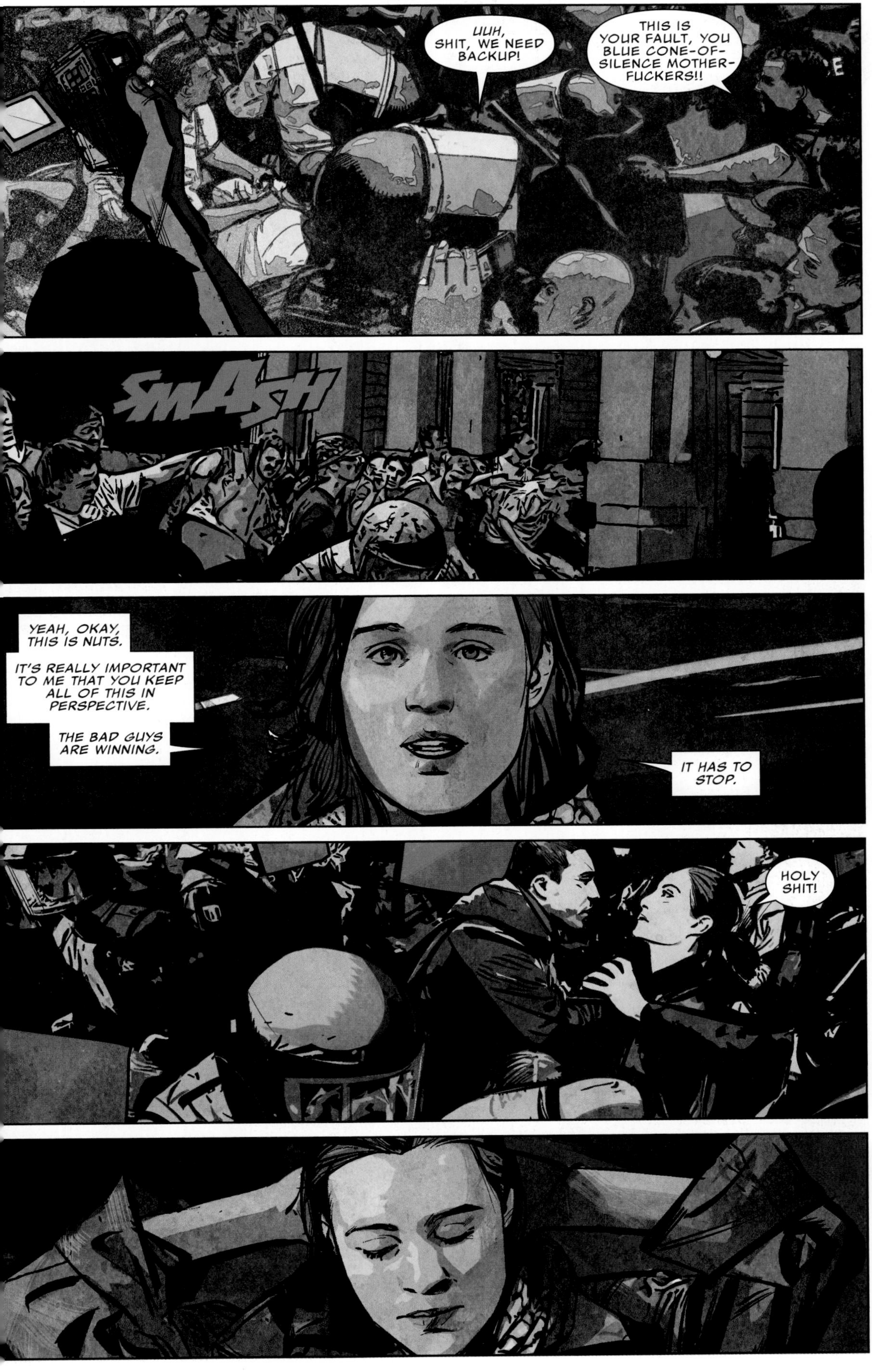
UUH, SHIT, WE NEED BACKUP!
THIS IS YOUR FAULT, YOU BLUE CONE-OF-SILENCE MOTHER-FUCKERS!!
SMASH
YEAH, OKAY, THIS IS NUTS.
IT'S REALLY IMPORTANT TO ME THAT YOU KEEP ALL OF THIS IN PERSPECTIVE.
THE BAD GUYS ARE WINNING.
IT HAS TO STOP.
HOLY SHIT!

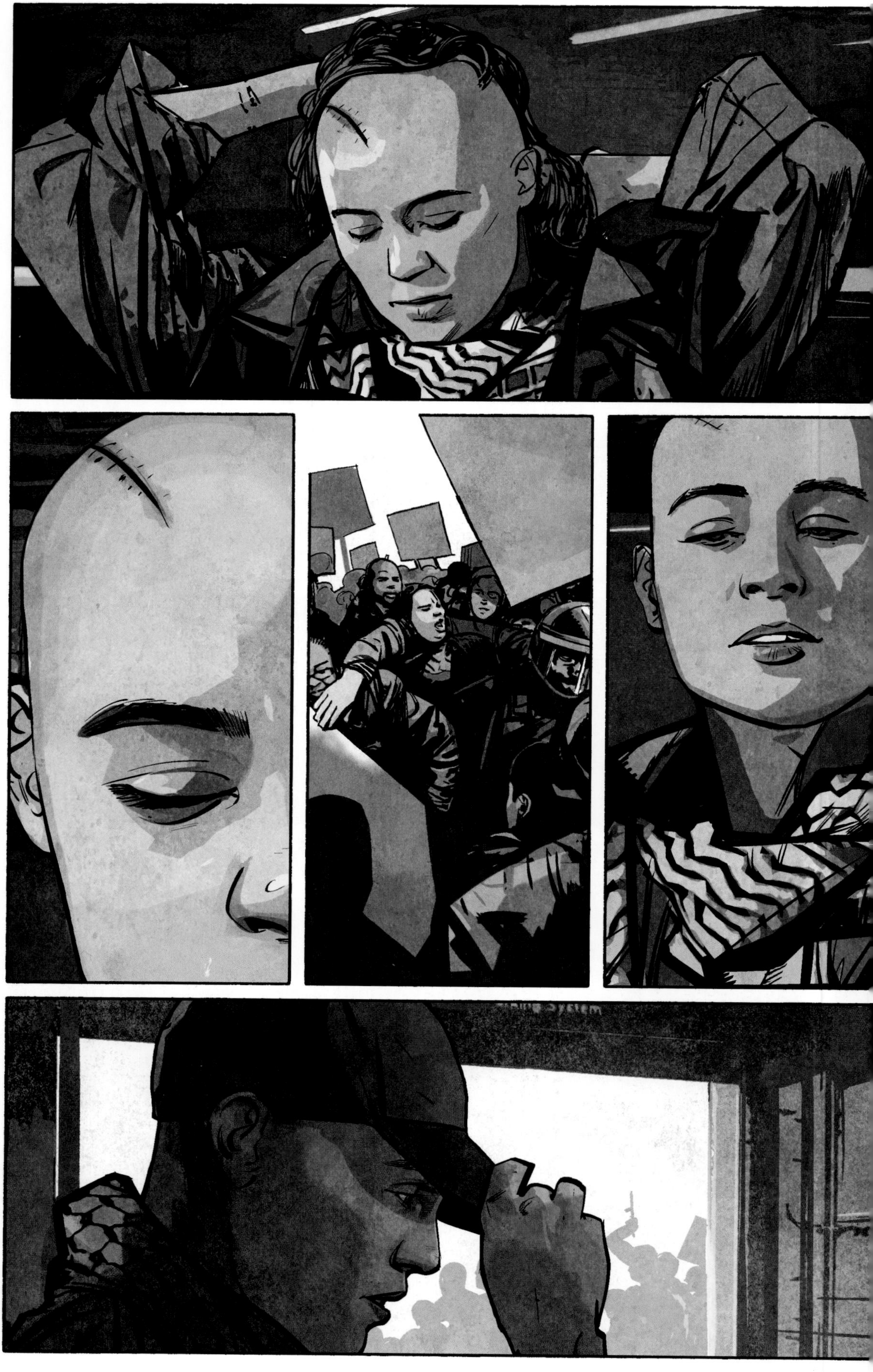
System

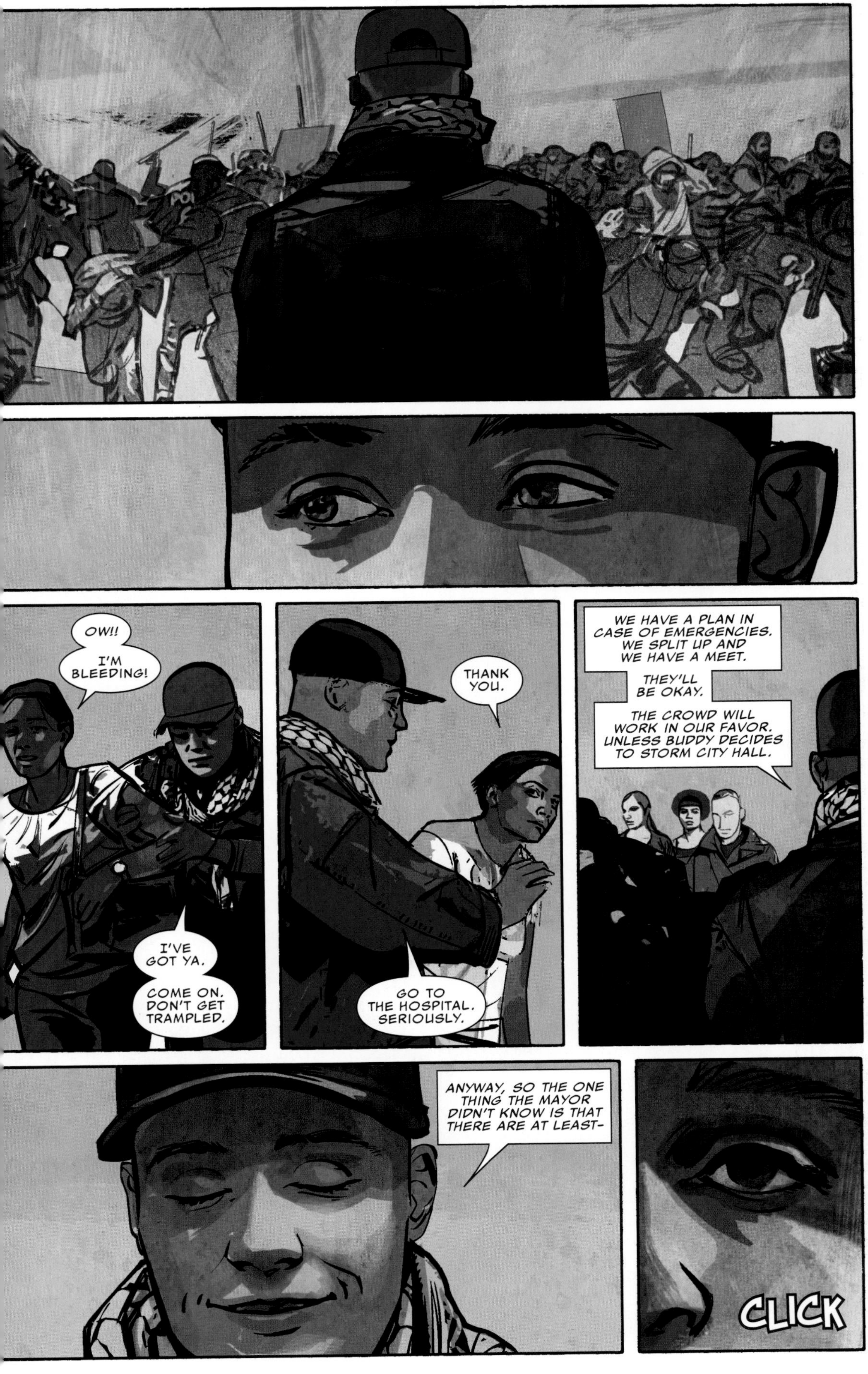
OW!!
I'M BLEEDING!
I'VE GOT YA.
COME ON. DON'T GET TRAMPLED.
THANK YOU.
GO TO THE HOSPITAL. SERIOUSLY.
WE HAVE A PLAN IN CASE OF EMERGENCIES. WE SPLIT UP AND WE HAVE A MEET.
THEY'LL BE OKAY.
THE CROWD WILL WORK IN OUR FAVOR. UNLESS BUDDY DECIDES TO STORM CITY HALL.
ANYWAY, SO THE ONE THING THE MAYOR DIDN'T KNOW IS THAT THERE ARE AT LEAST-
CLICK

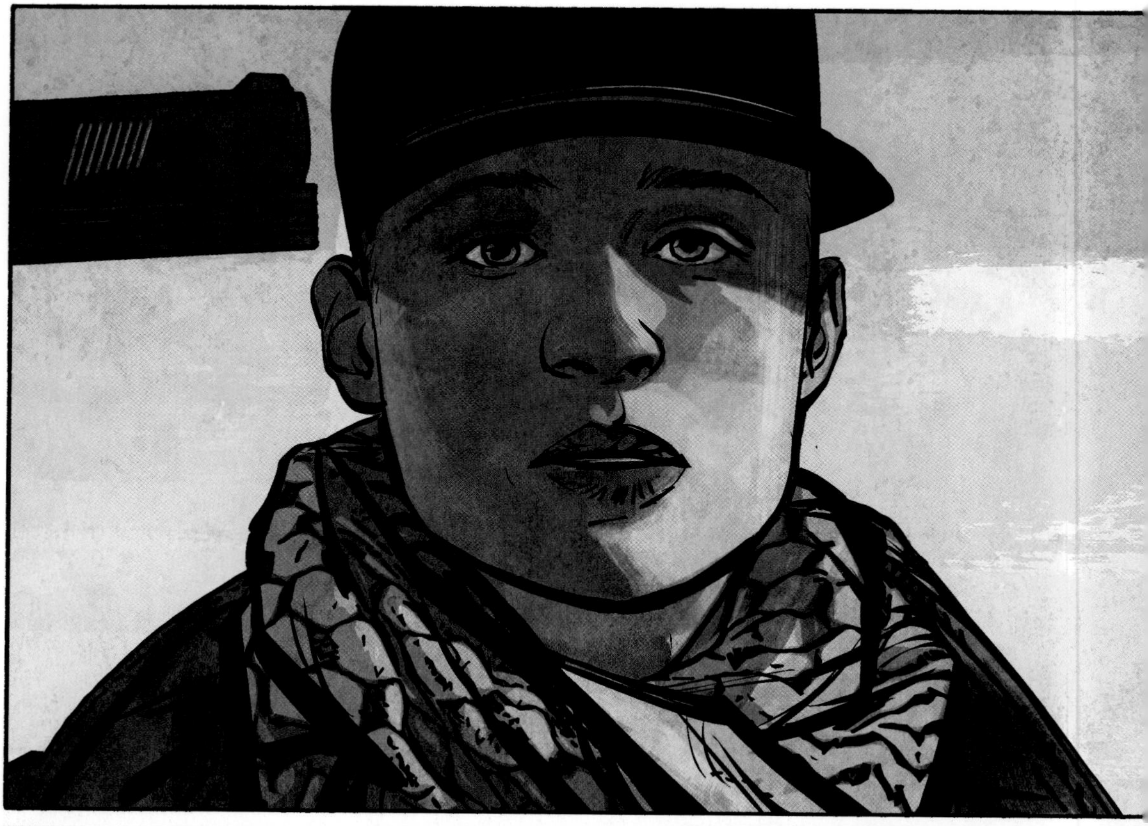

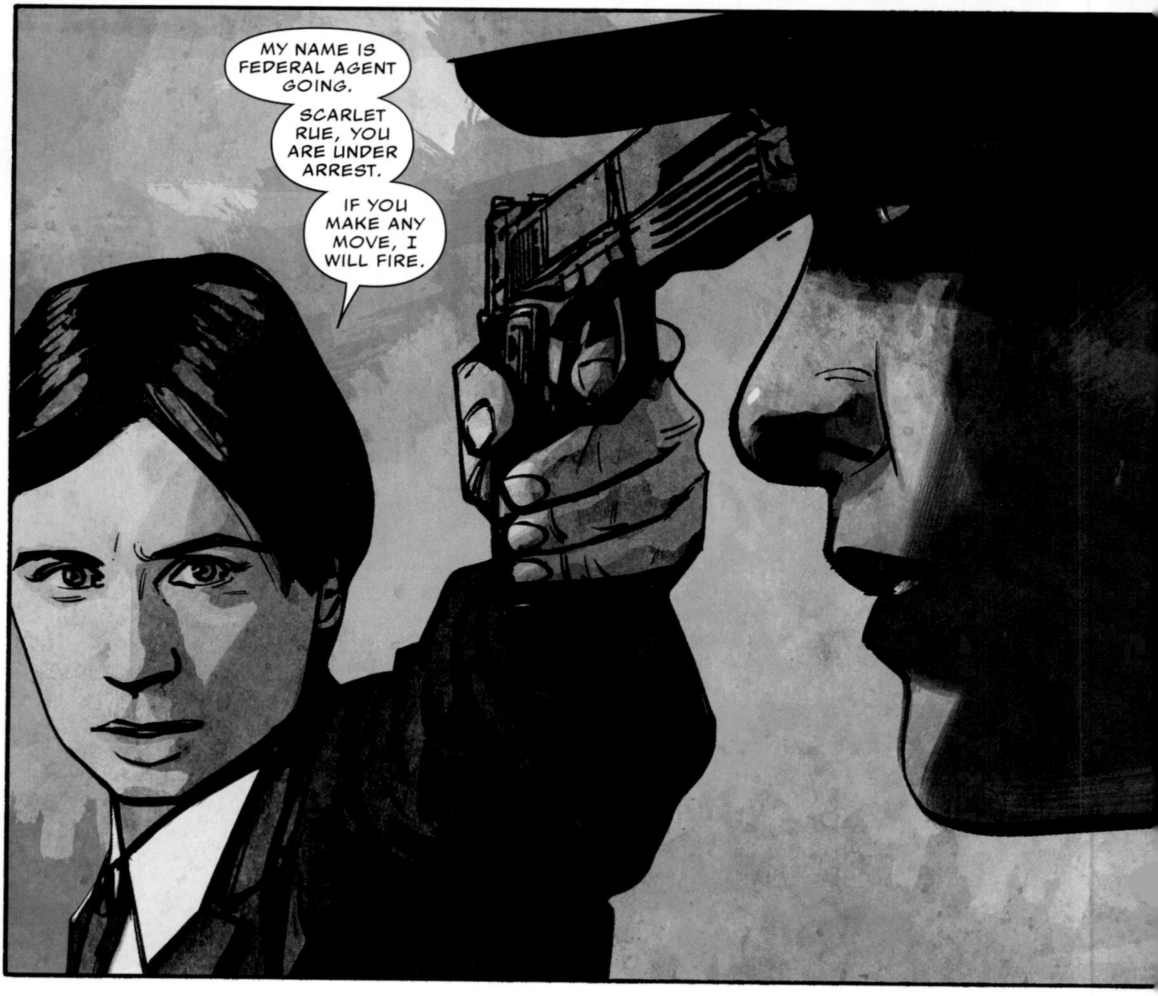

MY NAME IS FEDERAL AGENT GOING.
SCARLET RUE, YOU ARE UNDER ARREST.
IF YOU MAKE ANY MOVE, I WILL FIRE.

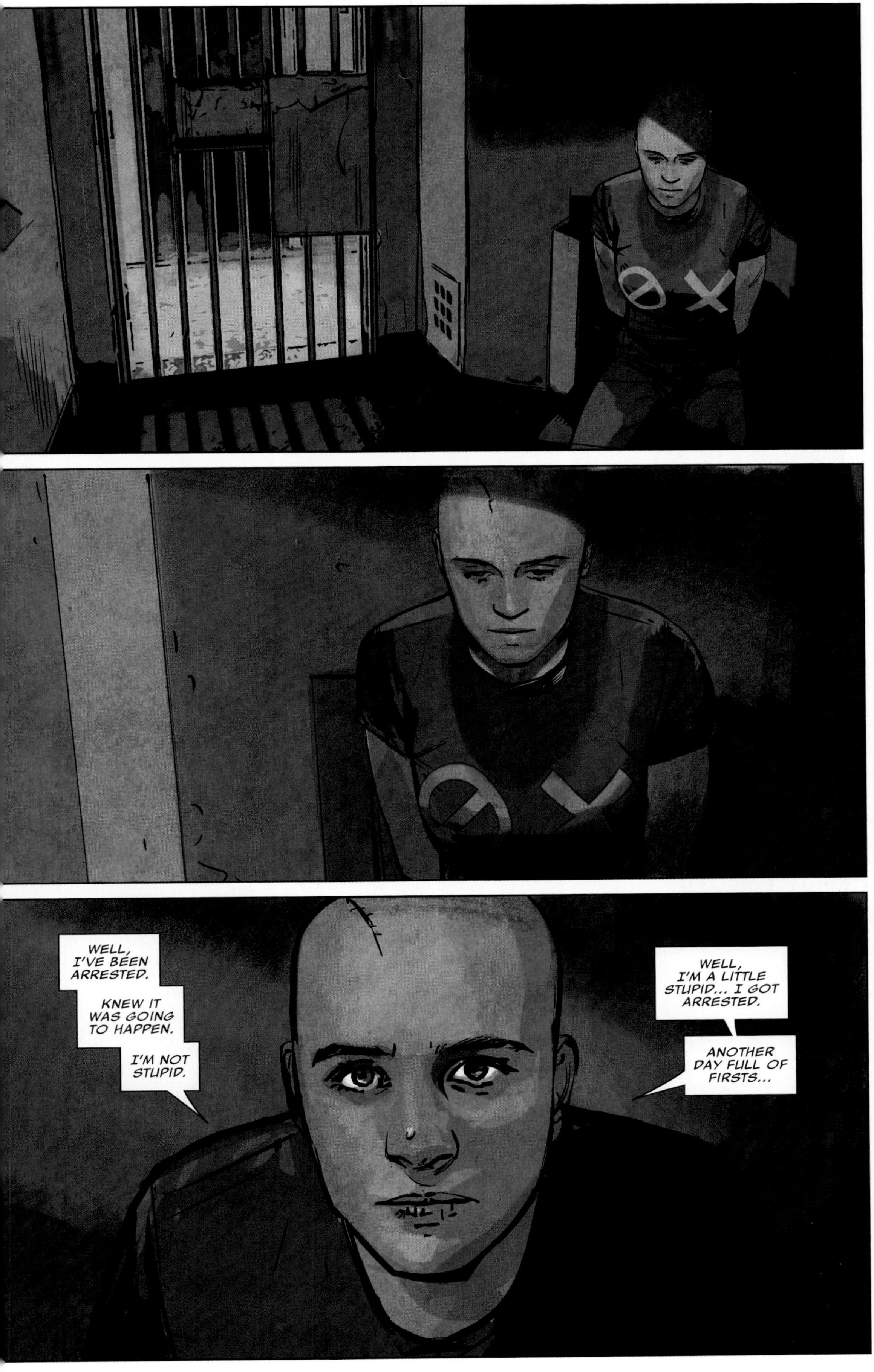
WELL, I'VE BEEN ARRESTED.
KNEW IT WAS GOING TO HAPPEN.
I'M NOT STUPID.
WELL, I'M A LITTLE STUPID... I GOT ARRESTED.
ANOTHER DAY FULL OF FIRSTS...

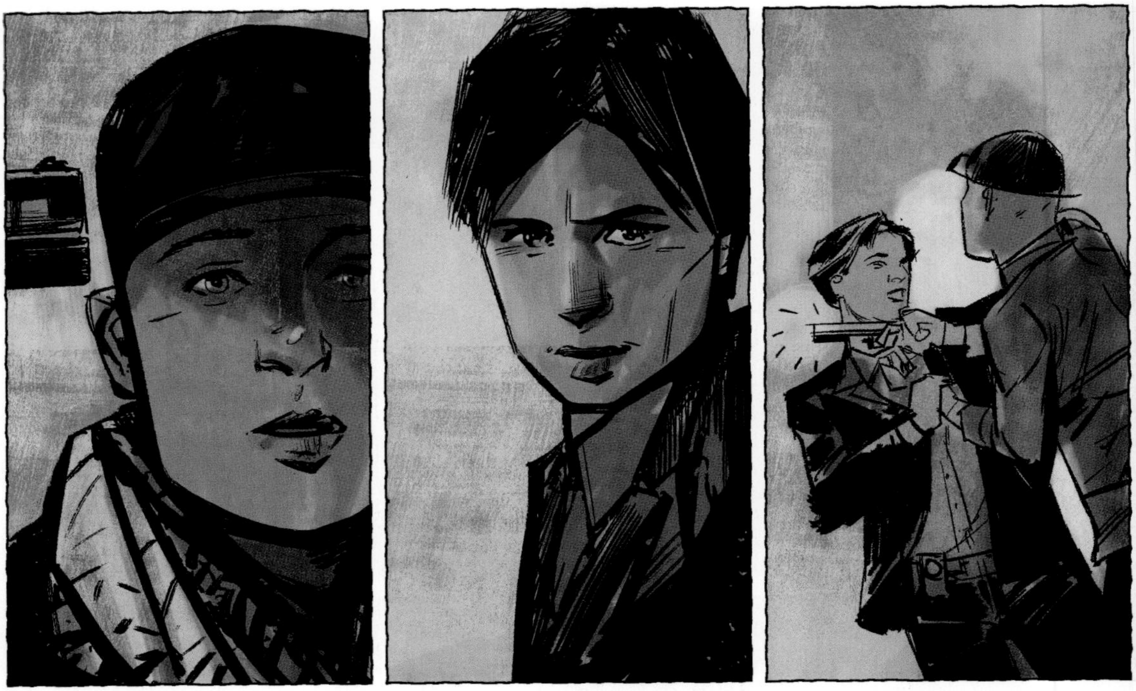

FIRST GUN TO MY HEAD

FIRST MEETING WITH FEDERAL AGENT ANGELA GOING

FIRST RESISTING ARREST

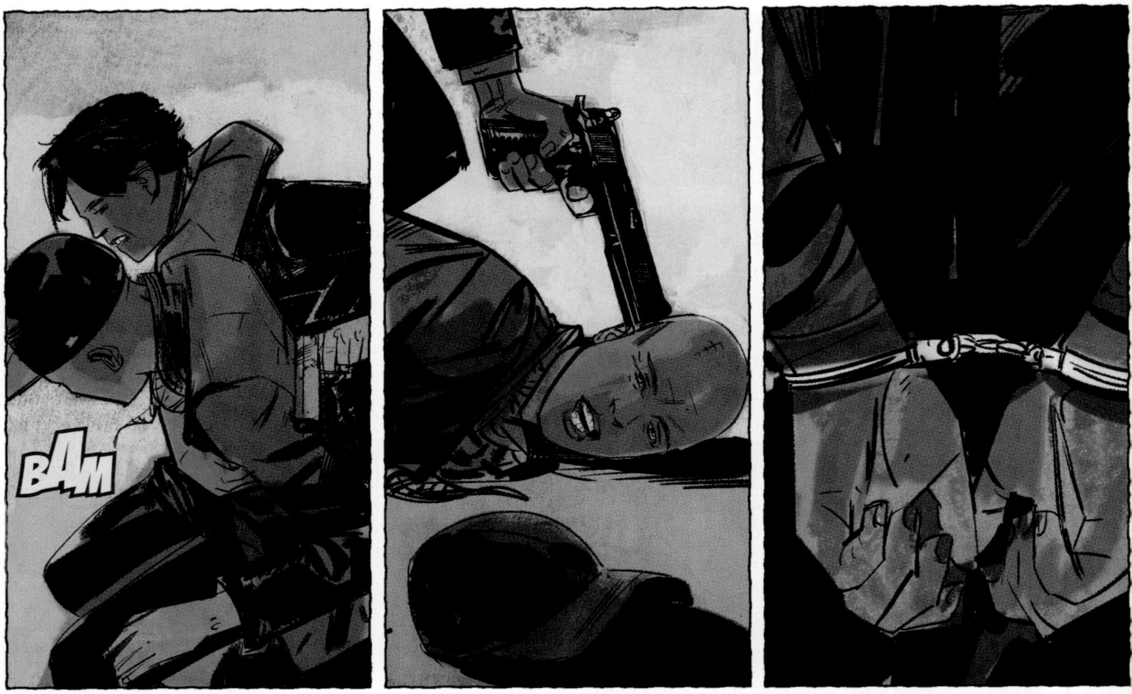
BAM

FIRST RESISTING ARREST FAIL

FIRST REALIZATION THAT THIS IS ACTUALLY HAPPENING

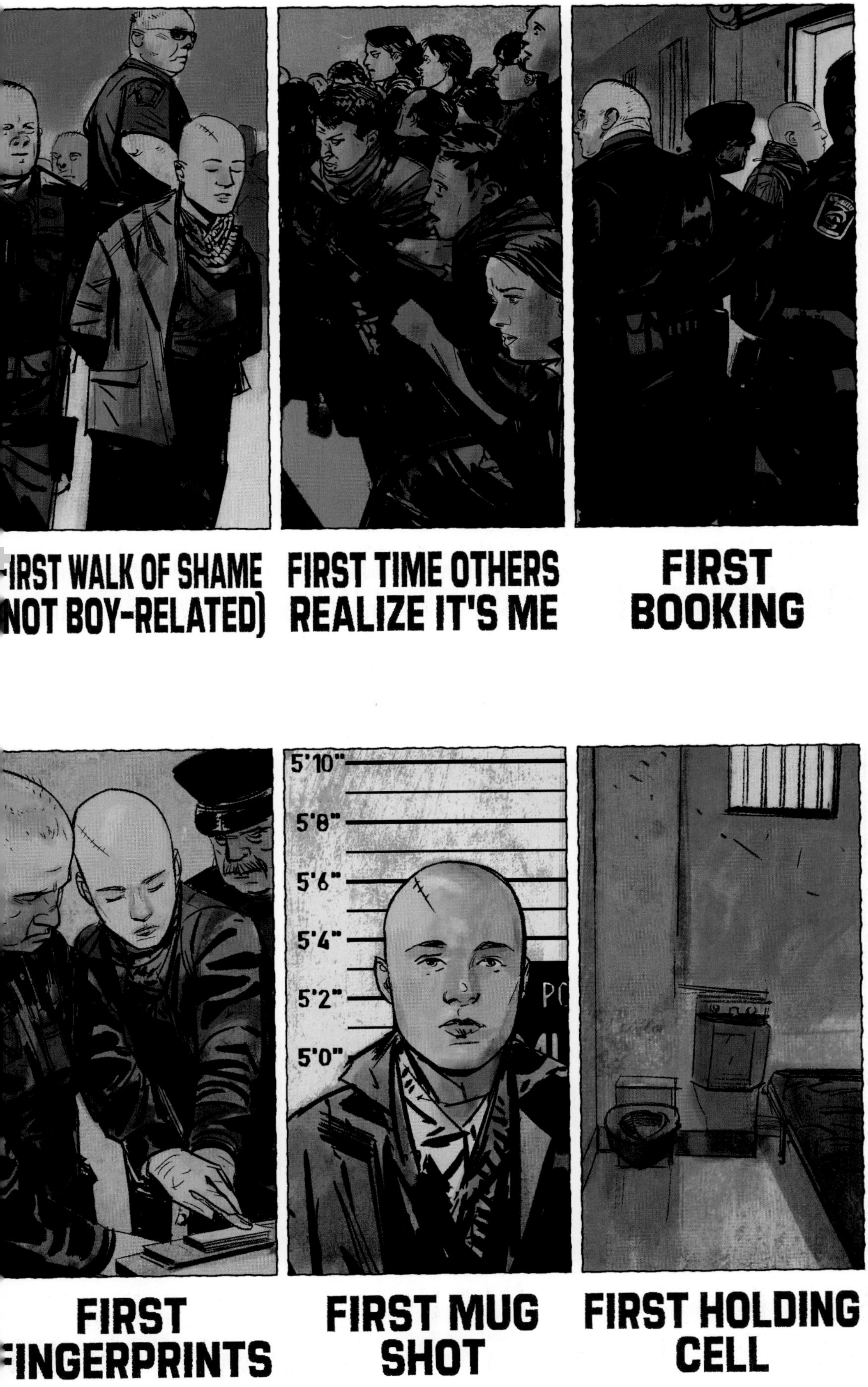
FIRST WALK OF SHAME (NOT BOY-RELATED)
FIRST TIME OTHERS REALIZE IT'S ME
FIRST BOOKING
5'10"
5'8"
5'6"
5'4"
5'2"
5'0"
FIRST FINGERPRINTS
FIRST MUG SHOT
FIRST HOLDING CELL

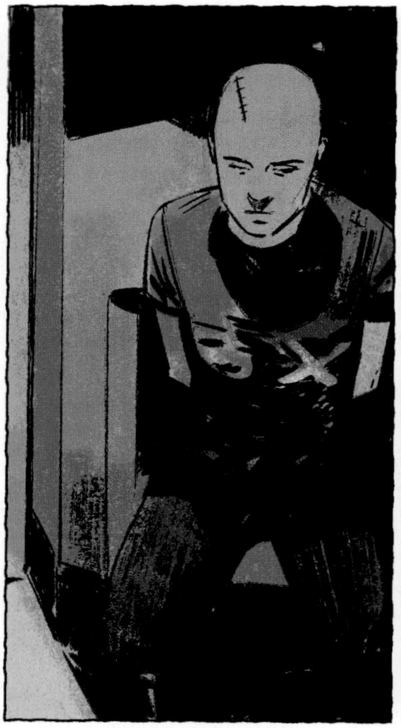

FIRST QUIET MOMENT IN A LONG TIME

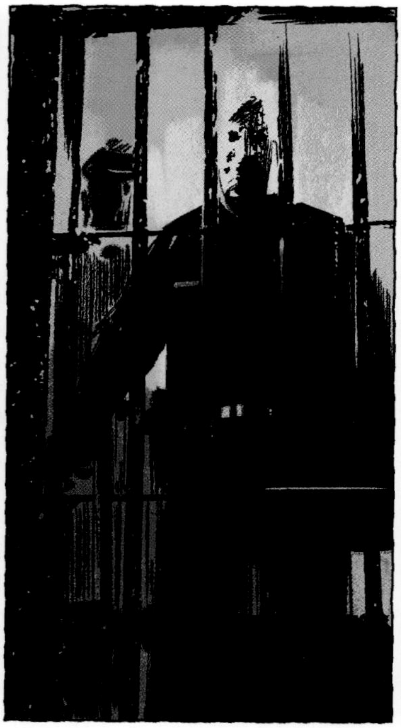

FIRST REALIZATION THAT THIS WAS INEVITABLE

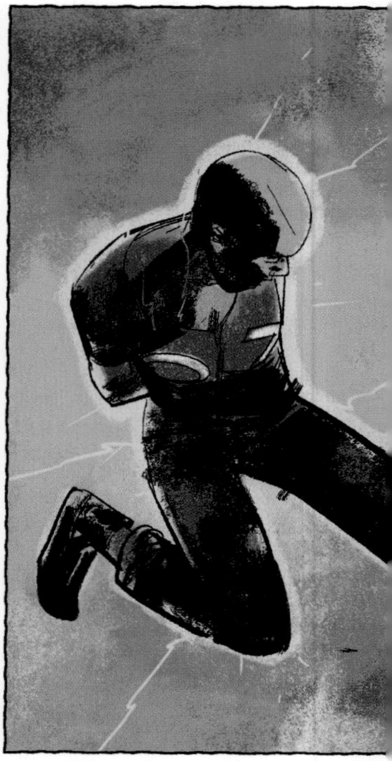

FIRST TASER

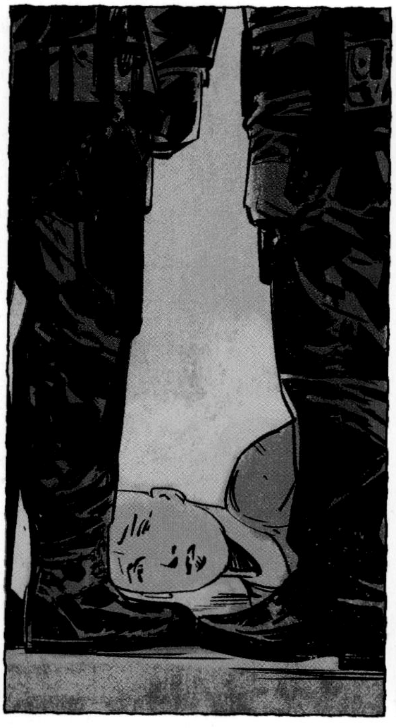

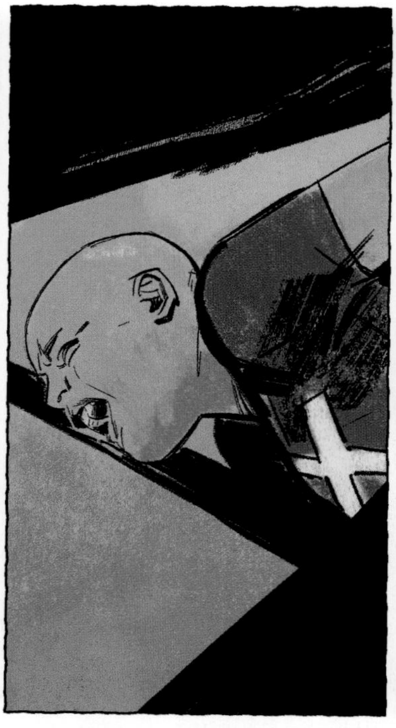

FIRST KICK IN THE CROTCH

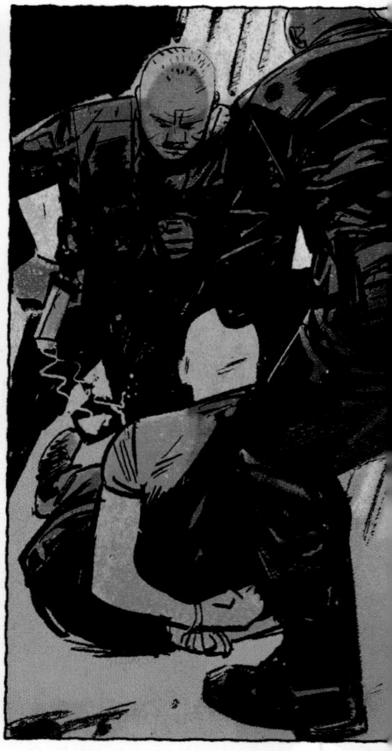

THEY ARE GOING TO KILL ME

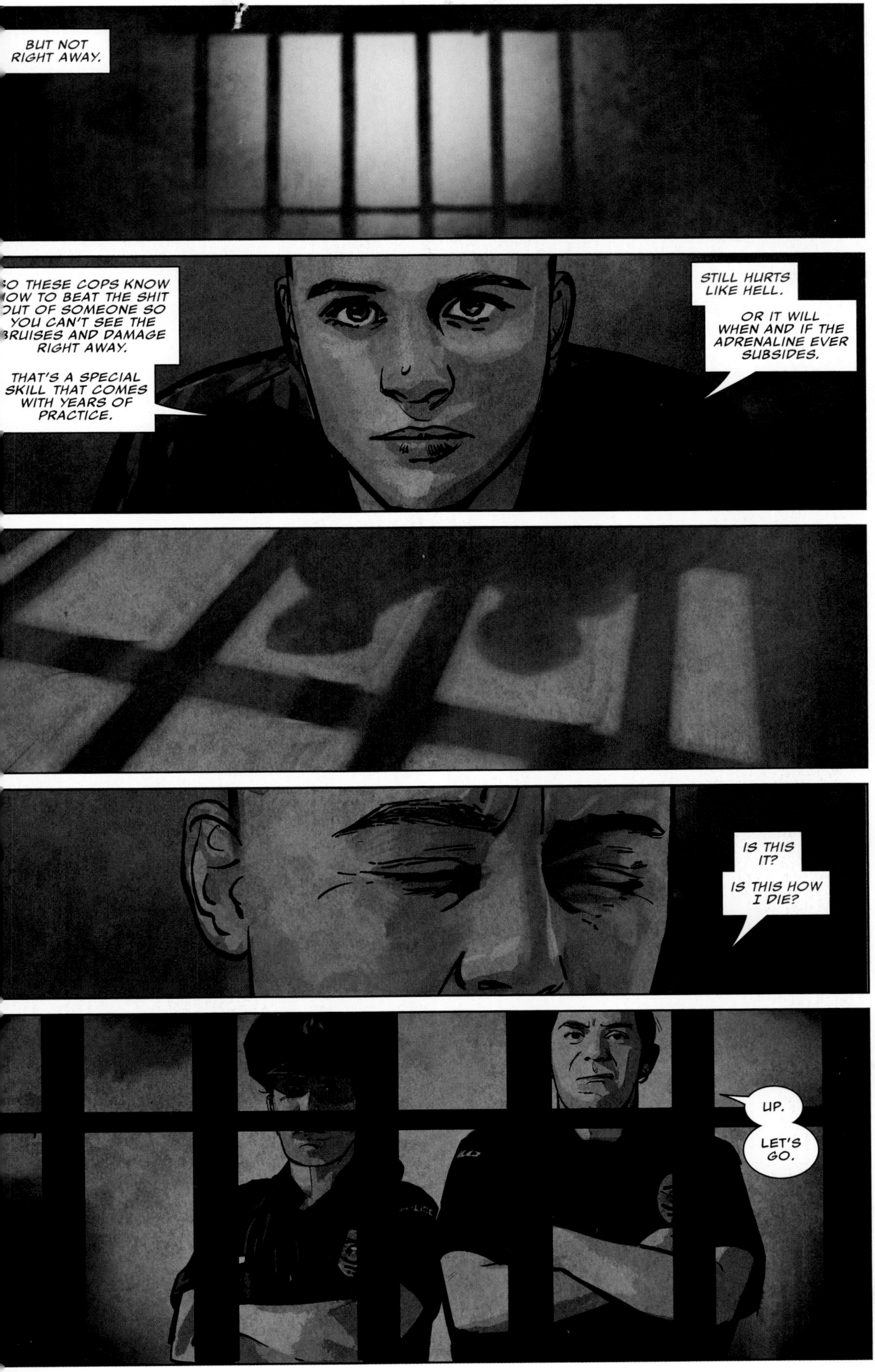
BUT NOT RIGHT AWAY.
SO THESE COPS KNOW HOW TO BEAT THE SHIT OUT OF SOMEONE SO YOU CAN'T SEE THE BRUISES AND DAMAGE RIGHT AWAY.
THAT'S A SPECIAL SKILL THAT COMES WITH YEARS OF PRACTICE.
STILL HURTS LIKE HELL.
OR IT WILL WHEN AND IF THE ADRENALINE EVER SUBSIDES.
IS THIS IT?
IS THIS HOW I DIE?
UP.
LET'S GO.

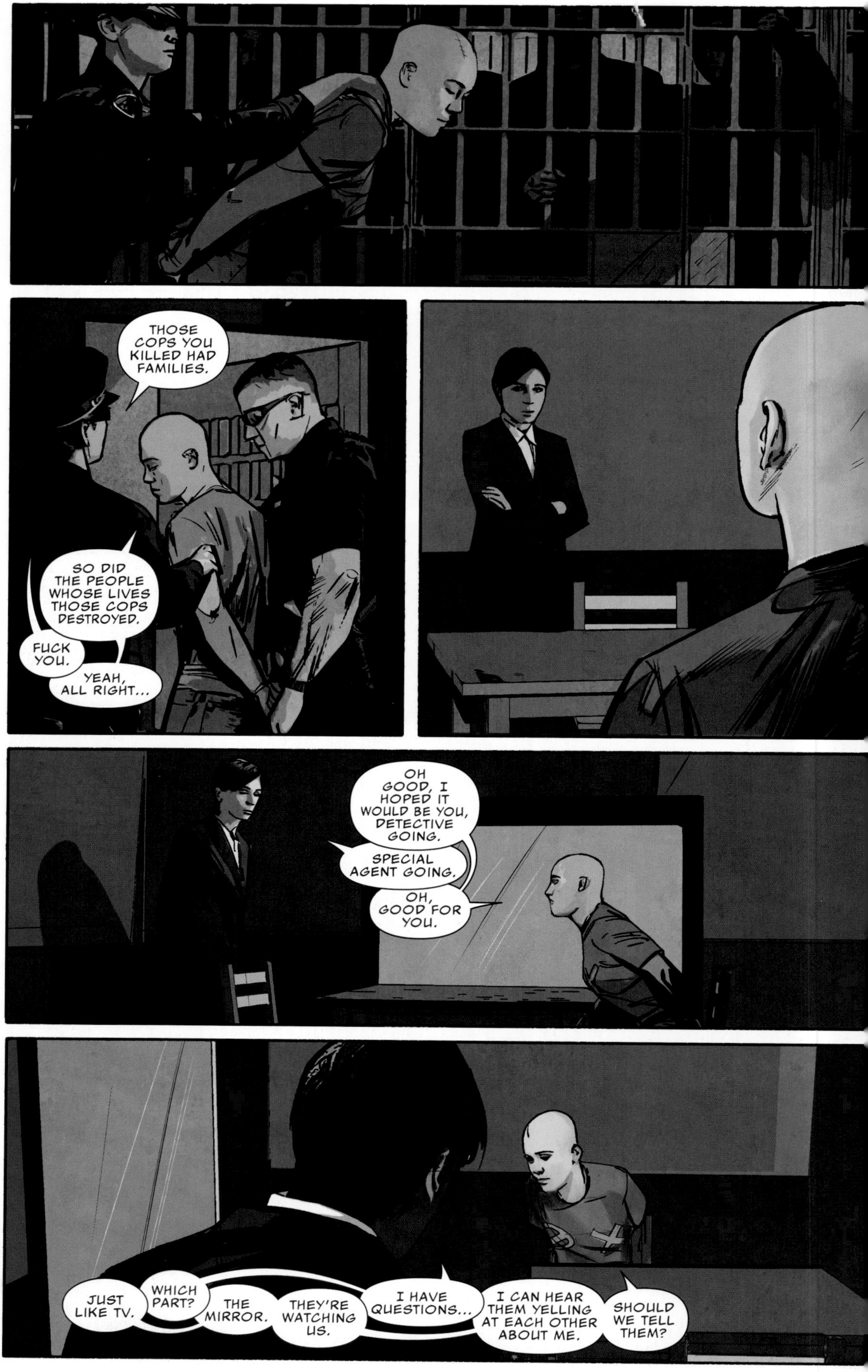
THOSE COPS YOU KILLED HAD FAMILIES.
SO DID THE PEOPLE WHOSE LIVES THOSE COPS DESTROYED.
FUCK YOU.
YEAH, ALL RIGHT...
OH GOOD, I HOPED IT WOULD BE YOU, DETECTIVE GOING.
SPECIAL AGENT GOING.
OH, GOOD FOR YOU.
JUST LIKE TV.
WHICH PART?
THE MIRROR.
THEY'RE WATCHING US.
I HAVE QUESTIONS...
I CAN HEAR THEM YELLING AT EACH OTHER ABOUT ME.
SHOULD WE TELL THEM?

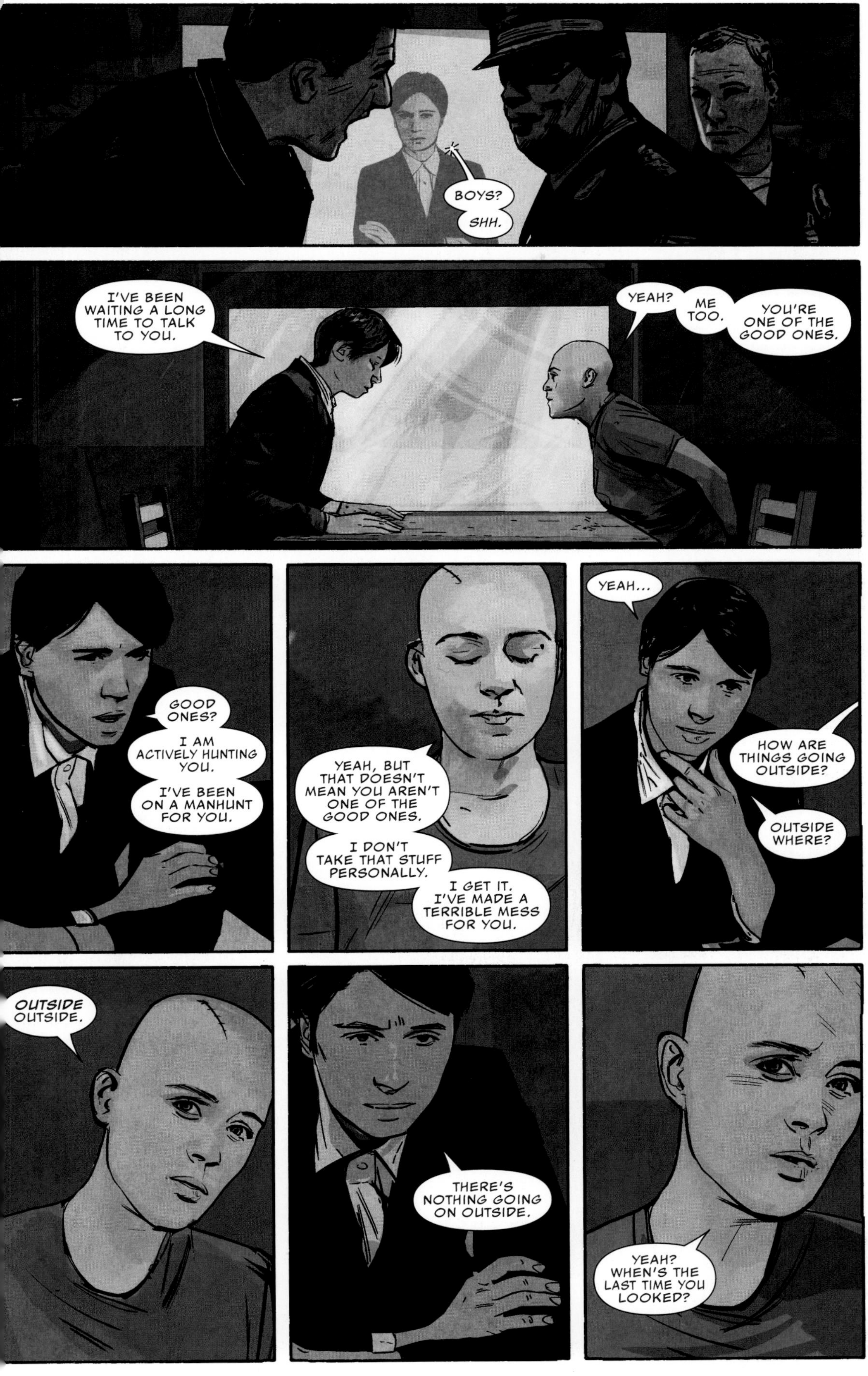
BOYS?
SHH.
I'VE BEEN WAITING A LONG TIME TO TALK TO YOU.
YEAH?
ME TOO.
YOU'RE ONE OF THE GOOD ONES.
GOOD ONES?
I AM ACTIVELY HUNTING YOU.
I'VE BEEN ON A MANHUNT FOR YOU.
YEAH, BUT THAT DOESN'T MEAN YOU AREN'T ONE OF THE GOOD ONES.
I DON'T TAKE THAT STUFF PERSONALLY.
I GET IT. I'VE MADE A TERRIBLE MESS FOR YOU.
YEAH...
HOW ARE THINGS GOING OUTSIDE?
OUTSIDE WHERE?
*OUTSIDE* OUTSIDE.
THERE'S NOTHING GOING ON OUTSIDE.
YEAH? WHEN'S THE LAST TIME YOU LOOKED?

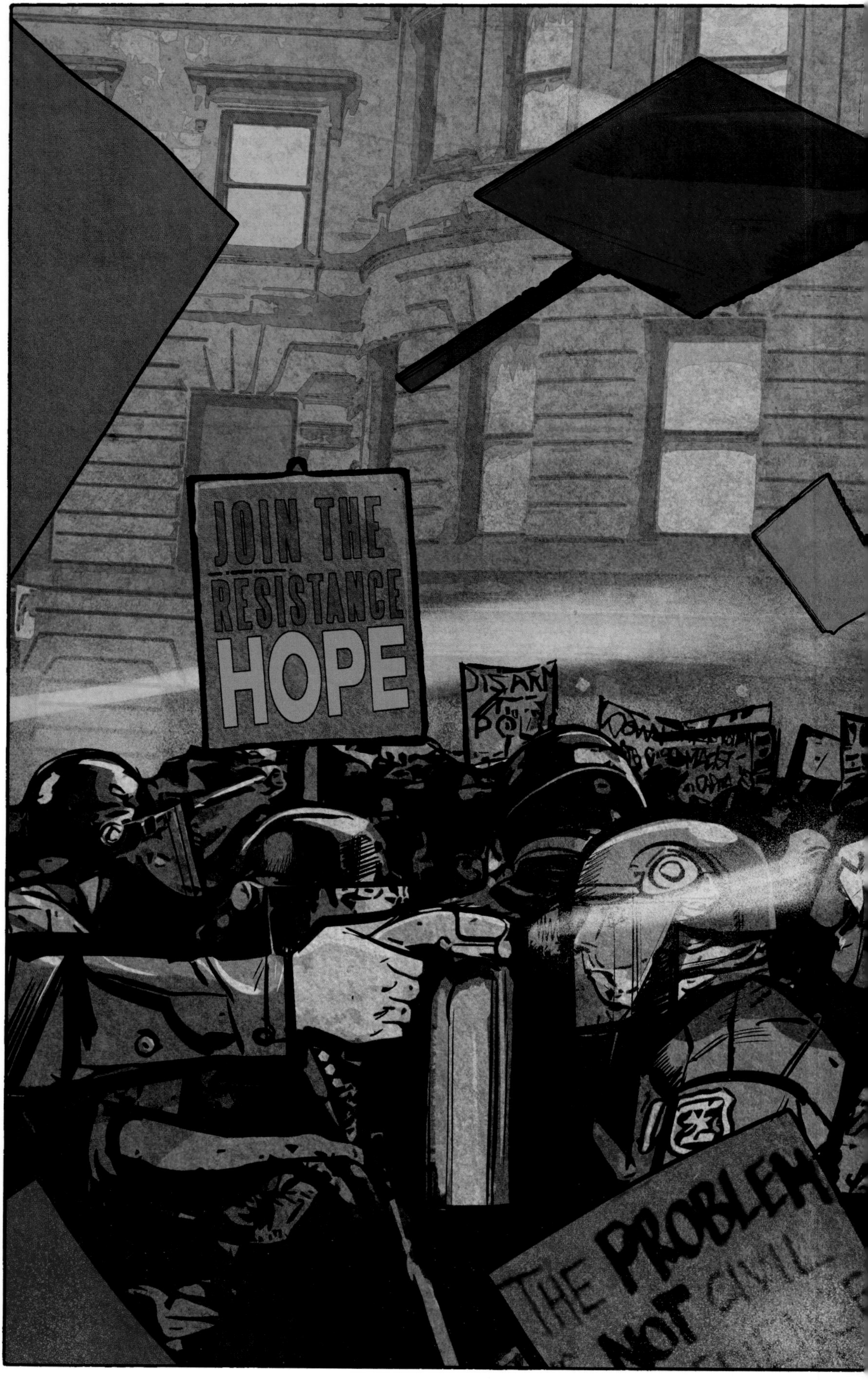
JOIN THE
RESISTANCE
HOPE
DISARM
THE PROBLEM
NOT CIVIL

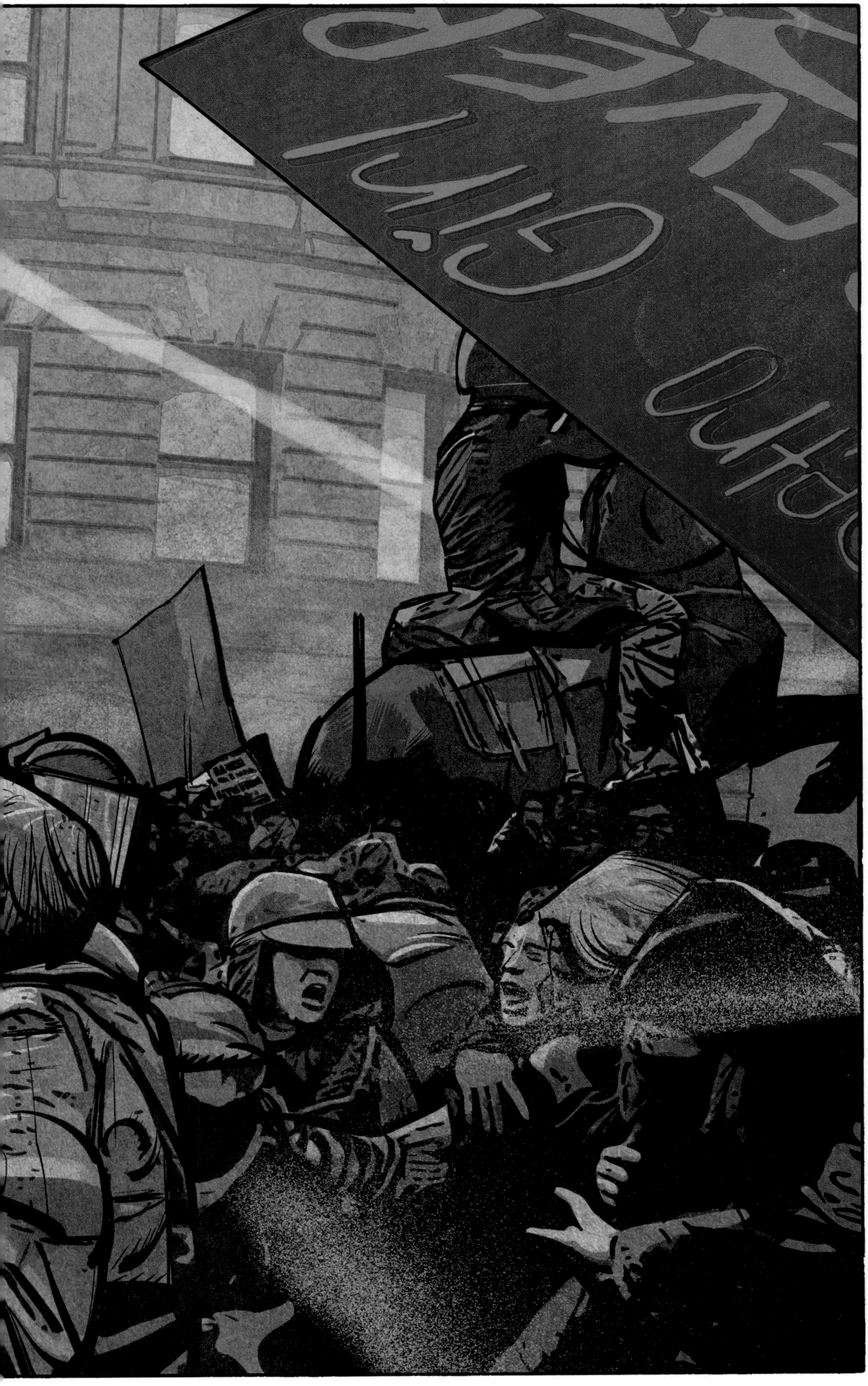

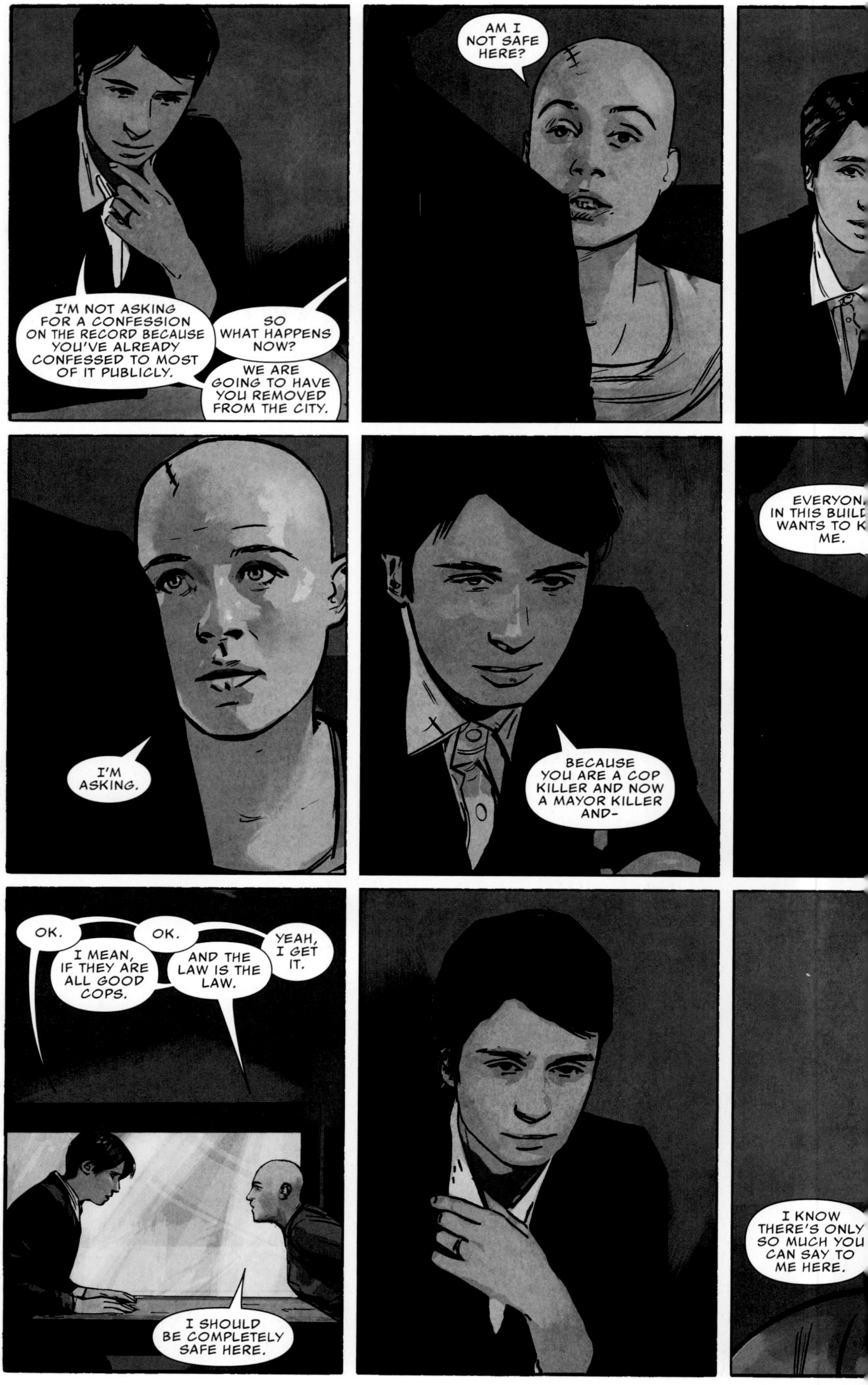
I'M NOT ASKING FOR A CONFESSION ON THE RECORD BECAUSE YOU'VE ALREADY CONFESSED TO MOST OF IT PUBLICLY.
SO WHAT HAPPENS NOW?
WE ARE GOING TO HAVE YOU REMOVED FROM THE CITY.
AM I NOT SAFE HERE?
I'M ASKING.
BECAUSE YOU ARE A COP KILLER AND NOW A MAYOR KILLER AND-
EVERYON IN THIS BUILD WANTS TO K ME.
OK.
I MEAN, IF THEY ARE ALL GOOD COPS.
OK.
AND THE LAW IS THE LAW.
YEAH, I GET IT.
I SHOULD BE COMPLETELY SAFE HERE.
I KNOW THERE'S ONLY SO MUCH YOU CAN SAY TO ME HERE.

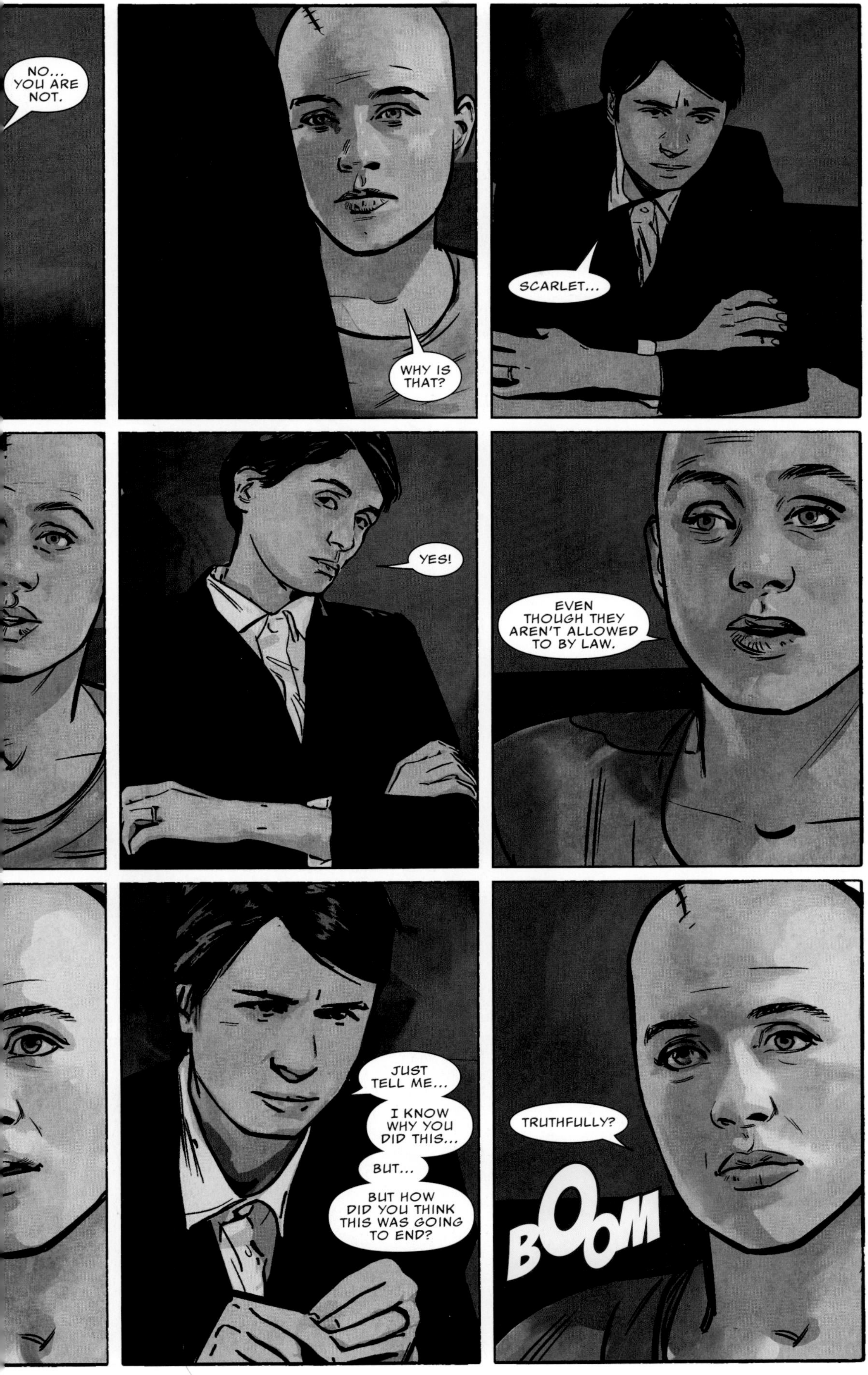
NO... YOU ARE NOT.
WHY IS THAT?
SCARLET...
YES!
EVEN THOUGH THEY AREN'T ALLOWED TO BY LAW.
JUST TELL ME...
I KNOW WHY YOU DID THIS...
BUT...
BUT HOW DID YOU THINK THIS WAS GOING TO END?
TRUTHFULLY?
BOOM

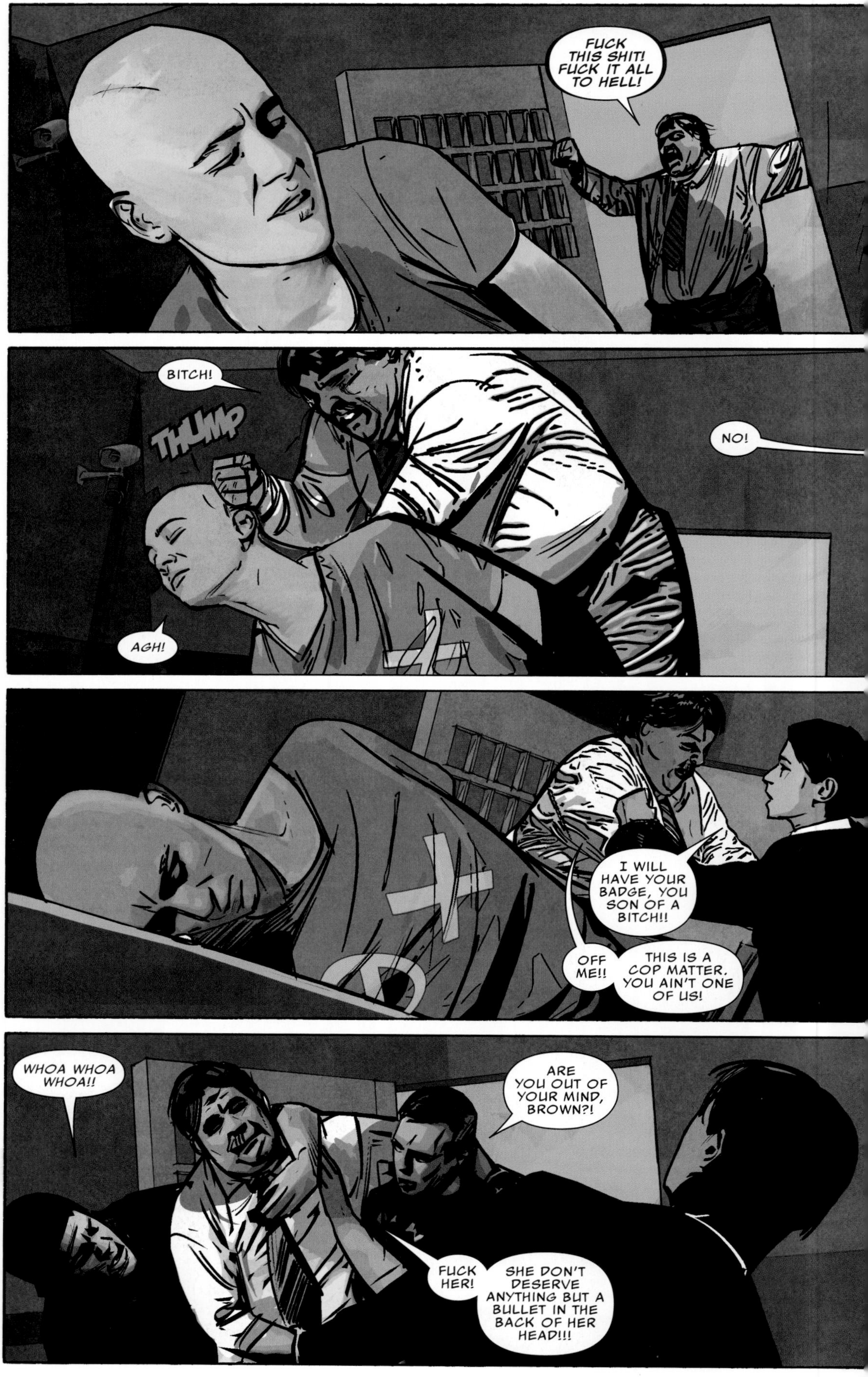
FUCK THIS SHIT! FUCK IT ALL TO HELL!
BITCH!
THUMP
NO!
AGH!
I WILL HAVE YOUR BADGE, YOU SON OF A BITCH!!
OFF ME!!
THIS IS A COP MATTER. YOU AIN'T ONE OF US!
WHOA WHOA WHOA!!
ARE YOU OUT OF YOUR MIND, BROWN?!
FUCK HER!
SHE DON'T DESERVE ANYTHING BUT A BULLET IN THE BACK OF HER HEAD!!!

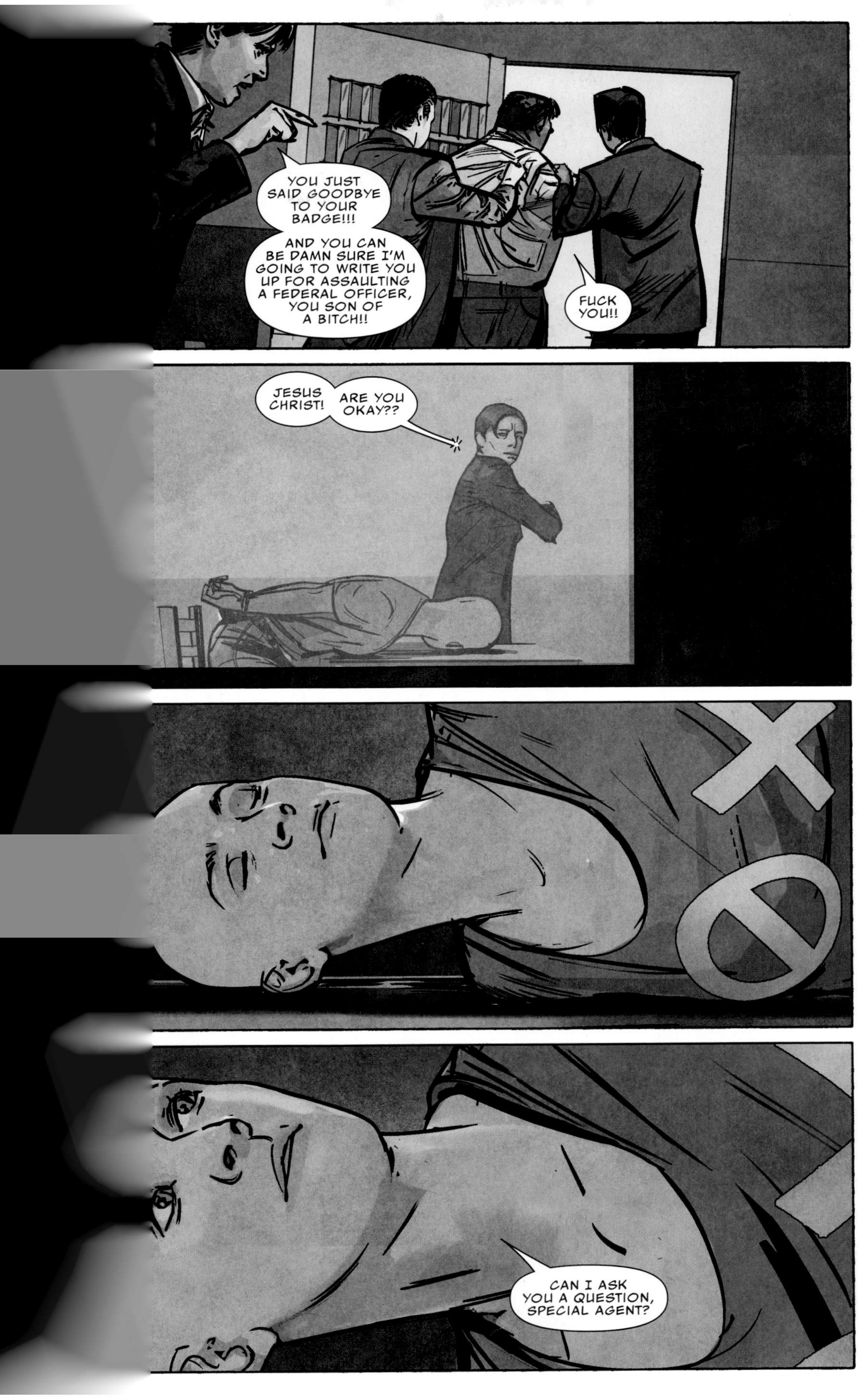
YOU JUST SAID GOODBYE TO YOUR BADGE!!!
AND YOU CAN BE DAMN SURE I'M GOING TO WRITE YOU UP FOR ASSAULTING A FEDERAL OFFICER, YOU SON OF A BITCH!!
FUCK YOU!!
JESUS CHRIST!
ARE YOU OKAY??
CAN I ASK YOU A QUESTION, SPECIAL AGENT?

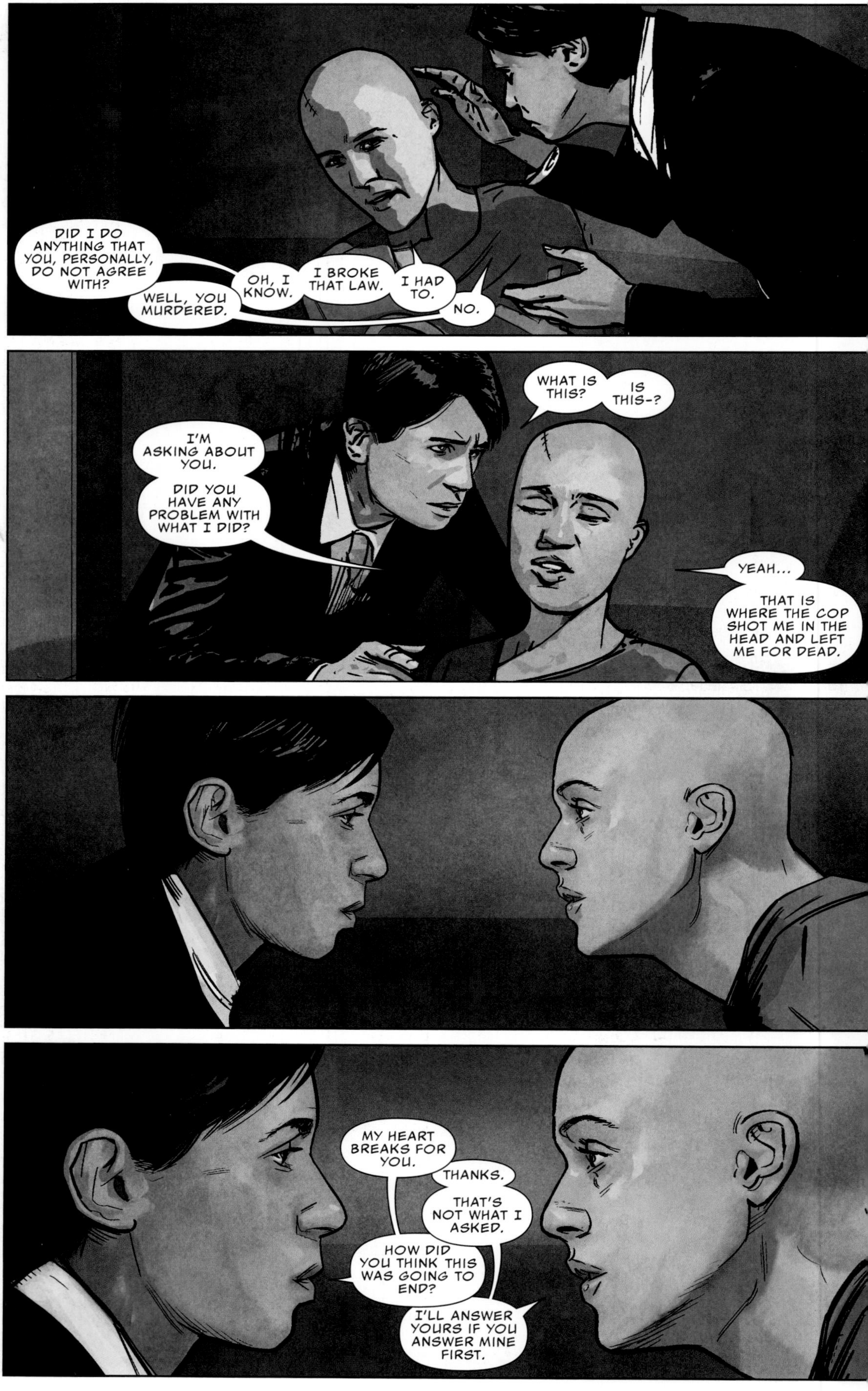
DID I DO ANYTHING THAT YOU, PERSONALLY, DO NOT AGREE WITH?
WELL, YOU MURDERED.
OH, I KNOW.
I BROKE THAT LAW.
I HAD TO.
NO.
WHAT IS THIS?
IS THIS-?
I'M ASKING ABOUT YOU.
DID YOU HAVE ANY PROBLEM WITH WHAT I DID?
YEAH...
THAT IS WHERE THE COP SHOT ME IN THE HEAD AND LEFT ME FOR DEAD.
MY HEART BREAKS FOR YOU.
THANKS.
THAT'S NOT WHAT I ASKED.
HOW DID YOU THINK THIS WAS GOING TO END?
I'LL ANSWER YOURS IF YOU ANSWER MINE FIRST.

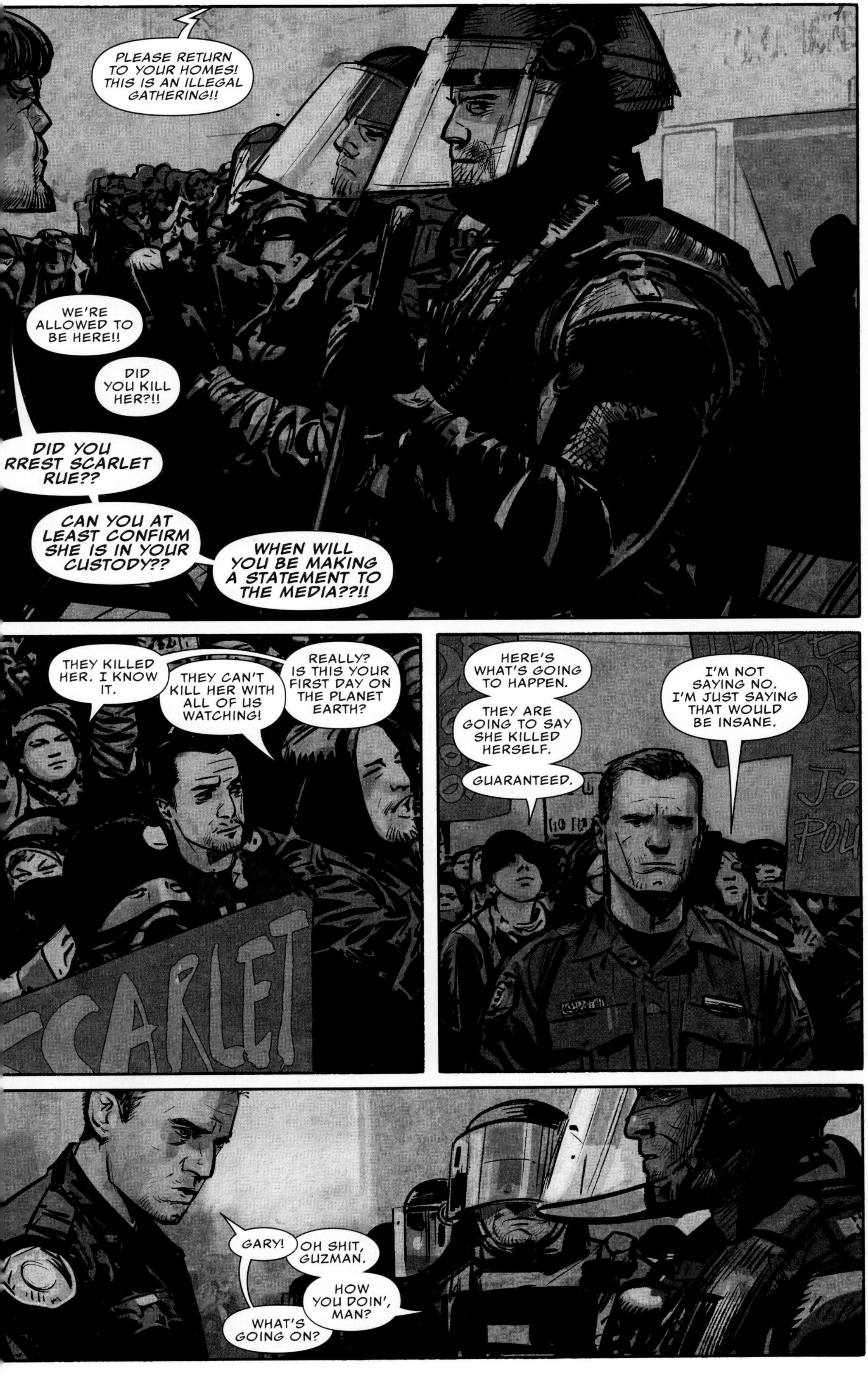

PLEASE RETURN TO YOUR HOMES! THIS IS AN ILLEGAL GATHERING!!
WE'RE ALLOWED TO BE HERE!!
DID YOU KILL HER?!!
DID YOU RREST SCARLET RUE??
CAN YOU AT LEAST CONFIRM SHE IS IN YOUR CUSTODY??
WHEN WILL YOU BE MAKING A STATEMENT TO THE MEDIA??!!
THEY KILLED HER. I KNOW IT.
THEY CAN'T KILL HER WITH ALL OF US WATCHING!
REALLY? IS THIS YOUR FIRST DAY ON THE PLANET EARTH?
HERE'S WHAT'S GOING TO HAPPEN.
THEY ARE GOING TO SAY SHE KILLED HERSELF.
GUARANTEED.
I'M NOT SAYING NO. I'M JUST SAYING THAT WOULD BE INSANE.
GARY!
OH SHIT, GUZMAN.
HOW YOU DOIN', MAN?
WHAT'S GOING ON?

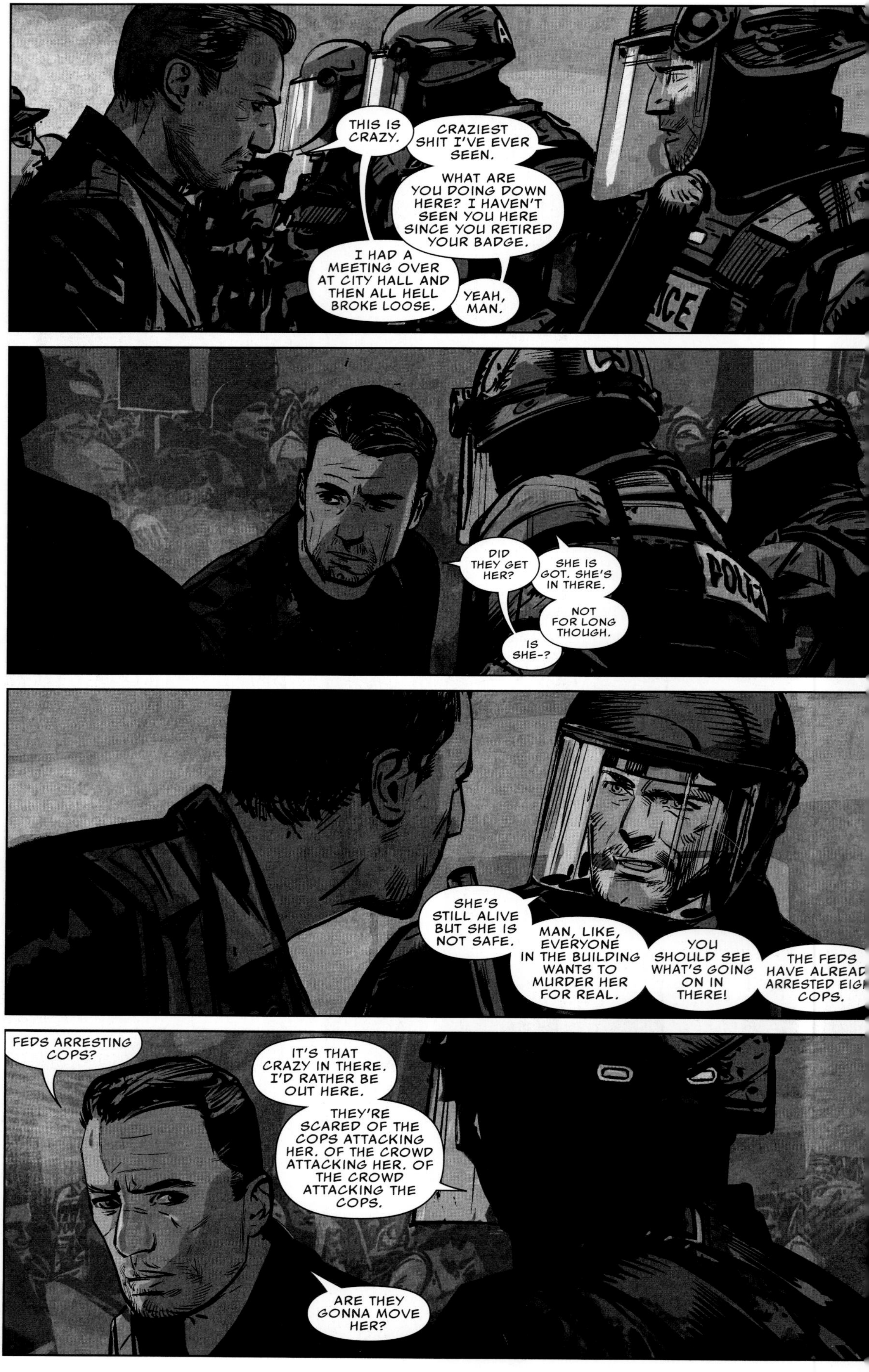
THIS IS CRAZY.
CRAZIEST SHIT I'VE EVER SEEN.
WHAT ARE YOU DOING DOWN HERE? I HAVEN'T SEEN YOU HERE SINCE YOU RETIRED YOUR BADGE.
I HAD A MEETING OVER AT CITY HALL AND THEN ALL HELL BROKE LOOSE.
YEAH, MAN.
POLICE
DID THEY GET HER?
SHE IS GOT. SHE'S IN THERE.
NOT FOR LONG THOUGH.
IS SHE-?
SHE'S STILL ALIVE BUT SHE IS NOT SAFE.
MAN, LIKE, EVERYONE IN THE BUILDING WANTS TO MURDER HER FOR REAL.
YOU SHOULD SEE WHAT'S GOING ON IN THERE!
THE FEDS HAVE ALREAD ARRESTED EIG COPS.
FEDS ARRESTING COPS?
IT'S THAT CRAZY IN THERE. I'D RATHER BE OUT HERE.
THEY'RE SCARED OF THE COPS ATTACKING HER. OF THE CROWD ATTACKING HER. OF THE CROWD ATTACKING THE COPS.
ARE THEY GONNA MOVE HER?

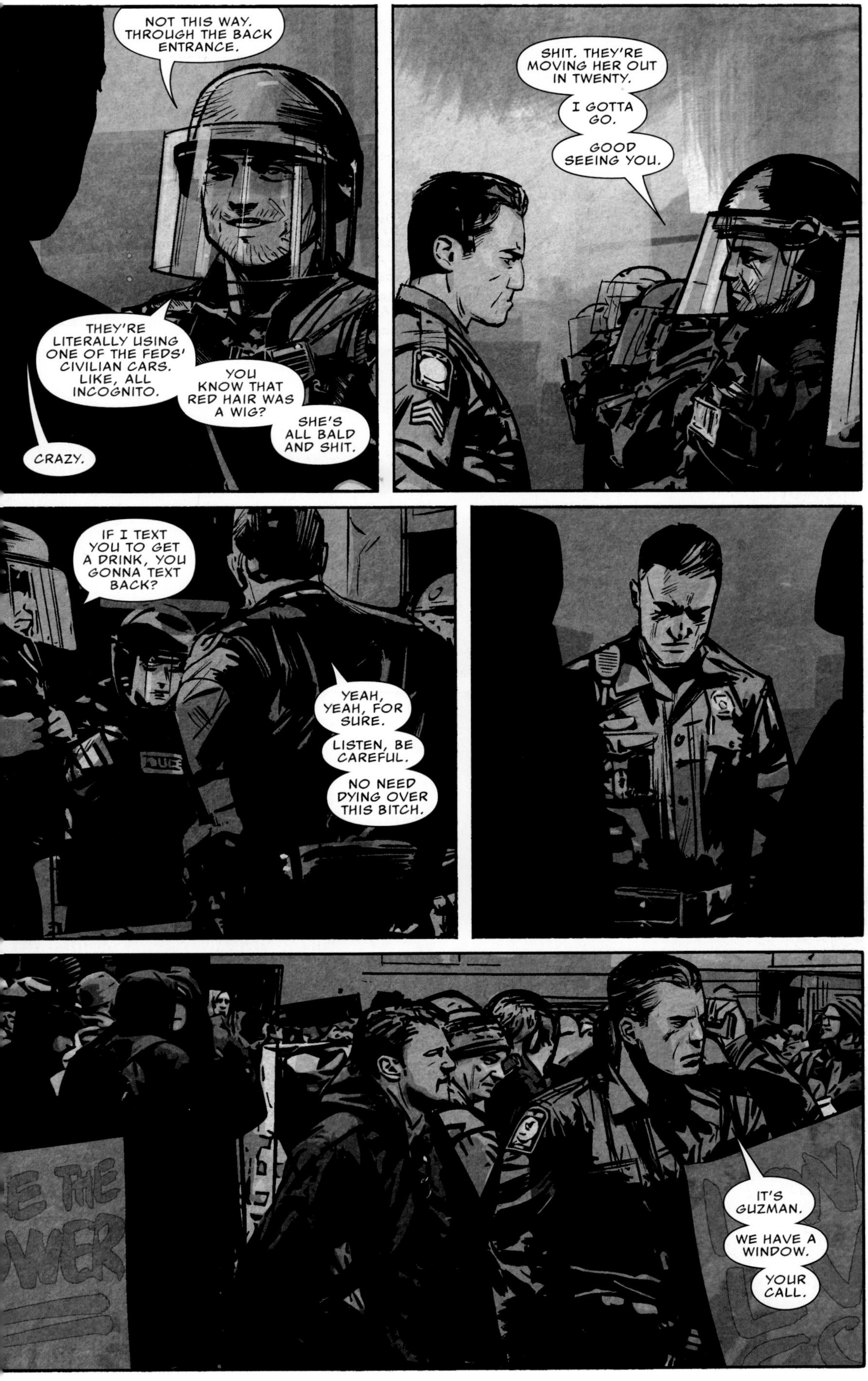
NOT THIS WAY. THROUGH THE BACK ENTRANCE.
THEY'RE LITERALLY USING ONE OF THE FEDS' CIVILIAN CARS. LIKE, ALL INCOGNITO.
CRAZY.
YOU KNOW THAT RED HAIR WAS A WIG?
SHE'S ALL BALD AND SHIT.
SHIT. THEY'RE MOVING HER OUT IN TWENTY.
I GOTTA GO.
GOOD SEEING YOU.
IF I TEXT YOU TO GET A DRINK, YOU GONNA TEXT BACK?
YEAH, YEAH, FOR SURE.
LISTEN, BE CAREFUL.
NO NEED DYING OVER THIS BITCH.
IT'S GUZMAN.
WE HAVE A WINDOW.
YOUR CALL.

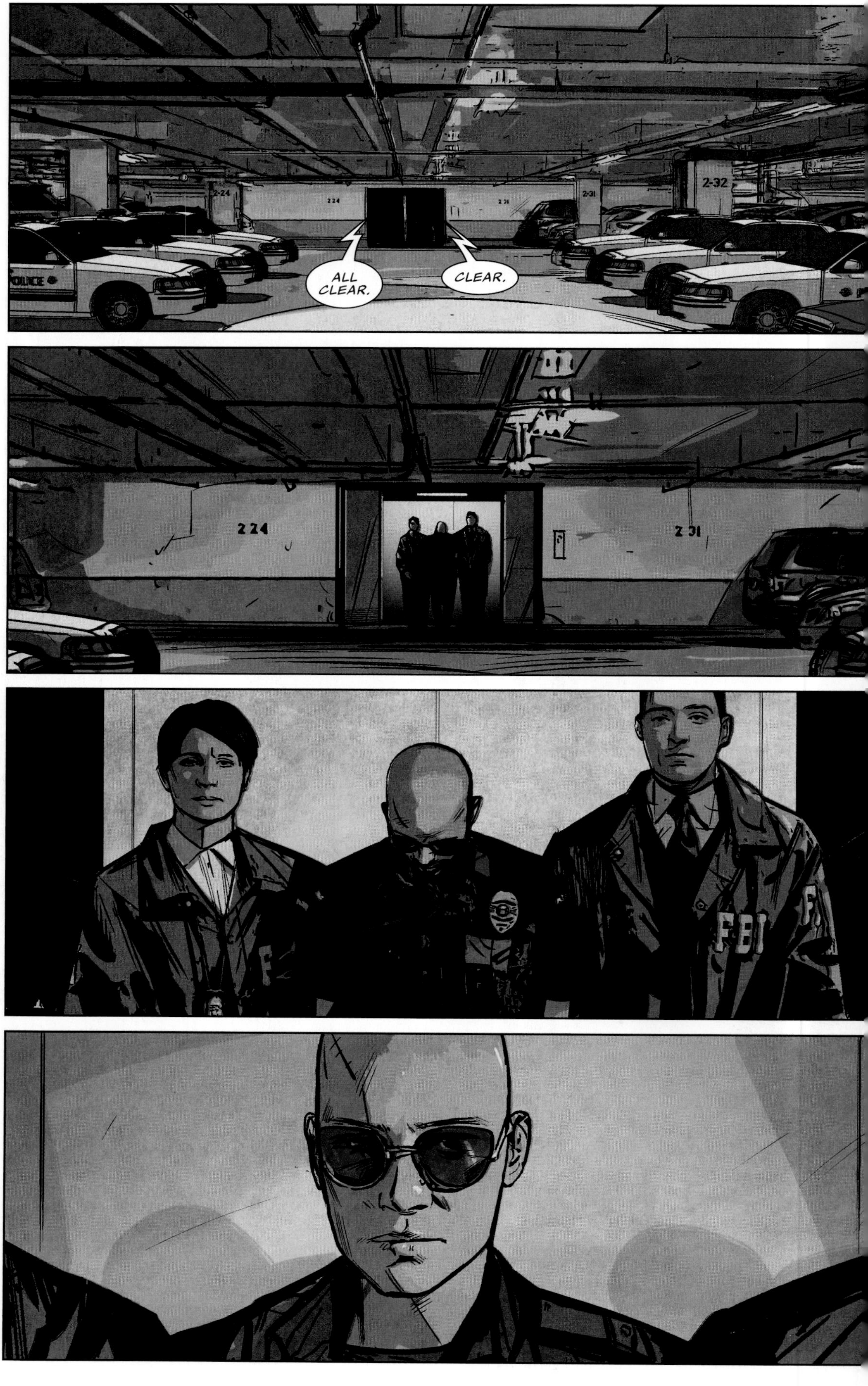

ALL CLEAR.
CLEAR.

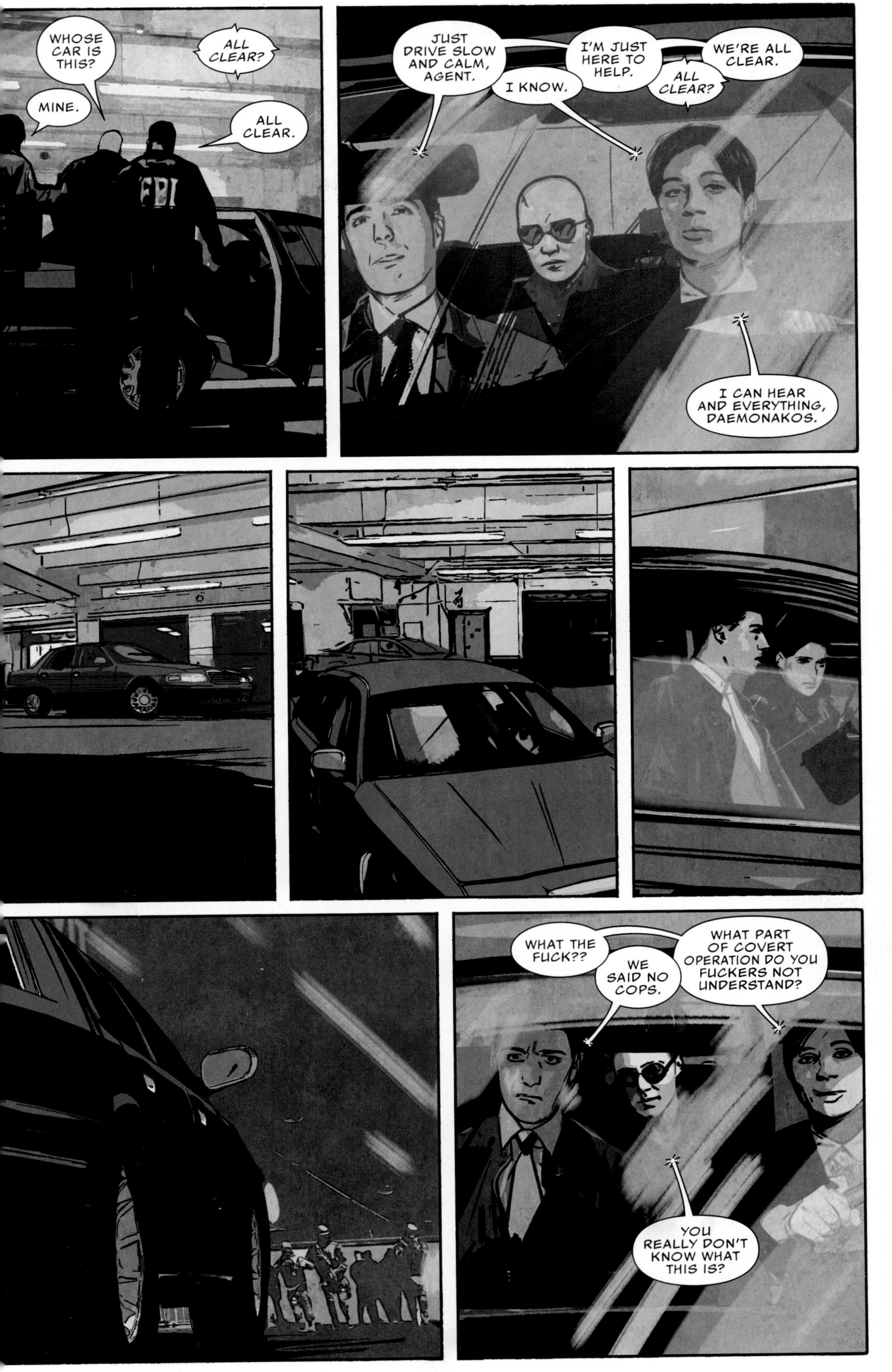
WHOSE CAR IS THIS?
ALL CLEAR?
MINE.
ALL CLEAR.
JUST DRIVE SLOW AND CALM, AGENT.
I KNOW.
I'M JUST HERE TO HELP.
ALL CLEAR?
WE'RE ALL CLEAR.
I CAN HEAR AND EVERYTHING, DAEMONAKOS.
WHAT THE FUCK??
WE SAID NO COPS.
WHAT PART OF COVERT OPERATION DO YOU FUCKERS NOT UNDERSTAND?
YOU REALLY DON'T KNOW WHAT THIS IS?

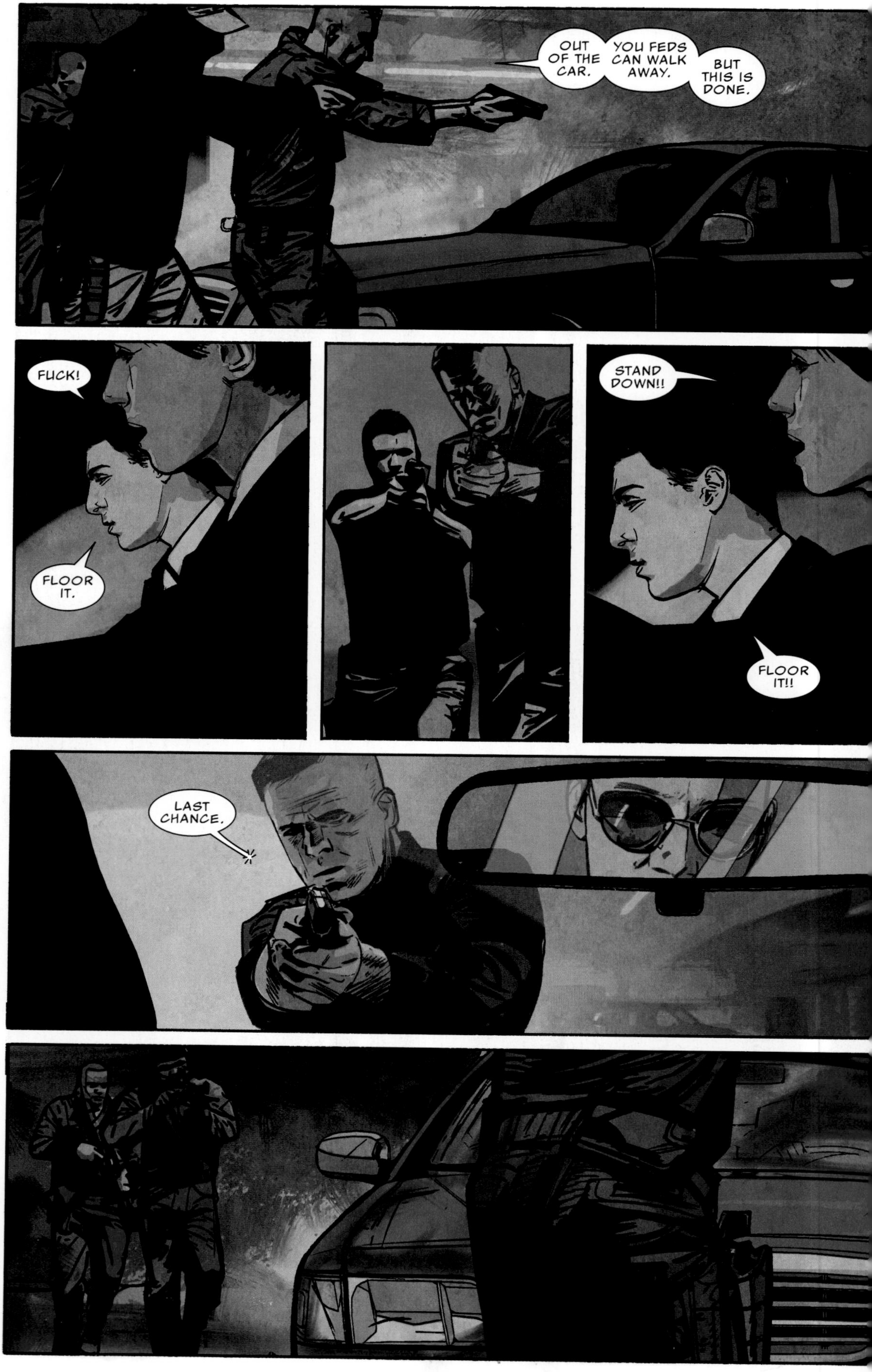
OUT OF THE CAR.
YOU FEDS CAN WALK AWAY.
BUT THIS IS DONE.
FUCK!
FLOOR IT.
STAND DOWN!!
FLOOR IT!!
LAST CHANCE.

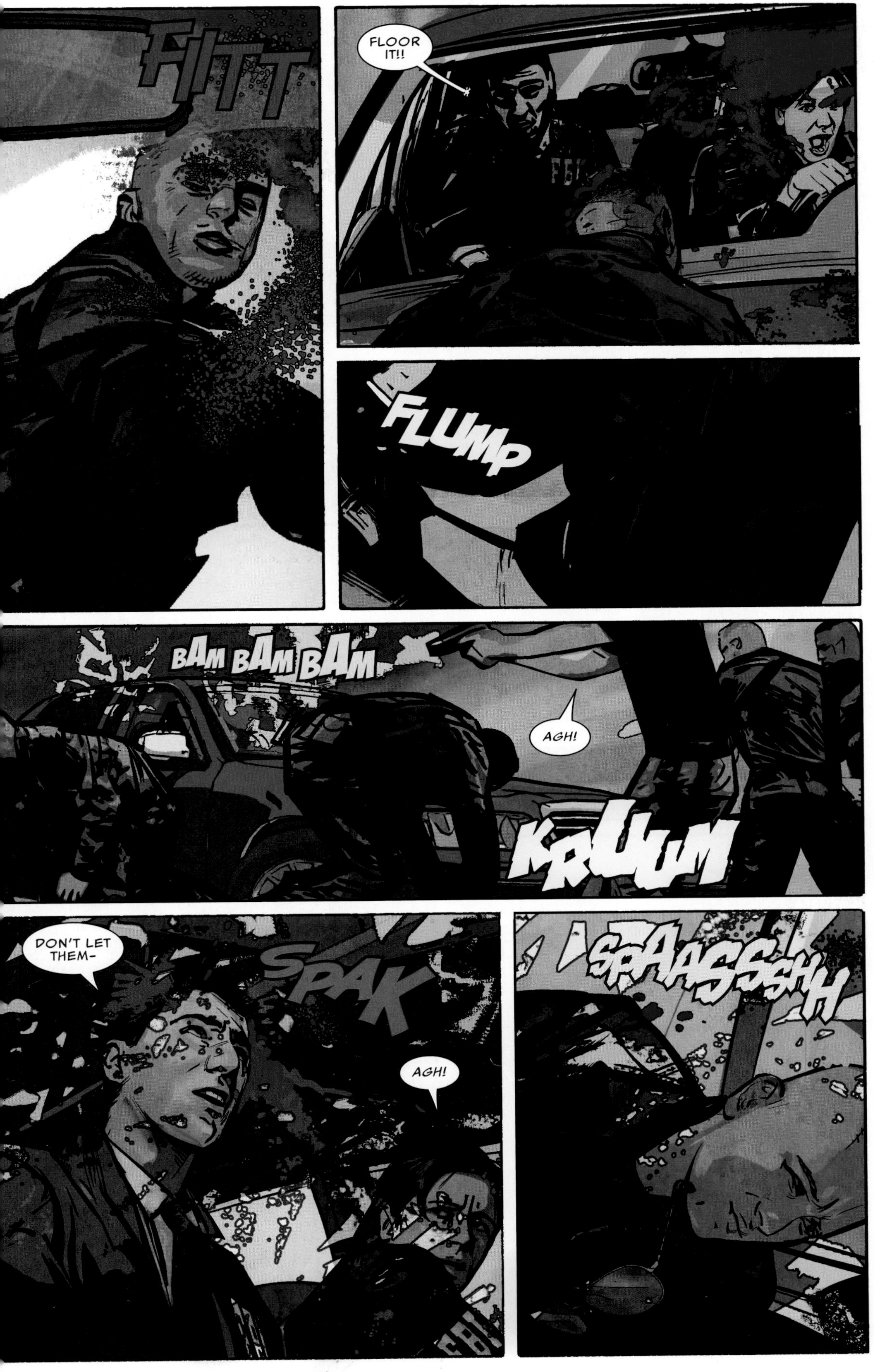
FITT
FLOOR IT!!
FLUMP
BAM BAM BAM
AGH!
KRUUUM
DON'T LET THEM-
SPAK
AGH!
SPAASSSHH

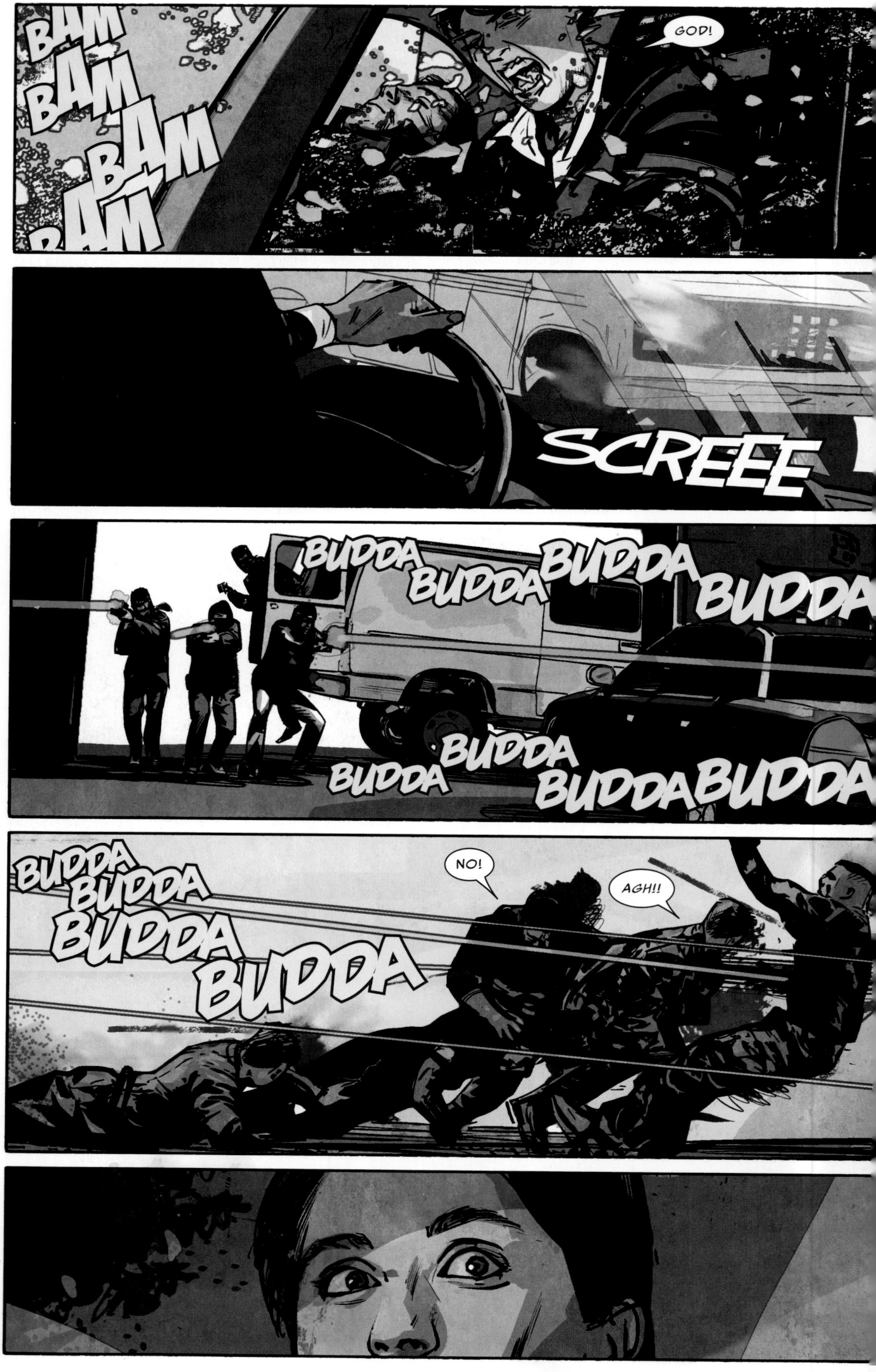
BAM
BAM
BAM
BAM
BAM
GOD!
SCREEE
BUDDA
BUDDA
BUDDA
BUDDA
BUDDA
BUDDA
BUDDA
BUDDA
BUDDA
BUDDA
BUDDA
BUDDA
NO!
AGH!!

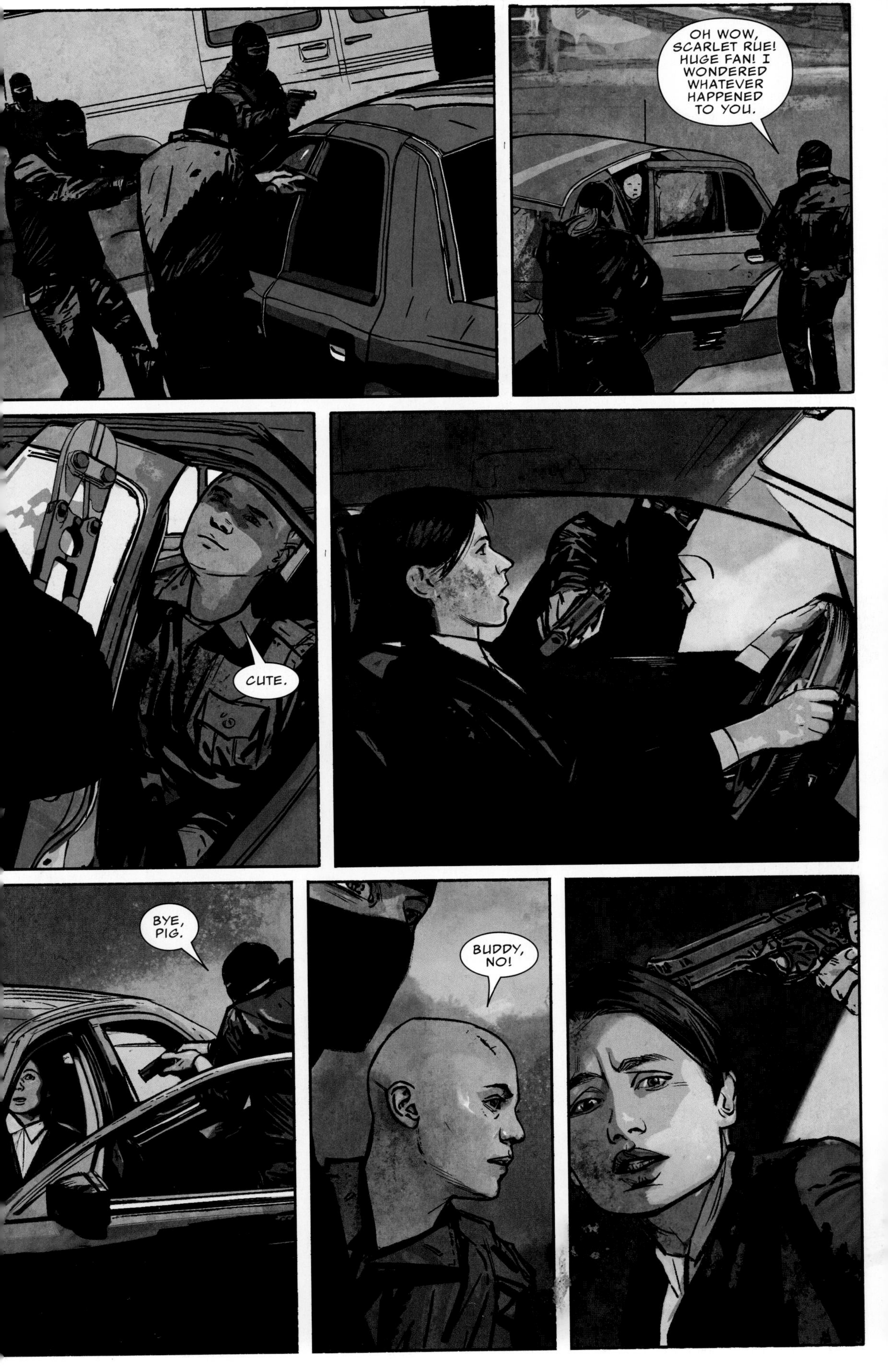
OH WOW, SCARLET RUE! HUGE FAN! I WONDERED WHATEVER HAPPENED TO YOU.
CUTE.
BYE, PIG.
BUDDY, NO!

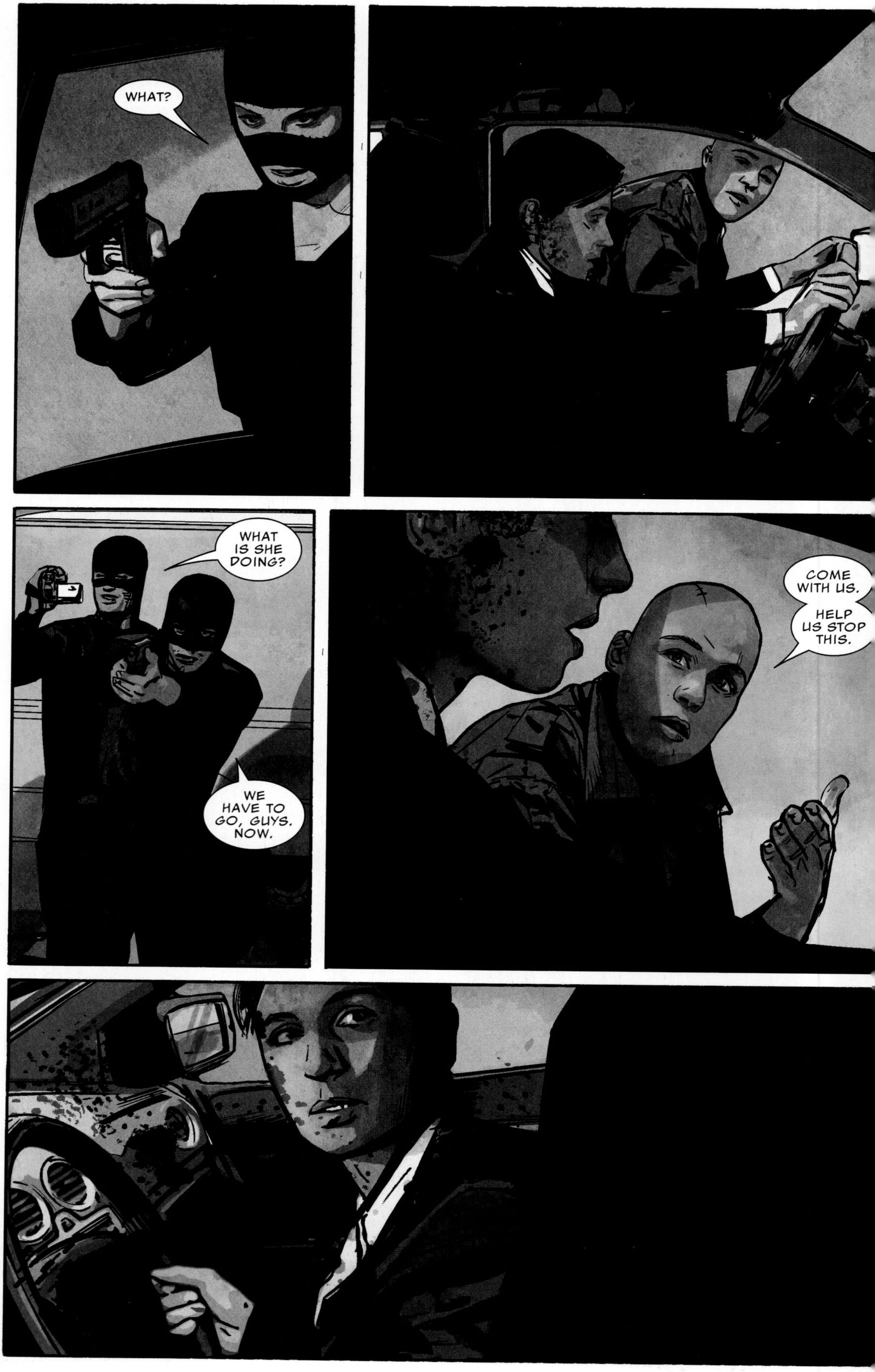
WHAT?
WHAT IS SHE DOING?
WE HAVE TO GO, GUYS. NOW.
COME WITH US.
HELP US STOP THIS.

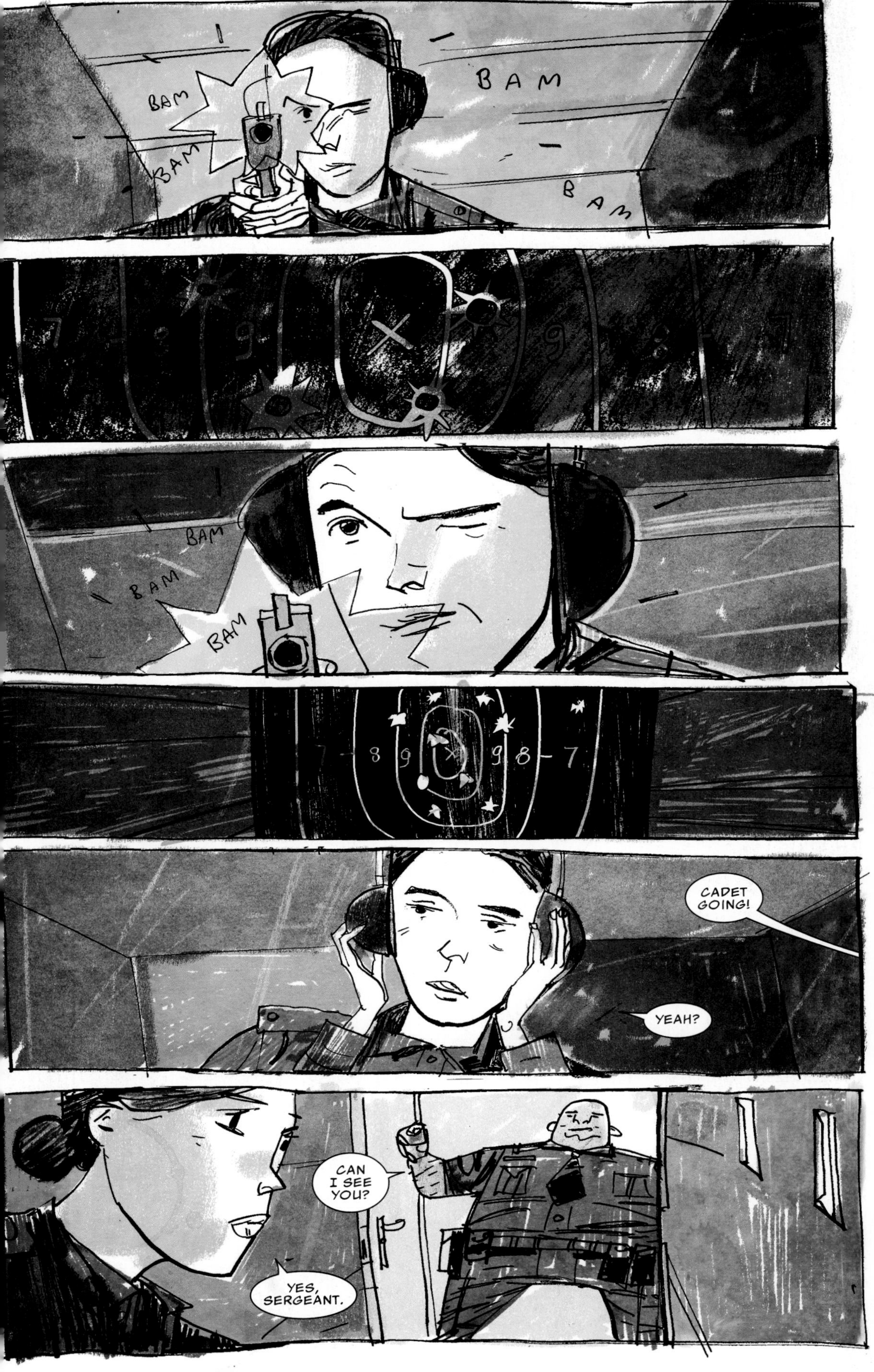
BAM
BAM
BAM
BAM
BAM
BAM
BAM
CADET GOING!
YEAH?
CAN I SEE YOU?
YES, SERGEANT.

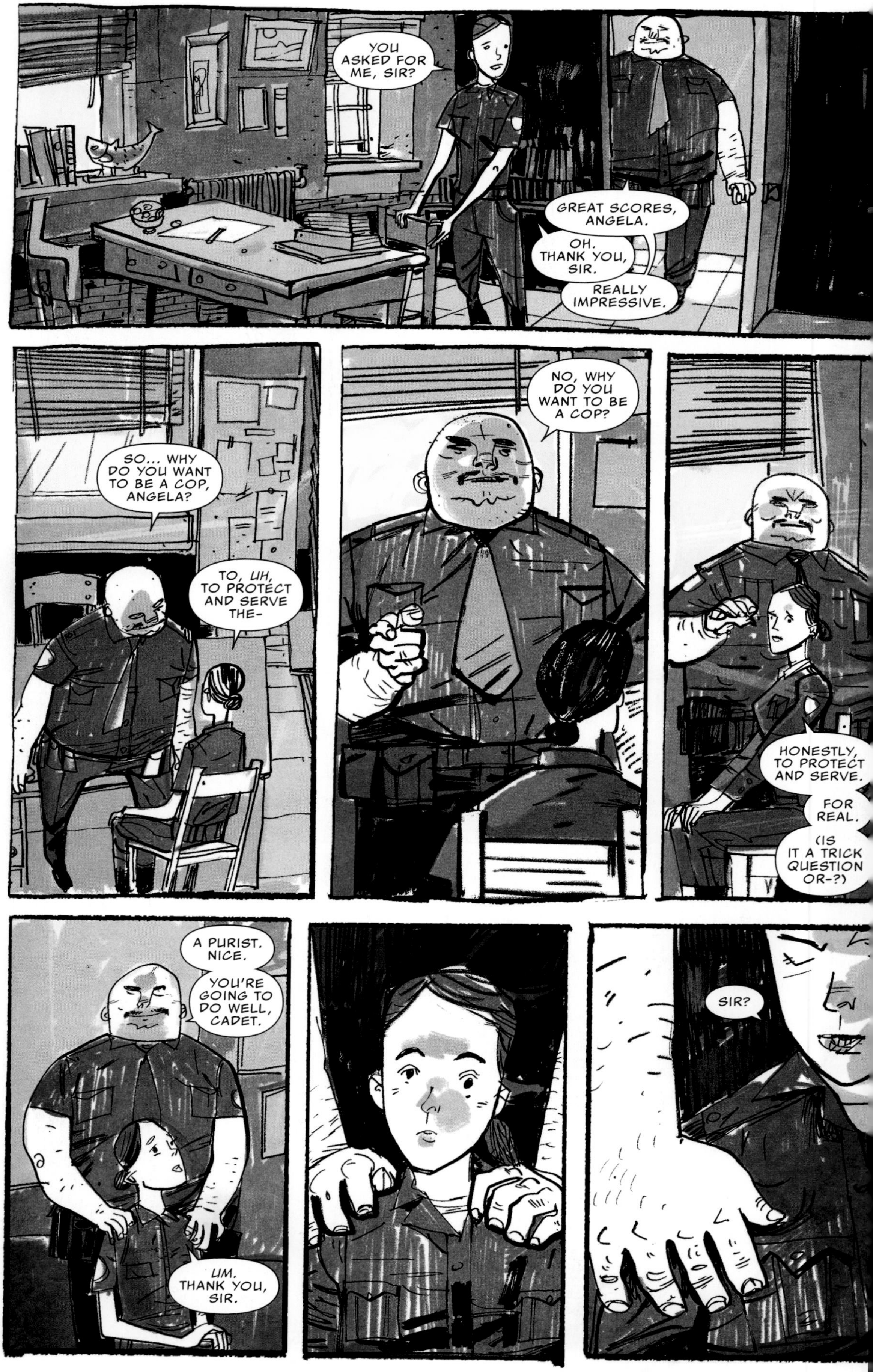
YOU ASKED FOR ME, SIR?
GREAT SCORES, ANGELA.
OH. THANK YOU, SIR.
REALLY IMPRESSIVE.
SO... WHY DO YOU WANT TO BE A COP, ANGELA?
TO, UH, TO PROTECT AND SERVE THE-
NO, WHY DO YOU WANT TO BE A COP?
HONESTLY, TO PROTECT AND SERVE.
FOR REAL.
(IS IT A TRICK QUESTION OR-?)
A PURIST. NICE.
YOU'RE GOING TO DO WELL, CADET.
UM. THANK YOU, SIR.
SIR?

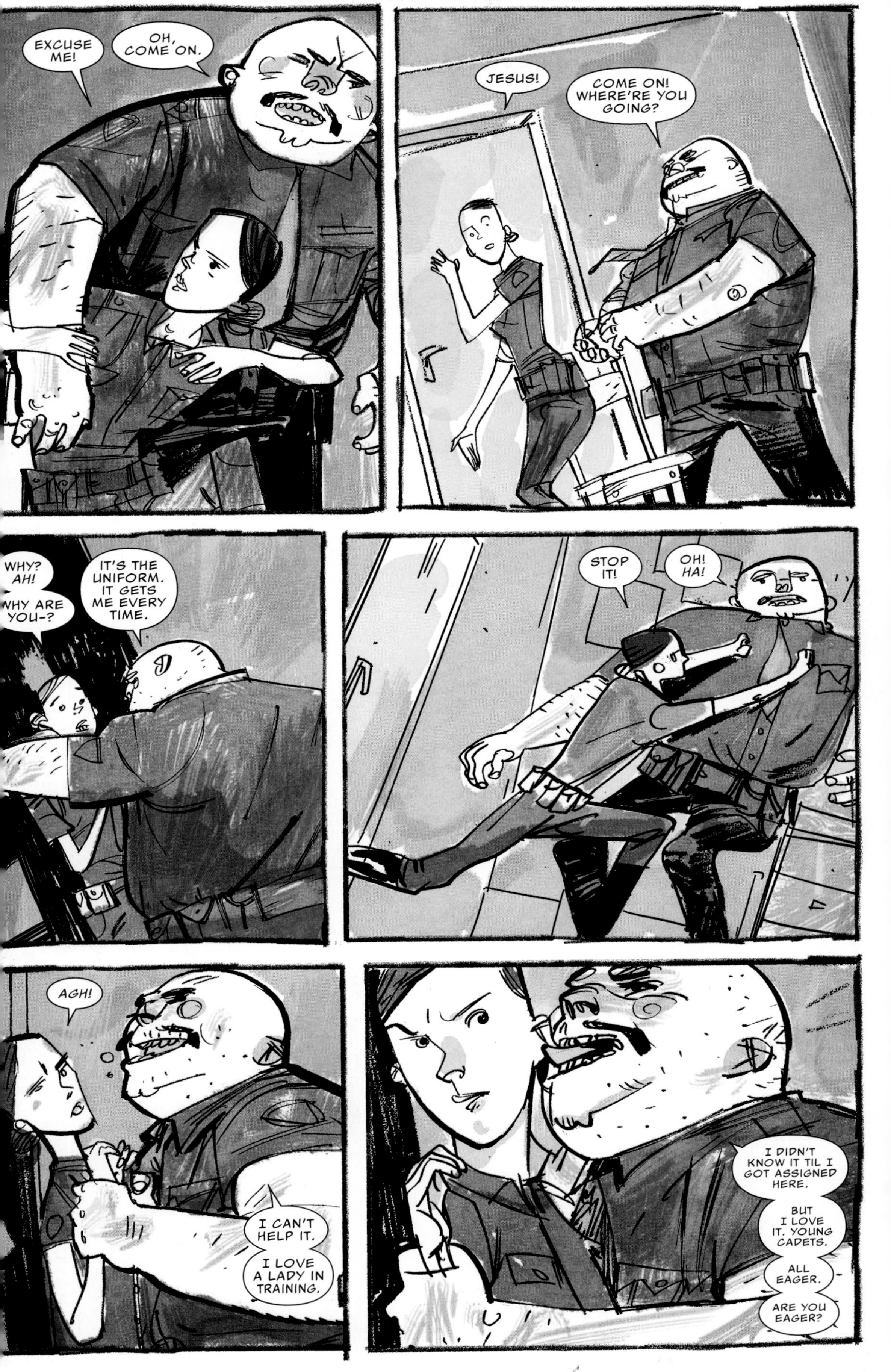
EXCUSE ME!
OH, COME ON.
JESUS!
COME ON! WHERE'RE YOU GOING?
WHY? AH!
WHY ARE YOU-?
IT'S THE UNIFORM. IT GETS ME EVERY TIME.
STOP IT!
OH! HA!
AGH!
I CAN'T HELP IT.
I LOVE A LADY IN TRAINING.
I DIDN'T KNOW IT TIL I GOT ASSIGNED HERE.
BUT I LOVE IT. YOUNG CADETS.
ALL EAGER.
ARE YOU EAGER?

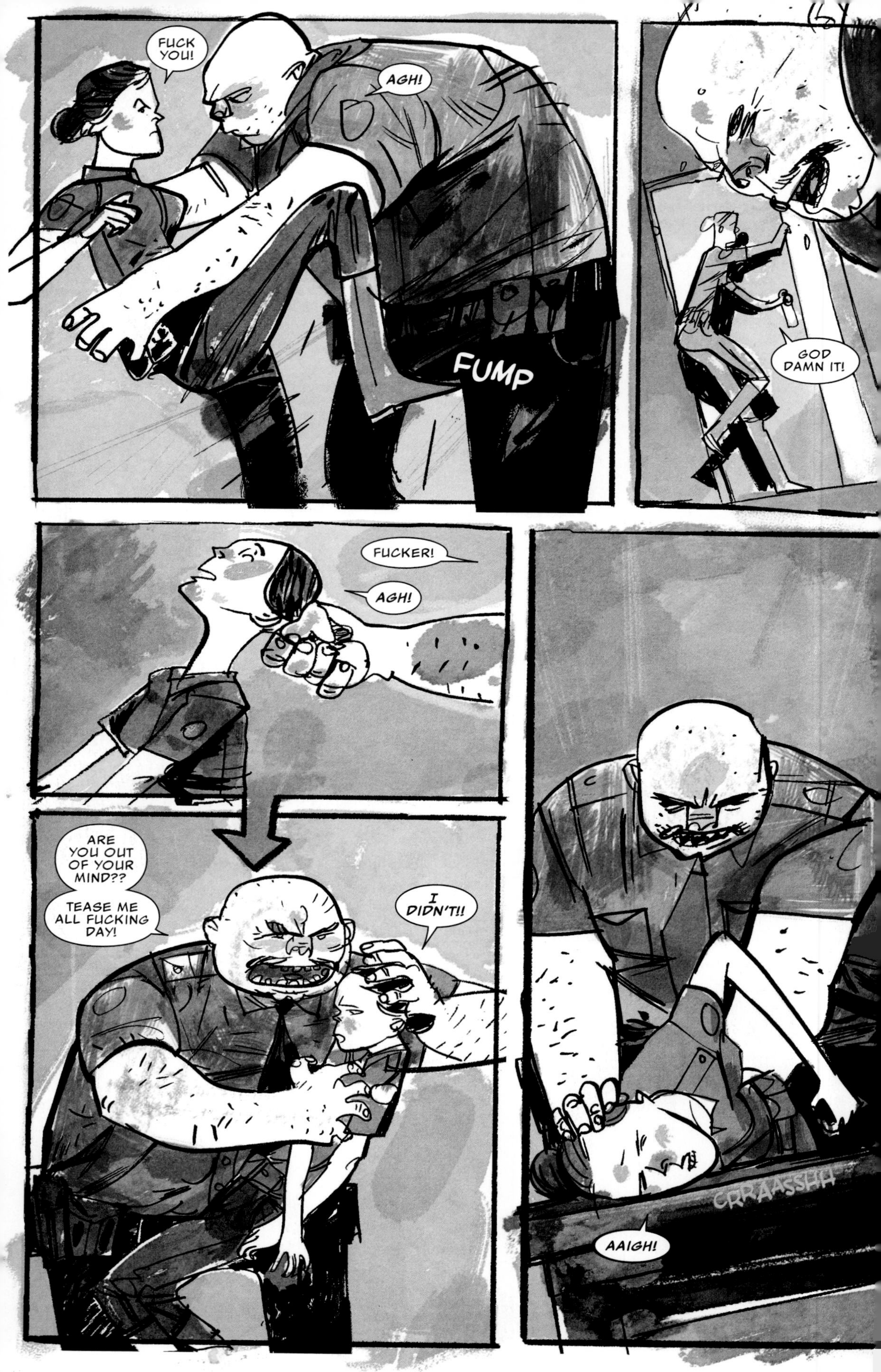
FUCK YOU!
AGH!
FUMP
GOD DAMN IT!
FUCKER!
AGH!
ARE YOU OUT OF YOUR MIND??
TEASE ME ALL FUCKING DAY!
I DIDN'T!!
CRRAASSHH
AAIGH!

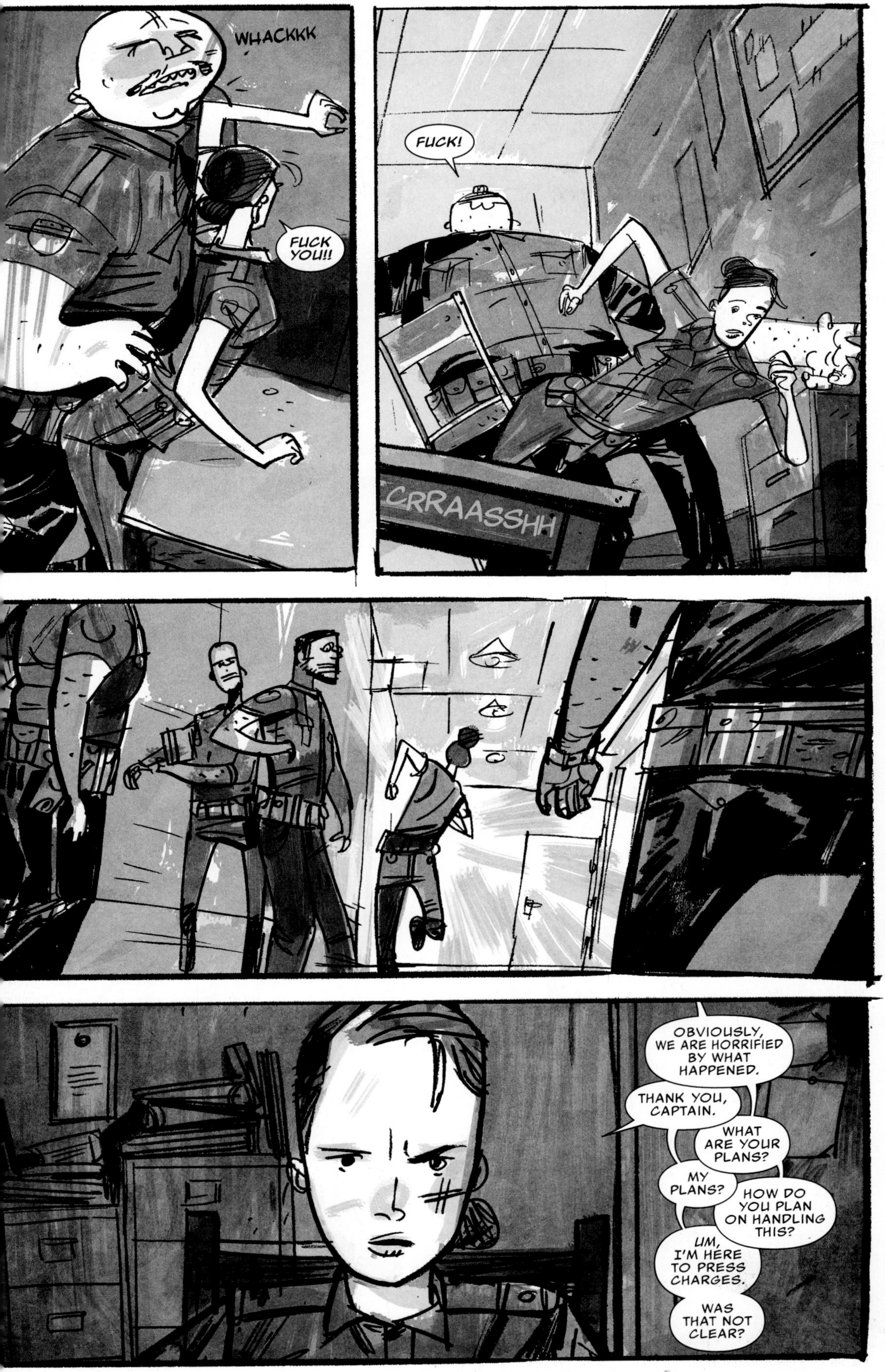
WHACKKK
FUCK YOU!!
FUCK!
CRRAASSHH
OBVIOUSLY, WE ARE HORRIFIED BY WHAT HAPPENED.
THANK YOU, CAPTAIN.
WHAT ARE YOUR PLANS?
MY PLANS?
HOW DO YOU PLAN ON HANDLING THIS?
UM, I'M HERE TO PRESS CHARGES.
WAS THAT NOT CLEAR?

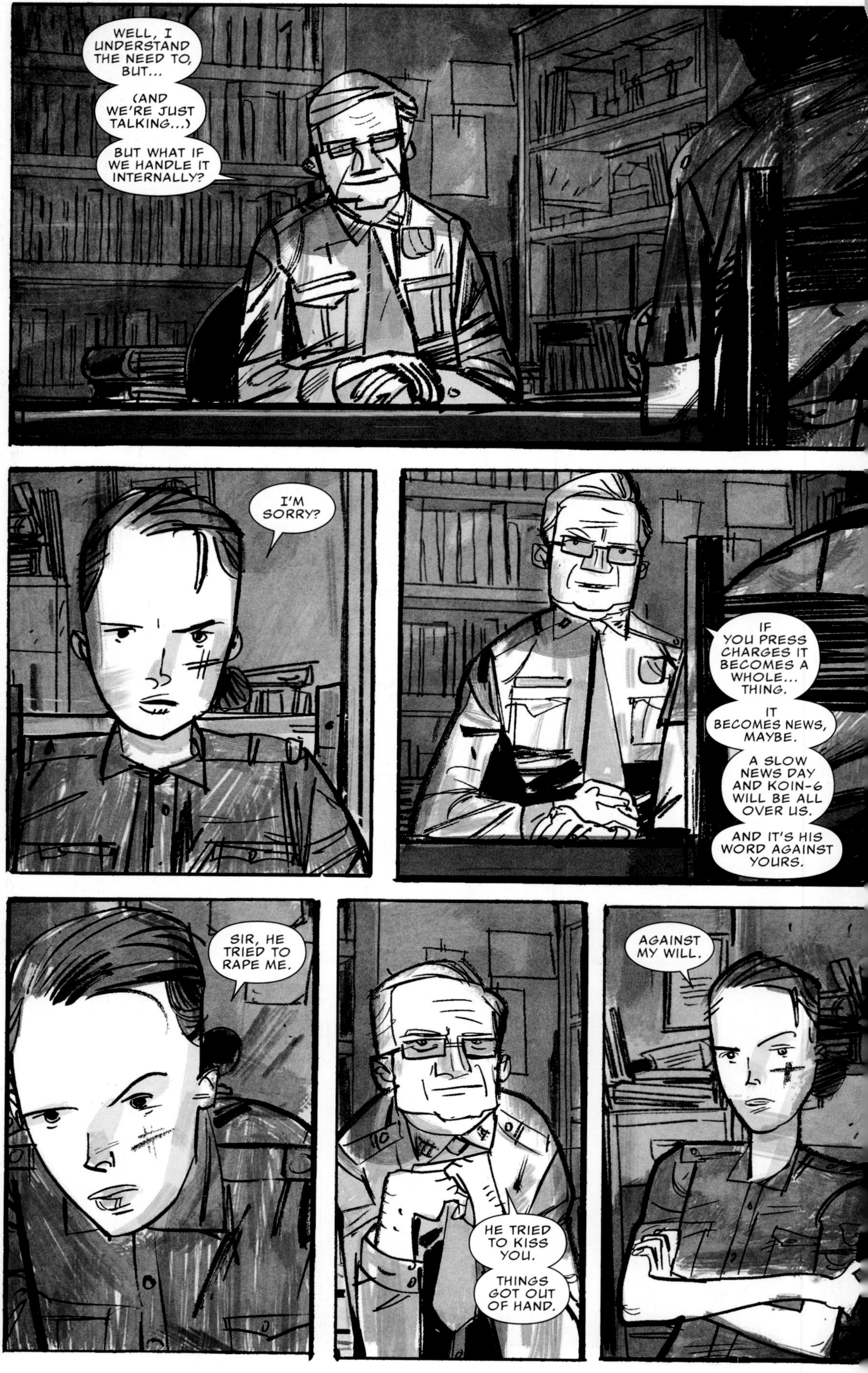
WELL, I UNDERSTAND THE NEED TO, BUT...
(AND WE'RE JUST TALKING...)
BUT WHAT IF WE HANDLE IT INTERNALLY?
I'M SORRY?
IF YOU PRESS CHARGES IT BECOMES A WHOLE... THING.
IT BECOMES NEWS, MAYBE.
A SLOW NEWS DAY AND KOIN-6 WILL BE ALL OVER US.
AND IT'S HIS WORD AGAINST YOURS.
SIR, HE TRIED TO RAPE ME.
HE TRIED TO KISS YOU.
THINGS GOT OUT OF HAND.
AGAINST MY WILL.

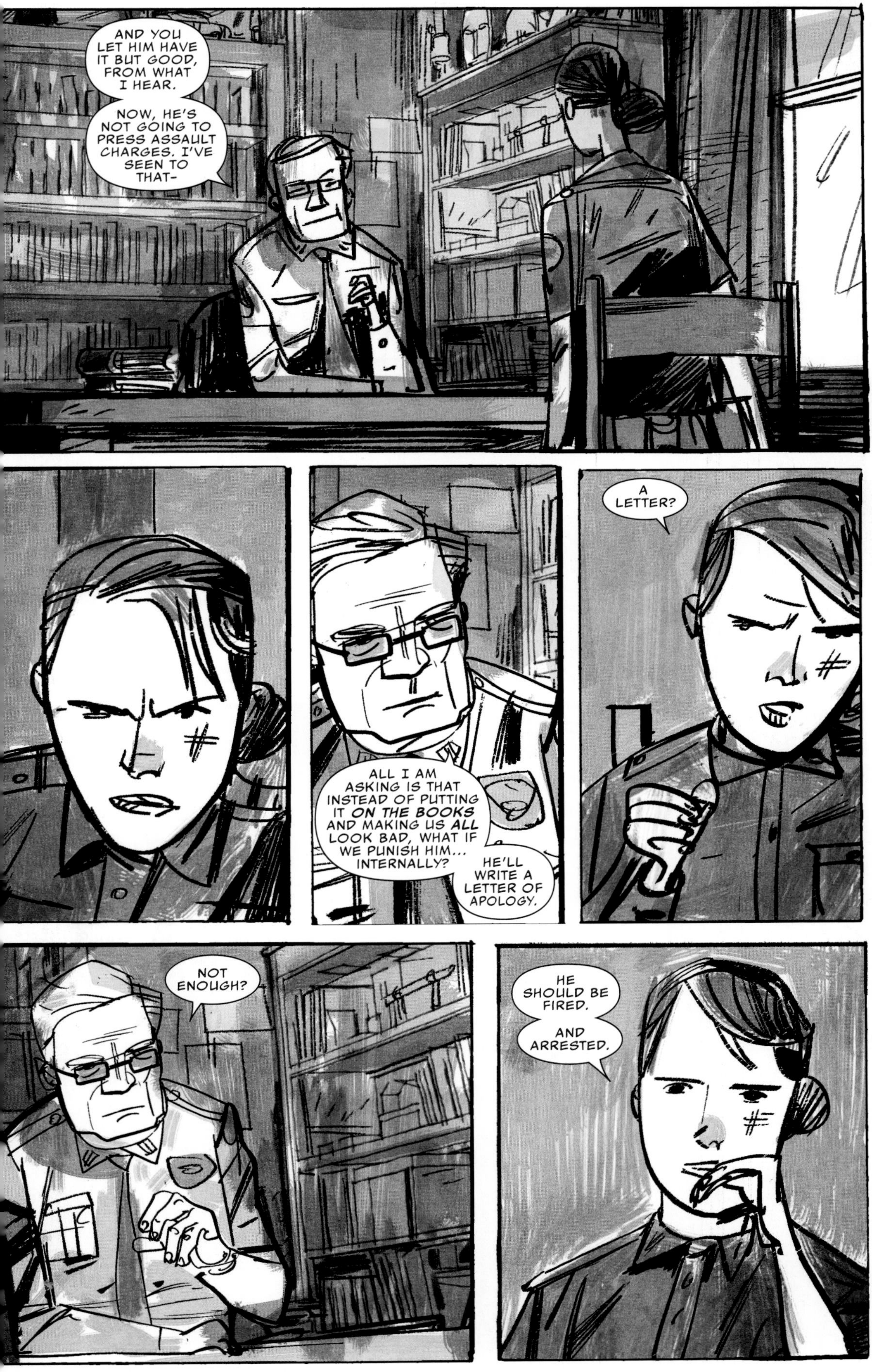
AND YOU LET HIM HAVE IT BUT GOOD, FROM WHAT I HEAR.
NOW, HE'S NOT GOING TO PRESS ASSAULT CHARGES. I'VE SEEN TO THAT-
ALL I AM ASKING IS THAT INSTEAD OF PUTTING IT ON THE BOOKS AND MAKING US ALL LOOK BAD, WHAT IF WE PUNISH HIM... INTERNALLY?
HE'LL WRITE A LETTER OF APOLOGY.
A LETTER?
NOT ENOUGH?
HE SHOULD BE FIRED.
AND ARRESTED.

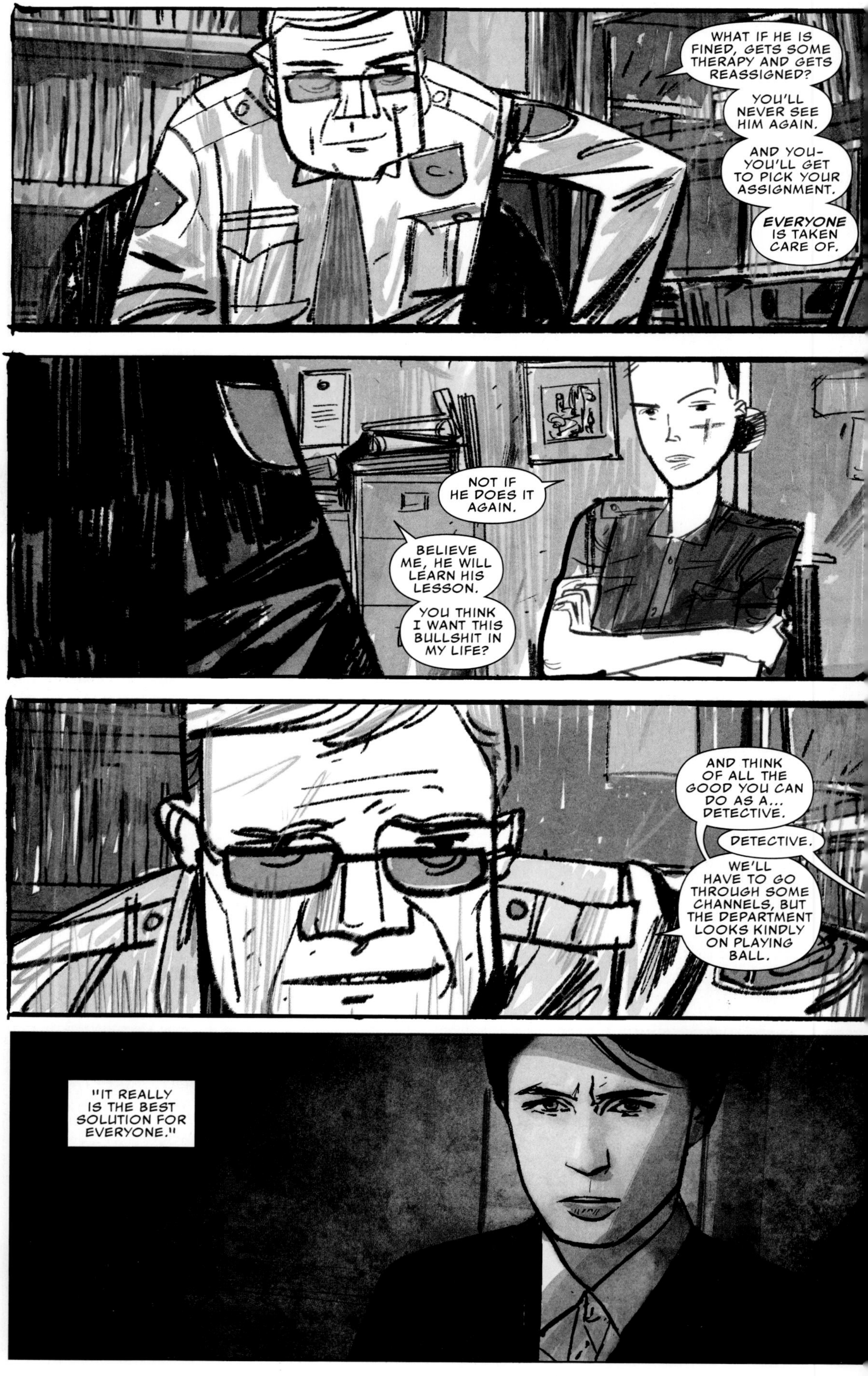
WHAT IF HE IS FINED, GETS SOME THERAPY AND GETS REASSIGNED?
YOU'LL NEVER SEE HIM AGAIN.
AND YOU-YOU'LL GET TO PICK YOUR ASSIGNMENT.
*EVERYONE* IS TAKEN CARE OF.
NOT IF HE DOES IT AGAIN.
BELIEVE ME, HE WILL LEARN HIS LESSON.
YOU THINK I WANT THIS BULLSHIT IN MY LIFE?
AND THINK OF ALL THE GOOD YOU CAN DO AS A... DETECTIVE.
DETECTIVE.
WE'LL HAVE TO GO THROUGH SOME CHANNELS, BUT THE DEPARTMENT LOOKS KINDLY ON PLAYING BALL.
"IT REALLY IS THE BEST SOLUTION FOR EVERYONE."

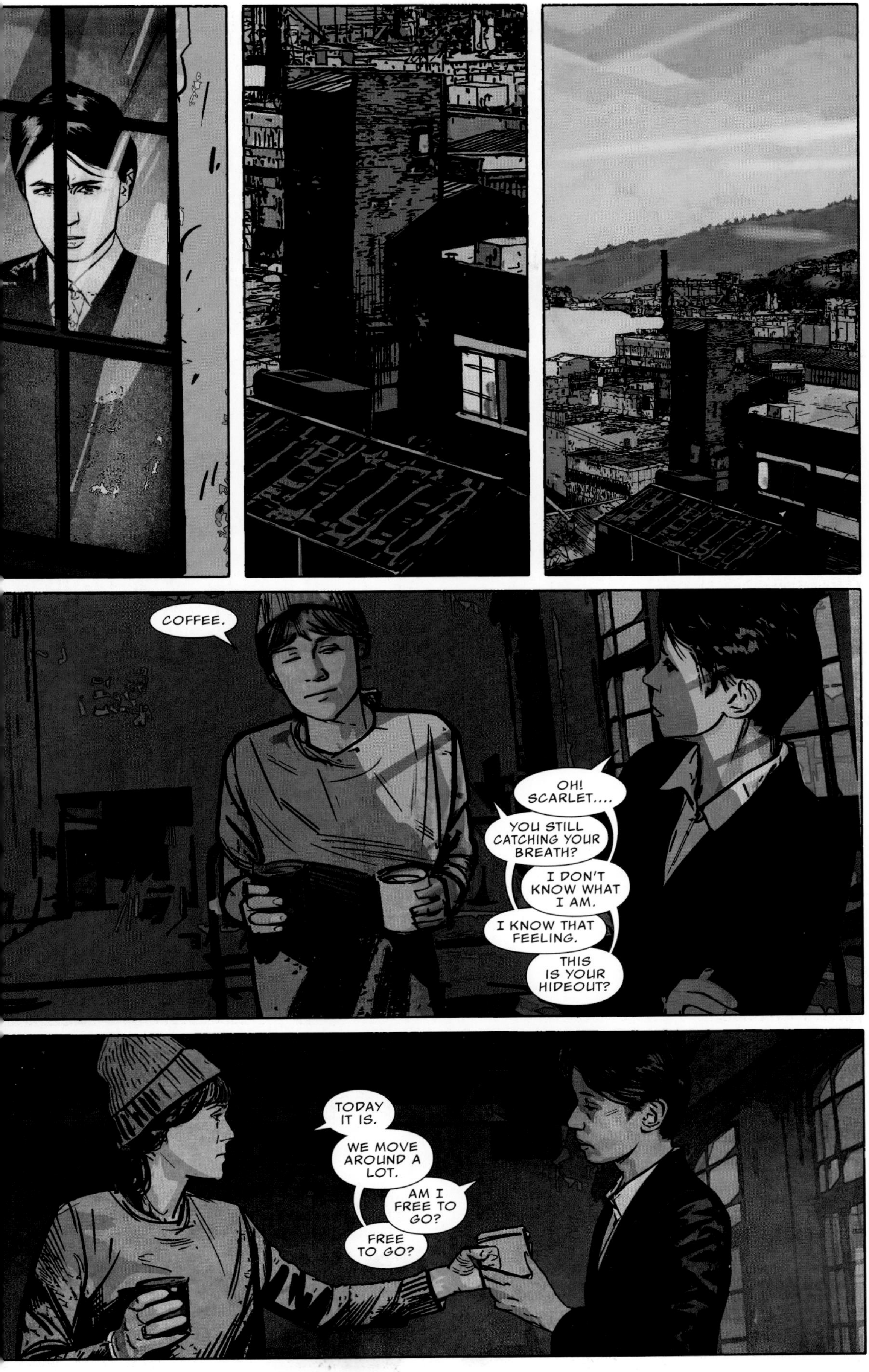
COFFEE.
OH! SCARLET....
YOU STILL CATCHING YOUR BREATH?
I DON'T KNOW WHAT I AM.
I KNOW THAT FEELING.
THIS IS YOUR HIDEOUT?
TODAY IT IS.
WE MOVE AROUND A LOT.
AM I FREE TO GO?
FREE TO GO?

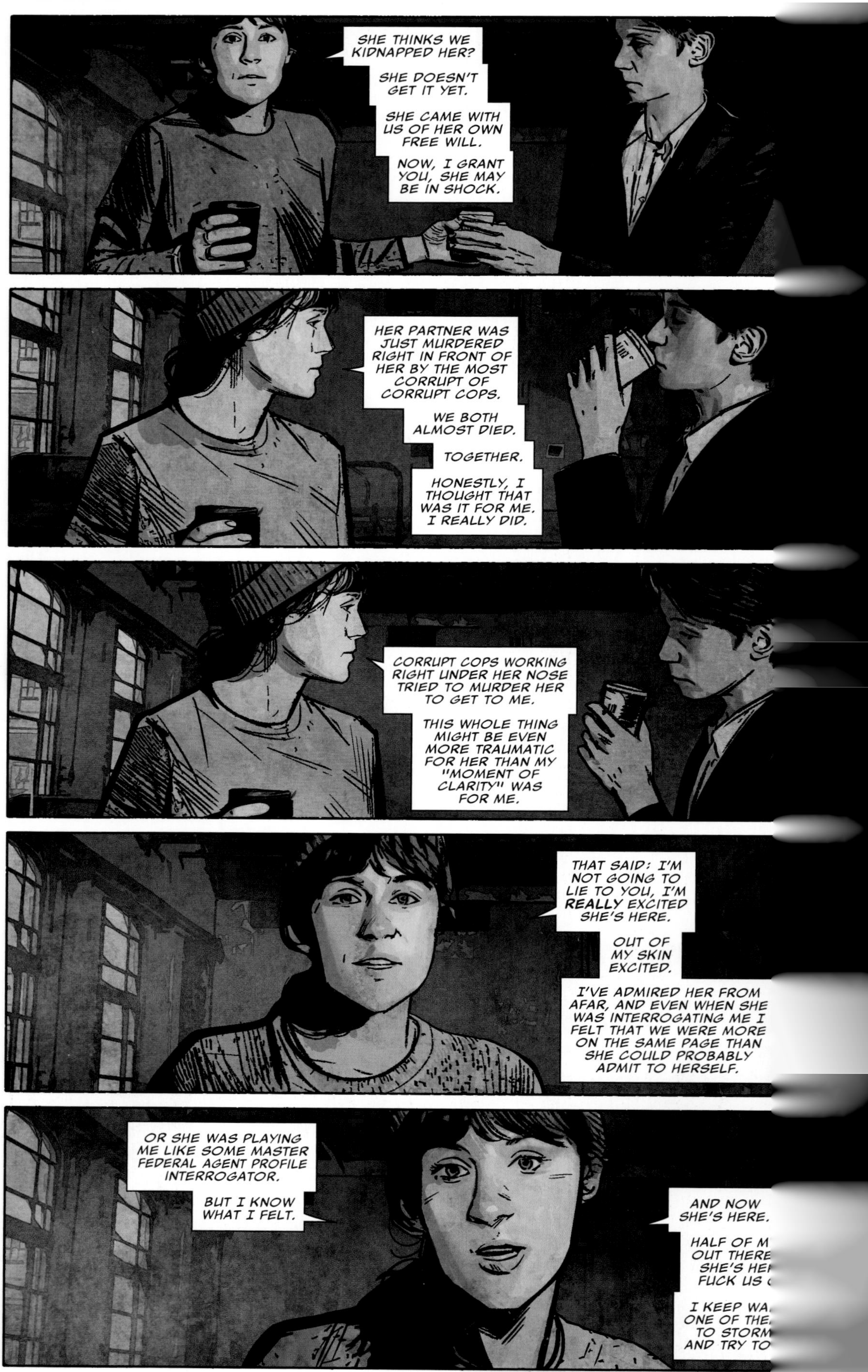
SHE THINKS WE KIDNAPPED HER?
SHE DOESN'T GET IT YET.
SHE CAME WITH US OF HER OWN FREE WILL.
NOW, I GRANT YOU, SHE MAY BE IN SHOCK.
HER PARTNER WAS JUST MURDERED RIGHT IN FRONT OF HER BY THE MOST CORRUPT OF CORRUPT COPS.
WE BOTH ALMOST DIED.
TOGETHER.
HONESTLY, I THOUGHT THAT WAS IT FOR ME. I REALLY DID.
CORRUPT COPS WORKING RIGHT UNDER HER NOSE TRIED TO MURDER HER TO GET TO ME.
THIS WHOLE THING MIGHT BE EVEN MORE TRAUMATIC FOR HER THAN MY "MOMENT OF CLARITY" WAS FOR ME.
THAT SAID: I'M NOT GOING TO LIE TO YOU, I'M REALLY EXCITED SHE'S HERE.
OUT OF MY SKIN EXCITED.
I'VE ADMIRED HER FROM AFAR, AND EVEN WHEN SHE WAS INTERROGATING ME I FELT THAT WE WERE MORE ON THE SAME PAGE THAN SHE COULD PROBABLY ADMIT TO HERSELF.
OR SHE WAS PLAYING ME LIKE SOME MASTER FEDERAL AGENT PROFILE INTERROGATOR.
BUT I KNOW WHAT I FELT.
AND NOW SHE'S HERE.
HALF OF M
OUT THERE
SHE'S HEI
FUCK US
I KEEP WA
ONE OF THE
TO STORM
AND TRY TO

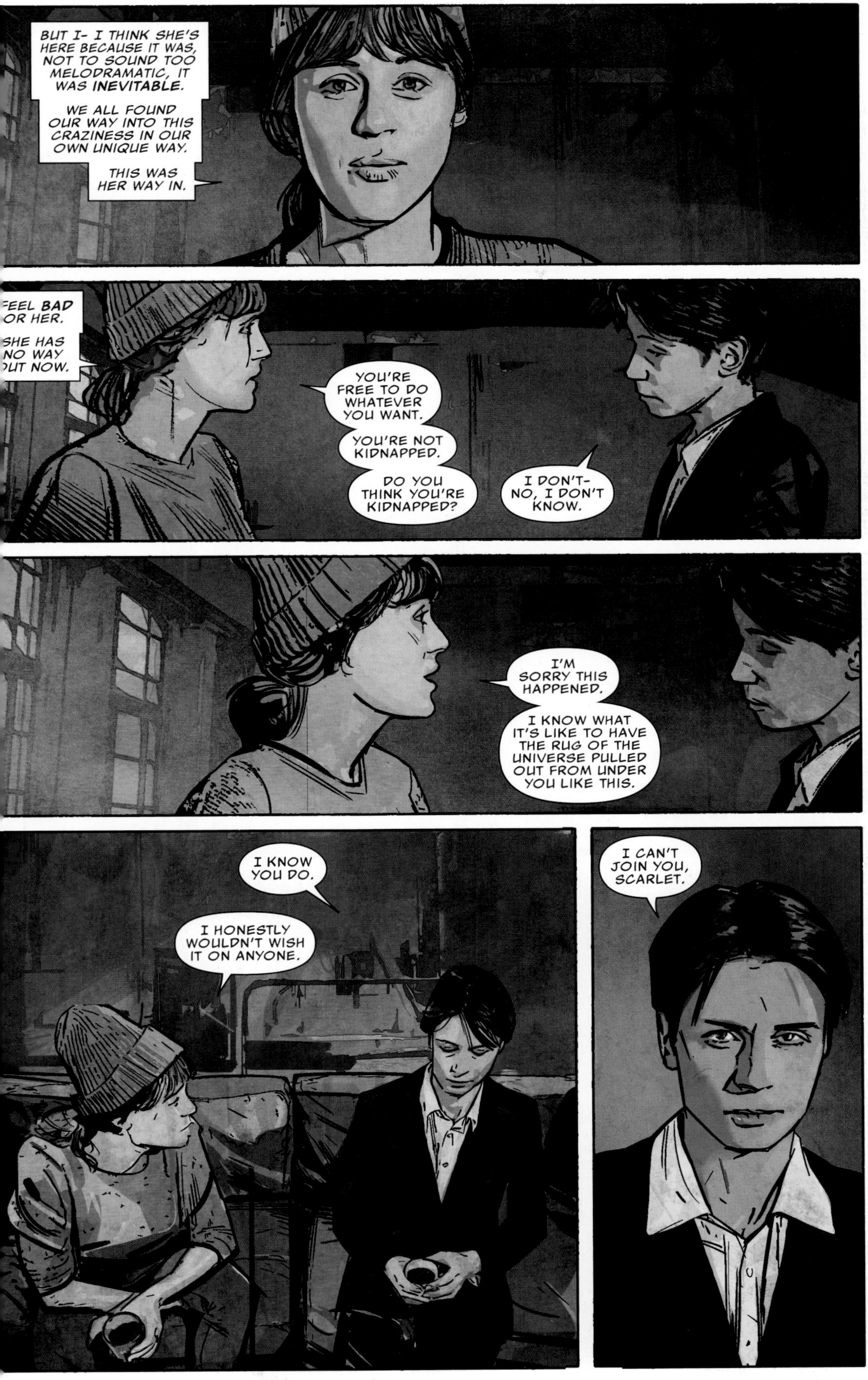
BUT I- I THINK SHE'S HERE BECAUSE IT WAS, NOT TO SOUND TOO MELODRAMATIC, IT WAS INEVITABLE.
WE ALL FOUND OUR WAY INTO THIS CRAZINESS IN OUR OWN UNIQUE WAY.
THIS WAS HER WAY IN.
FEEL BAD OR HER.
SHE HAS NO WAY UT NOW.
YOU'RE FREE TO DO WHATEVER YOU WANT.
YOU'RE NOT KIDNAPPED.
DO YOU THINK YOU'RE KIDNAPPED?
I DON'T- NO, I DON'T KNOW.
I'M SORRY THIS HAPPENED.
I KNOW WHAT IT'S LIKE TO HAVE THE RUG OF THE UNIVERSE PULLED OUT FROM UNDER YOU LIKE THIS.
I KNOW YOU DO.
I HONESTLY WOULDN'T WISH IT ON ANYONE.
I CAN'T JOIN YOU, SCARLET.

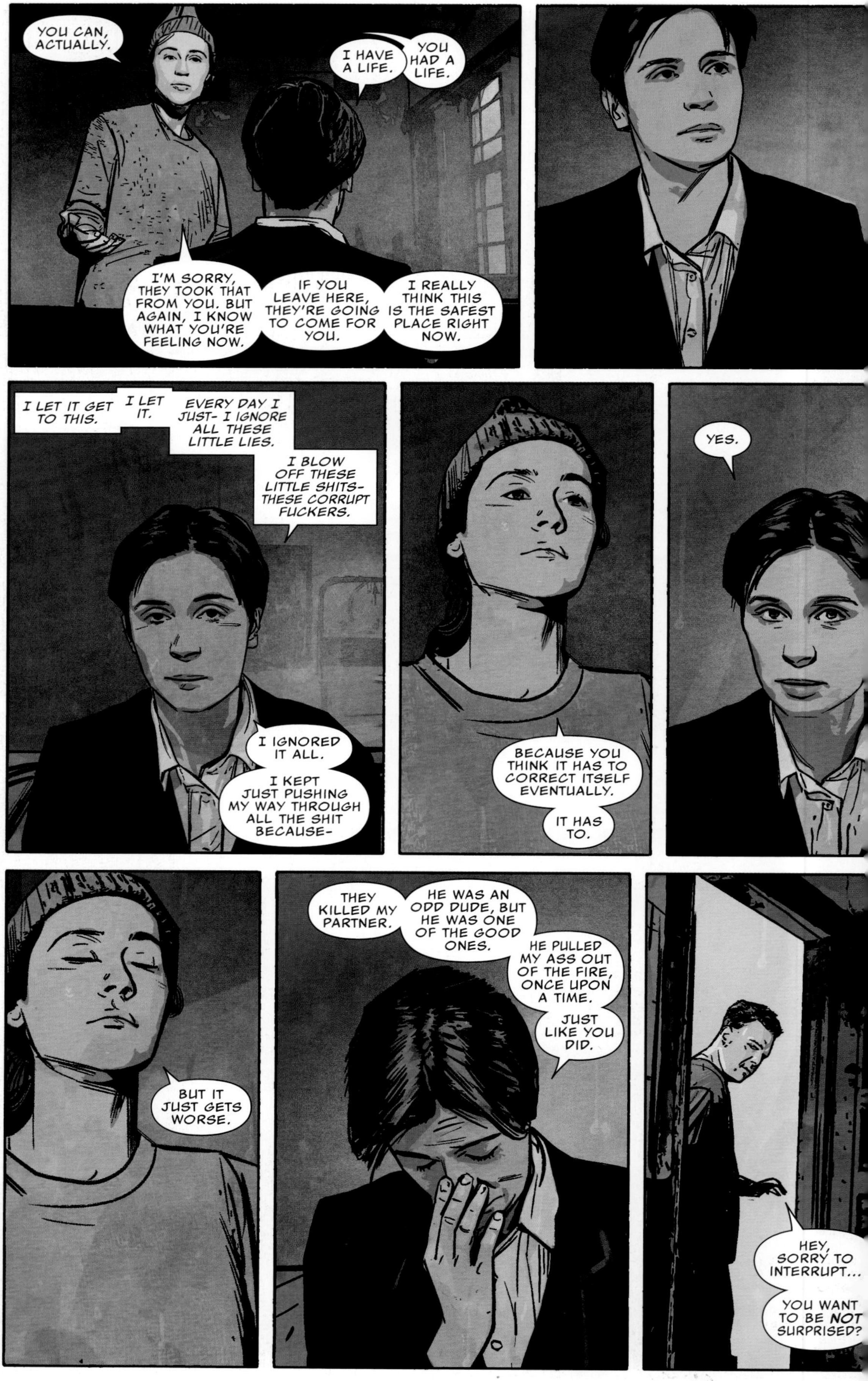
YOU CAN, ACTUALLY.
I HAVE A LIFE.
YOU HAD A LIFE.
I'M SORRY, THEY TOOK THAT FROM YOU. BUT AGAIN, I KNOW WHAT YOU'RE FEELING NOW.
IF YOU LEAVE HERE, THEY'RE GOING TO COME FOR YOU.
I REALLY THINK THIS IS THE SAFEST PLACE RIGHT NOW.
I LET IT GET TO THIS.
I LET IT.
EVERY DAY I JUST- I IGNORE ALL THESE LITTLE LIES.
I BLOW OFF THESE LITTLE SHITS- THESE CORRUPT FUCKERS.
I IGNORED IT ALL.
I KEPT JUST PUSHING MY WAY THROUGH ALL THE SHIT BECAUSE-
BECAUSE YOU THINK IT HAS TO CORRECT ITSELF EVENTUALLY.
IT HAS TO.
YES.
BUT IT JUST GETS WORSE.
THEY KILLED MY PARTNER.
HE WAS AN ODD DUDE, BUT HE WAS ONE OF THE GOOD ONES.
HE PULLED MY ASS OUT OF THE FIRE, ONCE UPON A TIME.
JUST LIKE YOU DID.
HEY, SORRY TO INTERRUPT...
YOU WANT TO BE NOT SURPRISED?

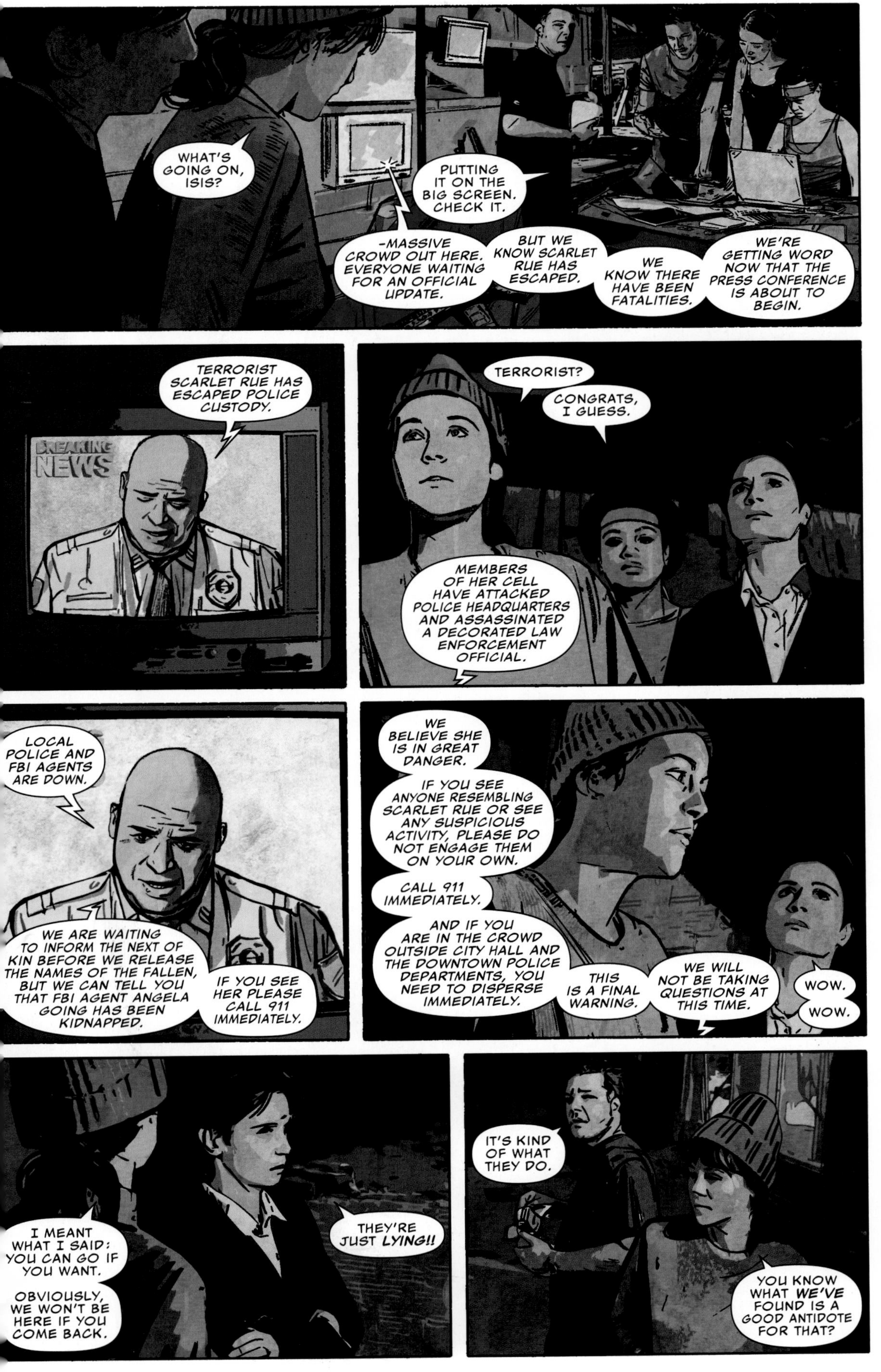

WHAT'S GOING ON, ISIS?
PUTTING IT ON THE BIG SCREEN. CHECK IT.
-MASSIVE CROWD OUT HERE. EVERYONE WAITING FOR AN OFFICIAL UPDATE.
BUT WE KNOW SCARLET RUE HAS ESCAPED.
WE KNOW THERE HAVE BEEN FATALITIES.
WE'RE GETTING WORD NOW THAT THE PRESS CONFERENCE IS ABOUT TO BEGIN.
TERRORIST SCARLET RUE HAS ESCAPED POLICE CUSTODY.
BREAKING NEWS
TERRORIST?
CONGRATS, I GUESS.
MEMBERS OF HER CELL HAVE ATTACKED POLICE HEADQUARTERS AND ASSASSINATED A DECORATED LAW ENFORCEMENT OFFICIAL.
LOCAL POLICE AND FBI AGENTS ARE DOWN.
WE ARE WAITING TO INFORM THE NEXT OF KIN BEFORE WE RELEASE THE NAMES OF THE FALLEN, BUT WE CAN TELL YOU THAT FBI AGENT ANGELA GOING HAS BEEN KIDNAPPED.
IF YOU SEE HER PLEASE CALL 911 IMMEDIATELY.
WE BELIEVE SHE IS IN GREAT DANGER.
IF YOU SEE ANYONE RESEMBLING SCARLET RUE OR SEE ANY SUSPICIOUS ACTIVITY, PLEASE DO NOT ENGAGE THEM ON YOUR OWN.
CALL 911 IMMEDIATELY.
AND IF YOU ARE IN THE CROWD OUTSIDE CITY HALL AND THE DOWNTOWN POLICE DEPARTMENTS, YOU NEED TO DISPERSE IMMEDIATELY.
THIS IS A FINAL WARNING.
WE WILL NOT BE TAKING QUESTIONS AT THIS TIME.
WOW.
WOW.
I MEANT WHAT I SAID: YOU CAN GO IF YOU WANT.
OBVIOUSLY, WE WON'T BE HERE IF YOU COME BACK.
THEY'RE JUST *LYING!!*
IT'S KIND OF WHAT THEY DO.
YOU KNOW WHAT *WE'VE* FOUND IS A GOOD ANTIDOTE FOR THAT?

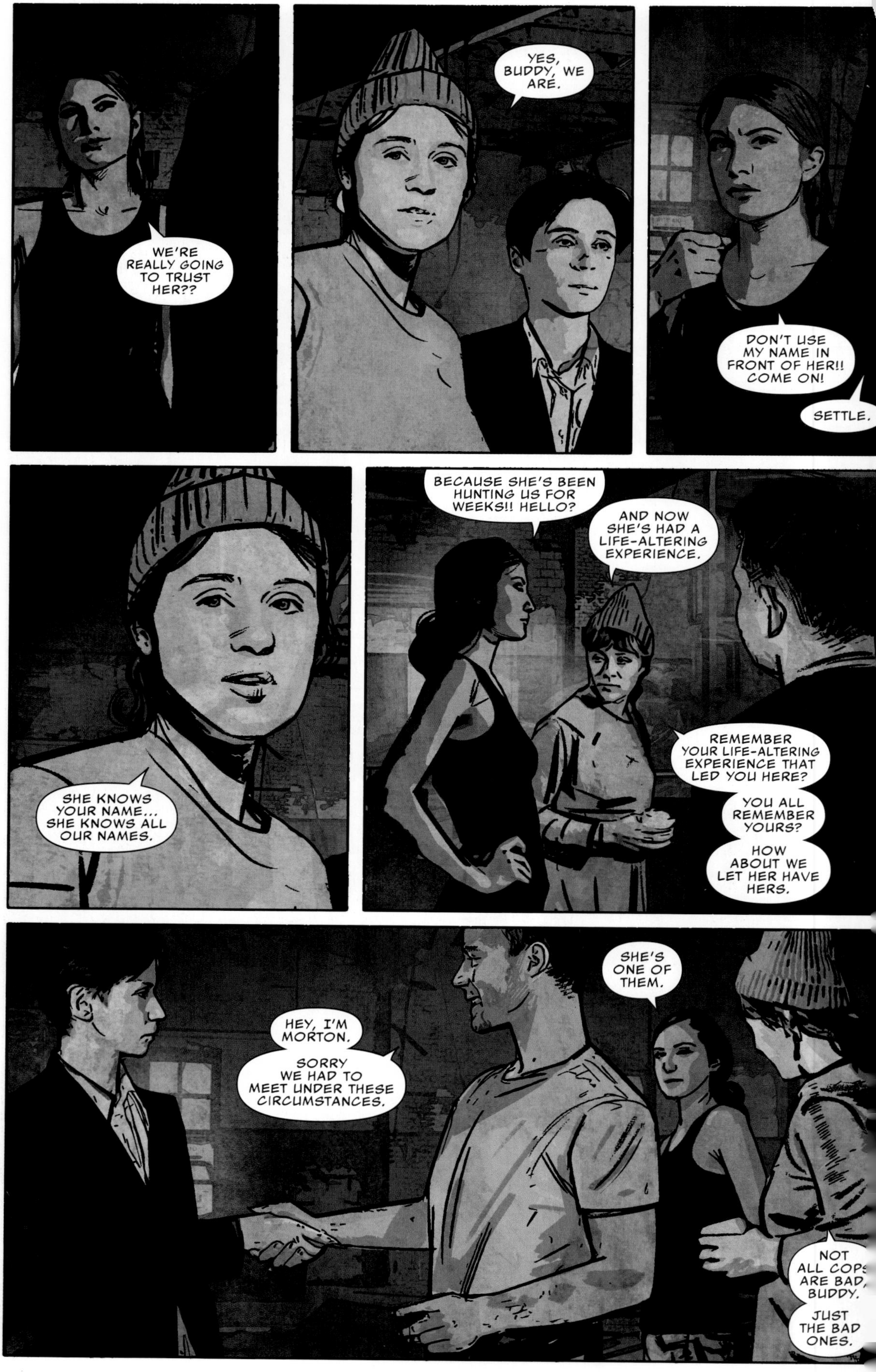
WE'RE REALLY GOING TO TRUST HER??
YES, BUDDY, WE ARE.
DON'T USE MY NAME IN FRONT OF HER!! COME ON!
SETTLE.
SHE KNOWS YOUR NAME... SHE KNOWS ALL OUR NAMES.
BECAUSE SHE'S BEEN HUNTING US FOR WEEKS!! HELLO?
AND NOW SHE'S HAD A LIFE-ALTERING EXPERIENCE.
REMEMBER YOUR LIFE-ALTERING EXPERIENCE THAT LED YOU HERE?
YOU ALL REMEMBER YOURS?
HOW ABOUT WE LET HER HAVE HERS.
HEY, I'M MORTON.
SORRY WE HAD TO MEET UNDER THESE CIRCUMSTANCES.
SHE'S ONE OF THEM.
NOT ALL COPS ARE BAD, BUDDY.
JUST THE BAD ONES.

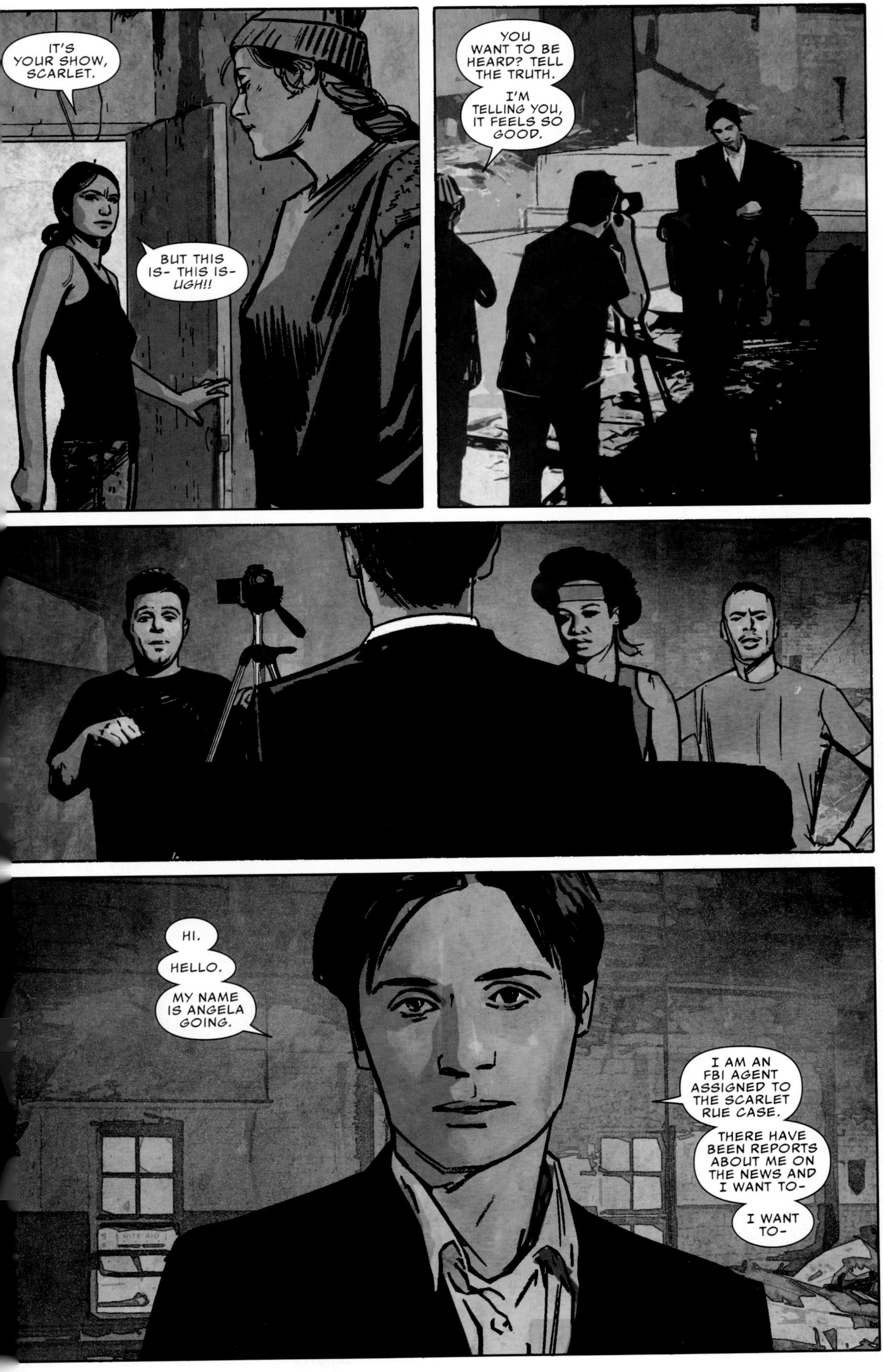
IT'S YOUR SHOW, SCARLET.
BUT THIS IS- THIS IS- UGH!!
YOU WANT TO BE HEARD? TELL THE TRUTH.
I'M TELLING YOU, IT FEELS SO GOOD.
HI.
HELLO.
MY NAME IS ANGELA GOING.
I AM AN FBI AGENT ASSIGNED TO THE SCARLET RUE CASE.
THERE HAVE BEEN REPORTS ABOUT ME ON THE NEWS AND I WANT TO-
I WANT TO-

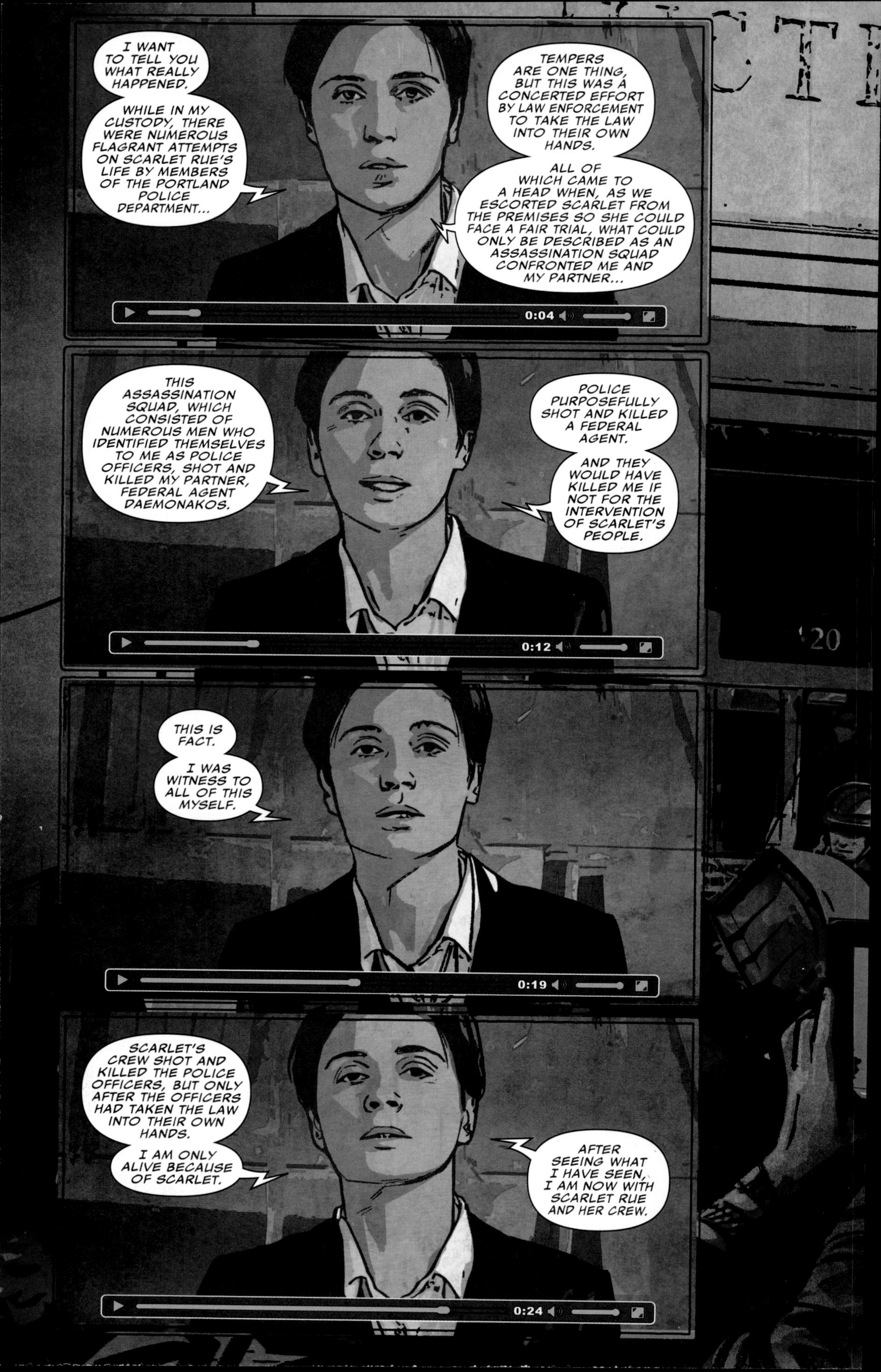
I WANT TO TELL YOU WHAT REALLY HAPPENED.
WHILE IN MY CUSTODY, THERE WERE NUMEROUS FLAGRANT ATTEMPTS ON SCARLET RUE'S LIFE BY MEMBERS OF THE PORTLAND POLICE DEPARTMENT...
TEMPERS ARE ONE THING, BUT THIS WAS A CONCERTED EFFORT BY LAW ENFORCEMENT TO TAKE THE LAW INTO THEIR OWN HANDS.
ALL OF WHICH CAME TO A HEAD WHEN, AS WE ESCORTED SCARLET FROM THE PREMISES SO SHE COULD FACE A FAIR TRIAL, WHAT COULD ONLY BE DESCRIBED AS AN ASSASSINATION SQUAD CONFRONTED ME AND MY PARTNER...
0:04
THIS ASSASSINATION SQUAD, WHICH CONSISTED OF NUMEROUS MEN WHO IDENTIFIED THEMSELVES TO ME AS POLICE OFFICERS, SHOT AND KILLED MY PARTNER, FEDERAL AGENT DAEMONAKOS.
POLICE PURPOSEFULLY SHOT AND KILLED A FEDERAL AGENT.
AND THEY WOULD HAVE KILLED ME IF NOT FOR THE INTERVENTION OF SCARLET'S PEOPLE.
0:12
THIS IS FACT.
I WAS WITNESS TO ALL OF THIS MYSELF.
0:19
SCARLET'S CREW SHOT AND KILLED THE POLICE OFFICERS, BUT ONLY AFTER THE OFFICERS HAD TAKEN THE LAW INTO THEIR OWN HANDS.
I AM ONLY ALIVE BECAUSE OF SCARLET.
AFTER SEEING WHAT I HAVE SEEN, I AM NOW WITH SCARLET RUE AND HER CREW.
0:24

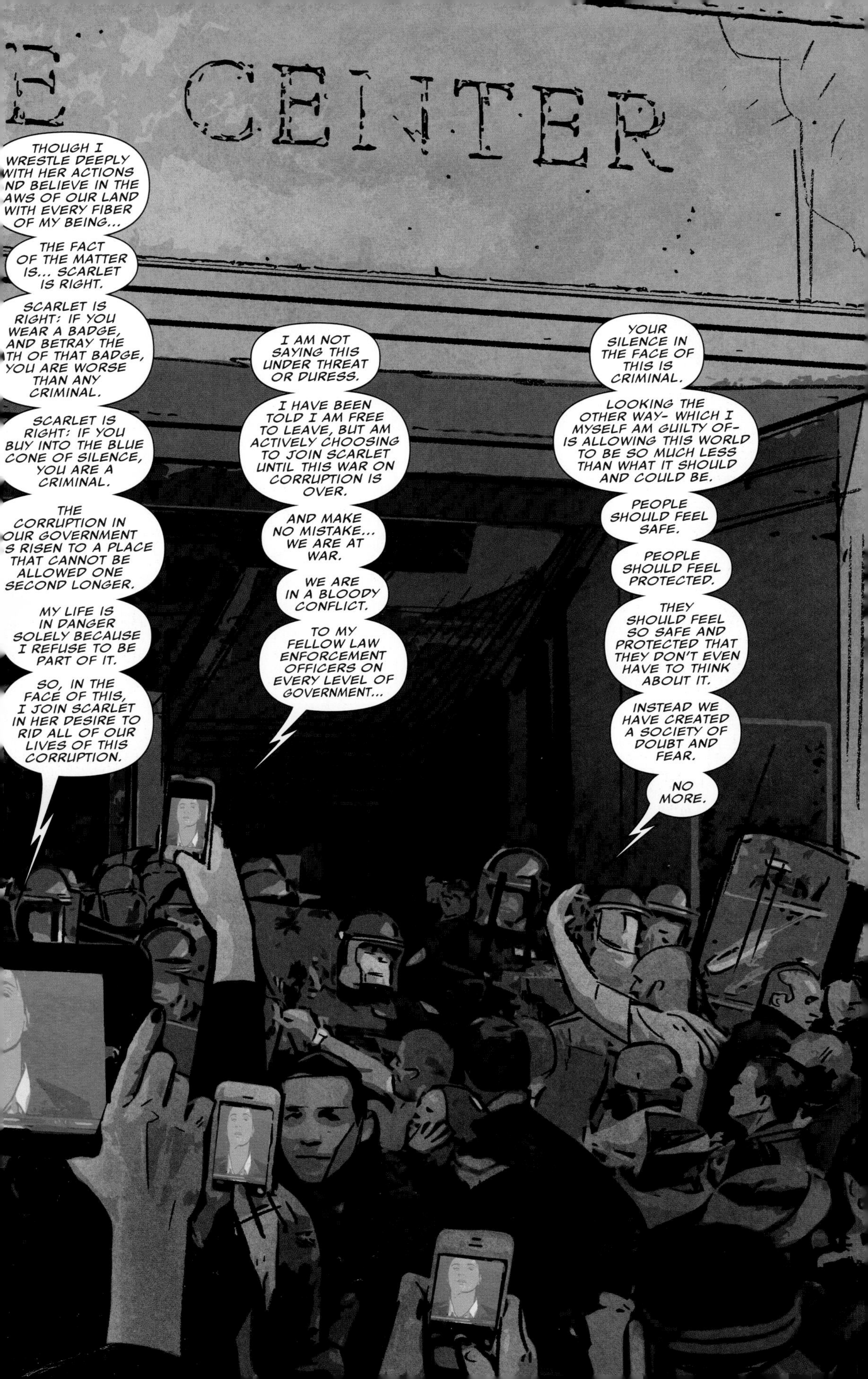
E CENTER
THOUGH I WRESTLE DEEPLY WITH HER ACTIONS ND BELIEVE IN THE AWS OF OUR LAND WITH EVERY FIBER OF MY BEING...
THE FACT OF THE MATTER IS... SCARLET IS RIGHT.
SCARLET IS RIGHT: IF YOU WEAR A BADGE, AND BETRAY THE TH OF THAT BADGE, YOU ARE WORSE THAN ANY CRIMINAL.
SCARLET IS RIGHT: IF YOU BUY INTO THE BLUE CONE OF SILENCE, YOU ARE A CRIMINAL.
THE CORRUPTION IN OUR GOVERNMENT S RISEN TO A PLACE THAT CANNOT BE ALLOWED ONE SECOND LONGER.
MY LIFE IS IN DANGER SOLELY BECAUSE I REFUSE TO BE PART OF IT.
SO, IN THE FACE OF THIS, I JOIN SCARLET IN HER DESIRE TO RID ALL OF OUR LIVES OF THIS CORRUPTION.
I AM NOT SAYING THIS UNDER THREAT OR DURESS.
I HAVE BEEN TOLD I AM FREE TO LEAVE, BUT AM ACTIVELY CHOOSING TO JOIN SCARLET UNTIL THIS WAR ON CORRUPTION IS OVER.
AND MAKE NO MISTAKE... WE ARE AT WAR.
WE ARE IN A BLOODY CONFLICT.
TO MY FELLOW LAW ENFORCEMENT OFFICERS ON EVERY LEVEL OF GOVERNMENT...
YOUR SILENCE IN THE FACE OF THIS IS CRIMINAL.
LOOKING THE OTHER WAY- WHICH I MYSELF AM GUILTY OF- IS ALLOWING THIS WORLD TO BE SO MUCH LESS THAN WHAT IT SHOULD AND COULD BE.
PEOPLE SHOULD FEEL SAFE.
PEOPLE SHOULD FEEL PROTECTED.
THEY SHOULD FEEL SO SAFE AND PROTECTED THAT THEY DON'T EVEN HAVE TO THINK ABOUT IT.
INSTEAD WE HAVE CREATED A SOCIETY OF DOUBT AND FEAR.
NO MORE.

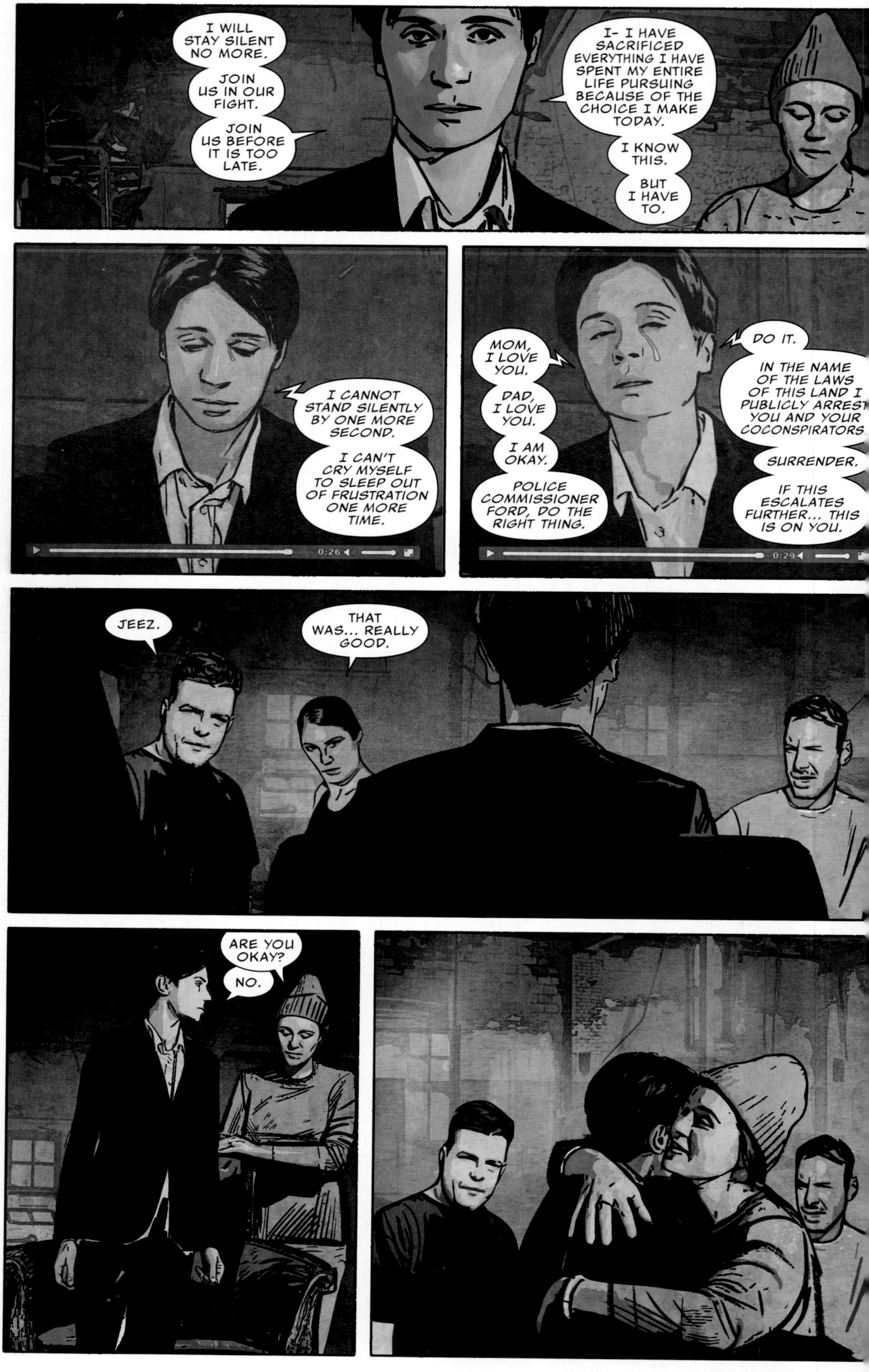
I WILL STAY SILENT NO MORE.
JOIN US IN OUR FIGHT.
JOIN US BEFORE IT IS TOO LATE.
I- I HAVE SACRIFICED EVERYTHING I HAVE SPENT MY ENTIRE LIFE PURSUING BECAUSE OF THE CHOICE I MAKE TODAY.
I KNOW THIS.
BUT I HAVE TO.
I CANNOT STAND SILENTLY BY ONE MORE SECOND.
I CAN'T CRY MYSELF TO SLEEP OUT OF FRUSTRATION ONE MORE TIME.
0:26
MOM, I LOVE YOU.
DAD, I LOVE YOU.
I AM OKAY.
POLICE COMMISSIONER FORD, DO THE RIGHT THING.
DO IT.
IN THE NAME OF THE LAWS OF THIS LAND I PUBLICLY ARREST YOU AND YOUR COCONSPIRATORS.
SURRENDER.
IF THIS ESCALATES FURTHER... THIS IS ON YOU.
0:29
JEEZ.
THAT WAS... REALLY GOOD.
ARE YOU OKAY?
NO.

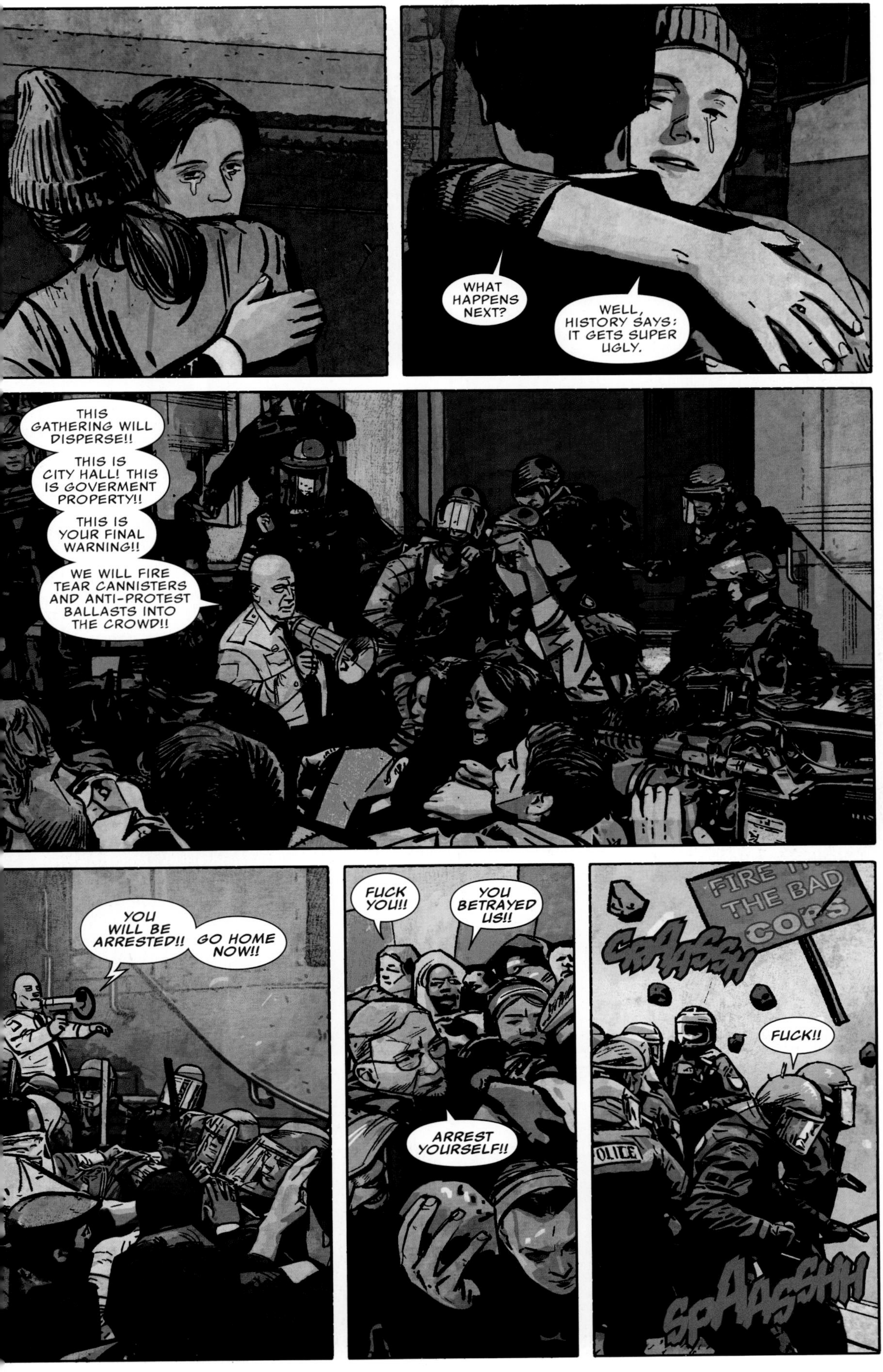
WHAT HAPPENS NEXT?
WELL, HISTORY SAYS: IT GETS SUPER UGLY.
THIS GATHERING WILL DISPERSE!!
THIS IS CITY HALL! THIS IS GOVERMENT PROPERTY!!
THIS IS YOUR FINAL WARNING!!
WE WILL FIRE TEAR CANNISTERS AND ANTI-PROTEST BALLASTS INTO THE CROWD!!
YOU WILL BE ARRESTED!!
GO HOME NOW!!
FUCK YOU!!
YOU BETRAYED US!!
ARREST YOURSELF!!
THE BAD COPS
GRAASSH
FUCK!!
POLICE
SPAASSHH

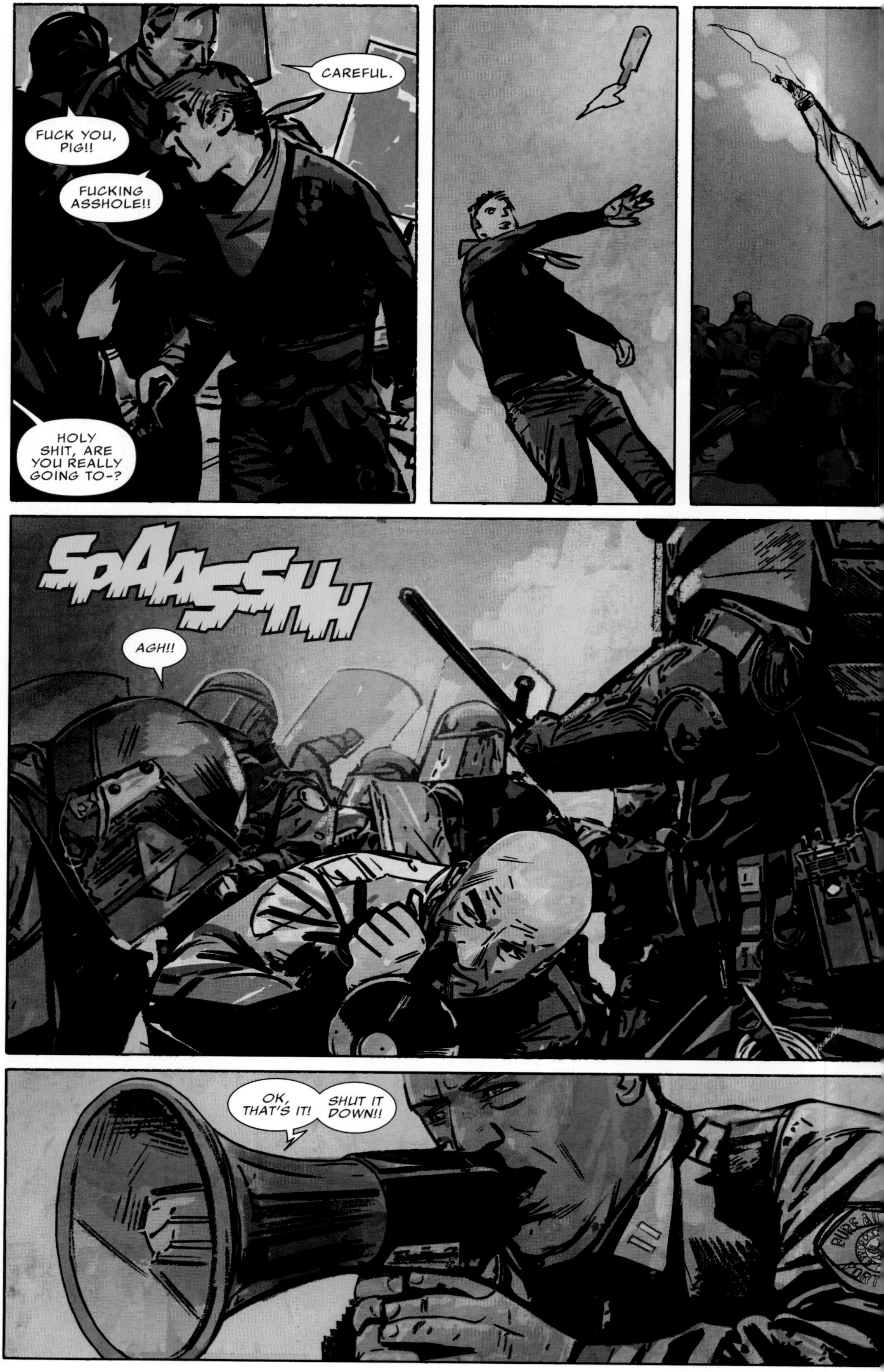
CAREFUL.
FUCK YOU, PIG!!
FUCKING ASSHOLE!!
HOLY SHIT, ARE YOU REALLY GOING TO-?
SPAASSHH
AGH!!
OK, THAT'S IT!
SHUT IT DOWN!!

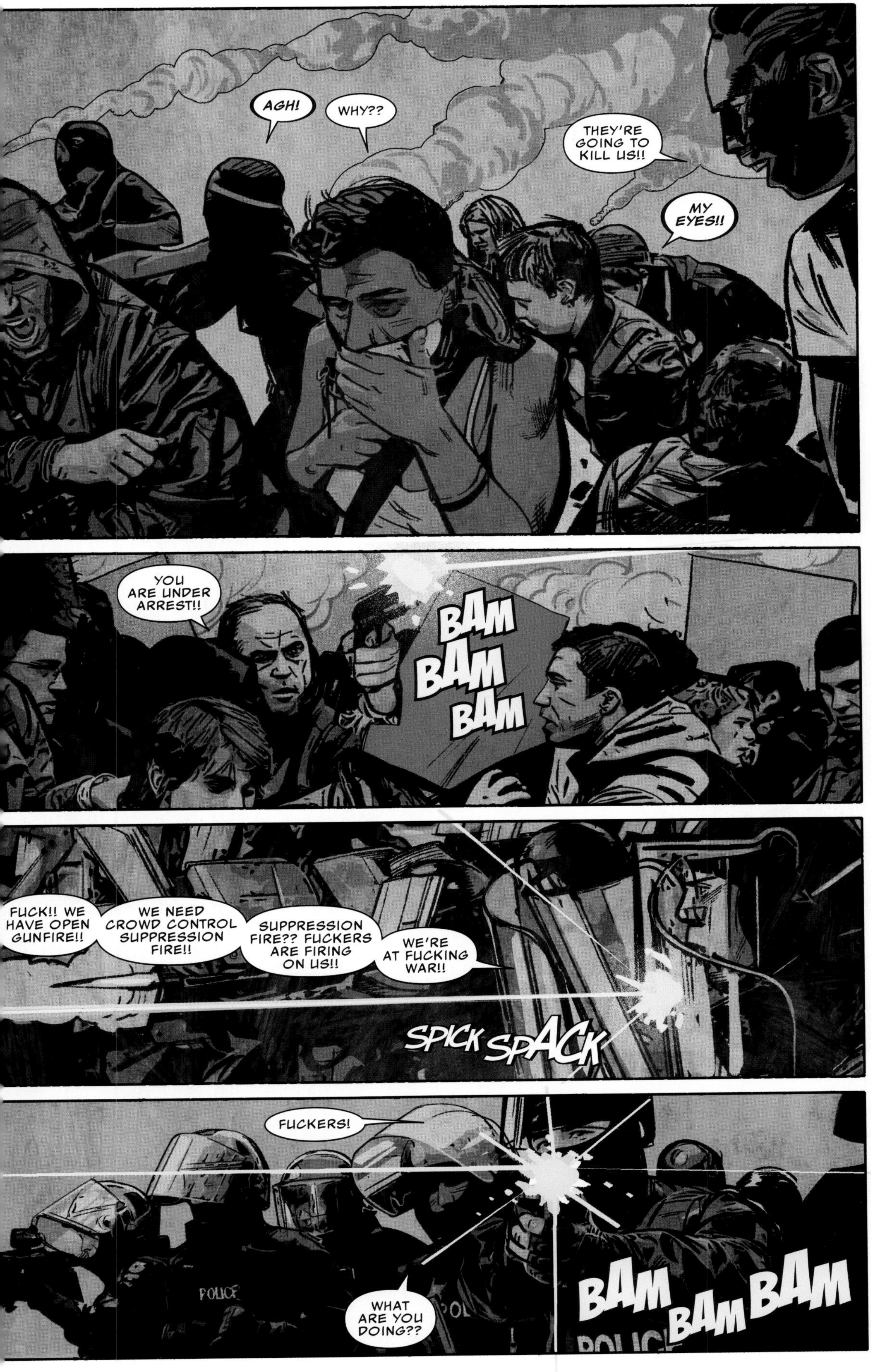
AGH!
WHY??
THEY'RE GOING TO KILL US!!
MY EYES!!
YOU ARE UNDER ARREST!!
BAM BAM BAM
FUCK!! WE HAVE OPEN GUNFIRE!!
WE NEED CROWD CONTROL SUPPRESSION FIRE!!
SUPPRESSION FIRE?? FUCKERS ARE FIRING ON US!!
WE'RE AT FUCKING WAR!!
SPICK SPACK
FUCKERS!
POLICE
WHAT ARE YOU DOING??
BAM BAM BAM
POLICE

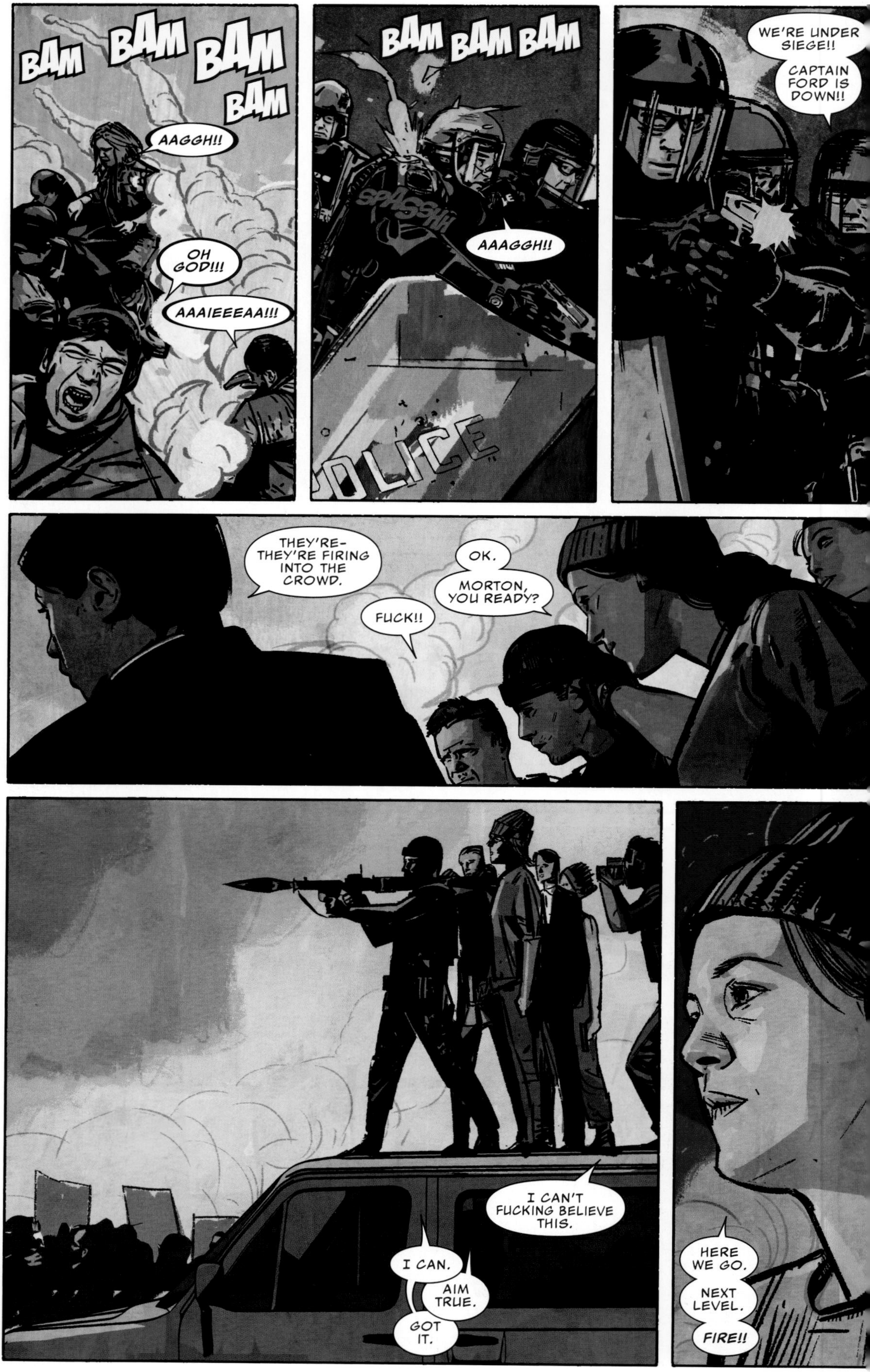
BAM BAM BAM BAM
AAGGH!!
OH GOD!!!
AAAIEEEAA!!!
BAM BAM BAM
SPASSHH
AAAGGH!!
WE'RE UNDER SIEGE!!
CAPTAIN FORD IS DOWN!!
THEY'RE-- THEY'RE FIRING INTO THE CROWD.
FUCK!!
OK.
MORTON, YOU READY?
I CAN'T FUCKING BELIEVE THIS.
I CAN.
AIM TRUE.
GOT IT.
HERE WE GO.
NEXT LEVEL.
FIRE!!

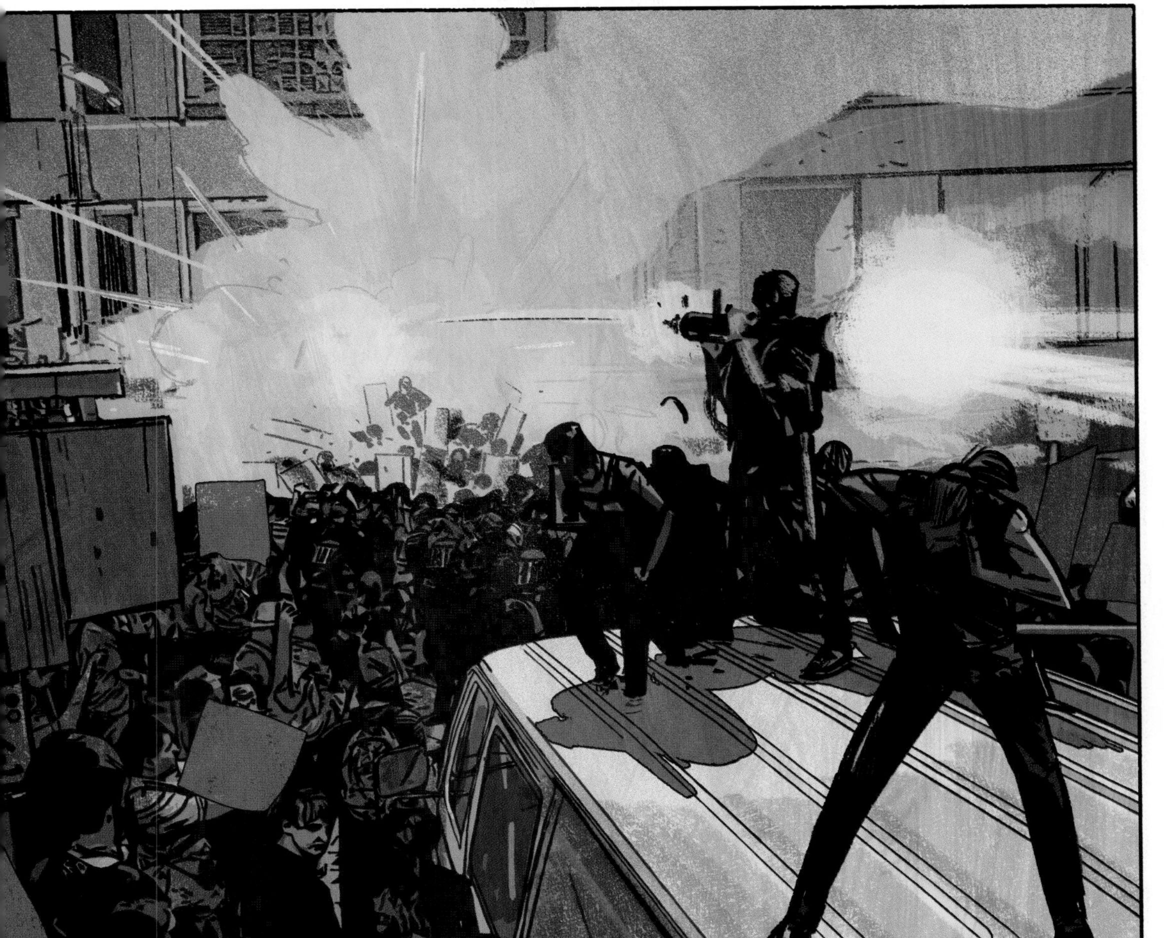

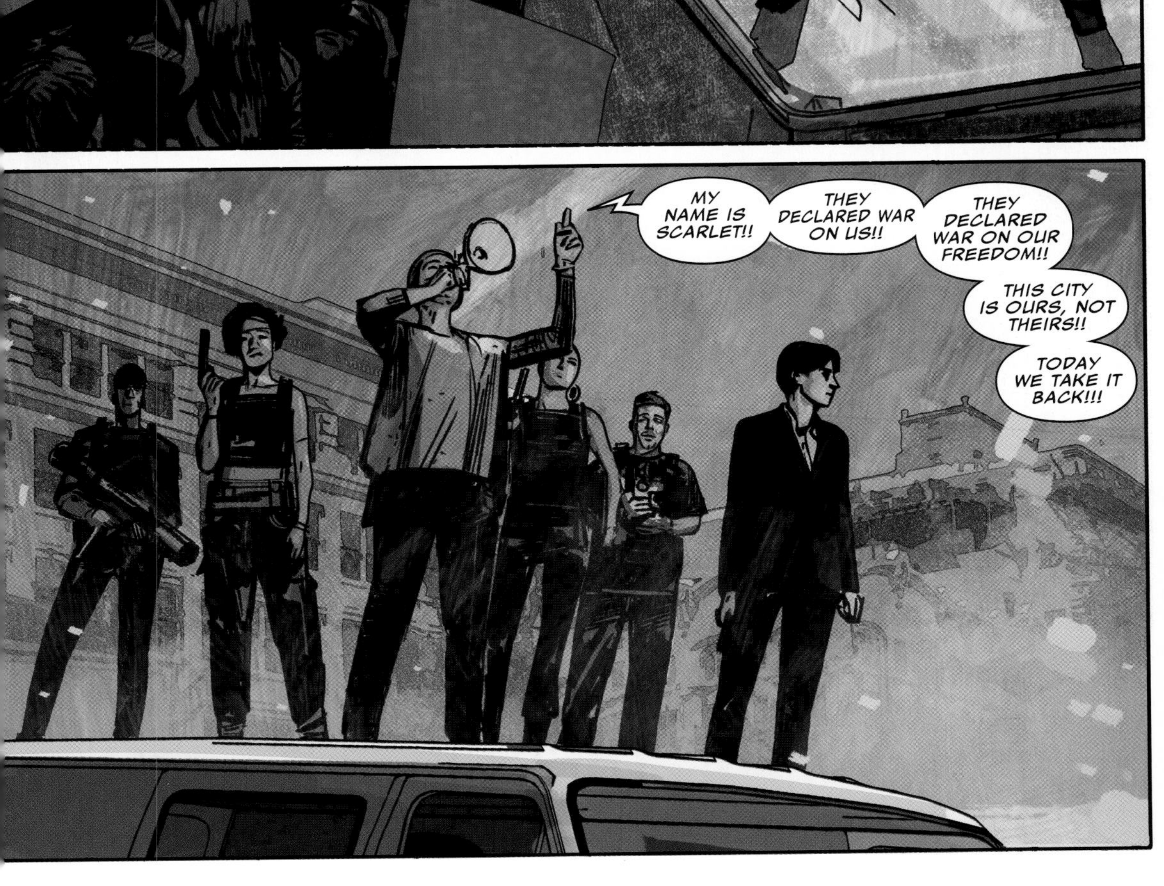

MY NAME IS SCARLET!!
THEY DECLARED WAR ON US!!
THEY DECLARED WAR ON OUR FREEDOM!!
THIS CITY IS OURS, NOT THEIRS!!
TODAY WE TAKE IT BACK!!!

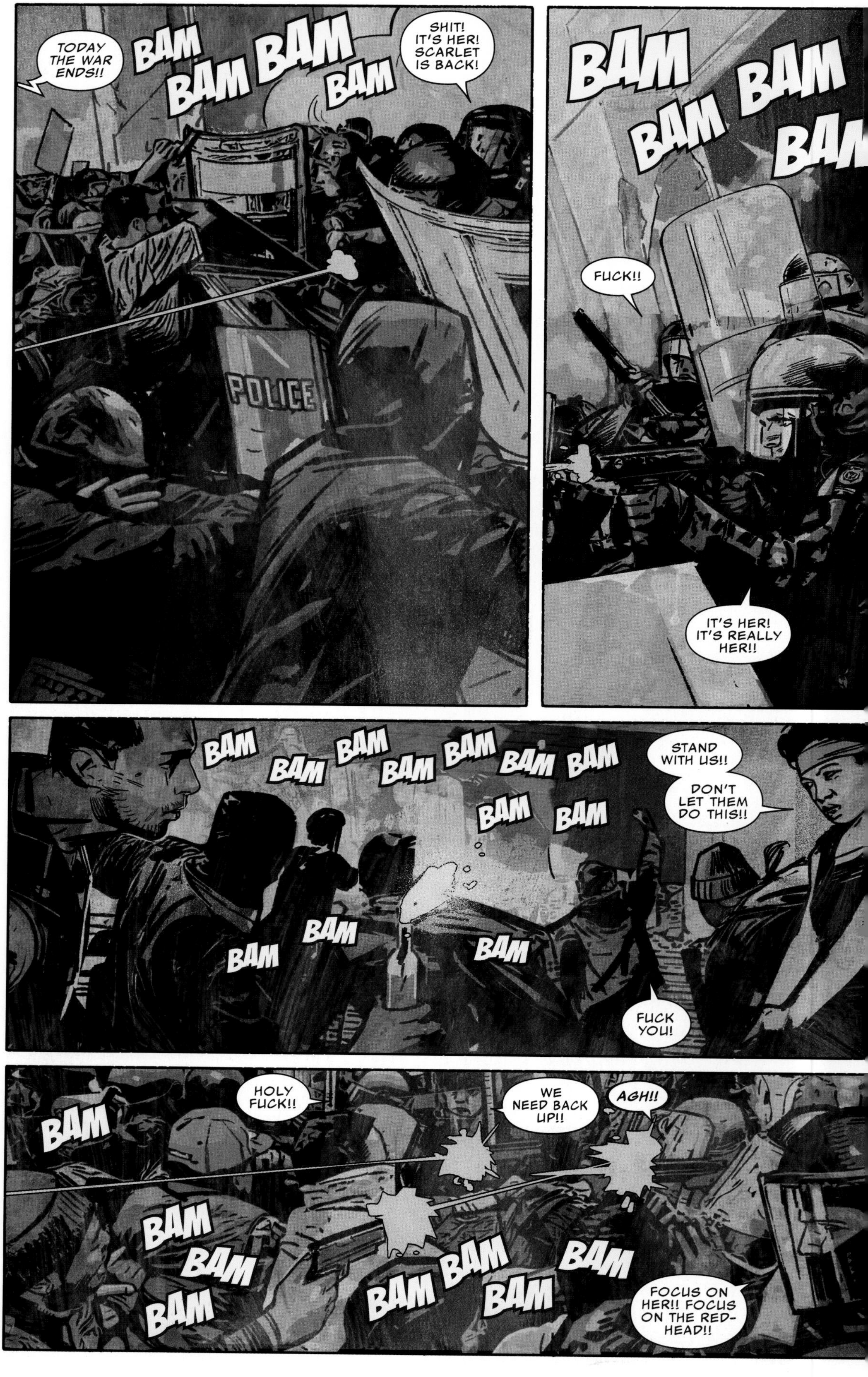
TODAY THE WAR ENDS!!
BAM
BAM BAM
BAM
SHIT! IT'S HER! SCARLET IS BACK!
POLICE
BAM
BAM BAM
BAM
FUCK!!
IT'S HER! IT'S REALLY HER!!
BAM BAM BAM BAM BAM BAM BAM BAM BAM
STAND WITH US!!
DON'T LET THEM DO THIS!!
BAM BAM BAM
FUCK YOU!
BAM
HOLY FUCK!!
WE NEED BACK UP!!
AGH!!
BAM BAM BAM
BAM BAM BAM BAM
FOCUS ON HER!! FOCUS ON THE RED-HEAD!!

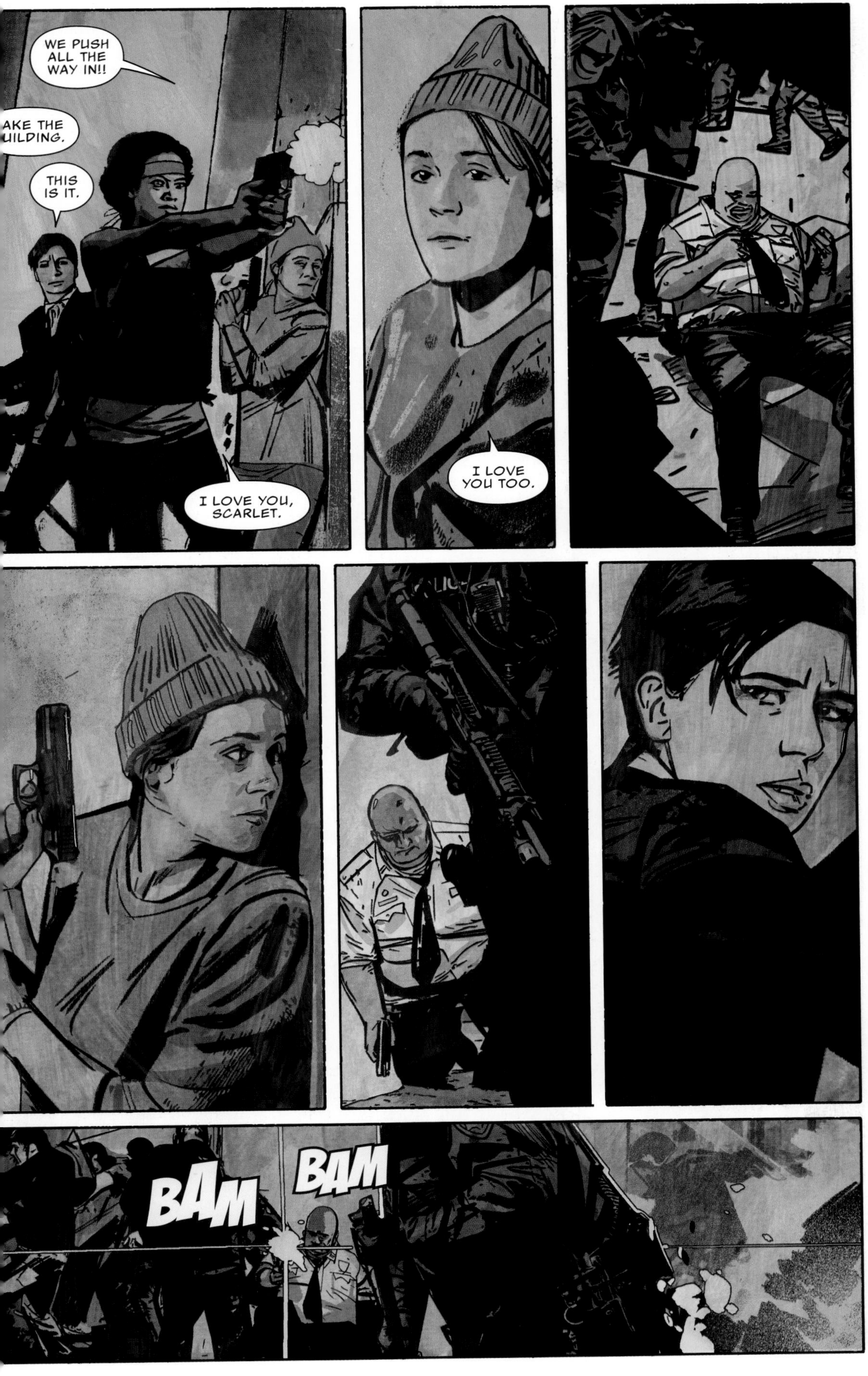
WE PUSH ALL THE WAY IN!!
AKE THE UILDING.
THIS IS IT.
I LOVE YOU, SCARLET.
I LOVE YOU TOO.
BAM
BAM

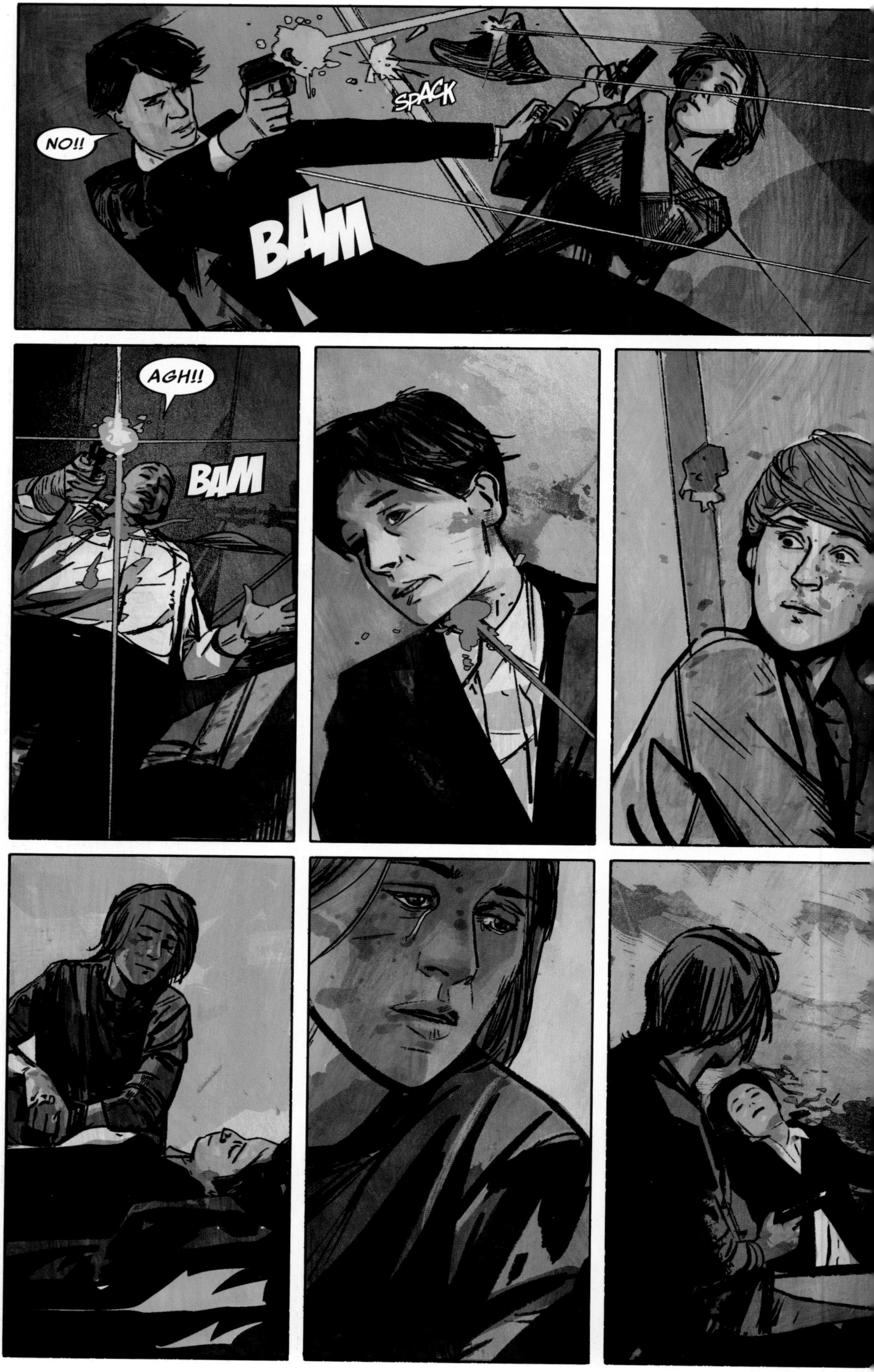
NO!!
SPACK
BAM
AGH!!
BAM

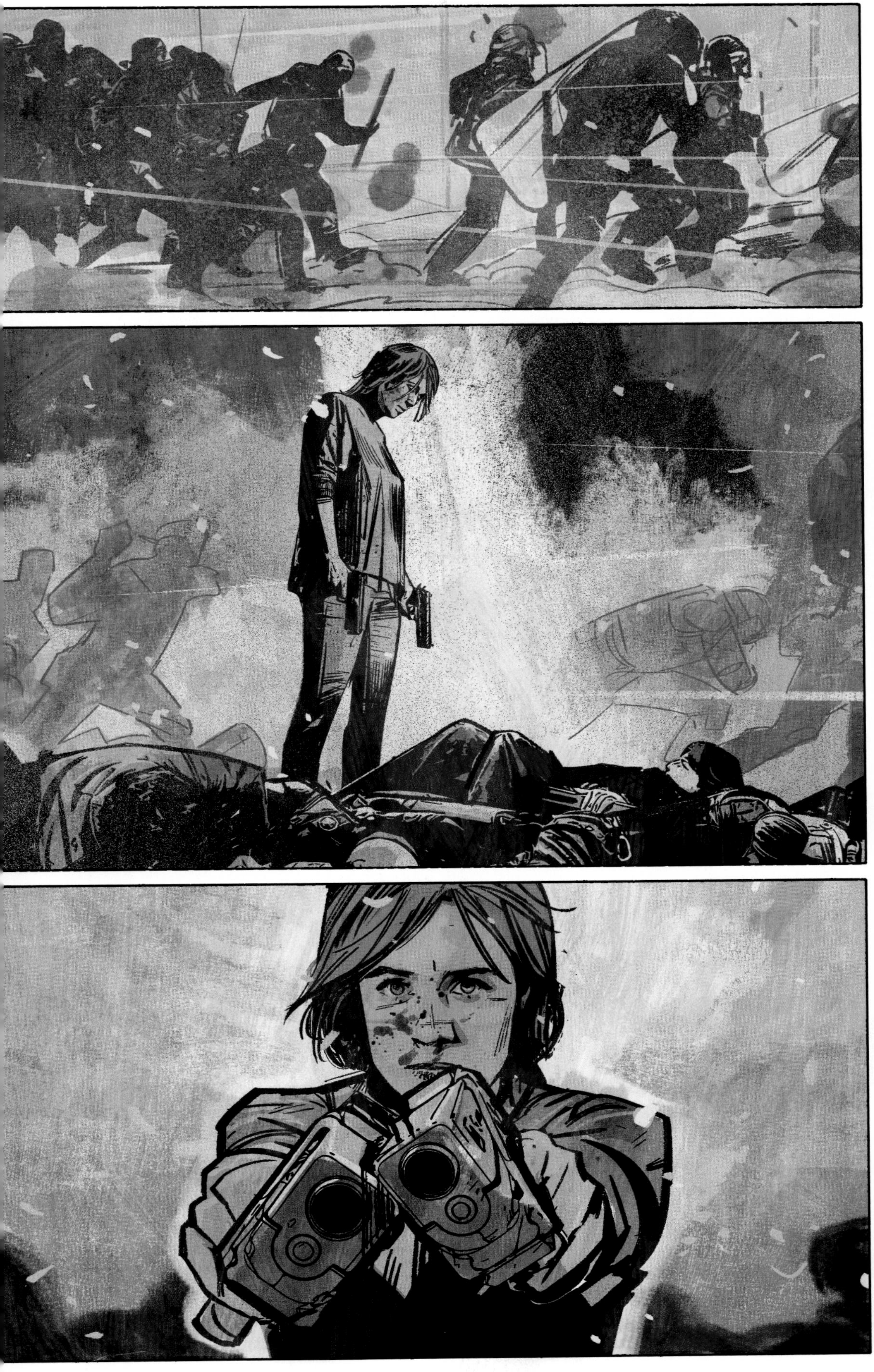

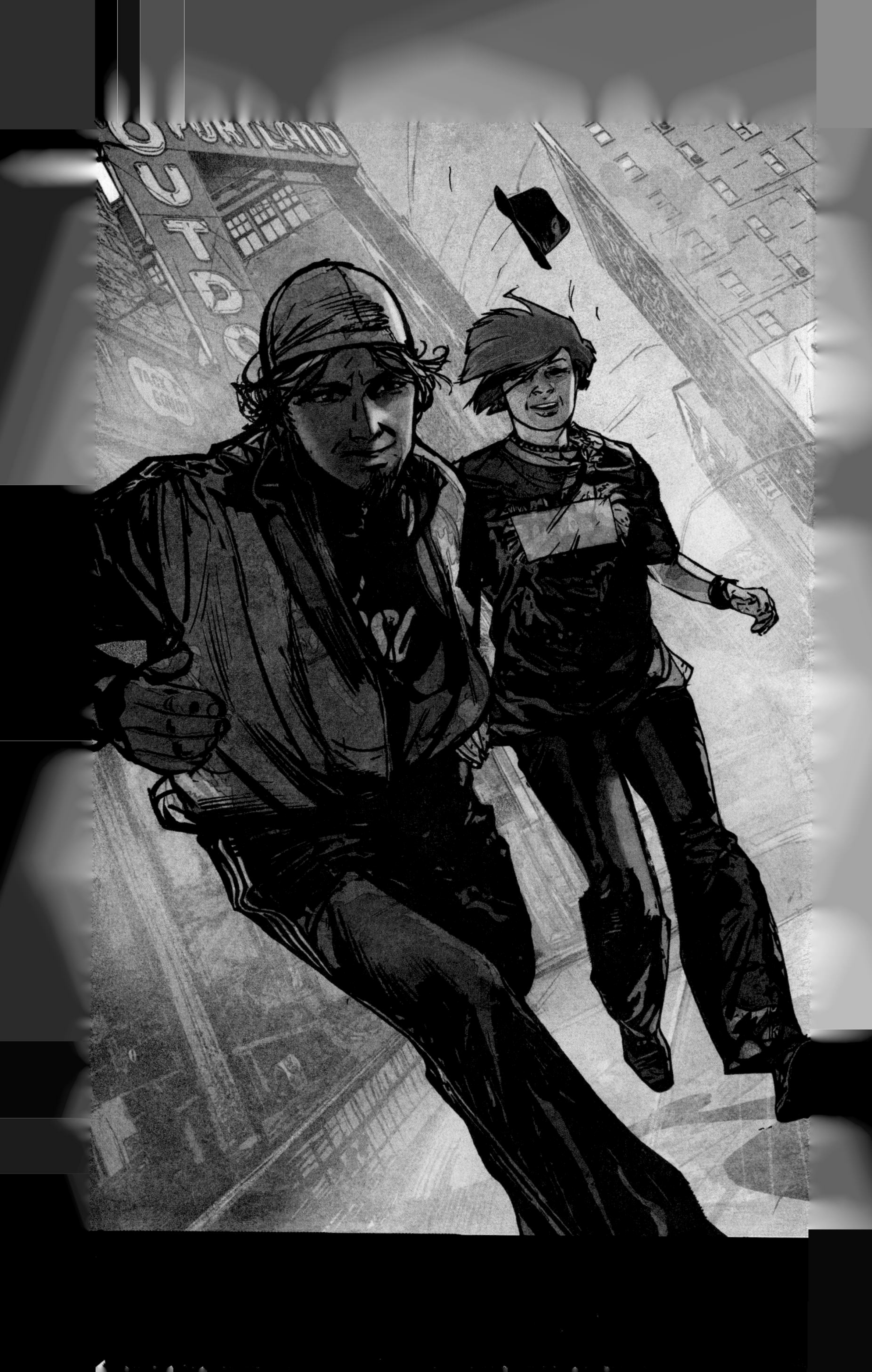

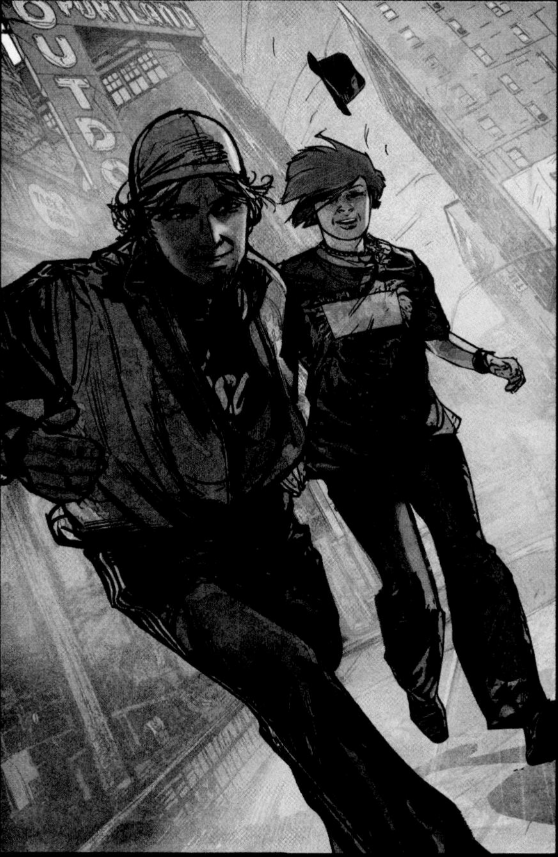
PORTLAND

TO BE CONTINUED... NEXT YEAR

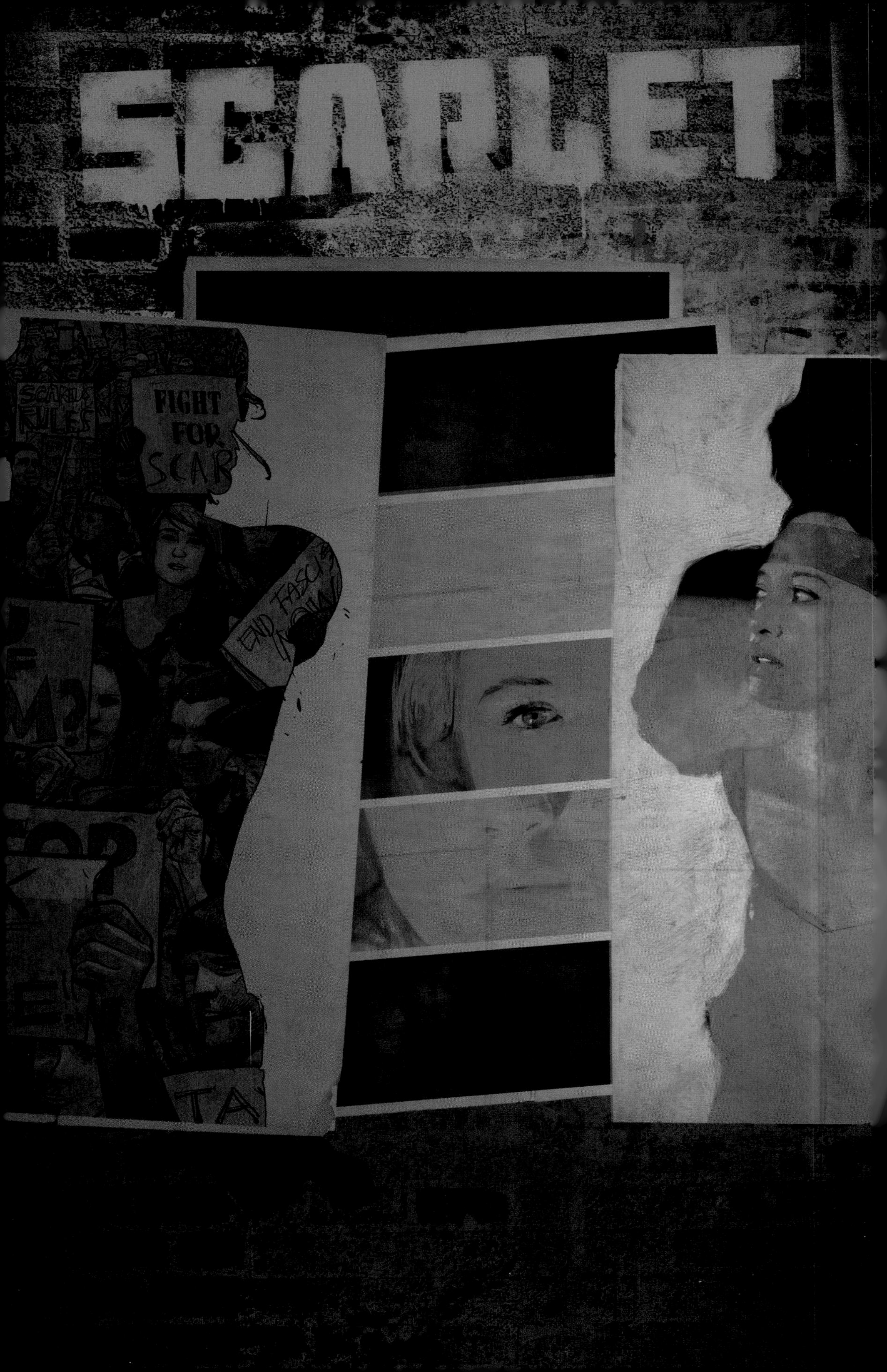
SCARLET
FIGHT FOR SCAR

# COVER GALLERY

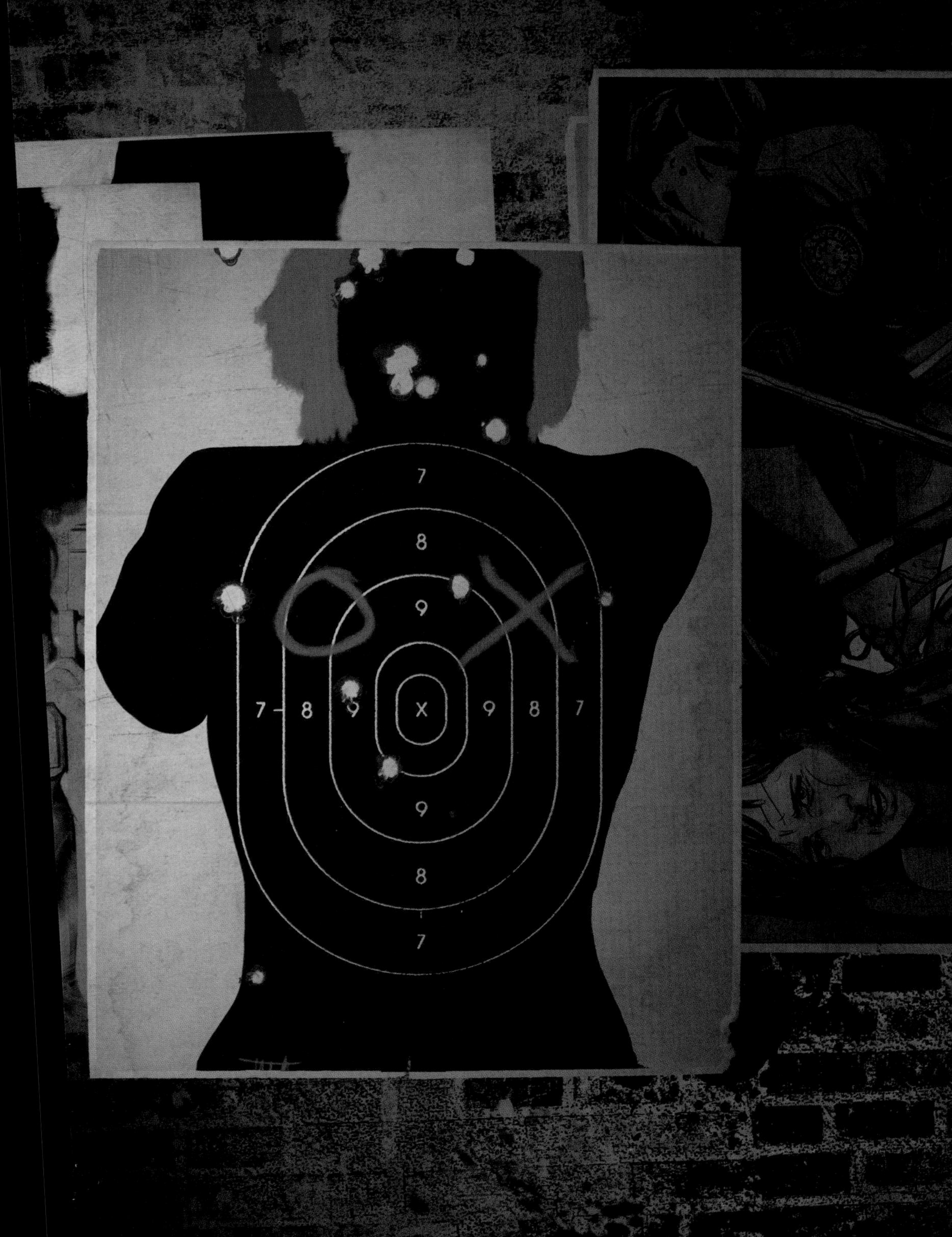

7
8
9
7 8 9 X 9 8 7
9
8
7

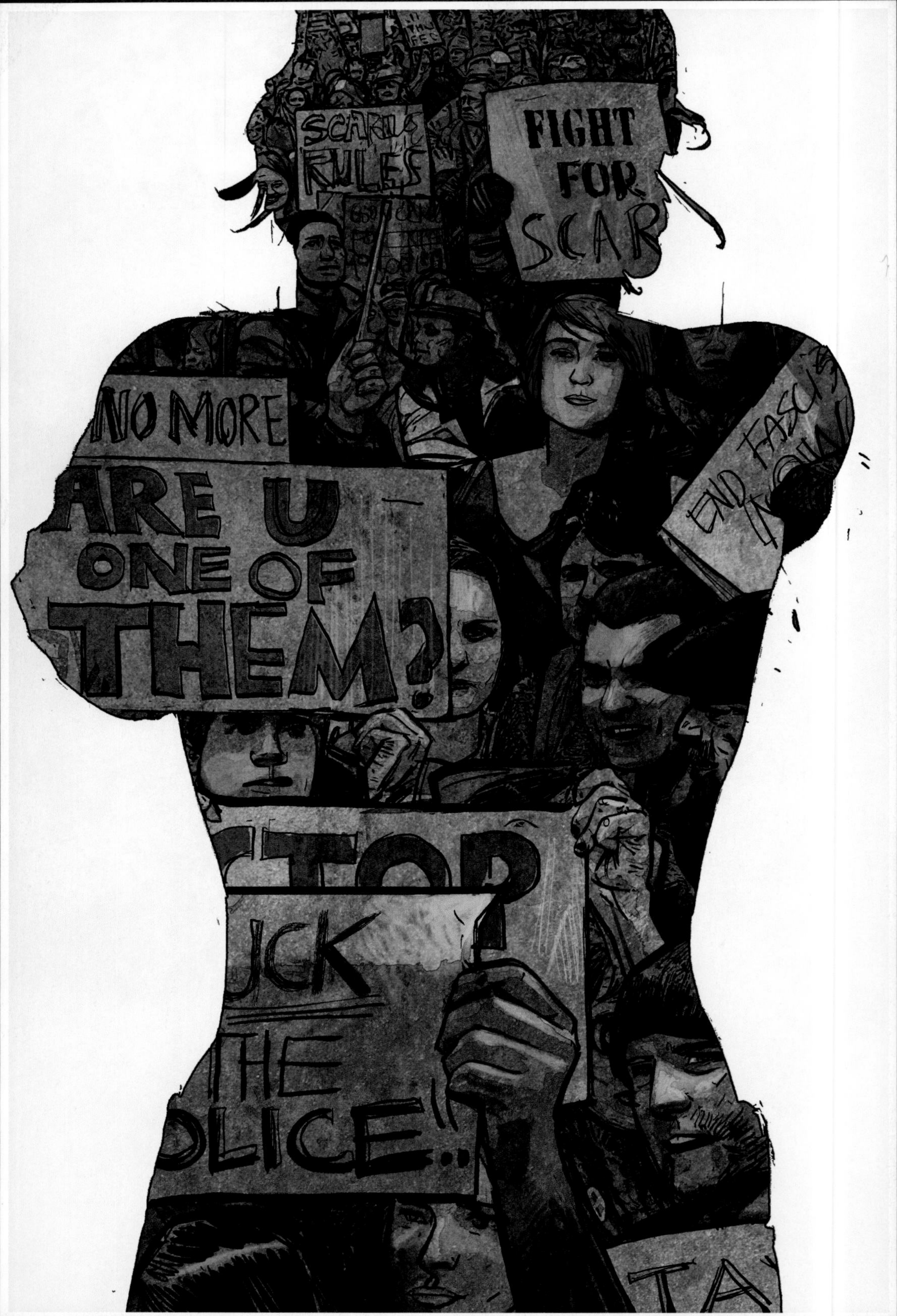
RULES
FIGHT FOR SCAR
NO MORE
ARE U ONE OF THEM?
THE

**SCARLET #6** BY **ALEX MALEEV**

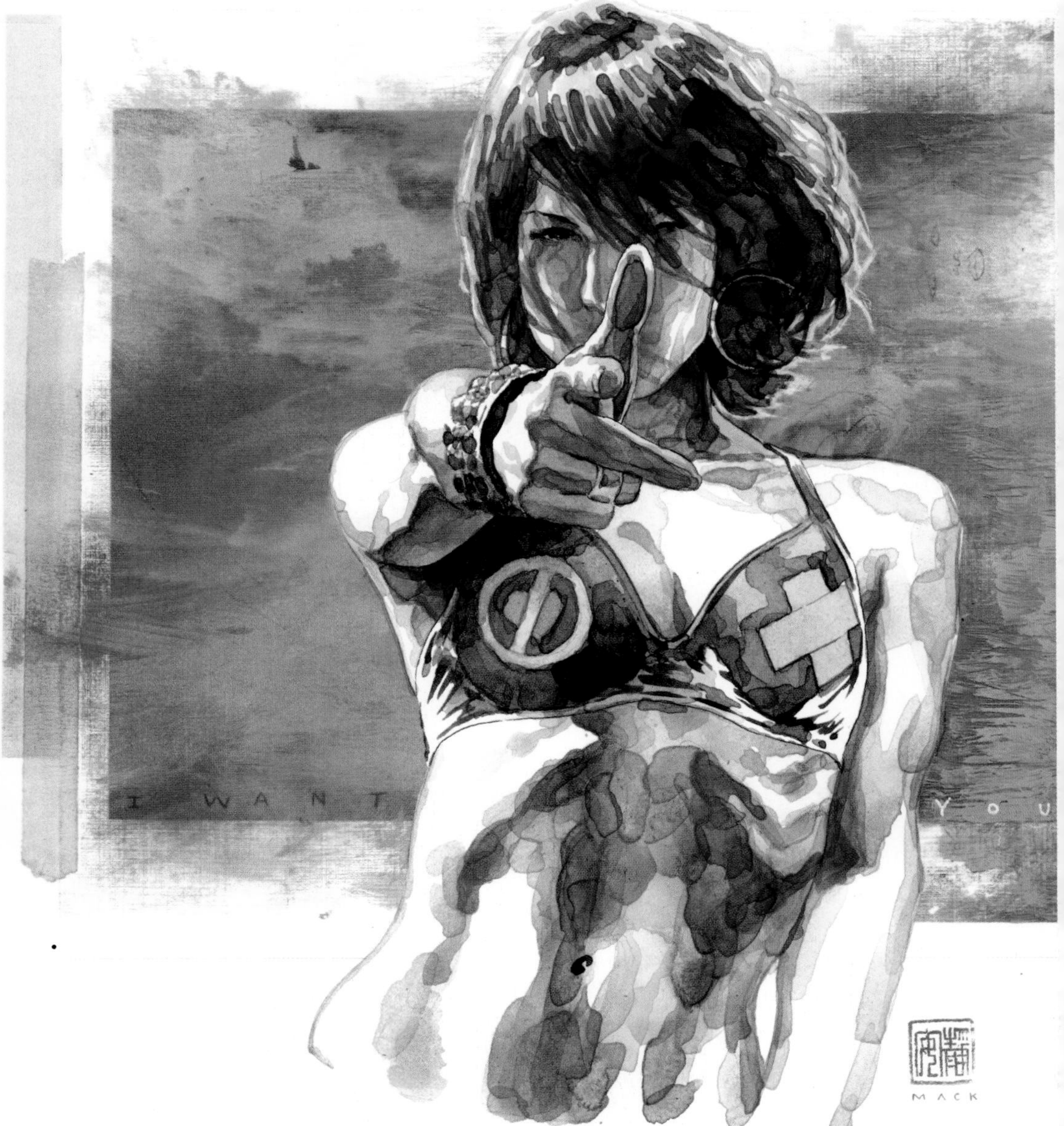
I WANT
YOU
MACK

BY DAVI

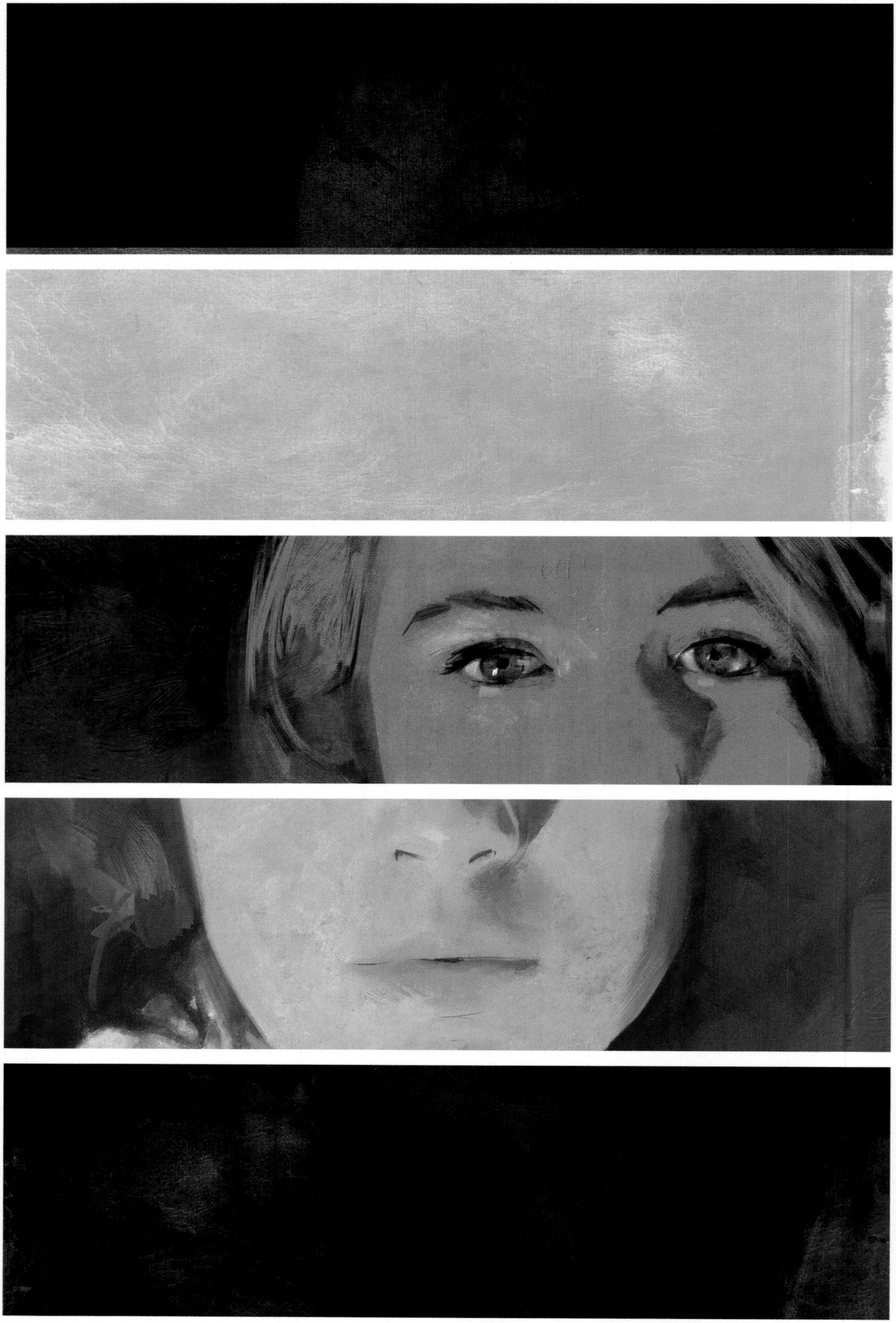

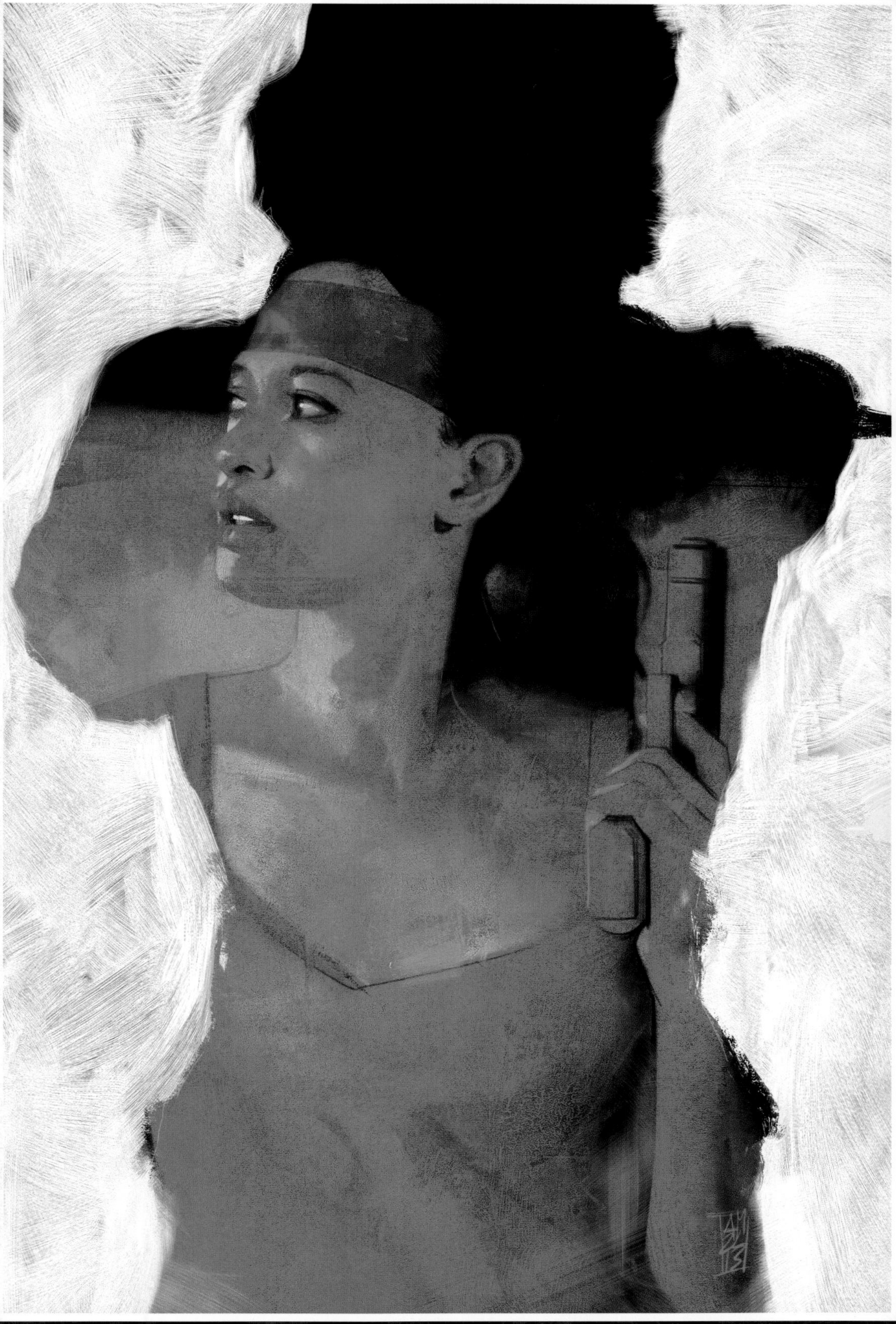

SCARLET #8 ALEX MALEEV

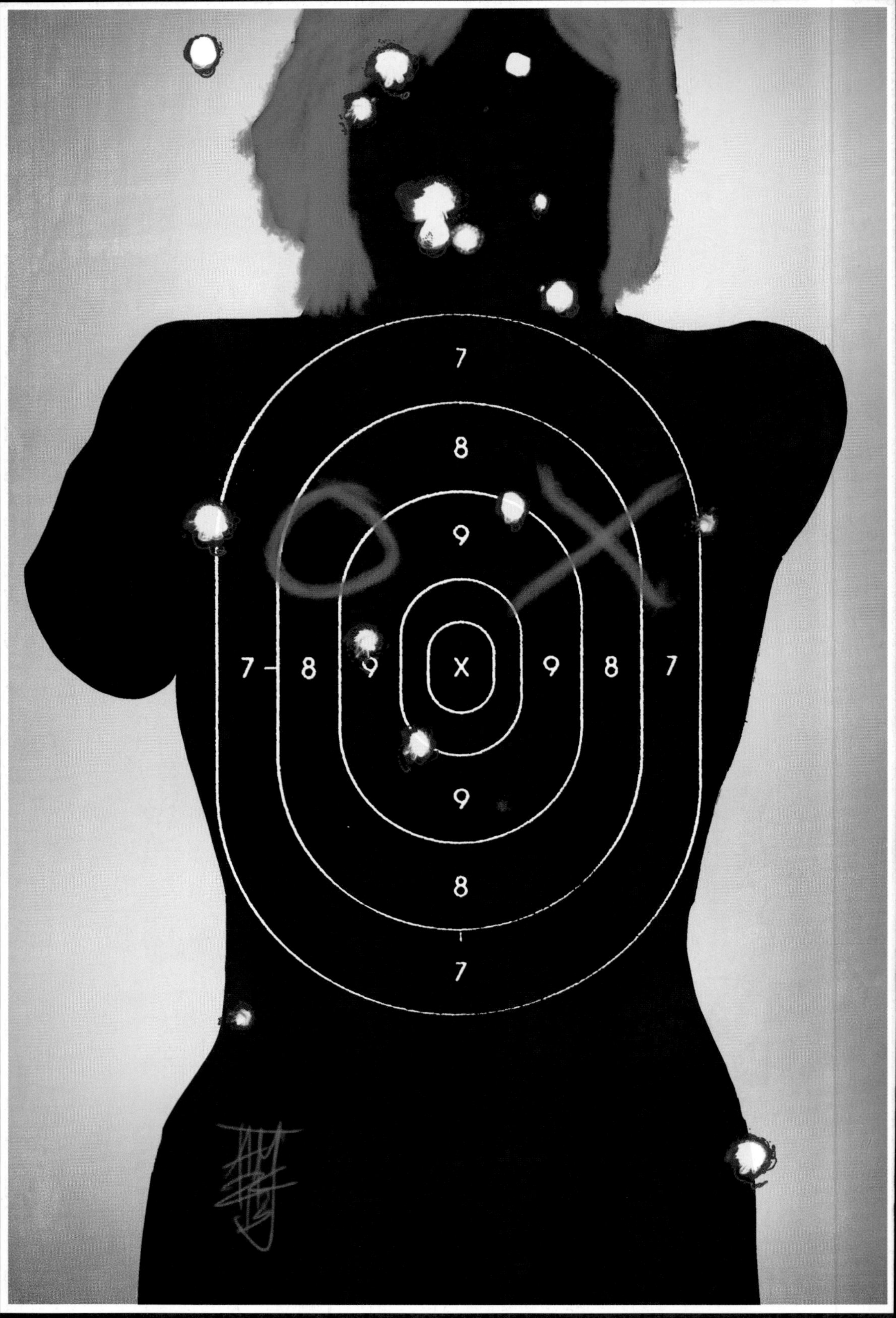
7
8
9
7
8
9
X
9
8
7
9
8
7

SCARLET #9 BY ALEX MALEEV

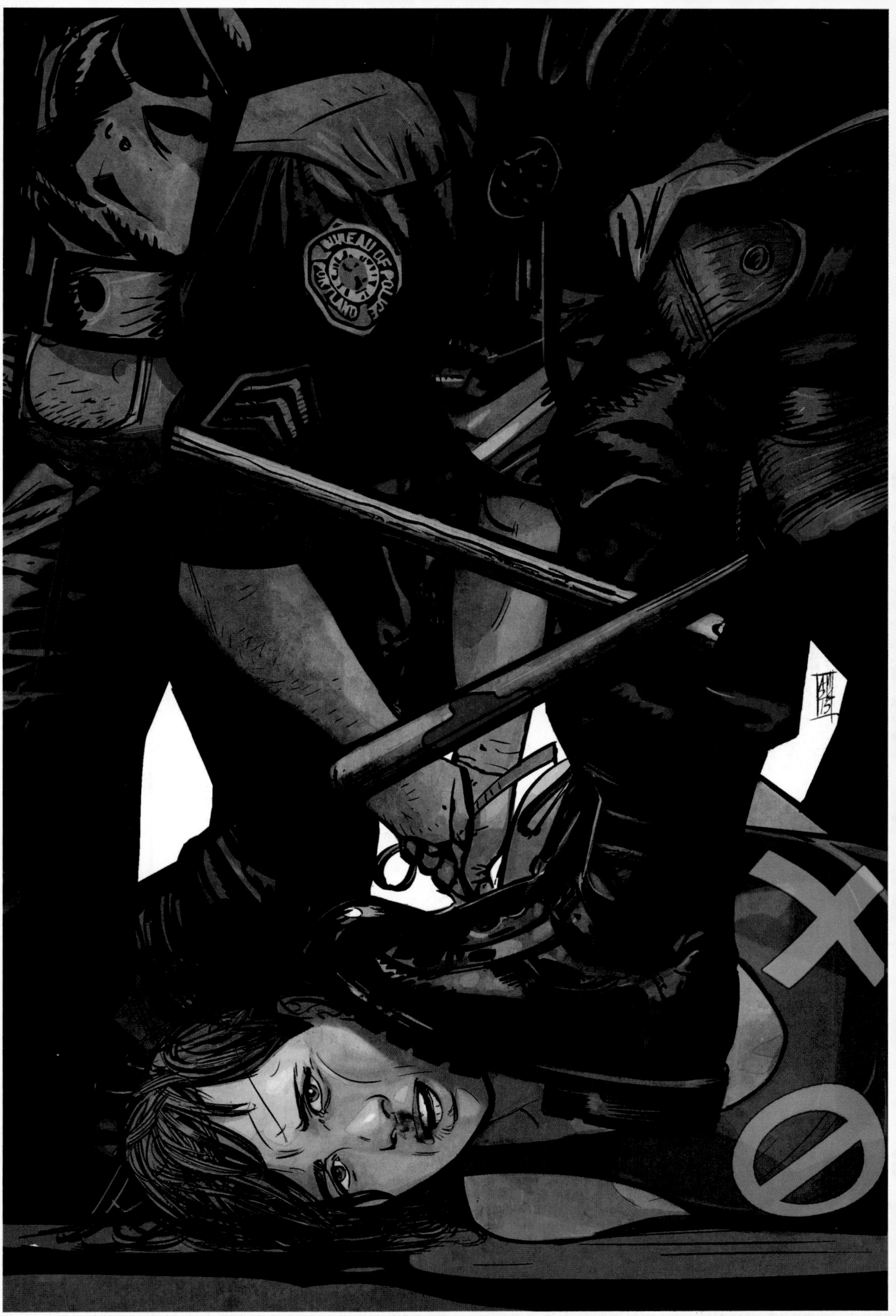

**BOOK TWO**
**ISSUE 10 SCRIPT**

# PAGE 1 —

Widescreen, quiet panels.

1- Int. Police academy/ firing range - DAY

A young, 20, angela Going, pony tail, is firing her service revolver right at us. She is a police cadet. Training. Working on her aim and gunmanship. She is wearing the big cans.

Like every flashback into Scarlet's world of characters lets give Going a new art style. Maybe something VERY stark. Shapes of black and white.

> **SPX:** *BAM BAM*

2- Going blasts the shit out of her target.

> **SPX:** *BAM BAM BAM*

3- Same as one but tighter. She fires well.

> **SPX:** *BAM BAM*

4- Going's p.o.v. The target is bullet ridden. Smolder. Great shot.

5- Going's proud of herself as takes off the glasses and cans.

> **SERGEANT RICK**
> *Cadet Going!*
> **GOING**
> *Yeah?*

6- Going turns to see a fat asshole of a desk sergeant waving her over to his office from down the hall. Other cadets mill about.

> **SERGEANT RICK**
> *Can I see you?*
> **GOING**
> *Yes, Sergeant.*

# PAGE 2 —

1- Int. Sergeant's office

His office is a small, shitty, very cluttered office. Fishing pictures and bowling trophies. Piles of paperwork surround his outdated computer.

She is coming into the office as he closes the door. He is checking her ass out as he does. She does not notice.

> **GOING**
> *You asked for me, sir?*
> **SERGEANT RICK**
> *Great scores, Angela.*
> **GOING**
> *Oh. Thank you sir.*
> **SERGEANT RICK**
> *Really impressive.*

2- Going has sat down. Rick sits at the edge on his desk right in her air space.

> **SERGEANT RICK**
> *So... Why do you want to be a cop, Angela?*
> **GOING**

3- Rick sits up and points at her. Knowing there is more.. Asking the real question.

**SERGEANT RICK**
*No, why do you want to be a cop?*

4- Angle on Going. Rick is walking behind her. She doesn't know why? She is kind of looking over her shoulder as she answers the question honestly

**GOING**
*Honestly, to protect and serve.*
*For real.*
*(Is it a trick question or-?)*

5- Same. Rick puts his hands on her shoulders. To massage her. She is instantly not happy but does not know what to do. This face is off panel. This is all on her.

**SERGEANT RICK**
*A purist. Nice.*
*You're going to do well, Cadet.*

**GOING**
*Um. Thank you, sir.*

6- Same. He is massaging her without speaking. She is officially creeped the fuck out. She has no idea what to do. Almost looking at us for help.

7- Closer. His hands start sliding down a little. Not to her boobs but he is seconds away from Going for it.

**GOING (CONT'D)**
*Sir?*

# PAGE 3 —

1- Same. Rick is about to go for it. Going grabs his hands JUST before he can.

**GOING (CONT'D)**
*Excuse me!*

**SERGEANT RICK**
*Oh, come on.*

2- Wide of the cluttered office. Going gets up to leave. Scrambling to her feet. He is almost laughing. He is playing a game. She is not.

**GOING**
*Jesus!*

**SERGEANT RICK**
*Come on! Where're you going?*

3- He presses Going against the door before she can open it.

**GOING**
*Why? Ah!*
*Why are you-?*

**SERGEANT RICK**
*It's the uniform. It gets me every time.*

4- Going panics and pushes him off.

**GOING**
*Stop it!*

**SERGEANT RICK**
*Oh! Ha!*

5- Rick grabs Going's wrists and pins her against the door. She is horrified. Looking into his smiling face.

**GOING**
*Agh!*

**SERGEANT RICK**
*I can't help it.*
*I love a lady in training.*

6- Closer. He tries to kiss her. Her lips are pursed and her face turned towards us. His tongue sticks out just a little. It's awful. We can imagine the stale coffee smell.

**SERGEANT RICK**
    *(whisper)*
    *I didn't know it til I got assigned here.*
    *But I love it. Young cadets.*
    *All eager.*
    *Are you eager?*

# PAGE 4 —

1- Wider. In a blind rage and panic. Going knees him in the balls as hard as she can. He keels over.

    **SPX:** *FUMP*

    **GOING**
    *Fuck you!*

    **SERGEANT RICK**
    *Agh!*

2- Frazzled, Going turns to storm out and grabs the doorknob. Not turning back. Just trying to leave. Rick is hunched over.

    **GOING**
    *God damn it!*

3- Rick reaches out and grabs Going by her pony tail just before she leaves. She is shocked. This is pain.

    **SERGEANT RICK**
    *Fucker!*

    **GOING**
    *Agh!*

4- Rick pulls her by her hair and back into him. She's terrified and confused. He's down right pissed. Sweating from the hit to the balls.

    **SERGEANT RICK**
    *Are you out of your mind??*
    *Tease me all fucking day!*

    **GOING**
    *I didn't!!*

5- Rick whips her around and throws her right into her desk. On her stomach. Stuff goes flying off his desk and right for us. He clearly is Going to have his way with her. She is saucer eyed. In shock.

    **SPX:** *CRRAASSHH*

    **GOING**
    *Aaigh!*

# PAGE 5 —

1- From behind Rick, Going swings around and punches him in the face with the back of her fist. Sloppy punch but it connects. She fights back.

    **SPX:** *WHACKKK*

    **GOING**
    *Fuck you!!*

2- Rick stumbles over the chair as Going storms out.

    **SERGEANT RICK**
    *Fuck!*

    **SPX:** *CRRAASSHH*

3- Int. Police academy Hallway
People see her run out. She's clearly crying even though she's run away from us.

4- Int. Captain's office
Cut to Going sitting there. It's the next day. A gash under her eye. She is pissed.

    **CAPTAIN HELFER**
    *Obviously, we are horrified by what happened.*

### GOING
*Thank you, Captain.*

### CAPTAIN HELFER
*What are your plans?*

### GOING
*My plans?*

### CAPTAIN HELFER
*How do you plan on handling this?*

### GOING
*Um, I'm here to press charges.*
*Was that not clear?*

## PAGE 6 —

1- Over Going's shoulder, she is in the police captain's office. Thing Ed Asner. Old cherub of a man. A lifetime of accomplishment on his walls.

### CAPTAIN HELFER
*Well, I understand the need to but...*
*(And we're just talking...)*
*But what if we handle it internally?*

2- Going is confused and not happy with what he is almost about to say.

### GOING
*I'm sorry?*

3- Similar to one. He treads lightly.

### CAPTAIN HELFER
*If you press charges it becomes a whole... thing.*
*It becomes news, maybe.*
*A slow news day and KOIN6 will be all over us.*
*And it's his word against yours.*

4- Going is getting really upset but trying to hold it together.

### GOING
*Sir, he tried to rape me.*

5- The captain is gentle. Trying keep it at a whisper.

### CAPTAIN HELFER
*He tried to kiss you.*
*Things got out of hand.*

6- Same as 4.

### GOING
*Against my will.*

## PAGE 7 —

1- Over Going's shoulder, The captain sits back and holds up his hands in mock surrender.

### CAPTAIN HELFER
*And you let him have it but good, from what I hear.*
*Now, he's not going to press assault charges. I've seen to that-*

### GOING
*He's not-?*

2 –

### CAPTAIN HELFER
*All I am asking is that instead of putting it ON THE BOOKS and making us ALL look bad, what if we punish him... internally?*
*He'll write a letter of apology.*

3- Going is stunned...

### GOING
*A letter?*

4- The captain tries to keep it cool.

**CAPTAIN HELFER**
*Not enough?*

5- Going is getting pissed. She's thinking about leaving.

**GOING**
*He should be fired.*
*And arrested.*

# PAGE 8 —

1- The captain in negotiating...

**CAPTAIN HELFER**
*What if he is fined, gets some therapy and gets reassigned?*
*You'll never see him again.*
*And you- you'll get to pick your assignment.*
*EVERYONE is taken care of.*

2- Going is being seduced by this but...

**GOING**
*Not if he does it again.*

3 The captain sits forward. Eager to land this. He feels he could.

**CAPTAIN HELFER**
*Believe me, he will learn his lesson.*
*You think I want this bullshit in my life?*
*And think of all the good you can do as a... detective.*

4- Going is taking the bait and she knows it. He is buying her silence. She's Going to go for it and she's already torn.

**GOING**
*Detective.*

**CAPTAIN HELFER**
*We'll have to go through some channels but the department favors kindly to playing ball.*

5- Int. Scarlet's hideout- night
Going, today, after the events of last issue. Staring at us. In Scarlet art style. So fucking tired. Haunted. Looking out a window. Sunlight on her face.

**CAPTAIN HELFER NARRATION**
*It really is the best solution for everyone.*

# PAGE 9 —

1- Ext. Warehouse- day
Same but now we're looking through what we will reveal to be a warehouse the window out to Going looking out to...

2- Wide shot of the warehouse and Going staring past us sadly from out the window. Sunny outside. Lovely actually.

3- Big panel. Wider shot. The warehouse is safe and snug amongst a bunch of other abandoned buildings near the waterfront. Not even an ounce of a hint of trouble.
Scarlet and crew are safe and sound and right in the city.

4- Int. Room- Same
Going turns to see Scarlet, worse for wear, wearing her hair, coming in with two coffees.
We now see we are in someone's old office. Long abandoned. A desk and a couple of chairs and the couch by the window that looks out to the Willamette river.
This was a fishing company. No one has been here so they took it over or Scarlet bought it and they keep it on the down low.

**SCARLET**
*Coffee.*

**GOING**
*Oh! Scarlet....*

**SCARLET**
*You still catching your breath?*

**GOING**
*I don't know what I am.*

**SCARLET**

*I know that feeling.*

**GOING**

*This is your hideout?*

5- Profile. Scarlet is holding out the coffee. Going is hesitant to take it for so many reasons.

This is such a surreal situation they find themselves in. Both of them. Scarlet is really happy it went this way but she doesn't want to push it.

**SCARLET**

*Today it is.*
*We move around a lot.*

**GOING**

*Am I free to go?*

**SCARLET**

*Free to go?*

# PAGE 10-11 —

Double page spread

1- Scarlet turns to us. Talking to us. Going sips her coffee. In her own thoughts.

**SCARLET NARRATION**

*She thinks we kidnapped her?*
*She doesn't get it yet.*
*She came with us of her own free will.*
*Now, I grant you, she may be in shock.*

2- Scarlet sips her coffee and admires Going who is lost in her own dark thoughts. Shaking a little.

**SCARLET NARRATION**

*Her partner was just murdered right in front of her by the most corrupt of corrupt cops.*
*We both almost died.*
*Together.*
*Honestly, I thought that was it for me. I really did.*

3- Going in holding her trembling hand. She is so overwhelmed.

**SCARLET NARRATION**

*Corrupt cops working right under her nose tried to murder her to get to me.*
*This whole thing might be even more traumatic for her than my "moment of clarity" was for me.*

4- Scarlet turns to us. Pretty optimistic.

**SCARLET NARRATION**

*That said: I'm not going to lie to you, I'm really excited she's here.*
*A little out of my skin excited.*
*I've admired her from afar and even when she was interrogating me I felt that we were more on the same page than she could probably admit to herself.*

5- Scarlet admits. This could be true too...

**SCARLET NARRATION**

*Or she was playing me like some*
*Master federal agent profile interrogator.*
*But I know what I felt.*
*And now she's here.*
*Half of my guys out there think she's here to fuck us over.*
*I keep waiting for one of them, Buddy, to storm in here and try to pop her.*

6- Scarlet shrugs. She really feels what she feels.

**SCARLET NARRATION**

*But I- I think she's here because it was, not to sound too melodramatic, it was inevitable.*
*We all found our way into this craziness in our own unique way.*
*This was her way in.*

7- Scarlet looks to her. Considering her. Going is lost in thought. Reliving the moment's of last issue.

8- Same.

**SCARLET NARRATION**

*I feel bad for her.*
*She has no way out now.*

**SCARLET**

*You're free to do whatever you want.*
*You're not kidnapped.*
*Do you think you're kidnapped?*

**GOING**

*I don't- no, I don't know.*

9- Scarlet sits down next to her. It just looks like two women enjoying coffee except for...

**SCARLET**

*I'm sorry this happened.*
*I know what it's like to have the rug of the universe pulled out from under you like this.*

**GOING**

*I know you do.*

**SCARLET**

*I honestly wouldn't wish it on anyone.*

10- Going looks right at us and says it so plainly. Like she's breaking up with her.

**GOING**

*I can't join you, Scarlet.*

# PAGE 12 —

1- Scarlet stands and offers her hand. Going doesn't take it.

**SCARLET**

*You can, actually.*

**GOING**

*I have a life.*

**SCARLET**

*You had a life.*
*I'm sorry, they took that from you. But again, I know what you're feeling now.*
*If you leave here, they're going to come for you.*
*I really think this is the safest place right now.*

2- Going looks at her trembling hand. Here is her only choice.

**GOING**

*Fuckers.*
*Fuck.*

3- Going looks at us and narrates.

**GOING NARRATION**

*I let it get to this.*
*I let it.*
*Every day I just- I ignore all these little lies.*
*I blow off these little shits- these corrupt fuckers.*

**GOING**

*I ignored it all.*
*I kept just pushing my way through all the shit because-*

4- Scarlet isn't looking at her but offers her own...

**SCARLET**

*Because you think it has to correct itself eventually.*
*It has to.*

5- Same as 3. Going knows the truth when she hears it...

**GOING**

*Yes.*

6- Same as 4.

**SCARLET**

*But it just gets worse.*

7- Going almost cries from the power of the truth.

**GOING**
> Yes.
> They killed my partner.
> He was an odd dude but he was one of the good ones.
> He pulled my ass out of the fire, once upon a time.
> Just like you did.

8- Brandon pops his head in. He is sincere in not wanting to interrupt but...

**BRANDON**
> Hey, sorry to interrupt...
> You want to be not surprised.

# PAGE 13 —

1- Int. Conference room

What was some fish company conference room is bow Scarlet's crew war room. Scarlet and Going come in from the next room. Scarlet's crew is there. Morton, buddy, frank, Brandon, Isis.

All of them giving Going a look. Not sure they can trust her. And Going feels it.

They are all armed. All tired. A real rebellion. Isis is on line with a lap top with a military grade protective cover/ signal blocker. She is typing as Brandon gestures for them to look at the computer.

On the far wall of this small shitty conference room is a flat screen for teleconferencing. She is putting the laptop image on the big screen for everyone to see.

On screen is the local news. Right outside city hall.

**SCARLET**
> What's going on, Isis?

**ISIS**
> Putting it on the big screen. Check it.

**TV ANCHOR**
> -massive crowd out here. Everyone waiting for an official update.
> But we know Scarlet Rue has escaped.
> We know there have been fatalities.
> We're getting word now that the press conference is about to begin.

2- On screen, active police captain Ford. The new police captain. Big guy, Brian Dennehy.

**POLICE CAPTAIN FORD**
> Terrorist Scarlet Rue has escaped police custody.

3- Angle on Scarlet, Isis and Going. Scarlet rolls her eye. Going is shocked by Isis' sarcasms.

**SCARLET**
> Terrorist?

**ISIS**
> Congrats, I guess.

**POLICE CAPTAIN FORD**
> Members of her cell have attacked police headquarters and assassinated decorated law enforcement official.

4- Same as 2.

**POLICE CAPTAIN FORD**
> Local police and FBI agents are down.
> We are waiting to inform the next of kin before we release the names of the fallen but we can tell you that FBI agent Angela Going has been kidnapped.
> If you see her please call 911 immediately.

5- Scarlet looks at Going as Going has the surreal experience of watching this...

**POLICE CAPTAIN FORD**
> We believe she is in great danger.
> If you see anyone resembling Scarlet Rue or see any suspicious activity,
> please do not engage them on your own.
> Call 911 immediately.
> And if you are in the crowd outside city hall and the downtown police departments, you need to disperse immediately.
> This is a final warning.
> We will not be taking questions at this time.

**SCARLET**
 *Wow.*

**GOING**
 *Wow.*

6- Scarlet turns to her. Sincere. Arms folded. Going is more stunned by...

**SCARLET**
 *I meant what I said: You can go if you want.*
 *Obviously, we won't be here if you come back.*

**GOING**
 *They're just lying!!*

7- Brandon is playing with a new high tech small video camera as Scarlet walks over and gestures to it.

**BRANDON**
 *It's kind of what they do.*

**SCARLET**
 *You know what we've found is a good antidote for that?*

# PAGE 14-15 —

Double page spread

1- Buddy, with Morton, is so agitated. She always is.

**BUDDY**
 *We're really going to trust her??*

2- Scarlet stands with Going.

**SCARLET**
 *Yes, Buddy, we are.*

3- Buddy gestures almost comically. She is so angry.

**BUDDY**
 *Don't use my name in front of her!! Come on!*

**MORTON**
 *Settle.*

4- Same as 4.

**SCARLET**
 *She knows your name... she knows all our names.*

5- Buddy gestures at Going and Scarlet approach. Buddy thinks she is the only sane one in the room.

**BUDDY**
 *Because she's been hunting us for weeks!! Hello?*

**SCARLET**
 *And now she's had a life-altering experience.*
 *Remember your life-altering experience that led you here?*
 *You all remember yours?*
 *How about we let her have hers.*

6- Morton steps up and shakes Going's hand. Going is weirded out. Scarlet is trying to settle Buddy down.
Going is not sure what to do or what is about to happen to her.

**MORTON**
 *Hey, I'm Morton.*
 *Sorry we had to meet under these circumstances.*

**BUDDY**
 *She's one of them.*

**SCARLET**
 *Not all cops are bad, Buddy.*
 *Just the bad ones.*

7- Buddy walks/ storms out of the room. Scarlet turns to Going.

**BUDDY**
 *It's your show, Scarlet.*
 *But this is- this is- ugh!!*

**SCARLET**
*You want to be heard? Tell the truth.*
*I'm telling you, it feels so good.*

8- Going looks at the little camera Brandon puts on the table in front of her.

9- Wide of the room. They are watching her thinking about it. What is she going to do?

10- Going looks right at us. This is her cross road.

**GOING**
*Hi.*
*Hello.*
*My name is Angela Going.*
*I am an FBI agent assigned to the Scarlet Rue case.*
*There have been reports about me on the news and I want to –*
*I want to-*

# PAGE 16-17 —

Double page spread

Four equal sized screen panels on left giving way to a huge protest panel that takes up the rest of the spread.

1- Screen. Going talks to us. A you tube viral video. She is so nervous but so serious.

**GOING**
*I want to tell you what really happened.*
*While in my custody, there were numerous flagrant attempts on Scarlet Rue's life by members of the Portland Police department...*
*Tempers are one thing but this was a concerted effort by law enforcement to take the law into their own hands.*
*All of which came to a head when, as we escorting Scarlet from the premises so she could face a fair trial- what could only be described as an assassination squad- confronted me and my partner...*

2- Screen. Going talks to us. A you tube viral video. She is so nervous but so serious.

**GOING**
*This assassination squad, that consisted of numerous men who identified themselves to me as police officers, shot and killed my partner Federal agent Daemonakos.*
*Police purposefully shot and killed a federal agent.*
*And they would have killed me if not for the intervention of Scarlet's people.*

3- Screen. Going talks to us. A you tube viral video. She is so nervous but so serious.. Less with every second.

**GOING (CONT'D)**
*This is fact.*
*I was witness to all of this myself.*

4- Going talks to us. A you tube viral video. She is so nervous but so serious.. Less with every second.

**GOING**
*Scarlet's crew shot and killed the police officers but only after the officers had taken the law into their own hands.*
*I am only alive because of Scarlet.*
*After seeing what I have seen, I am now with Scarlet Rue and her crew.*

5- Ext. City hall- dusk

Huge panel. The entire spread. Outside is a madhouse.

A crowd as big as the city has ever seen. The protest from the waterfront has officially moved here and grown.

There are cops blocking the doorway in a row of Swat gear.

The signs. The chaos. The media. It is growing by the second. The story of the year is happening right inside.

It is a sea of chaos and she has created all of it.

In the crowd we see dozens of little screens watching the video. Everyone is seeing the video. It is spreading all over the world like wild fire.

**GOING (CONT'D)**
*Though I wrestle deeply with her actions and believe in the laws of our land with every fibre of my being...*
*The fact of the matter is... Scarlet is right.*
*Scarlet is right: If you wear a badge and betray the oath of that badge you are worse than any criminal.*
*Scarlet is right: if you buy into the blue cone of silence, you are a criminal.*
*The corruption in our government has risen to a place that cannot be allowed one second longer.*
*My life is in danger solely because I refuse to be part of it.*
*So, in the face of this I join Scarlet in her desire to rid all of our lives of this corruption.*
*I am not saying this under threat or duress.*

*I have been told I am free to leave but am actively choosing to join Scarlet until this war on corruption is over.*
*And make no mistake... We are at war.*
*We are in a bloody conflict.*
*To my fellow law enforcement officers on every level of government...*
*Your silence in the face of this is criminal.*
*Looking the other way- of which I myself am guilty of- is allowing this world to be so much less than what it should and could be.*
*People should feel safe.*
*People should feel protected.*
*They should feel so safe and protected that they don't even have to think about it.*
*Instead we have created a society of doubt and fear.*
*No more.*

# PAGE 18 —

1- Going is talking to us. Scarlet is behind her. Backing her up.

> **GOING**
> *I will stay silent no more.*
> *Join us in our fight.*
> *Join us before it is too late.*
> *I- I have sacrificed everything I have spent my entire life pursuing because of the choice I make today.*
> *I know this.*
> *But I have to.*

2- On screen. Going has a tear in her eye as she tries to hold it together.

> **GOING**
> *I cannot stand silently by one more second.*
> *I can't cry myself to sleep out of frustration one more time.*

3- Going in going to war and she knows it. She is tearing up.

> **GOING**
> *Mom, I love you.*
> *Dad, I love you.*
> *I am ok.*
> *Police Commissioner Ford, do the right thing.*
> *Do it.*
> *In the name of the laws of this land I publicly arrest you and your coconspirators.*
> *Surrender.*
> *If this escalates further... this is on you.*

4- Wide of the room. Going sits back and exhales as Brandon puts down the camera.
Everyone is stunned. That was so powerful. Everyone is shocked.

5- Buddy is stunned. Brandon and Morton are too.

> **BRANDON**
> *Jeez.*

> **BUDDY**
> *That was... really good.*

5- Going stands up. Wobbly. Scarlet and Going are face to face.

> **SCARLET**
> *Are you ok?*

> **GOING**
> *No.*

6- Going hugs her. She has to. Scarlet takes the hug. Everyone watches.

# PAGE 19 —

1- They are both tearing up in the embrace. This is crazy emotional and it comes out of nowhere.

2- Scarlet and Going look at each other. Scarlet is not happy to be right about this.

> **GOING**
> *What happens next?*

> **SCARLET**
> *Well, history says: It gets super ugly.*

3- Ext. City hall- dusk

Huge panel. Outside is the growing madhouse.

A wall of swat with riot guard shields block the entrance.

A crowd as big as the city has ever seen.

There are cops blocking the doorway. The signs. The chaos. The media. It is growing by the second. The story of the year is happening right inside.

It is a sea of chaos and she has created all of it.

In the crowd we see dozens of little screens watching the going and Scarlet videos.

>       **POLICE CAPTAIN FORD**
>           *This gathering will disperse!!*
>           *This is your final warning!!*
>           *We will fire tear canisters and anti-protest ballasts into the crowd!!*

4- A wall of guards. Ford is barking into a megaphone.

>       **POLICE CAPTAIN FORD**
>           *You will be arrested!!*
>           *Go home now!!*

5- The crowd is angry and rushing and pushing. It is overheating fast and furious. Real rage. People are throwing things.

>       **MAN**
>           *Fuck you!!*

>       **WOMAN**
>           *You betrayed us!!*

>       **MAN**
>           *Arrest yourself!!*

6- The swat team on the city hall steps are being pelted by batteries and rocks and pipes. Overwhelmed.

>           **SPX:** *CRAASSH*

>           **SPX:** *SPAASSHH*

>       **SWAT**
>           *Fuck!!*

# PAGE 20 —

1- A college aged kid lights a Molotov cocktail. Holding it low as he does it. Others see him doing it and are stunned.

>       **WOMAN**
>           *Fuck you, pig!!*

>       **COLLEGE KID**
>           *Fucking asshole!!*

>       **MAN**
>           *Careful.*

>       **WOMAN**
>           *Holy shit, are you really going to-?*

2- The young man throws the Molotov cocktail into the air with all his might.

3- It arcs over the crowd. Tumbling. On fire.

4- And crashes right into the shields of the armed and armored swat force.
Ford is almost hit. He dives behind the shields but fire splashes all over all of them.

>           **SPX:** *SPAASSHH*

>       **SWAT**
>           *Agh!!*

5- Ford is on the bull horn. Snarls. He's had enough.

>       **POLICE CAPTAIN FORD**
>           *Ok, that's it!*
>           *Shut it down!!*

1- Wide. Multiple Tear gas launches into the crowd. People are choking and falling over each other. It's crazy panic in the streets.

> **WOMAN**
>> *Agh!*

> **TEEN**
>> *Why??*

> **MAN**
>> *They're going to kill us!!*

> **TEEN**
>> *My eyes!!*

2- An older man in the crowd, covers his mouth and fires a pistol at the swat team.

> **SPX:** *BAM BAM BAM*

> **MAN**
>> *You are under arrest!!*

3- The bullets deflect on the shield but the swat team line is freaked out and fucking pissed.

> **SPX:** *SPICK SPACK*

> **SWAT**
>> *Fuck!! We have open gun fire!!*

> **SWAT**
>> *We need crowd control suppression fire!!*

> **SWAT**
>> *Suppression fire?? Fuckers are firing on us!!*

> **SWAT**
>> *We're at fucking war!!*

4- One of the swat members pulls his semi automatic and opens fire at us/ the crowd. The others are stunned.

> **SWAT**
>> *Fuckers!*

> **SWAT**
>> *What are you doing??*

> **SPX:** *BAM BAM BAM*

1- The crowd is being fired upon and tear gas is pouring all over them. A couple of innocent protestors are hit with bullets. Shoulders and legs. Blood spurts. People fall over each other.

> **SPX:** *BAM BAM BAM BAM*

> **WOMAN**
>> *Aaggh!!*

> **MAN**
>> *Oh god!!!*

> **WOMAN**
>> *Aaaieeeaa!!!*

2- Another Molotov cocktail hits the firing swat member. He gets tagged in the shoulder by fire and his gun drops as it fires.

> **SPX:** *BAM BAM BAM*

> **SPX:** *SPASSHH*

> **SWAT**
>> *Aaaggh!!*

3- Another couple of panicked swat members opens fire. Real bullets.

> **SWAT**
>> *We're under siege!!*
>> *Captain Ford is down!!*

4- In what we will reveal is the back of the crowd, in the back of the madness and chaos, Scarlet has angry tears in her eyes as she barks her orders. Brandon is filming.

Scarlet's crew is wearing protective vests and are armed to the teeth. Thy are hear to fight.

> **BRANDON**
> *Fuck!!*

> **GOING**
> *They're- they're firing into the crowd.*

> **SCARLET**
> *Ok.*
> *Morton, you ready?*

5- Wider. Morton has a huge military bazooka on his shoulder and Buddy is helping him steady it. Going, Isis, Frank and the rest are there. Armed. On top of their van.

> **FRANK**
> *I can't fucking believe this.*

> **MORTON**
> *I can.*

> **SCARLET**
> *Aim true.*

> **MORTON**
> *Got it.*

6- Scarlet knows this is the next level shit.

> **SCARLET**
> *Here we go.*
> *Next level.*
> *Fire!!*

# PAGE 23 —

1- Half page spread. The bazooka shell sails over the crowd and explodes right on the steps and into the front door of the city hall court house.

Swat members go flying. A fall of fire erupts.

The tear gassed and hurt crowd are stunned by the fireball. Now this is war.

2- Scarlet steps up and barks into a megaphone. Going, Isis and the group behind her. She is charging. Going to war. Guns out.

Everyone nearby turns and is shocked to see her.

> **SCARLET**
> *My name is Scarlet!!*
> *They declared war on us!!*
> *They declared war on our freedom!!*
> *This city is ours, not theirs!!*
> *Today we take it back!!!*

# PAGE 24 —

1- Charge!! The insanely huge crowd backs Scarlet and rushes the burning steps of the court house/ police headquarters.

Police have guns up and firing back. Bullets and tear gas.

> **SPX:** *BAM BAM BAM BAM*

> **SCARLET**
> *Today the war ends!!*

2- On the steps, scrambling armed Police open fire on the pushing crazed crowd. The steps were hit by a bazooka and it shows.

> **SPX:** *BAM BAM BAM BAM*

> **SWAT**
> *Fuck!!*

> **SWAT**
> *It's her! It's really her!!*

3- At the bottom of the steps, Scarlet and her crew open fire back and the protestors rush the halls. Trashing the place.

**ISIS**
*Stand with us!!*
*Don't let them do this!!*

**BUDDY**
*Fuck you!*

**SPX:** *BAM BAM BAM BAM*

**SPX:** *BAM BAM BAM BAM*

**SPX:** *BAM BAM BAM BAM*

4- The Swat team and police force is either running away or being overwhelmed by the sheer force of numbers.

**SPX:** *BAM BAM BAM BAM*

**SPX:** *BAM BAM BAM BAM*

**POLICE CAPTAIN**
*Holy fuck!!*

**SWAT**
*We need back up!!*

**POLICE OFFICER**
*Agh!!*

**SWAT**
*Focus on her!! Focus on the red head!!*

## PAGE 25 —

1- At the blown up entrance, Scarlet is behind a pillar with her gun. Ready to push forward even as the crowd already does. Chaos around them in every panel.
Isis and Going are with her. Isis is firing.

**SCARLET**
*We push all the way in!!*

**MORTON**
*Take the building.*

**GOING**
*This is it.*

**ISIS**
*I love you, Scarlet.*

2- Scarlet can't help but look at Isis. Moved by it. Even in the chaos.

**SCARLET**
*I love you too.*

3- Across the way, Ford is bleeding and stomped on by the maddened crowd. Smoldering from a fire that whipped by him. And he sees...

4- Scarlet behind a pillar with Isis and Going.

5- Same as 3, but tighter, in the chaos Ford pulls his gun.

6- Going turns and sees...

7- Going's p.o.v. Ford is aiming at Scarlet/ us.

**SPX:** *BAM BAM*

## PAGE 26 —

1- Going pushes Scarlet down and fires back at him/ us. Ford's bullet hits the pillar instead of the back of Scarlet's head.

**GOING**
*No!!*

**SPX:** *SPACK*

**SPX:** *BAM*

2- Ford takes a Going bullet to the cheek and lunges back hard. His gun fires as he does.

      **POLICE CAPTAIN FORD**
        *Agh!!*

      **SPX:** *BAM*

3- And Going takes a Ford bullet to the neck. It goes right through her. She doesn't even feel it.

4- Low looking up, Scarlet is horrified and she sees...

5- Looking down, over Scarlet's shoulder, she bends down to Going. Going is down and bleeding out of her neck. She's Going to die.

6- Low looking up, Scarlet has tears in her wide eyes even as bullets and madness whizzes over her head. No last words.

7- Over Scarlet's shoulder, Going looks at her with blank eyes.

# PAGE 27 —

1- Wide, profile. Lobby of the police department, dozens of protestors crash through everything. Cops are being over powered in their own department.
College kids are leaping over turnstiles and protective glass. Guns firing. A couple of protestors get hit. a big garbage can is being used as a battering ram,
An older cop/ desk sergeant is surrendering.

2- Scarlet has both her gun and Goings. Blood on her. She has a moment of calm as the chaos whips around her.
Tear gas fumes. Shells. Smoke. Fire.

3- Scarlet turns into the fight and opens fire with both guns. Right for us.
It's the cover of issue one. Tears in her eyes for all that she has lost.
Chaos all around her.

# PAGE 28 —

Full page spread
Reprinting the Gabriel/ Scarlet page of issue one.
Her last true moment of happiness. The moment she has lost. The moment she is fighting for.
To be continued...

# ALEX MALEEV SKETCHBOOK

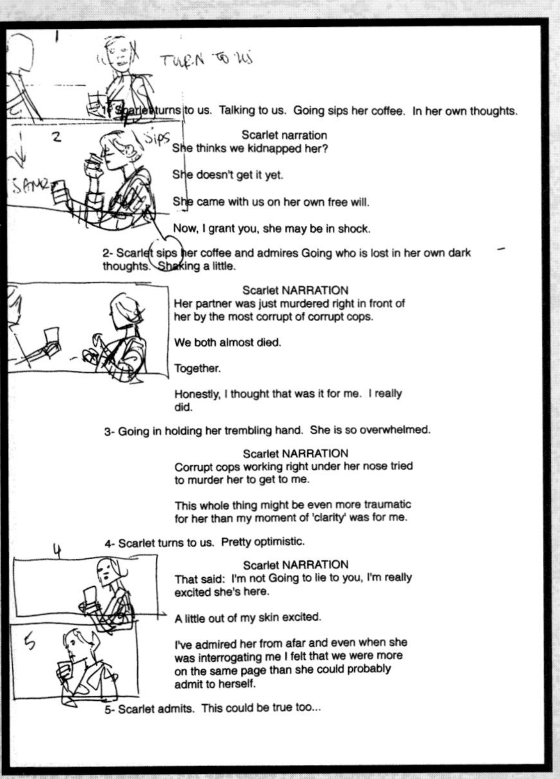
1- Scarlet turns to us. Talking to us. Going sips her coffee. In her own thoughts.

Scarlet narration
She thinks we kidnapped her?

She doesn't get it yet.

She came with us on her own free will.

Now, I grant you, she may be in shock.

2- Scarlet sips her coffee and admires Going who is lost in her own dark thoughts. Shaking a little.

Scarlet NARRATION
Her partner was just murdered right in front of her by the most corrupt of corrupt cops.

We both almost died.

Together.

Honestly, I thought that was it for me. I really did.

3- Going in holding her trembling hand. She is so overwhelmed.

Scarlet NARRATION
Corrupt cops working right under her nose tried to murder her to get to me.

This whole thing might be even more traumatic for her than my moment of 'clarity' was for me.

4- Scarlet turns to us. Pretty optimistic.

Scarlet NARRATION
That said: I'm not Going to lie to you, I'm really excited she's here.

A little out of my skin excited.

I've admired her from afar and even when she was interrogating me I felt that we were more on the same page than she could probably admit to herself.

5- Scarlet admits. This could be true too...

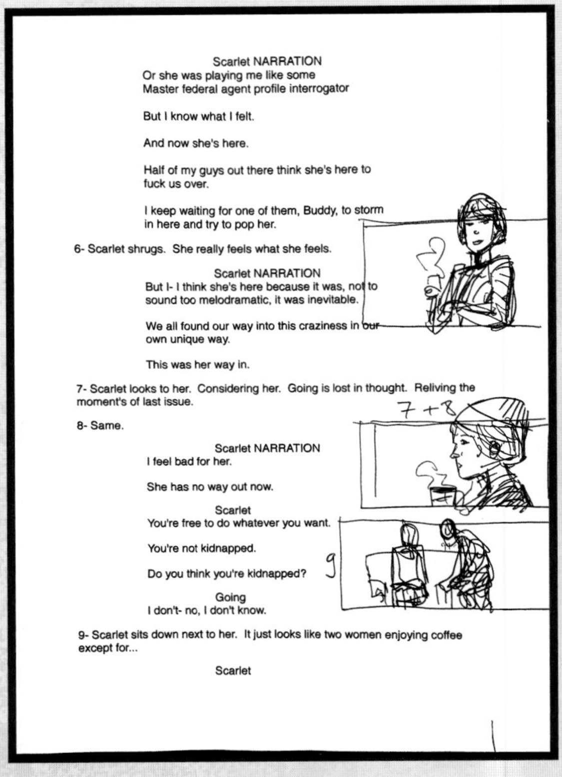
Scarlet NARRATION
Or she was playing me like some Master federal agent profile interrogator

But I know what I felt.

And now she's here.

Half of my guys out there think she's here to fuck us over.

I keep waiting for one of them, Buddy, to storm in here and try to pop her.

6- Scarlet shrugs. She really feels what she feels.

Scarlet NARRATION
But I- I think she's here because it was, not to sound too melodramatic, it was inevitable.

We all found our way into this craziness in our own unique way.

This was her way in.

7- Scarlet looks to her. Considering her. Going is lost in thought. Reliving the moment's of last issue.

8- Same.

Scarlet NARRATION
I feel bad for her.

She has no way out now.

Scarlet
You're free to do whatever you want.

You're not kidnapped.

Do you think you're kidnapped?

Going
I don't- no, I don't know.

9- Scarlet sits down next to her. It just looks like two women enjoying coffee except for...

Scarlet

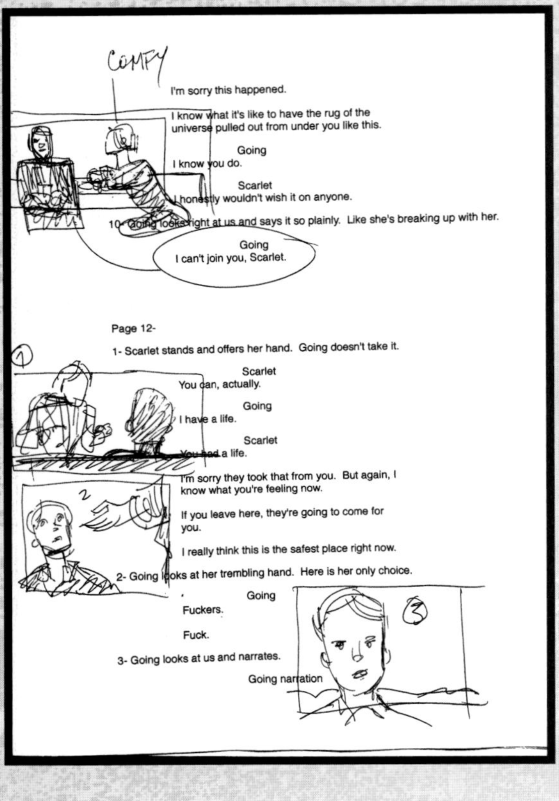
I'm sorry this happened.

I know what it's like to have the rug of the universe pulled out from under you like this.

Going
I know you do.

Scarlet
I honestly wouldn't wish it on anyone.

10- Going looks right at us and says it so plainly. Like she's breaking up with her.

Going
I can't join you, Scarlet.

Page 12-

1- Scarlet stands and offers her hand. Going doesn't take it.

Scarlet
You can, actually.

Going
I have a life.

Scarlet
You had a life.

I'm sorry they took that from you. But again, I know what you're feeling now.

If you leave here, they're going to come for you.

I really think this is the safest place right now.

2- Going looks at her trembling hand. Here is her only choice.

Going
Fuckers.

Fuck.

3- Going looks at us and narrates.

Going narration

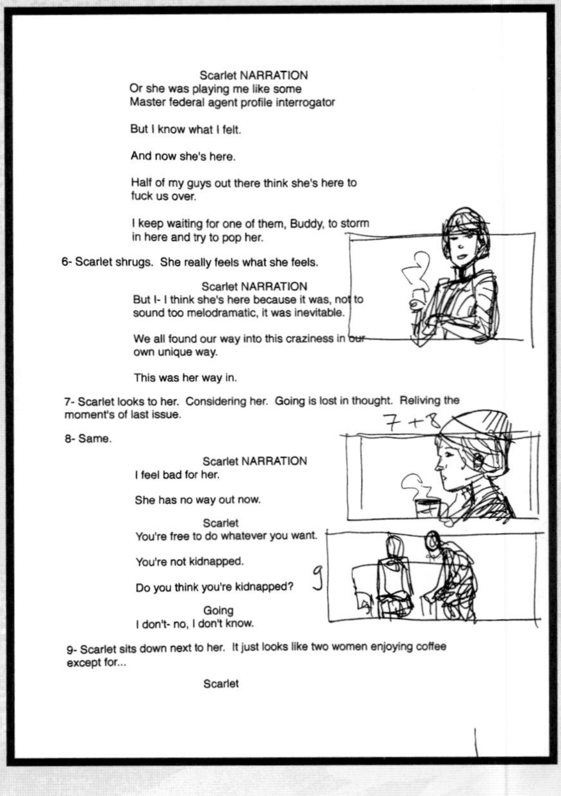

Scarlet NARRATION
Or she was playing me like some Master federal agent profile interrogator

But I know what I felt.

And now she's here.

Half of my guys out there think she's here to fuck us over.

I keep waiting for one of them, Buddy, to storm in here and try to pop her.

6- Scarlet shrugs. She really feels what she feels.

Scarlet NARRATION
But I- I think she's here because it was, not to sound too melodramatic, it was inevitable.

We all found our way into this craziness in our own unique way.

This was her way in.

7- Scarlet looks to her. Considering her. Going is lost in thought. Reliving the moment's of last issue.

8- Same.

Scarlet NARRATION
I feel bad for her.

She has no way out now.

Scarlet
You're free to do whatever you want.

You're not kidnapped.

Do you think you're kidnapped?

Going
I don't- no, I don't know.

9- Scarlet sits down next to her. It just looks like two women enjoying coffee except for...

Scarlet

I let it get to this.

I let it.

Every day I just- I ignore all these little lies

I blow off these little shits- these corrupt fuckers.

Going
I ignored it all.

I kept just pushing my way through all the shit because-

4- Scarlet isn't looking at her but offers her own...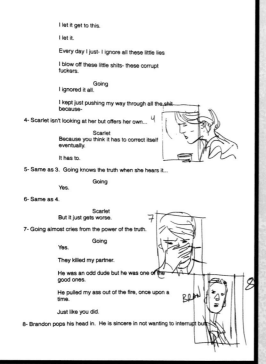

Scarlet
Because you think it has to correct itself eventually.

It has to.

5- Same as 3. Going knows the truth when she hears it...

Going
Yes.

6- Same as 4.

Scarlet
But it just gets worse.

7- Going almost cries from the power of the truth.

Going
Yes.

They killed my partner.

He was an odd dude but he was one of the good ones.

He pulled my ass out of the fire, once upon a time.

Just like you did.

8- Brandon pops his head in. He is sincere in not wanting to interrupt but-

---

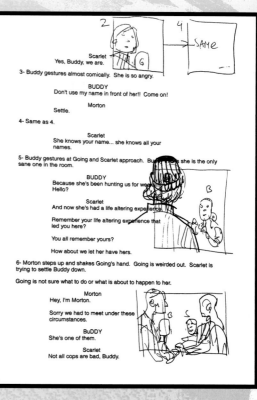

Scarlet
Yes, Buddy, we are.

3- Buddy gestures almost comically. She is so angry.

BUDDY
Don't use my name in front of her!! Come on!

Morton
Settle.

4- Same as 4.

Scarlet
She knows your name... she knows all your names.

5- Buddy gestures at Going and Scarlet approach. Buddy thinks she is the only sane one in the room.

BUDDY
Because she's been hunting us for weeks? Hello?

Scarlet
And now she's had a life altering experience.

Remember your life altering experience that led you here?

You all remember yours?

How about we let her have hers.

6- Morton steps up and shakes Going's hand. Going is weirded out. Scarlet is trying to settle Buddy down.

Going is not sure what to do or what is about to happen to her.

Morton
Hey, I'm Morton.

Sorry we had to meet under these circumstances.

BuDDY
She's one of them.

Scarlet
Not all cops are bad, Buddy.

---

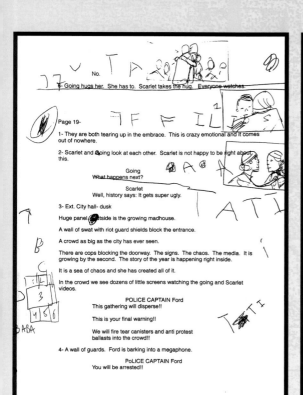

No.

5- Going hugs her. She has to. Scarlet takes the hug. Everyone watches.

Page 19-

1- They are both tearing up in the embrace. This is crazy emotional and it comes out of nowhere.

2- Scarlet and Going look at each other. Scarlet is not happy to be right about this.

Going
What happens next?

Scarlet
Well, history says: It gets super ugly.

3- Ext. City hall- dusk

Huge panel outside is the growing madhouse.

A wall of swat with riot guard shields block the entrance.

A crowd as big as the city has ever seen.

There are cops blocking the doorway. The signs. The chaos. The media. It is growing by the second. The story of the year is happening right inside.

It is a sea of chaos and she has created all of it.

In the crowd we see dozens of little screens watching the going and Scarlet videos.

POLICE CAPTAIN Ford
This gathering will disperse!!

This is your final warning!!

We will fire tear canisters and anti protest ballasts into the crowd!!

4- A wall of guards. Ford is barking into a megaphone.

PoLICE CAPTAIN Ford
You will be arrested!!

---

6- Scarlet knows this is the next level shit.

Scarlet
Here we go.

Next level.

Fire!!

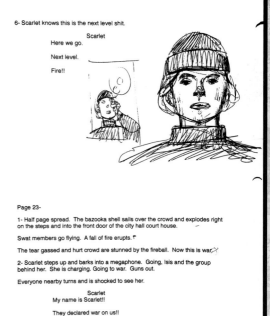

Page 23-

1- Half page spread. The bazooka shell sails over the crowd and explodes right on the steps and into the front door of the city hall court house.

Swat members go flying. A fall of fire erupts.

The tear gassed and hurt crowd are stunned by the fireball. Now this is war.

2- Scarlet steps up and barks into a megaphone. Going, Isis and the group behind her. She is charging. Going to war. Guns out.

Everyone nearby turns and is shocked to see her.

Scarlet
My name is Scarlet!!

They declared war on us!!

They declared war on our freedom!!

IN CHARGE →

This city is ours, not theirs!!

Today we take it back!!!

Page 24-

1- Charge!! The insanely huge crowd backs Scarlet and rushes the burning steps of the court house/ police headquarters.

Police have guns up and firing back. Bullets and tear gas.

Spx: bam bam bam bam

        Scarlet
        Today the war ends!!

2- On the steps, scrambling armed Police open fire on the pushing crazed crowd. The steps were hit by a bazooka and it shows.

Spx: bam bam bam bam

        SwAT
      Fuck!!

        SwAT
      It's her! It's really her!!

3- At the bottom of the steps, Scarlet and her crew open fire back and the protestors rush the halls. Trashing the place.

        Isis
      Stand with us!!

      Don't let them do this!!

        BuDDY
      Fuck you!

Spx: bam bam bam bam

Spx: bam bam bam bam

Spx: bam bam bam bam

4- The Swat team and police force is either running away or being overwhelmed

---

2- Scarlet can't help but look at Isis. Moved by it. Even in the chaos.

        Scarlet
      I love you too.

3- Across the way, Ford is bleeding and stomped on by the maddened crowd. Smoldering from a fire that whipped by him. And he sees...

4- Scarlet behind a pillar with Isis and Going.

5- Same as 3, but tighter, in the chaos Ford pulls his gun.

6- Going turns and sees...

7- Going's p.o.v. Ford is aiming at Scarlet/ us.

Spx: bam bam

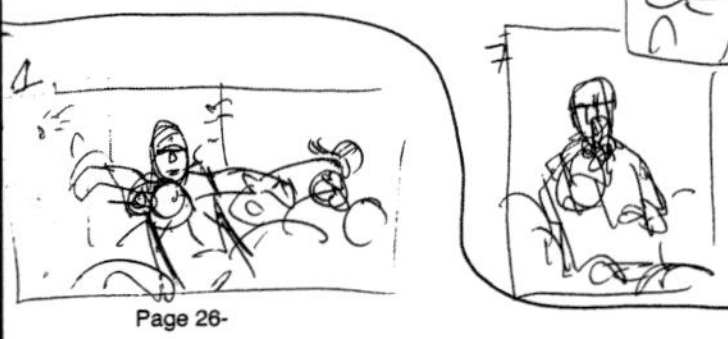

Page 26-

1- Going pushes Scarlet down and fires back at him/ us. Ford's bullet hits the pillar instead of the back of Scarlet's head.

        Going
      No!!

Spx: spack

Spx: bam

2- Ford takes a Going bullet to the cheek and lunges back hard. His gun fires as he does.

        PoLICE CAPTAIN Ford
      Agh!!

Spx; bam

---

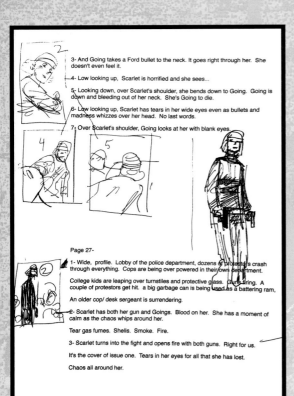

3- And Going takes a Ford bullet to the neck. It goes right through her. She doesn't even feel it.

4- Low looking up, Scarlet is horrified and she sees...

5- Looking down, over Scarlet's shoulder, she bends down to Going. Going is down and bleeding out of her neck. She's Going to die.

6- Low looking up, Scarlet has tears in her wide eyes even as bullets and madness whizzes over her head. No last words.

7- Over Scarlet's shoulder, Going looks at her with blank eyes.

Page 27-

1- Wide, profile. Lobby of the police department, dozens of protestors crash through everything. Cops are being over powered in their own department.

College kids are leaping over turnstiles and protective glass. Guns firing. A couple of protestors get hit. a big garbage can is being used as a battering ram,

An older cop/ desk sergeant is surrendering.

2- Scarlet has both her gun and Goings. Blood on her. She has a moment of calm as the chaos whips around her.

Tear gas fumes. Shells. Smoke. Fire.

3- Scarlet turns into the fight and opens fire with both guns. Right for us.

It's the cover of issue one. Tears in her eyes for all that she has lost.

Chaos all around her.

---

Page 28-

Full page spread

Reprinting the Gabriel/ Scarlet page of issue one.

Her last true moment of happiness. The moment she has lost. The moment she is fighting for.

To be continued...

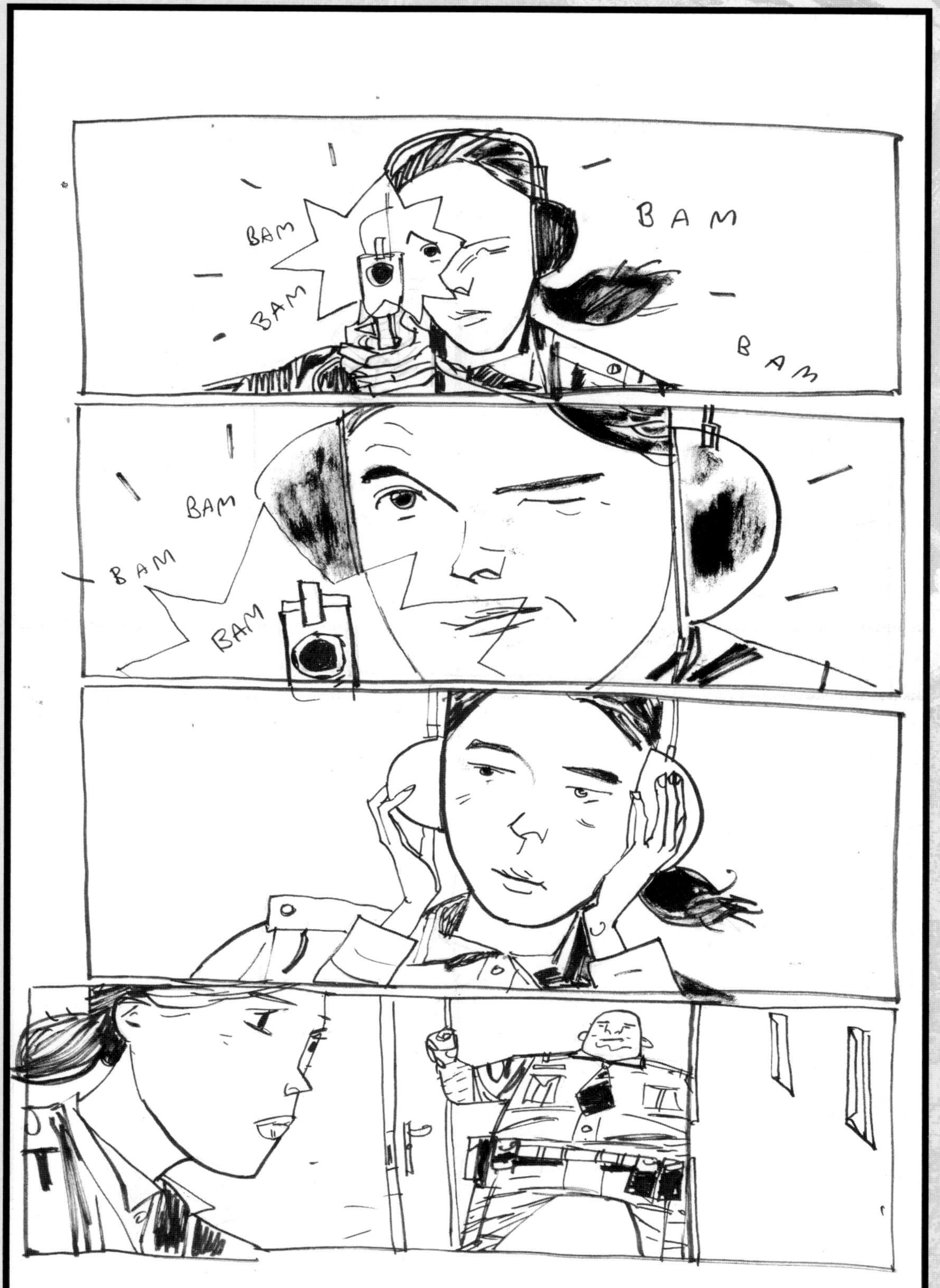

BAM
BAM
BAM
BAM
BAM
BAM
BAM
BAM

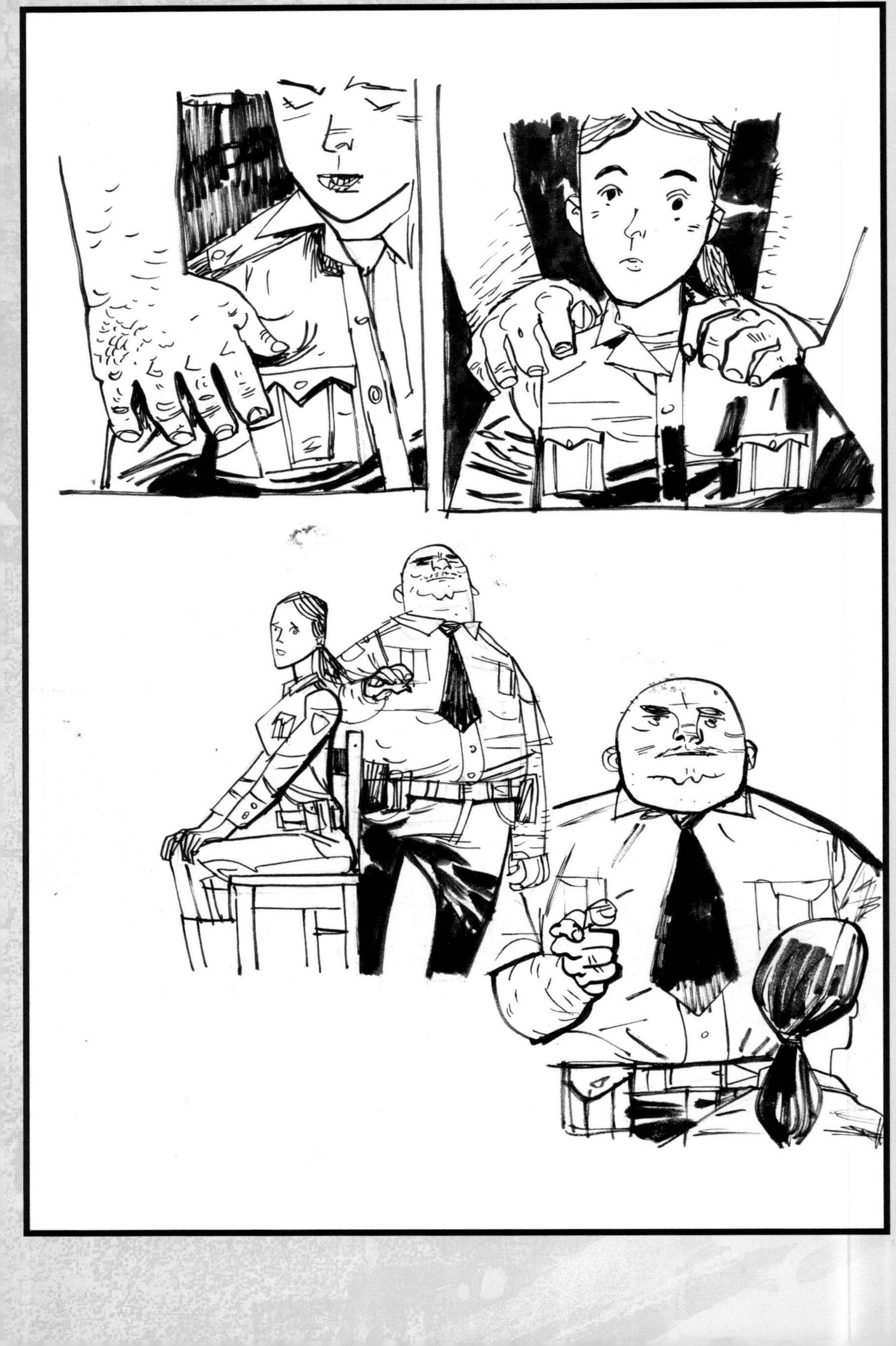

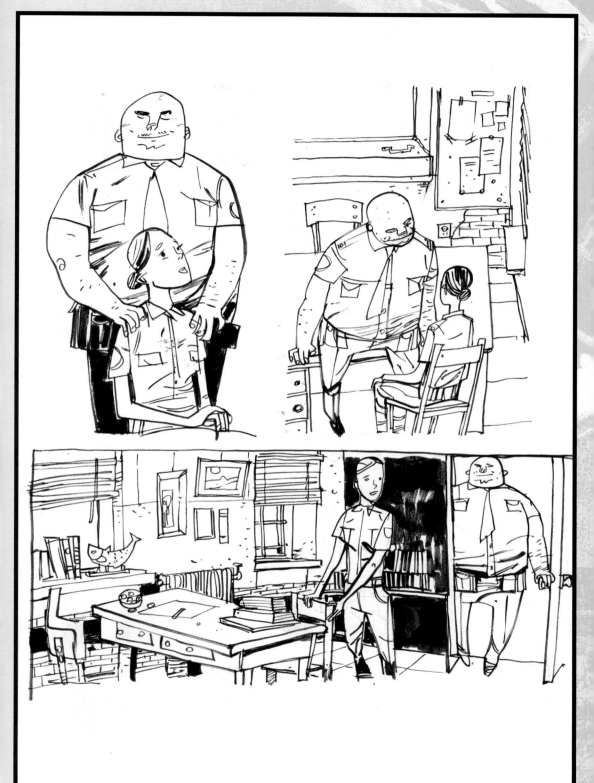

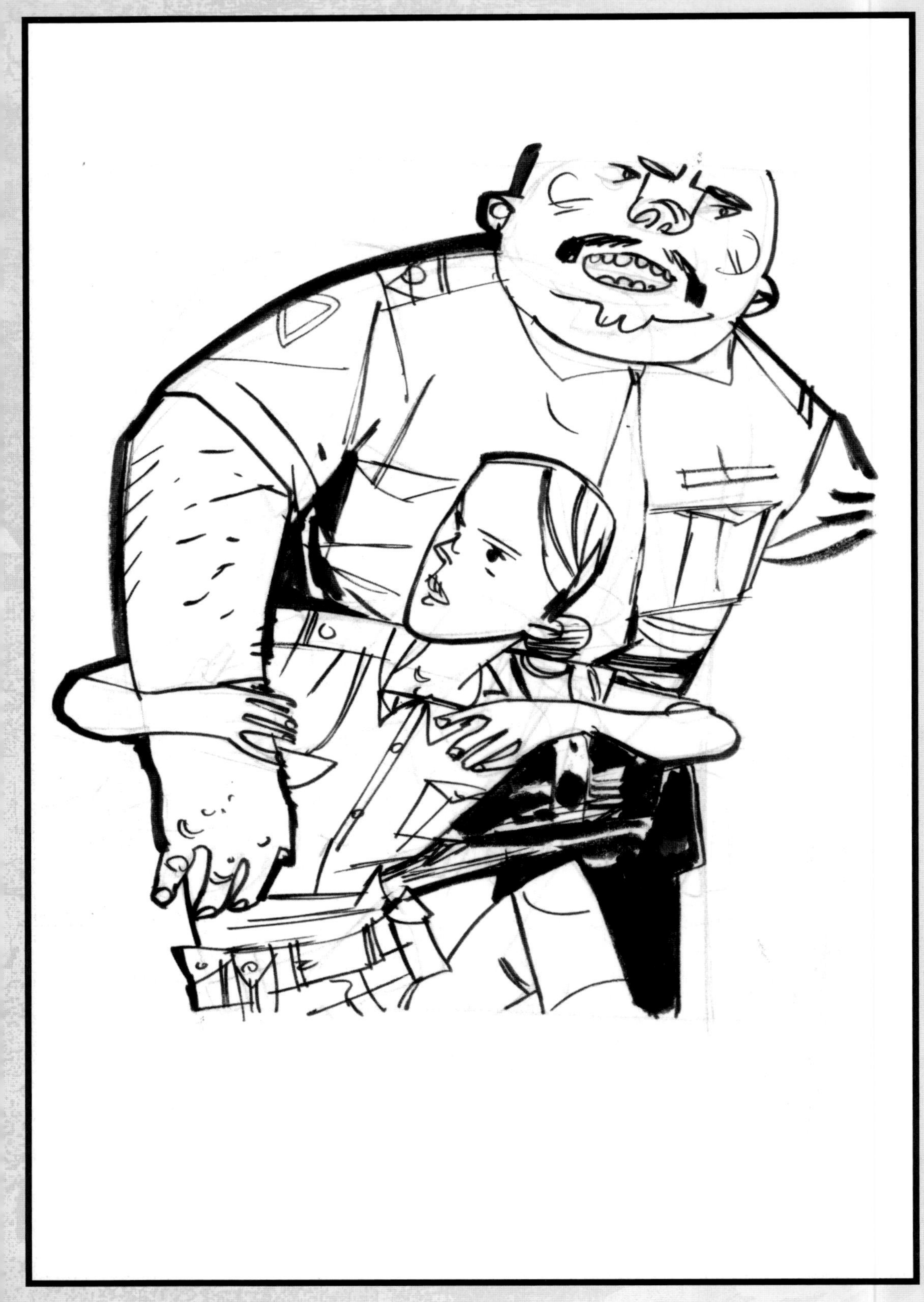

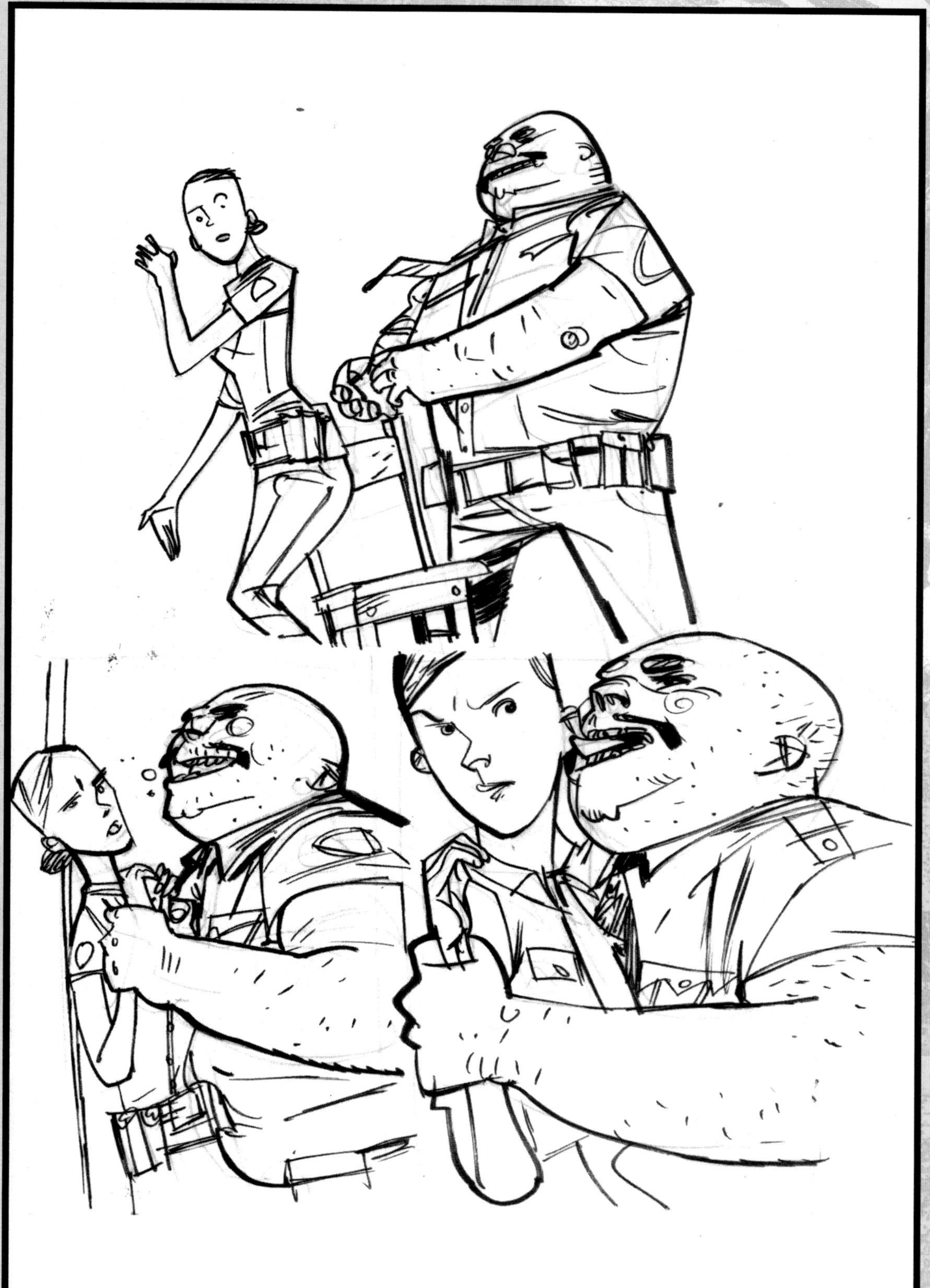

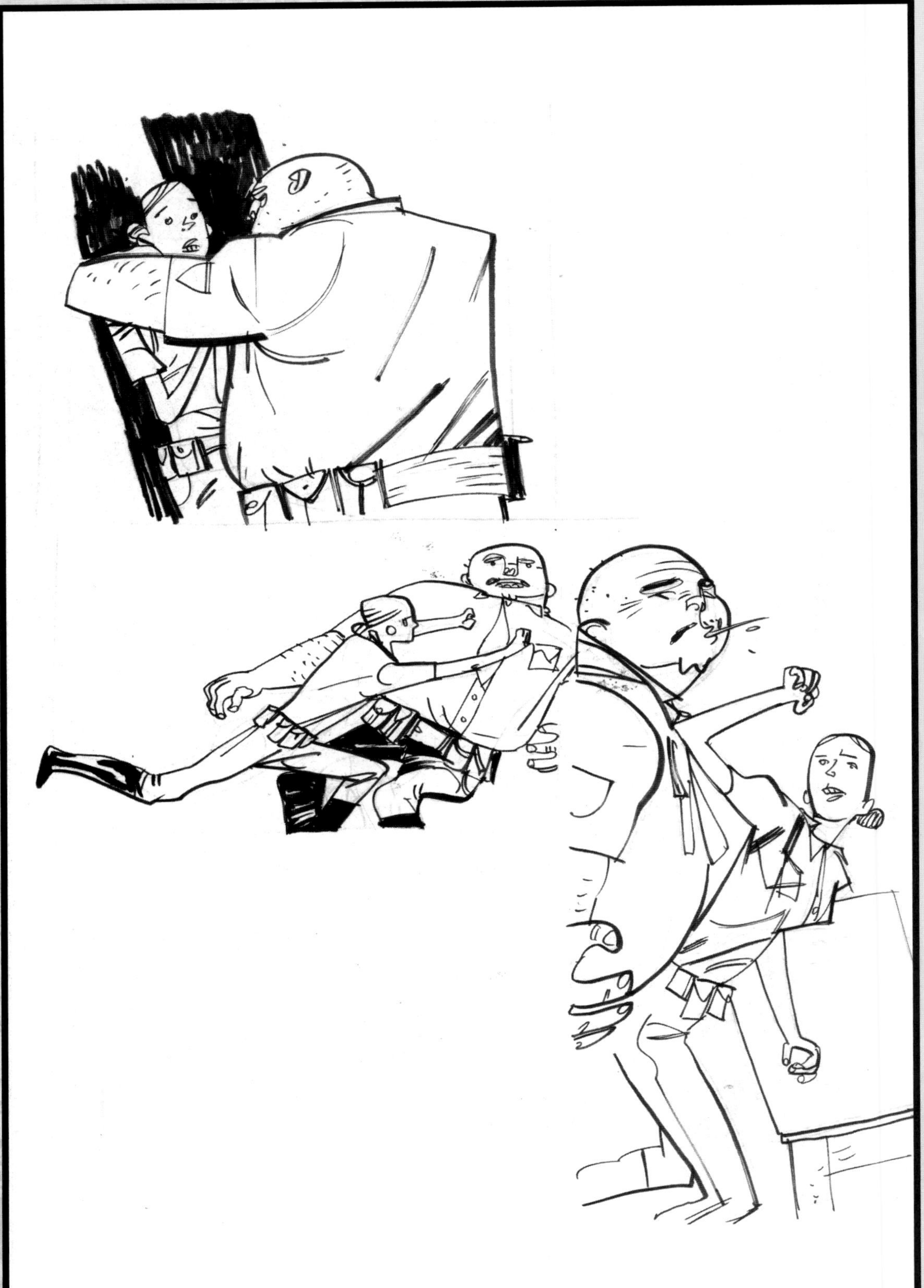

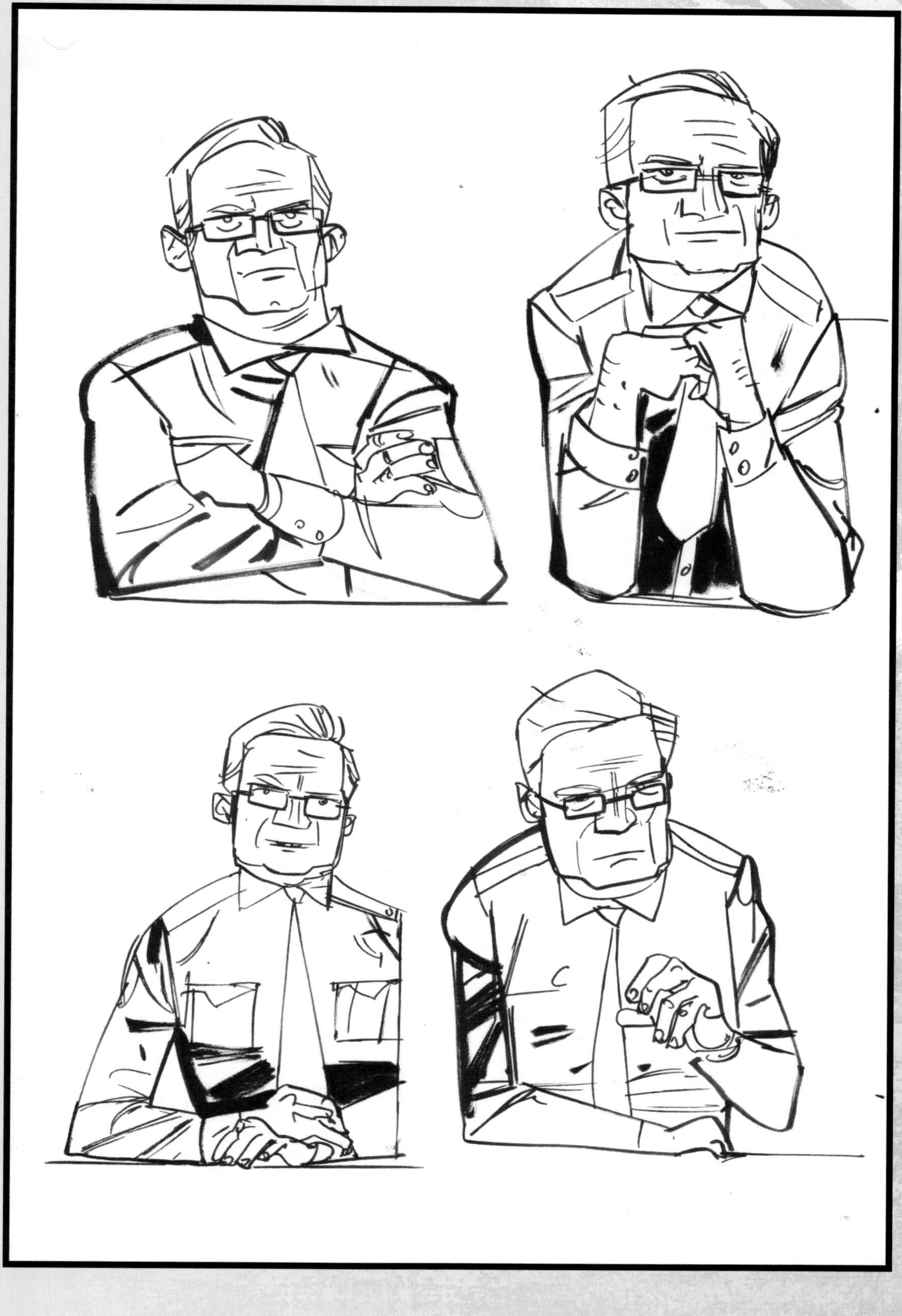

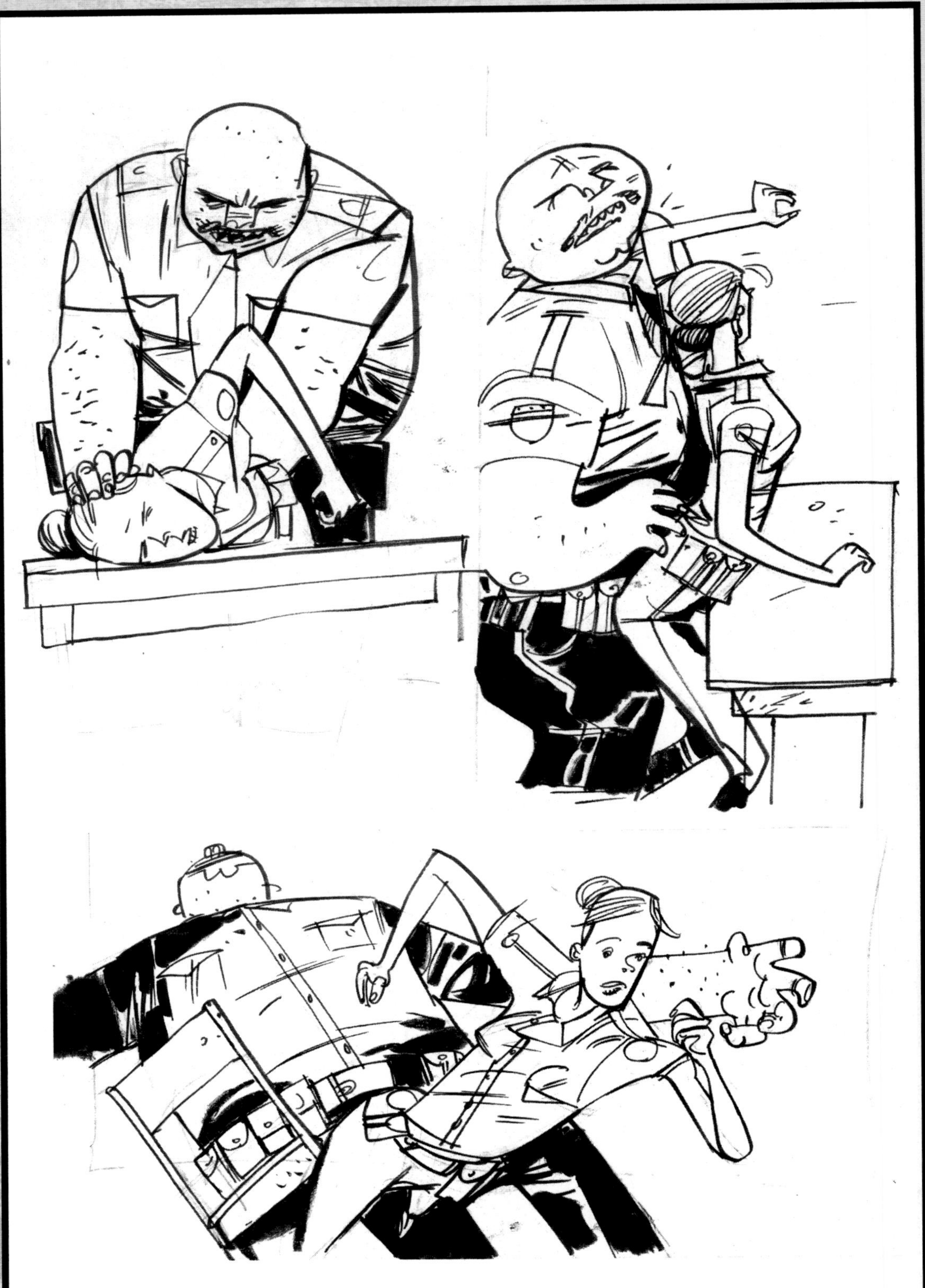

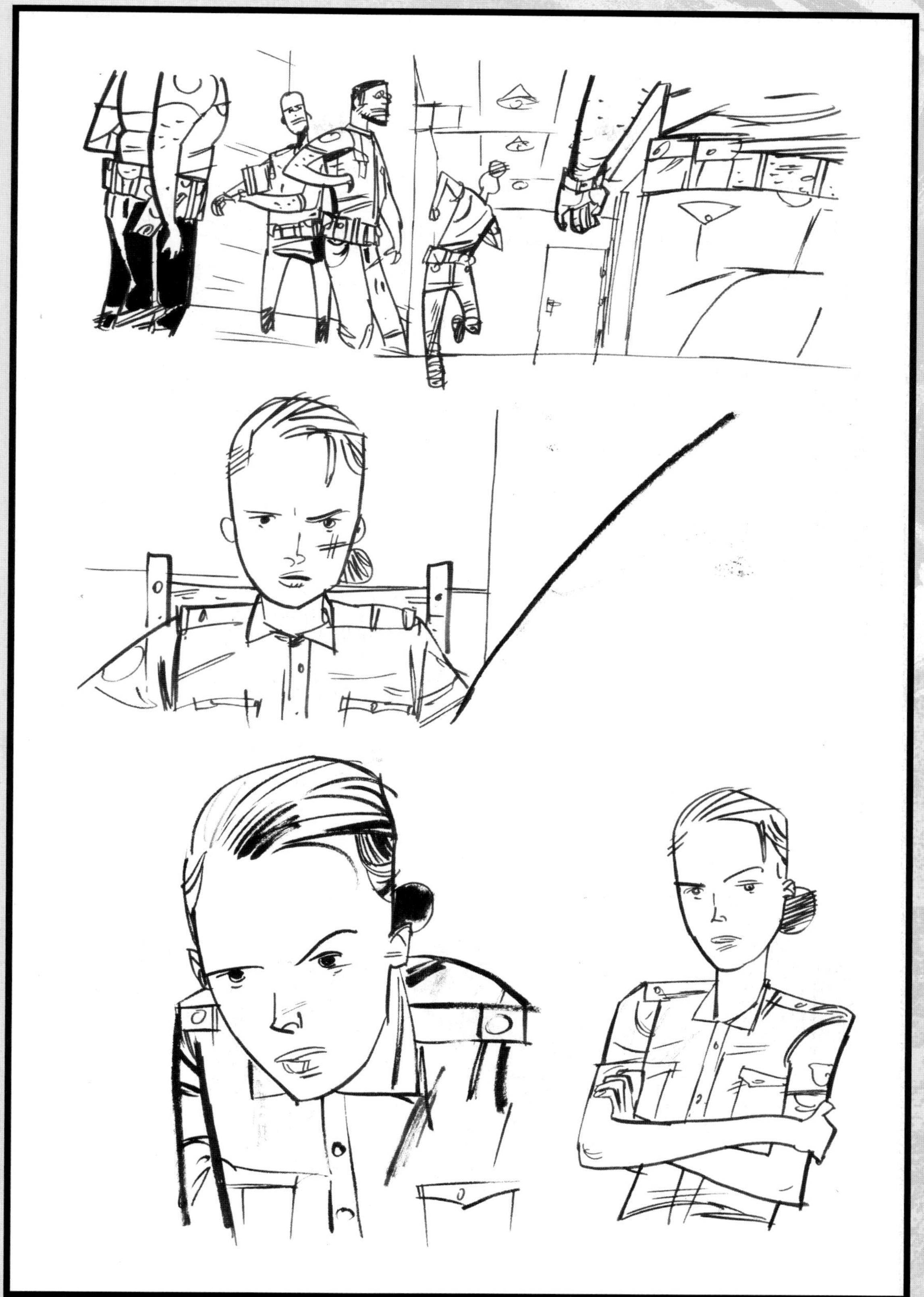

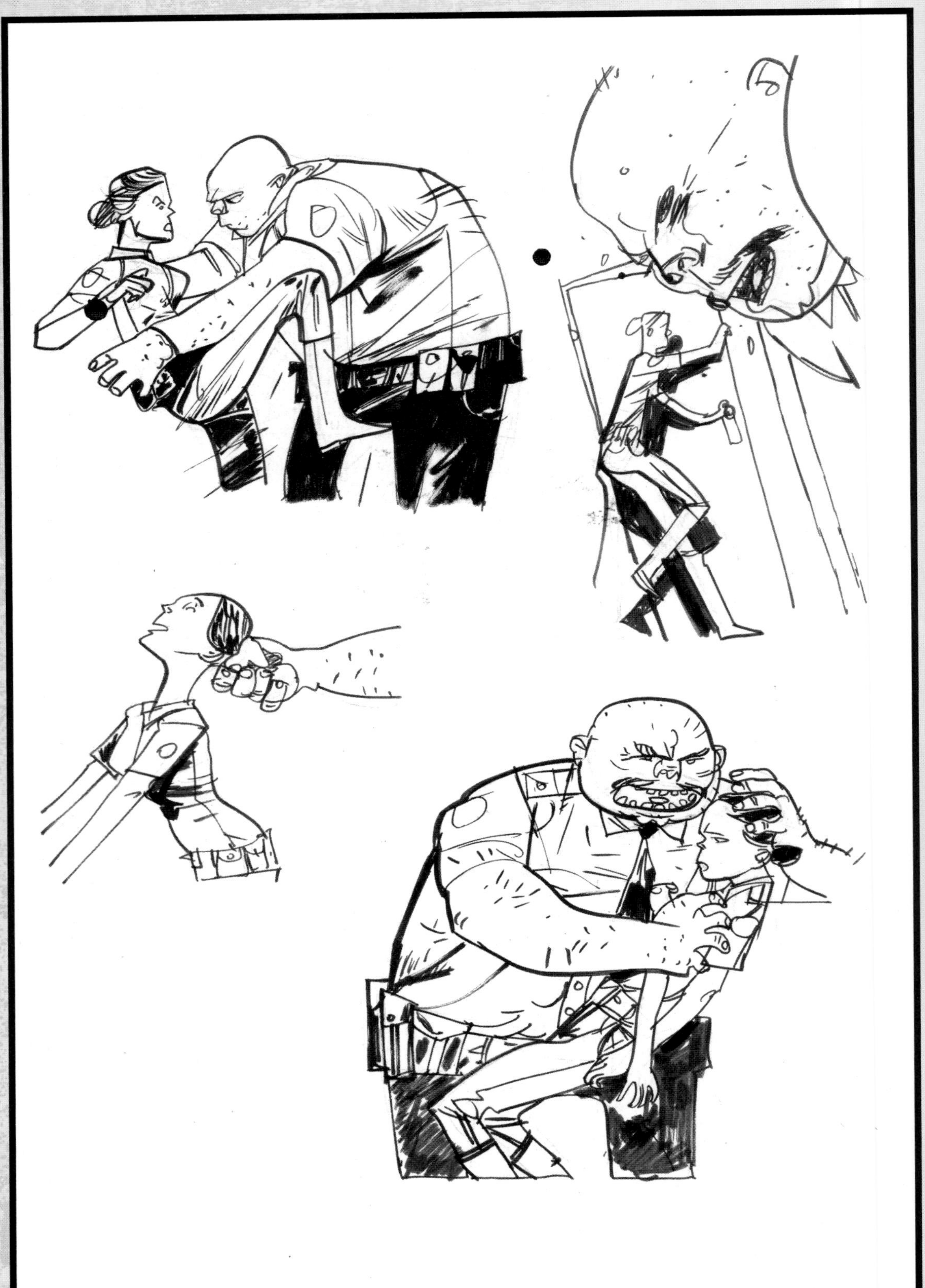

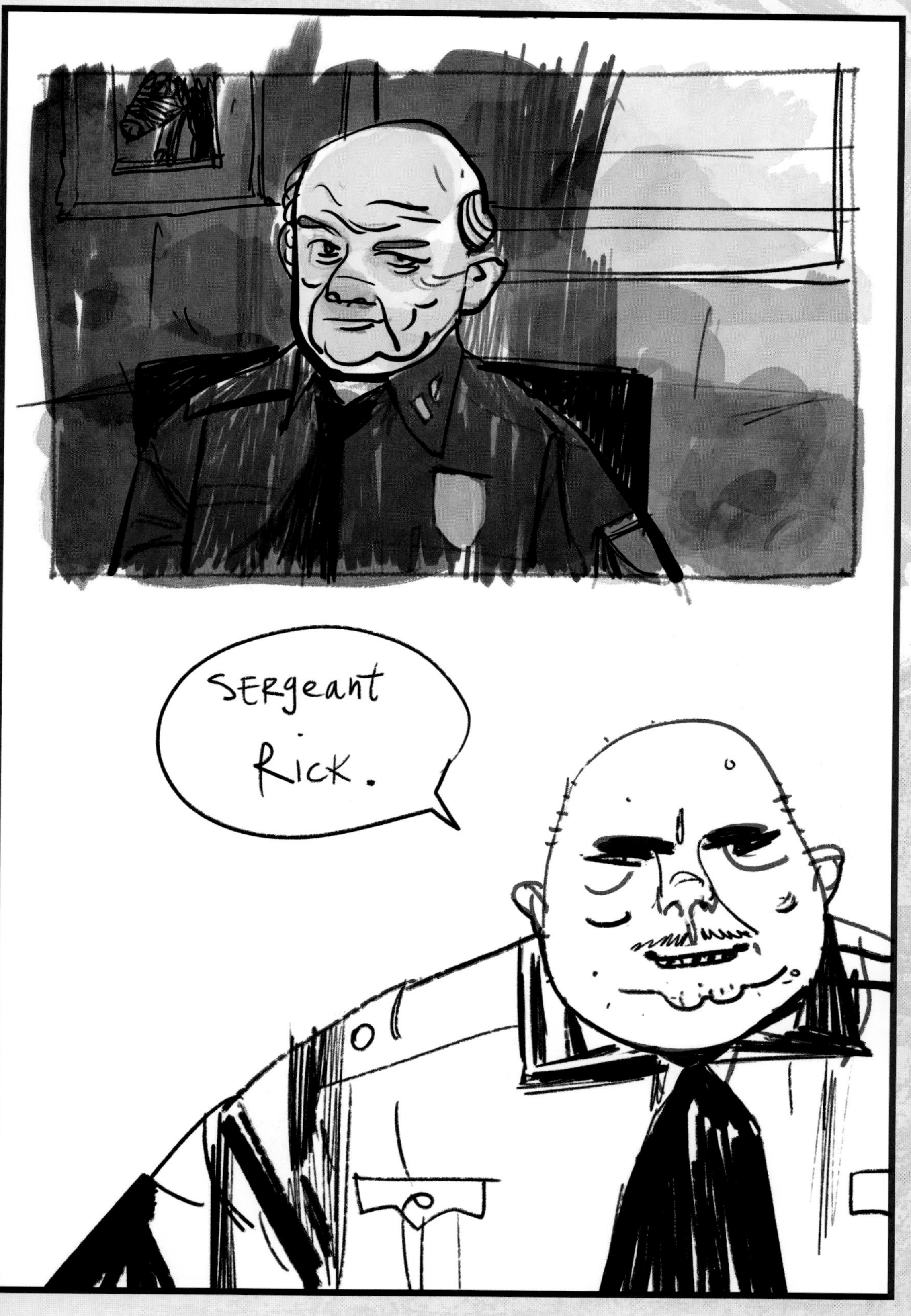
SERgeant Rick.

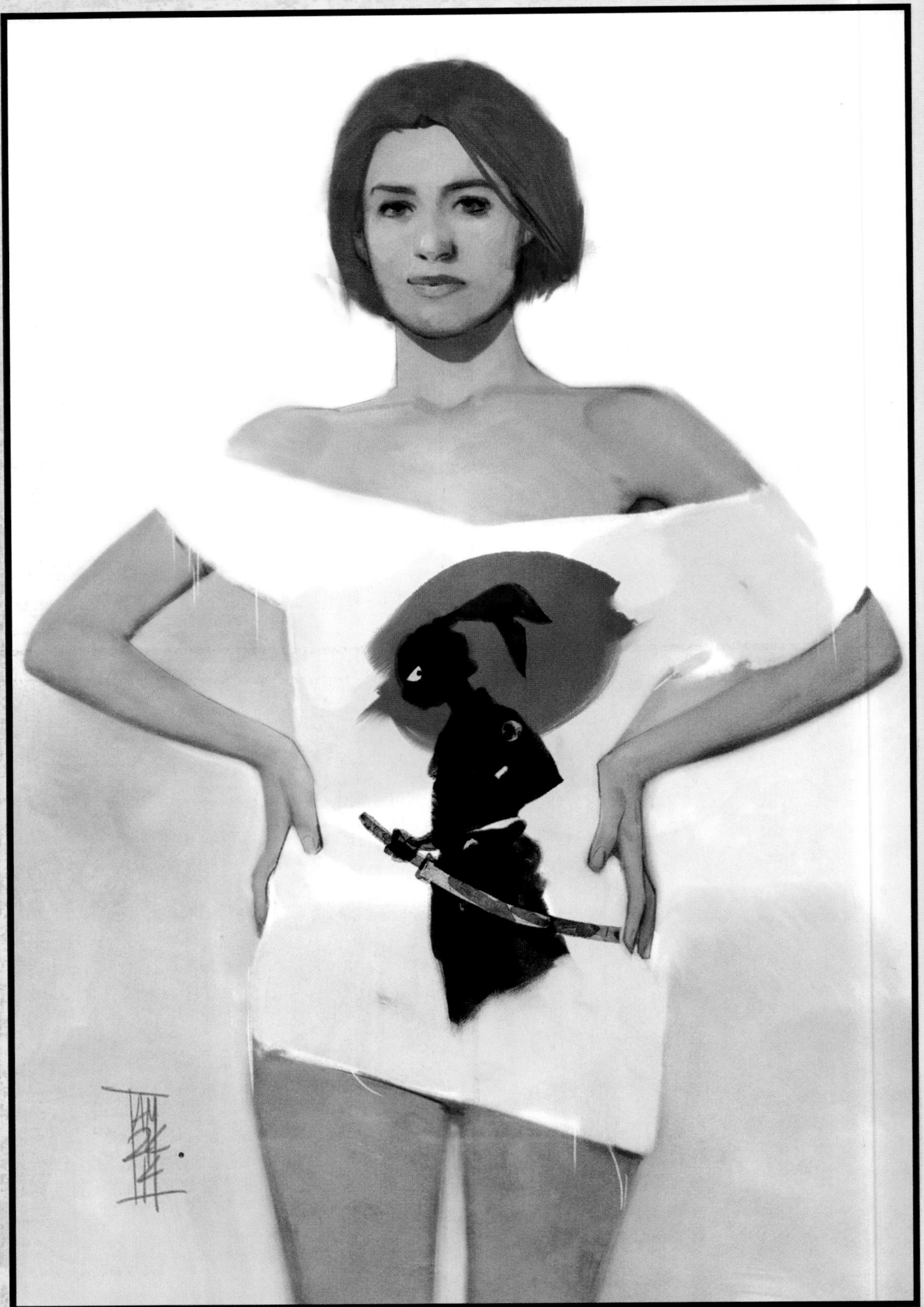

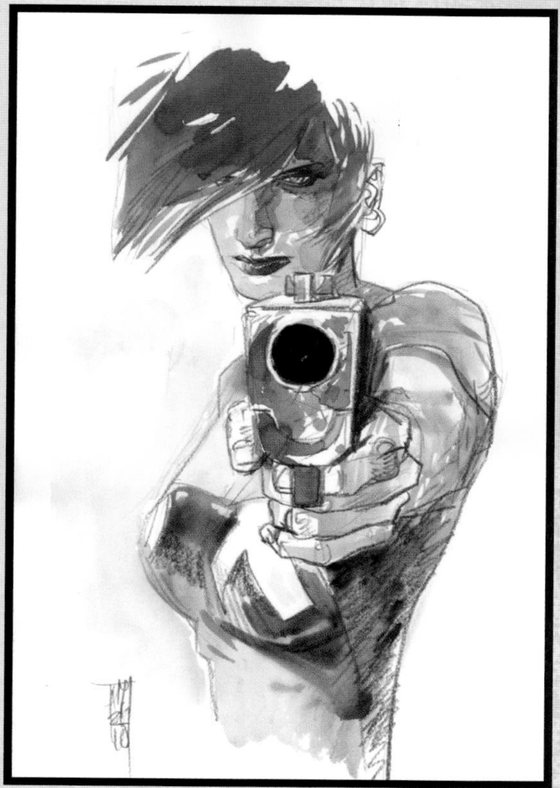

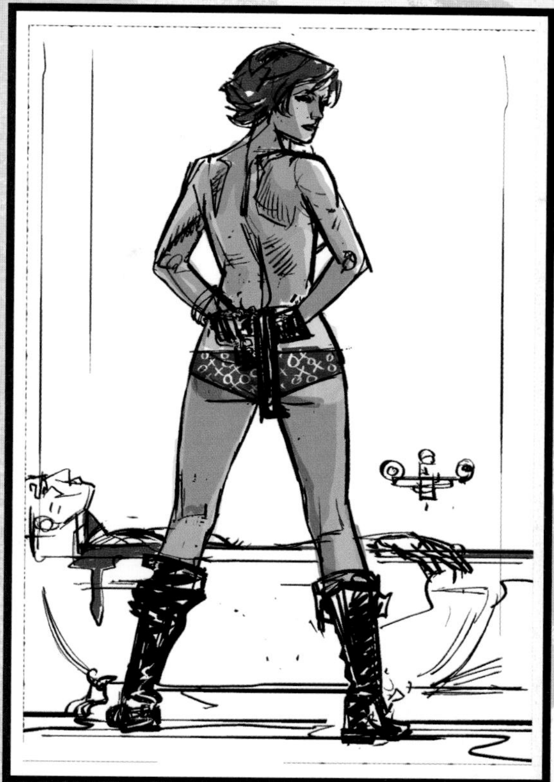

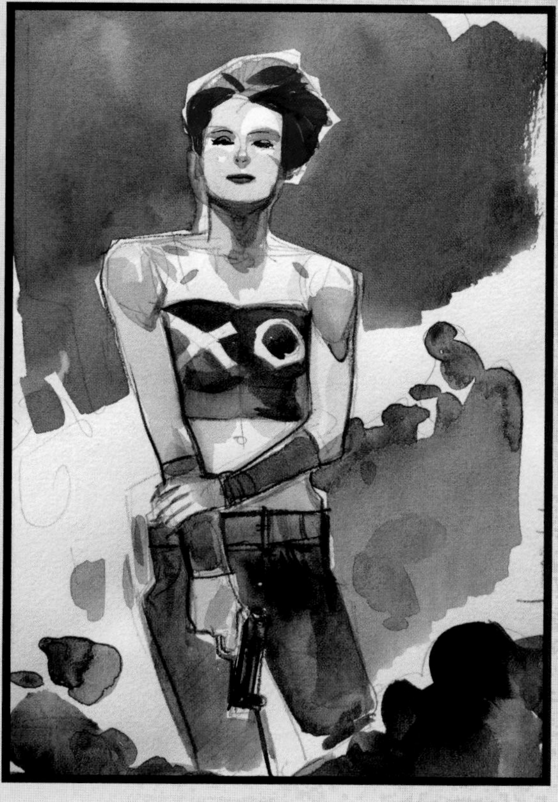

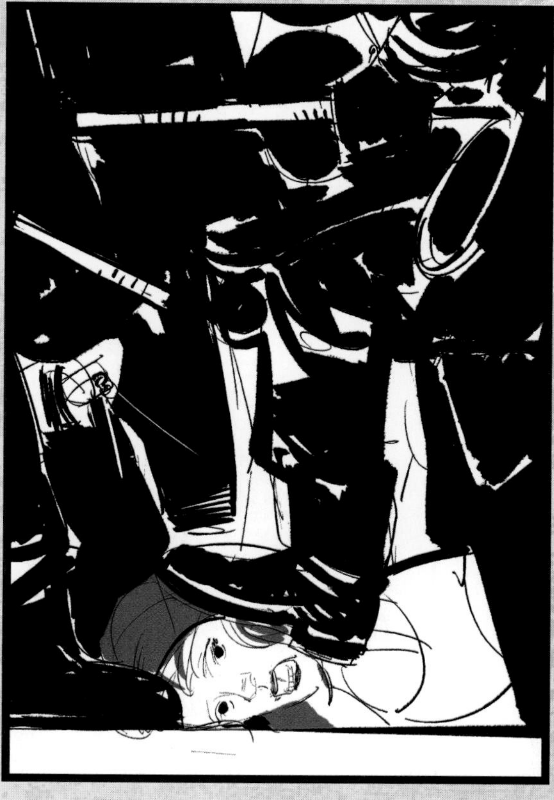

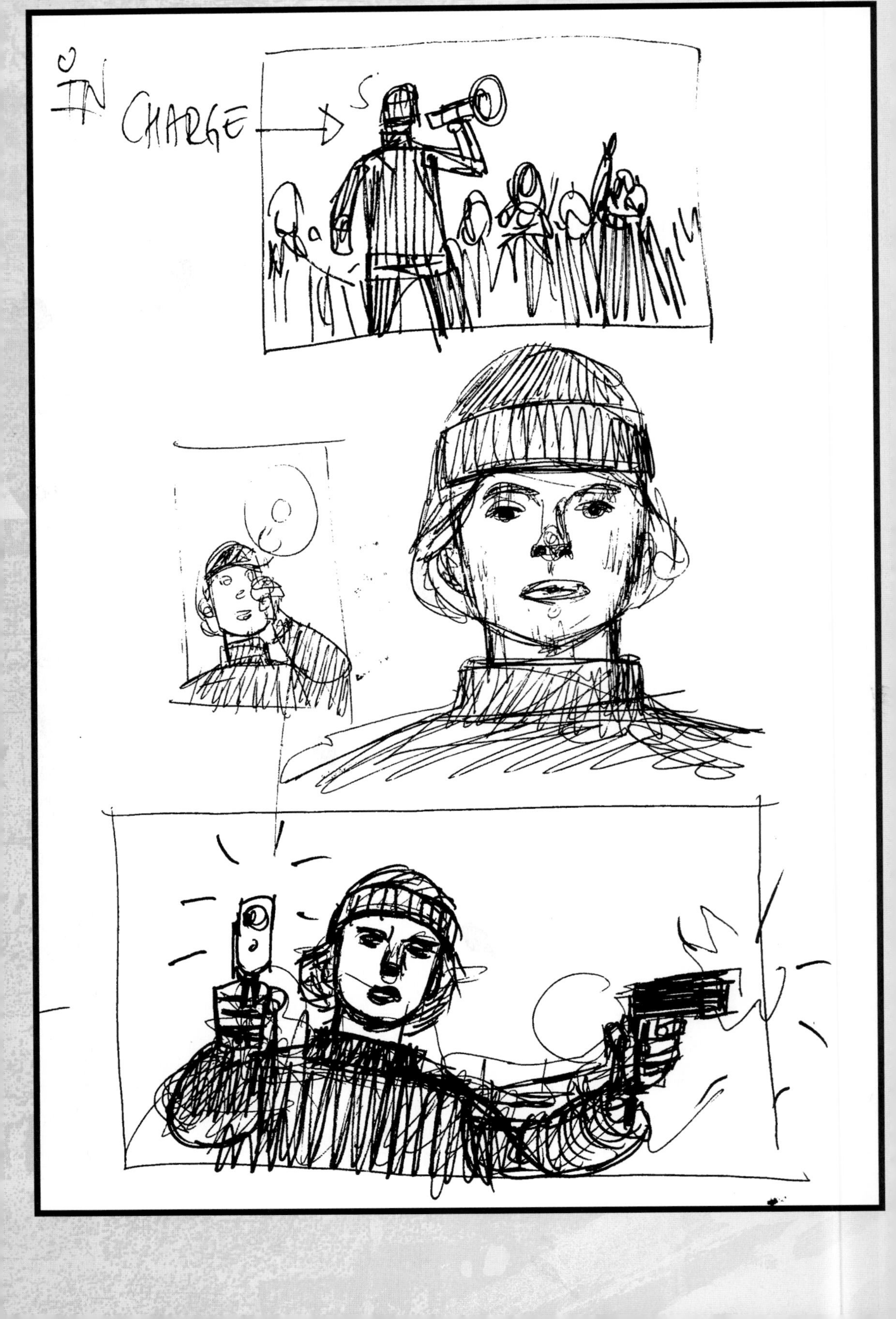

IN CHARGE